WORKING MEN'S COLLEGE.

LIBRARY REGULATIONS.

The Library is open every week-day evening, from 6.30 to 10 o'clock, except on Saturdays, when it closes at 9.

This book may be kept for three weeks. If not returned within that period, the borrower will be liable to a fine of one penny per week.

If lost or damaged, the borrower will be required to make good such loss or damage.

Only one book may be borrowed at a time.

Why Was Lincoln Murdered?

WHY WAS LINCOLN MURDERED?

by
OTTO EISENSCHIML

FABER AND FABER
24 Russell Square
London

*First Published in September Mcmxxxvii
by Faber and Faber Limited
24 Russell Square London W.C. 1
Printed in Great Britain
at the Bowering Press Plymouth
All Rights Reserved*

Smudges

One day in the year 1896 a French chemist named Becquerel took a photographic plate, which had been wrapped in light-proof paper, from one of the drawers of his laboratory. When it was developed it showed dark smudges for which he could find no immediate explanation. His curiosity was aroused, and he did not rest until it was satisfied. The result of his inquisitiveness was the discovery of radium.[1]

Historians, in developing the story of Lincoln's assassination, have encountered smudges equally baffling. Why did General Grant suddenly alter his plans and decide not to go to Ford's Theatre on the evening of Lincoln's assassination? Who, during the same night, tampered with the telegraph wires leading out of Washington? Why was the President's bodyguard at the playhouse, guilty of the grossest negligence, not punished nor even questioned?

Perhaps the most serious reproach against historical writers is not that they have left such questions unanswered, but that they have failed to ask them.

[1] *Transactions Chemical Society*, 1912, vol. 101 , also Floyd L. Darrow, *Masters of Science and Invention* (Harcourt, Brace & Co., New York, 1923), p. 241.

Contents

7

Contents

Illustrations

9

Illustrations

Why Was Lincoln Murdered?

CHAPTER I
The Fourteenth of April

The fourteenth of April 1865, dawning on the city of Washington, found the Capital gaudily bedecked with flags; for on the preceding night Lee's surrender had been celebrated by a grand illumination. The end of the long war was at last in sight.

In the forenoon a regular meeting of the Cabinet was held, at which General Grant was present as a distinguished guest. The victor of Appomattox Court House was a medium-sized, stoop-shouldered, taciturn man, then at the zenith of his military glory. At the White House he met all the members of Lincoln's official family, except Secretary of State Seward, who had been the President's closest rival at the Chicago Republican Convention of 1860. Seward had been thrown from his carriage a few days before and was lying at home under the care of physicians. The framework of steel which encased his face and neck, agonizing though it must have been, was destined that night to save his life.

Secretary of the Navy Gideon Welles was there; a kindly-looking man with a long white beard, who was gifted with a shrewd insight into the character of men. Thoroughly loyal to his chief, and with a finely balanced judgement, he kept close watch on the events of his era and faithfully recorded them in his diary.

The President himself seemed in unusually good spirits. Before the opening of the formal meeting he spoke freely of his plans for reconciling the conquered South. So far as he was concerned, he promised, there would be no persecution; he even hoped that the fallen leaders of the Confederacy would leave the country and thereby make it unnecessary for him to take direct action against them. He then told of a dream that had come to him during the night, the same that had so often in the past presaged a portentous happening. This time he hoped that it foretold the surrender to General Sherman of the last Confederate army. As Lincoln was describing his dream Stanton entered. The President stopped abruptly. 'Gentlemen,' he said, 'let us proceed to business.'[1]

Stanton did not often attend Cabinet meetings, and when he came he usually came late. It was his way of indicating the superiority he felt over his colleagues, if not over Lincoln himself. Gideon Welles distrusted him intensely, considering him an unscrupulous intriguer. 'He has cunning and skill,' the head of the Navy Department once wrote in his diary, 'dissembles his feelings . . . is a hypocrite. . . . '[2] Small of stature, with a long beard which he kept perfumed, the Secretary of War had an air of sternness; but Welles always believed that this outward semblance concealed the heart of a coward. The two secretaries had crossed swords only once. On that occasion Welles had shown plainly that he would brook no interference in his department, and Stanton had since treated him with an obsequiousness in sharp contrast to his imperious manner toward the other Cabinet members.[3]

With Stanton's entrance the pleasant flow of informal conversation ceased. The Secretary of War had brought with him an outline of the first step that he thought should be taken along the road to reconstruction. He contemplated the creation of a military territory combining Virginia and North Carolina, and the placing of this district under the supervision of his own department. Welles immediately offered objections. He declared that state lines should be inviolate and that the plan submitted would aggravate, rather than harmonize, the feelings of the two hostile sections. Lincoln sided with Welles, but tactfully suggested that Stanton should furnish a copy of his scheme, for

[1] Clara E. Laughlin, *The Death of Lincoln* (Doubleday Page, New York, 1909), pp. 71, 72 (footnote).
[2] Gideon Welles, *Diary* (Houghton Mifflin Co., Boston, 1911), II, pp. 16, 58; I, p. 127.
[3] Ibid., I, p. 67.

study and future discussion, to all the Cabinet officials. Soon afterward the meeting adjourned.[1]

On the same day, early in the morning, a shambling little man, whose head seemed wedged between his shoulders, rented a room at the Kirkwood House on the corner of Pennsylvania Avenue and Twelfth Street. With an unpractised hand he wrote his name on the register: G. A. Atzerodt.[2]

In the afternoon a handsome young actor walked into the lobby of the same hotel and asked for Vice-President Andrew Johnson. When informed that he was not in his apartment, the visitor left with the clerk a card on which he had scribbled these words:

> 'Don't wish to disturb you Are you at home?
> J. WILKES BOOTH[3]

The young man then left and mingled with the crowds on the avenue.

Had any one been able at that time to read the significance of these two incidents he would have recognized in them the shadow which all great events are said to cast before them; for they were the only outward evidence of a conspiracy that was then afoot against the life of the President.

That evening John Wilkes Booth shot Abraham Lincoln during a performance at Ford's Theatre.

[1] Welles, *Diary*, II, pp. 281–2.
[2] Benn Pitman, *The Assassination of President Lincoln* (Moore, Wilstach & Baldwin, Cincinnati, 1865), p. 144.
[3] Ibid., p. 70; quoted from original card, War Department Archives, Washington.

CHAPTER II

Assassination

The story of Lincoln's assassination has never been more concisely told than through the official telegrams in which Secretary of War Stanton informed the world of that tragedy. These messages, in conformity with a rule established earlier in the war, were sent to General John A. Dix in New York, from whose headquarters they were given to the Press for wider dissemination.

Here are the dispatches[1] of that memorable night:

(No. 1)

War Department
15 *April* 1865—1.30 a.m.
(Sent 2.15 a.m.)

MAJOR-GENERAL DIX,
New York:

Last evening, about 10.30 p.m., at Ford's Theatre, the President, while sitting in his private box with Mrs. Lincoln, Miss Harris, and Major Rathbone, was shot by an assassin, who suddenly entered the box and approached behind the President. The assassin then leaped upon the stage, brandishing a large dagger or knife, and made his escape in the rear of the theatre. The pistol-ball entered the back of the President's head, and penetrated nearly through the head. The wound is mortal. The President has been insensible ever since it was inflicted, and is now dying.

About the same hour an assassin (whether the same or another) entered Mr. Seward's home, and, under pretense of having a

---

[1] *Official Records*, Series I, vol. 46, part 3, pp. 780, 781.

16

prescription, was shown to the Secretary's sick chamber. The Secretary was in bed, a nurse and Miss Seward with him. The assassin immediately rushed to the bed, inflicted two or three stabs on the throat and two on the face. It is hoped the wounds may not be mortal; my apprehension is that they will prove fatal. The noise alarmed Mr. Frederick Seward, who was in an adjoining room, and hastened to the door of his father's room, where he met the assassin, who inflicted upon him one or more dangerous wounds. The recovery of Frederick Seward is doubtful.

It is not probable that the President will live through the night. General Grant and wife were advertised to be at the theater this evening, but he started to Burlington at 6 o'clock this evening. At a Cabinet meeting yesterday, at which General Grant was present, the subject of the state of the country and the prospects of speedy peace was discussed. The President was very cheerful and hopeful; spoke very kindly of General Lee and others of the Confederacy, and the establishment of government in Virginia. All the members of the Cabinet except Mr. Seward are now in attendance upon the President. I have seen Mr. Seward, but he and Frederick were both unconscious.

EDWIN M. STANTON,

Secretary of War.

(No. 2)   *Washington City*
                    No. 458 Tenth Street, 15 April 1865—3 a.m.
                              (Sent 3.20 a.m.)

MAJOR-GENERAL DIX
(*Care Horner, New York*):

The President still breathes, but is quite insensible, as he has been ever since he was shot. He evidently did not see the person who shot him, but was looking on the stage as he was approached behind.

Mr. Seward has rallied, and it is hoped he may live. Frederick Seward's condition is very critical. The attendant who was present was stabbed through the lungs, and is not expected to live. The wounds of Major Seward are not serious. Investigation strongly indicates J. Wilkes Booth as the assassin of the President. Whether it was the same or a different person that attempted to murder Mr. Seward remains in doubt. Chief-Justice

Cartter is engaged in taking the evidence. Every exertion has been made to prevent the escape of the murderer. His horse has been found on the road, near Washington.

EDWIN M. STANTON,
Secretary of War.

(No. 3)
Washington City
No. 458 Tenth Street, 15 April, 1865—4.10 a.m.
(Sent 4.44 a.m.)

MAJOR-GENERAL DIX:

The President continues insensible and is sinking. Secretary Seward remains without change. Frederick Seward's skull is fractured in two places, besides a severe cut upon the head. The attendant is still alive but hopeless. Major Seward's wounds are not dangerous.

It is now ascertained with reasonable certainty that two assassins were engaged in the horrible crime, Wilkes Booth being the one that shot the President, the other a companion of his whose name is not known, but whose description is so clear that he can hardly escape. It appears from a letter found in Booth's trunk that the murder was planned before the 4th of March, but fell through then because the accomplice backed out until 'Richmond could be heard from.'

Booth and his accomplice were at the livery stable at 6 this evening, and left there with their horses about 10 o'clock, or shortly before that hour. It would seem that they had for several days been seeking their chance, but for some unknown reason it was not carried into effect until last night. One of them has evidently made his way to Baltimore, the other has not yet been traced.

EDWIN M. STANTON,
Secretary of War.

(No. 4)
Washington City
15 April 1865.

MAJOR-GENERAL DIX,
New York:

Abraham Lincoln died this morning at 22 minutes after 7 o'clock.

EDWIN M. STANTON,
Secretary of War.

18

On the following forenoon, Stanton, in an official letter to the American minister at London, gave a more detailed account of Lincoln's death. Considering the circumstances under which this communication was composed, it is a masterly effort.[1]

> *War Department*
> *Washington City*
> 15 *April* 1865—11.40 a.m.

HON. CHARLES FRANCIS ADAMS,
Minister of the United States to Her Britannic Majesty:

SIR: It has become my distressing duty to announce to you that last night His Excellency Abraham Lincoln, President of the United States, was assassinated about the hour of 10.30 o'clock in his private box at Ford's Theater in this city. The President about 8 o'clock accompanied Mrs. Lincoln to the theater. Another lady and gentleman were with them in the box. About 10.30, during a pause in the performance, the assassin entered the box, the door of which was unguarded, hastily approached the President from behind, and discharged a pistol at his head. The bullet entered the back of his head and penetrated nearly through. The assassin then leaped from the box upon the stage, brandishing a large knife or dagger and exclaiming '*Sic semper tyrannis*', and escaped in the rear of the theater. Immediately upon the discharge the President fell to the floor insensible, and continued in that state until 7.20 o'clock this morning, when he breathed his last.

About the same time this murder was being committed at the theater another assassin presented himself at the door of Mr. Seward's residence, gained admission by pretending he had a prescription from Mr. Seward's physician, which he was directed to see administered, hurried up to the third-story chamber, where Mr. Seward was lying. He here encountered Mr. Frederick Seward, struck him over the head, inflicting several wounds, and fracturing the skull in two places, inflicting, it is feared, mortal wounds. He then rushed into the room where Mr. Seward was in bed, attended by a young daughter and a male nurse. The male attendant was stabbed through the lungs, and it is believed will die. The assassin then struck Mr. Seward with a knife or

---

[1] *Official Records*, Series I, vol. 46, part 3, pp. 784–5.

dagger twice in the throat and twice in the face, inflicting terrible wounds. By this time Major Seward, the eldest son of the Secretary, and another attendant reached the room, and rushed to the rescue of the Secretary. They were also wounded in the conflict, and the assassin escaped. No artery or important blood vessel was severed by any of the wounds inflicted upon him, but he was for a long time insensible from the loss of blood. Some hopes of his possible recovery are entertained.

Immediately upon the death of the President notice was given to Vice-President Johnson, who happened to be in the city, and upon whom the office of President now devolves. He will take the office and assume the functions of President to-day. The murderer of the President has been discovered, and evidence obtained that these horrible crimes were committed in execution of a conspiracy deliberately planned and set on foot by rebels, under pretense of avenging the South and aiding the rebel cause. It is hoped that the immediate perpetrators will be caught. The feeling occasioned by these atrocious crimes is so great, sudden, and overwhelming that I cannot at present do more than communicate them to you at the earliest moment.

Yesterday the President called a Cabinet meeting, at which General Grant was present. He was more cheerful and happy than I had ever seen, rejoiced at the near prospect of firm and durable peace at home and abroad, manifested in marked degree the kindness and humanity of his disposition, and the tender and forgiving spirit that so eminently distinguished him. Public notice had been given that he and General Grant would be present at the theater, and the opportunity of adding the lieutenant-general to the number of victims to be murdered was no doubt seized for the fitting occasion of executing plans that appear to have been in preparation for some weeks. But General Grant was compelled to be absent, and thus escaped the designs upon him.

It is needless for me to say anything in regard to the influence which this atrocious murder of the President may exercise upon the affairs of this country, but I will only add that horrible as are the atrocities that have been resorted to by the enemies of this country, they are not likely in any degree to impair that public spirit or postpone the complete and final overthrow of the rebellion.

In profound grief for the events which it has become my duty to communicate to you, I have the honor to be, very respectfully, your obedient servant,

Edwin M. Stanton[1]

[1] *Official Records*, Series I, vol. 46, part 3, pp. 784–5.

CHAPTER III

The Strange Career of John F. Parker

In his dispatches to the Press Stanton made no mention of any measures that had been taken to protect the life of the President. In his letter to Adams he merely stated that the door to Lincoln's box had been left unguarded.

Historians have touched but lightly on the fact that the Chief Magistrate was accompanied by an armed bodyguard on the night of his assassination. Some writers have chosen to disregard this escort completely; others have vaguely referred to him as a messenger, as an attendant, or as a servant.[1] The truth is that he was a veteran member of the Metropolitan Police Force, one of four officers specially detailed for White House duty. Although wearing civilian clothes, he was armed with a .38 Colt revolver. His orders were to stand at the entrance of the box and to permit no unauthorized person to enter it; his duty, to quote one of his comrades, was to remain at his post and to protect the President at all hazards.[2] The name of this guard was John F. Parker. Although he held a key position on the evening of that fatal fourteenth of April, and could easily have foiled the plans of the murderer, our knowledge of him is woefully inadequate. In all probability the little that is known of his life has never been fully set forth before.

Parker was born on 19 May 1830 in Frederick County, Virginia. He later became a carpenter in the city of Washington, and enlisted in the army shortly after the outbreak of the war.

[1] See supplementary note to chapter iii, 'The Elusiveness of Mr. Parker'.
[2] William H. Crook, *Memories of the White House* (Little, Brown & Co., Boston, 1911), p. 41.

When the Metropolitan Police Force was organized in September 1861 he became one of its first patrolmen. At that time he was married, had three children, and lived at 750 L Street.[1]

His record as a police officer is not one that inspires great confidence. Perhaps few of the Washington patrolmen of that day were paragons of virtue. In any case, Mr. Parker certainly was no exception to the rule. About a year after joining the Force he was charged with conduct unbecoming an officer and with the use of violent, coarse, and insolent language. It appears that the owner of a grocery store had complained that officers were embarrassing him by loafing in front of his establishment. One of Parker's superiors explained this matter to a recruit, whom he had found with Parker in front of the shop. Parker took personal offence, thinking that the remarks had reference to himself. In clearing the case, the Police Board found that Parker had shown a disposition to be insubordinate. 'The language he used', says the report, 'was exceedingly violent and disrespectful, and, if permitted to be continued, must lead to insubordination.' Parker maintained, however, that he had been jesting, and had not intended to be disrespectful to his superior; whereupon, this being his first offence, he was reprimanded and transferred to another precinct.[2]

On 16 March 1863 Parker again found himself before the Police Board, charged with wilful violation of the rules and regulations, and with conduct unbecoming an officer. This time he was accused not only of having used highly offensive language toward an officer named Pumphrey, but also of having visited a house of prostitution, kept by a Miss Annie Wilson. It was stated that he had been intoxicated, that he had been put to bed, and that he had fired a pistol through the window. According to the official charges, Parker had, 'after coming off of his beat at twelve o'clock, gone to the said house and to bed, with one of the inmates, Miss Ada Green'.[3]

Upon investigation of this report, the Board learned that Parker 'was at a house of ill fame with no other excuse than that he was sent for by the Keeper . . .', although there was

[1] Records of the Metropolitan Police Department, Washington, D.C.
[2] Ibid.; see also supplementary note to chapter iii, 'The Metropolitan Police'.
[3] Ibid.

'no Evidence that there was any robbery there or disturbance of the peace or quiet of that neighbourhood . . .'. The witnesses, employees of the house in question, proved staunch champions for the defendant, one of them going so far as to declare that he had never in his life seen Parker drunk, 'and he had been in that house for five weeks'. In the face of this solid phalanx, the Board found that no evidence could be produced to show that Parker had been 'drunk or had fired a Pistol there as charged'.[1] The Board thereupon figuratively shrugged its shoulders, remarked that there was a seeming intimacy between the officer and the inmates, and turned its attention to other cases on its docket.

Parker once more ran foul of the police regulations only a fortnight later. This time he was accused of being found asleep on a street car when he should have been walking his rounds; but the charges were dismissed upon Mr. Parker's statement that he and a brother officer, named Williams, had heard the squawking of ducks, and that they thereupon had entered the car to ascertain the cause of this unusual commotion.

Scarcely three months passed before Parker had to appear before the Police Board again. This time it was said of him that he had refused to restrain some disorderly negroes, and had used insulting language to the lady making the complaint. These charges were also dismissed.

Some weeks later Parker received a severe kick from a man he was endeavouring to arrest. His injuries required the visit of a police physician, and therefore the incident is registered in the reports of the Washington Police Department.[2]

After this Parker's career seems to have been uneventful until the beginning of April 1865. Then a great change came into his life; for, strangely enough, a request was made in his behalf that he be excused from the draft, taken off his beat, and detailed for duty at the Executive Mansion.

Parker may have been a fairly efficient patrolman in spite of his shortcomings, but his record certainly was not one that would entitle him to special promotion. Nor could his educational background, as indicated by the language that he was in the habit of using and by the hand that he wrote, be called a

[1] Records of the Metropolitan Police Department, Washington, D.C.
[2] Ibid.

Executive Mansion,

Washington, *April 3ᵈ 1865*

This is to certify that John F. Parker, a member of the Metropolitan Police has been detailed for duty at the Executive Mansion by order of

Mrs Lincoln

Facsimile of letter written by Mrs. Lincoln pertaining to the appointment of John F. Parker, the bodyguard whose negligence allowed Booth easy access to the President's box in Ford's Theatre.

Original Letter in possession of author

recommendation. Most other White House guards had also been picked from the ranks of the oldest police officers of Washington and, so far as the files show, they were among the best behaved and the most respected members of the Force. Thomas Pendel and William Crook, two of the men selected to watch over the President, remained in the White House for over a generation after the death of Lincoln. How, then, did a man of John F. Parker's character find his way into this select company?

The answer to this query is as mystifying as the query itself. Parker was chosen for his duty as bodyguard by none other than President Lincoln's own wife. In a letter written by her on 3 April 1865 to James R. O'Beirne, provost-marshal of the District of Columbia, she asked that Parker be excused from the draft.[1]

'This is to certify [she stated in a note written on White House stationery] that John F. Parker, a member of the Metropolitan Police has been detailed for duty at the Executive Mansion by order of,
Mrs Lincoln'

On the same day she wrote a certificate detailing one Joseph Sheldon for duty at the Executive Mansion, and on 4 April Major O'Beirne replied:

'Will Mrs. Lincoln be pleased to state on the accompanying certificate whether it is intended that Mr Sheldon shall be excused from the Draft, in order that I may have the necessary authority to exempt him.'

Mrs. Lincoln quickly settled the matter by her endorsement, asking to, 'Please have them both exem from the Draft'.

What prompted the wife of the President to make this unusual request in behalf of an obscure and mediocre patrolman like Parker will probably remain a moot question.

That Parker seriously failed in his duty during the performance of *Our American Cousin* is a matter beyond dispute,

---

[1] O'Beirne papers. A collection of documents left by Major (later General) James Rowan O'Beirne, in possession of the author. The papers also include a diary kept by O'Beirne while the pursuit of Booth was in progress, and some letters of Captain Beckwith.

but it is not exactly known to what extent he was technically guilty. On 1 May 1865 A. C. Richards, superintendent of the Metropolitan Police Force, preferred charges of neglect of duty against him, the specification reading as follows:

'In this, that Said Parker was detailed to attend and protect the President Mr. Lincoln, that while the President was at Fords Theatre on the night of the 14 of April last, Said Parker allowed a man to enter the Presidents private Box and Shoot the President.'

As witnesses were cited A. C. Richards himself and Charles Forbes of the President's house.[1]

The police archives afford no proof that Parker was really tried. If any transcripts of the case existed, they have been removed, and even the eventual findings of the Board are available only through subsequent records. These show that, although Parker was tried on 3 May, the complaint was dismissed on 2 June 1865. The minutes of this trial before the Board would make one of the most interesting chapters in the story of Lincoln's assassination.

Many peculiar things, which history has seen fit to overlook, happened in and around the presidential box that evening. This was the only time that the searchlight of an official investigation was trained on them; it is, therefore, a matter of the deepest regret that none of the testimony has been preserved for posterity.

The War Office archives have yielded only one more piece of information concerning Parker. Francis Burns, Lincoln's coachman, stated that he 'stayed at the door until the tragedy occurred. The special police officer and the footman of the President came up to him and asked him to take a drink with them; which he did. . . .' This would indicate that Parker and the footman Forbes had approached the coachman during an intermission in the play. It was practically the only time at which such a convivial meeting seemed feasible. Of course, the danger to the President during a pause in the play would be many times greater than while the performance was in progress, and Parker's carelessness in leaving his post at such a moment, taking the

[1] O'Beirne papers.

President's valet with him, is so extraordinary as to be almost beyond belief.[1]

What Parker did immediately after the assassination has not been definitely ascertained. The police blotter of that night shows that at 6 a.m., 15 April, only a few hours after Lincoln was shot, Parker brought to headquarters a woman by the name of Lizzie Williams. One can visualize the pathetic figure of the patrolman, made desperate by the tragedy he should have and could have prevented, roaming the streets of the Capital all night long, trying to find the murderer as an atonement for his negligence. When morning dawned the assassin was still at large. Not willing to report empty-handed to headquarters, Parker reverted to type and brought in a woman of the streets, who, by the way, was promptly discharged.[2]

Even those only superficially acquainted with the history of the Civil War period would probably surmise that this policeman, guilty of criminal neglect while on important duty, was promptly court-martialled and executed. Stanton was in complete control of the situation, and, without Lincoln's gentler hands to stay him, one would have expected the austere Secretary of War to make sure that the delinquent officer was summarily dealt with. Had not Stanton acquired a reputation for merciless severity toward poor country lads in uniform who had fallen asleep on sentry duty after long, weary marches? Had he not repeatedly and violently remonstrated with Lincoln for undermining the discipline of the army by letting clemency supersede justice? Now that his Chief was dead, murdered through the unbelievable carelessness of a special guard, for whom no mitigating circumstances could be pleaded, one would certainly have expected that Stanton would have had Parker shot at dawn.

But Stanton did exactly nothing. Parker was not shot; nor was he court-martialled. He not only kept his life, he also kept his position. He was not reprimanded, not dismissed, not even immediately relieved of his White House appointment. This inexplicable failure on the part of the authorities to act brought

[1] War Department Archives, Washington, D.C.
[2] Records of the Metropolitan Police Department, Washington, D.C.

forth no burst of indignation from the populace. It elicited no diligent research among questioning newspapermen. In short, it has remained one of the unexplained mysteries of those eventful days.

Mrs. Lincoln herself believed that Parker was involved in the conspiracy to murder her husband. A few days after the assassination she upbraided the poor man in a most tempestuous manner, accusing him of the crime of which she thought him guilty and hardly giving him a chance to defend himself. The unhappy police officer could only stammer that he was innocent of anything worse than negligence, and then shuffle out of Mrs. Lincoln's room to resume his watch.[1] But the President's wife must have rued the day when she meddled in state affairs to the extent of selecting that bodyguard, and her violent grief was no doubt intensified by the secret knowledge of her own folly which had carried with it such tragic and unforeseen consequences.

There is no evidence that Parker was in any way involved in the murder conspiracy. The plot to assassinate Lincoln was a well thought out affair in which nothing was left to chance. There was no place in these plans for a man of Parker's type, nor could it have been known in advance that he would be chosen that night to guard the President.

The rest of Parker's career is quickly told. It is not known on what day he was put back on his beat, but on 24 May he again picked up a woman for soliciting on the streets. This time he was more fortunate in proving his charges, as the police records show. The lady was found guilty and was sentenced to pay a fine of ten dollars.[2]

Another complaint against Parker for unbecoming conduct was put on file on 22 November 1865. By 27 July 1868 this officer had tried the patience of his superiors once too often. He was found asleep on his beat by his sergeant and, although he claimed that he had been ill, and although another sergeant gave the lieutenant in charge a good report about him up to that

[1] Elizabeth Keckley, *Behind the Scenes* (G. W. Carleton & Co., New York, 1868), pp. 193 ff.
[2] Records of the Metropolitan Police Department, Washington, D.C.

time, he was promptly discharged from the service on 13 August 1868 for 'gross neglect of duty'. Under this cloud he disappears for ever from the roster of Washington policemen and from the pages of history.[1]

Parker's last offence was perhaps the least important one among his many infringements of the police rules and regulations. That he really was sick when found asleep was attested to even by the sergeant who preferred the charges against him, and all the witnesses summoned before the Board confirmed the statement. Yet the official axe fell promptly and relentlessly. In his earlier years in the Force, complaint had followed complaint, but the final result had only been a promotion. Now, after three years of good behaviour, the Police Board was inexorable, and he was dishonourably discharged.

A few weeks prior to Parker's dismissal, Secretary of War Stanton had finally been ousted from his position, and had returned to private life. Of course, it is a far cry from the resignation of a Cabinet officer to the dismissal of a Washington patrolman, and there is no evidence that these two events were in any way related to each other; nor is there any proof that Stanton's protective hand had safeguarded Parker up to that time.

Curiously, no contemporary historian or journalist found it of interest to throw any light on John F. Parker and the part he played during the night of 14 April 1865. This could not have been due to ignorance of his existence. As early as Monday, 17 April, attention was called to him through a story related in the *New York Tribune* by a Captain Theodore McGowan of General Augur's office. On the night of the performance Captain McGowan and his friend Lieutenant Crawford had occupied seats about five feet from the door of the presidential box. Some time during the third act McGowan was disturbed in his seat by the approach of a man who desired to pass up the aisle. This man drew a number of visiting cards from his pocket, from which, with some attention, he selected one. 'These things',—McGowan stresses the point—'I saw distinctly. I saw him stoop, and, I think, descend to the level with the messenger . . . and as my attention was then more closely fixed upon the play, I do not

[1] Records of the Metropolitan Police Department, Washington, D.C.

know whether the card was carried in by the messenger, or his consent given to the entrance of the man who presented it.'[1]

Captain McGowan repeated this tale on the witness stand during the conspiracy trial a few weeks later,[2] so that the public was given two chances to hear it. Yet no one sensed the unusual news value of his evidence or seemed anxious to ask him questions.

Whose card was it that Booth handed to Parker? Was it that of some senator or other dignitary whose name might lull the suspicions of the guard? Or did Booth have enough bravado to produce a card of his own? And what became of it? Did Parker keep it or not? Was there any writing on this piece of pasteboard whereon the fate of a nation trembled for a fraction of a minute? Did Booth speak to the guard, and if so, what did he say? These and other equally pertinent queries have never been answered.

Parker's name does not appear in any official story of Lincoln's death. He was not called to the witness stand in the conspiracy trial nor in any subsequent investigation. Silence settled like a merciful fog around the person of this unfortunate policeman who had so egregiously missed his opportunity to win eternal fame. Only one of the other guards at the White House worried about his case. 'I have often wondered', he wrote many years later, 'why the negligence of the guard who accompanied the President to the theatre on the night of the 14th has never been divulged. So far as I know, it was not even investigated by the police department. Yet, had he done his duty, I believe President Lincoln would not have been murdered by Booth.'[3]

[1] *New York Tribune*, 17 Apr. 1865.
The Terrible Tragedy at Washington—Assassination of Abraham Lincoln (Barclay & Co., Philadelphia, 1865), p. 39.
[2] Pitman, op. cit., p. 78.
[3] William H. Crook, *Through Five Administrations* (Harper & Bros., New York, 1907), pp. 71–2.

CHAPTER IV

What Really Happened at Ford's Theatre

The sequence of events on the night of 14 April has been clearly established. The presidential carriage left the White House about ten minutes after eight o'clock. In it were President and Mrs. Lincoln and Charles Forbes, Lincoln's footman. Ten minutes later it arrived at the residence of Senator Harris. There Miss Harris and Major Rathbone entered the conveyance and, about half-past eight, they all alighted in front of Ford's Theatre. Parker had preceded the carriage on foot. The party ascended to the balcony, from which a small corridor led into the two boxes, which had been thrown into one for the occasion. A chair had been placed for Parker outside this corridor, but he failed to use it, as he could not have followed the play from there.[1]

Up to the time of Booth's appearance, at about thirteen minutes after ten, nothing noteworthy occurred. Then things happened with lightning-like rapidity. Unheard and unseen, the assassin entered the box, and before the slightest suspicion was aroused he had fatally wounded Lincoln. Major Rathbone grappled with the murderer, but could not prevent his escape. It was all over in less than thirty seconds. Neither Mrs. Lincoln nor Miss Harris had even left their seats.[2]

According to Rathbone's sworn statement before Justice Olin on 17 April, the box in Ford's Theatre assigned to the President was occupied by President and Mrs. Lincoln, Miss Harris, and

[1] Crook, *Memories of the White House*, p. 29; *Through Five Administrations*, p. 72.
[2] Pitman, op. cit., p. 78.

himself, '*and by no other person*', as he averred with emphasis. Miss Harris confirmed the affidavit of her fiancé in a statement of her own, saying that 'she has read the foregoing affidavit of Major Rathbone, and knows the contents thereof . . . and . . . that the facts stated in the foregoing affidavit, so far as the same came to the knowledge or notice of this deponent, are accurately stated therein'.[1]

Most authorities have, therefore, concluded that only the four above-named persons occupied Lincoln's box, and that no one else entered or left it previous to Booth's intrusion. There certainly is nothing in any official reports which runs counter to these conclusions. Yet, there is every reason to believe that neither is correct. The occupants of the box did not number four, but five; and at least one other person entered it during the course of the performance.

The fifth occupant of the box was Charles Forbes, Lincoln's footman and personal attendant. He was not only present during the performance, but was also there when the fatal shot was fired. For this we have his own sworn statement.[2] If this be deemed insufficient, there is no lack of verification from other sources.

One of those who corroborate Forbes's affidavit is A. C. Richards, the superintendent of the Metropolitan Police. It was he who summoned Forbes as the only witness against John F. Parker, the neglectful guard, thereby showing that he knew Forbes's presence near the scene of the murder to be an undisputed fact. The day of the summons was 2 May, hence enough time had elapsed to eliminate any error, such as might have crept into hastily conceived proceedings.[3]

Further confirmation of Forbes's presence in the box comes to us from the editor of the *Washington National Republican*, a contemporary daily newspaper. This journalist, a man named S. P. Hanscom, in a little-known story throws additional light on what transpired around Lincoln's loge that evening:

'The Editor of the REPUBLICAN [so Hanscom's story runs]

---

[1] Laughlin, op. cit., pp. 289, 294, 295. Italics are the author's.
[2] Affidavit of Charles Forbes, used by courtesy of Mr. Frank G. Logan and the Chicago Historical Society.
[3] Records of Metropolitan Police Department, Washington, D.C.

was, probably, the last person at the box of the President prior to the assassin's entry of it. We went there for the purpose of delivering to the President a message, which we were requested to convey from the White House. Upon approaching the door of the box we found the passage-way leading to it blockaded by two gentlemen who were seated upon chairs, about six or eight feet from the door. We requested them to allow us to pass. They did so, and upon reaching the door we found no other person belonging to the Presidential household than Mr. CHARLES FORBES, one of Mrs. LINCOLN'S footmen and messengers, who was always in the habit of attending the President and Mrs. LINCOLN at the theatre. As the play was progressing we requested FORBES to hand the dispatch to the President. It was the last he ever received. At that time there were no guards, watchmen, sentinels, or ushers about the door of the President, and anyone could have passed in without molestation.'[1]

Of course, Hanscom does not state positively where Forbes was when he handed him the dispatch. He only says that 'upon reaching the door . . . we found no other person . . . than Mr. CHARLES FORBES'. But if Forbes had been outside the box, Hanscom probably would not have asserted so impressively that 'at that time there were no guards, and anyone could have passed in without molestation'. Forbes could very well have acted as a barrier to Booth's progress had he been outside the box and, what is more, would undoubtedly have done so. He had been in Lincoln's employ since 1861, and although not a native of the United States, was a faithful follower of his and greatly devoted to the presidential family.[2]

There is another point which leads to the inference that Forbes was with the Chief Executive when Hanscom approached him; had he been outside he would have detected Parker's absence and in all probability have called him back to his proper place, without a moment's delay.

[1] *Washington National Republican*, 8 June 1865.
[2] Forbes's affidavit; Thomas F. Pendel, *Thirty-Six Years in the White House* (Neale Publishing Co., Washington, 1902), p. 32; see also supplementary note to chapter iv, 'The Forbes Affidavit'.

To go back to Hanscom's story. Is there any evidence to verify his rather surprising revelations? Does it seem probable that they can be true?

Testimony from several witnesses proves that Hanscom's tale was founded on fact and was not the product of an over-wrought imagination. Lieutenant Crawford, a spectator whom Hanscom had to pass on his way to the box, appeared before Stanton and Judge Cartter, while, only a few hours after the event, they were carrying on a preliminary investigation at the Petersen House and mentioned the editor's arrival.

'There was a dispatch brought to the President about twenty Minutes before this [the assassination] occurred,' he testified. 'I think the name of the bearer was HANSCOMBE. He asked me where the President was. I showed him and he went in and gave it to him.'[1]

Lieutenant Crawford's companion, Captain Theodore Mc-Gowan, also saw Hanscom and was quite excited about him when quoted by the *Tribune* on 17 April.

'I remember that a man . . . passed me and inquired of one sitting near who the President's messenger was, and learning, exhibited to him an envelope, apparently official, having a printed heading and superscribed in a bold hand. I could not read the address, and did not try. *I think now it was meant for Lieut.-Gen. Grant.* That man went away.'[2]

Still further confirmation of Hanscom's entrance into the loge comes unexpectedly from Miss Clara Harris. In a statement made previous to her affidavit before Justice Olin and published in the *New York Herald*, 16 April, she reported that 'Nearly one hour before the commission of the deed the assassin came to the door of the box, and looked in to take a survey of the position of its occupants. It was supposed at the time that it was either a mistake or the exercise of an impertinent curiosity. The circumstance attracted no particular attention at the time. Upon his entering the box again Major Rathbon[e] arose and asked the intruder his business. He rushed past the Major without making a reply, and . . . fired. . . .'[3]

[1] Crawford's testimony—from papers of Corporal James Tanner in the Philadelphia Union League.
[2] *New York Tribune*, 17 Apr. 1865.
[3] *New York Herald*, 16 Apr. 1865.

The supposed assassin making his survey was probably none other than the editor of the *National Republican,* and his survey nothing worse than a search for the President, to whom he wanted to hand his message. This further substantiates the assumption that Forbes was inside the box and not at the door or outside of it.

What makes Miss Harris's statement to the Press doubly remarkable is that it differs so radically from the sworn statement she made before an official investigator two days later. Then she made no mention of the unknown visitor whom she had taken for the murderer. She must have forgotten the man as completely as she did the fact that her fiancé had risen to question him.

Or was it something other than forgetfulness which changed her testimony almost overnight? If she had seen the editor, Rathbone must have seen him too. Then why, people might ask, did he not react energetically to the obvious absence of the bodyguard? When Miss Harris appeared before Justice Olin she merely stated that the sworn statement of her fiancé was substantially correct, so far as she knew. She was careful not to go beyond that; and by doing so she not only shielded her future husband, but incidentally prevented any further inquiry relative to the appearance of the mysterious intruder. Such an investigation unquestionably would have thrown Parker's actions into full relief, and might have led to further disclosures in regard to the curious story of his appointment, and to the still more curious fact of his immunity from punishment. Miss Harris probably was easily influenced to modify her original story. The young lady was the daughter of an ex-senator and could be depended on to know when silence was golden. In this case, the interests of her fiancé clearly outweighed those of historical accuracy.

All this would be of minor interest were it not for the fact that Miss Harris's deposition was not the only one to undergo a remarkable change in the days that followed the death of the President. Major Rathbone also suffered a lapse of memory between the time he stood before Justice Olin on 17 April and the moment he took the witness stand in the conspiracy trial on 15 May. On 17 April he was emphatic in declaring that no one but Mr. and Mrs. Lincoln, Miss Harris, and himself had been in the presidential box. On the 15 May he omitted all reference to this point. This is the more noteworthy as the two statements are otherwise almost identical in wording.[1] The repetition of the same phrases on both occasions even suggests that Major Rathbone read his statement before the military commission from a prepared memorandum. An assertion made in the first account and deleted in the second must have been stricken out deliberately and for good reasons. For what reasons?

The next person to forget that he had ever seen either Hanscom or Forbes was Captain McGowan. On 16 April he had described with minute care Hanscom's appearance on the scene and had evidently been much impressed with the importance of his observation, for the *New York Tribune* published in italics his remarks about the man with the envelope, while all the rest of his story was printed in ordinary type. But on 15 May the witness McGowan did not seem to remember anything about this person and made no mention whatsoever of him.[2]

Lieutenant Crawford's statement never was given to the public, and therefore it is not known whether he still remembered in May what he had told Stanton and Judge Cartter about Hanscom a month earlier.

To insure Forbes's silence in regard to the event he had witnessed should not have been difficult. Although his loyalty was unquestioned in the opinion of all who knew him, he had been forced to play an unenviable, passive role which could easily have been misinterpreted by an enraged public. At any rate, Lincoln's footman was not heard from until he disclosed his presence at the theatre in an affidavit twenty-seven years later.

All the testimony involving the editor of the *National Republican* would probably have been completely forgotten, if he himself had not brought it forth in his paper on 8 June. What finally made him divulge the story is as much of a riddle as what had made him keep it under cover in the first place. Here we have the editor of a metropolitan daily in possession of a sensational and exclusive news story actually withholding it from his public, from the authorities, from the world.

[1] Laughlin, op. cit., p. 289; Pitman, op. cit., p. 78.
[2] Ibid.

As to Stanton, he should have had Hanscom arrested on the spot for suppressing important evidence. Was not the Secretary of War moving heaven and earth to gather all the facts which could be used as evidence against the conspirators? It was bad enough to fight the resistance of the Southern sympathizers— did he also have to tolerate lack of help in his own camp? But again Stanton did nothing. So far as he was concerned the issue of the *National Republican* of 8 June 1865 remained entirely unheeded, though scarcely unnoticed.

Not that Hanscom seemed particularly anxious to bring out the really sensational parts of his tale—that he was the last man to go into the box before the assassination; that he brought a message for the President, the last he ever received; that a fifth person whose name had been omitted from all published Press accounts was present in the box. These matters he alluded to only parenthetically; his main theme was an article which had appeared in the June number of *Harper's Magazine* and which greatly aroused his ire because of some alleged minor misstatements.

'It is not surprising', he lamented, 'that those who had to write on that night and the following day for the daily Press should have made mistakes, but it is hardly excusable that great errors should occur in the history of the affair published in a June monthly, written certainly one month after the occurrence.' He then went on to complain that no one could have known that Booth had barred the door to the presidential box behind him. He made this the motif of his whole column, although *Harper's Monthly* had at no time stressed the statement to which Hanscom took such violent exception.

One cannot help wondering why Hanscom, who appears so anxious to establish historical truths, was himself so slow in furnishing a veracious account of what he himself had seen; one must wonder still more why this historically minded editor did not favour future students with an elaboration of his report. He went to the box, he said, for the purpose of delivering to the President a message which he was requested to convey from the White House. But who requested Hanscom to act as a messenger? What became of the letter? What could have been the contents of this document that was carried to Lincoln in such an unorthodox manner and under such unusual conditions?

It is difficult to envisage a trained news-reporter, on the scene of a great national calamity, leaving these questions uninvestigated, unanswered. If Hanscom was any kind of newspaperman, why did he not interview Forbes and Parker—not to mention himself—and thereby secure for his paper the great scoop of the century and for himself a prominent place in history?

There is no answer to all this. If a document was found on Lincoln's body, the story has never been told. If Forbes failed to deliver it, he never disclosed the fact. Thomas Pendel, the doorkeeper of the White House, who wrote in detail of the happenings at the Executive Mansion on the night of Lincoln's death, made no reference to Hanscom nor to any document that had to be delivered to the President while he was at the theatre; least of all did he explain why such a message could not have been taken there through the ordinary channels.[1]

By writing his editorial in the *National Republican*, Hanscom effectively cleared his record of all suspicion of having suppressed pertinent evidence; if there were any rumours connecting his known presence at the box with the crime itself, the article squelched them. Yet so cleverly were his disclosures hidden beneath the smoke-screen of an attack on *Harper's Magazine* that the casual reader's attention is entirely diverted from the sensational confession which Hanscom in reality was recording.

There was nothing extraordinary, *per se*, in either Hanscom's or Forbes's presence in or near Lincoln's loge on the night of the murder. Even the mystery of the message may have a simple explanation, as will be shown later. The strangest part of the whole episode was that such efforts were made to hush it up.

Is it only a coincidence that Hanscom withheld his contribution to history long enough to escape the possibility of being summoned as a witness at the conspiracy trial? The prosecution had closed its case on 23 May, and the last rebuttal testimony for the defence closed formally on 10 June. The editorial in the *National Republican* appeared on 8 June. Furthermore, if Hanscom wanted his editorial to create as little stir as possible, he could not have chosen a better time. The whole country was watching the great trial that was to make the conspirators atone

[1] Pendel, *Thirty-Six Years in the White House*, p. 40.

for their bloody deeds, and but little attention was being paid to matters that had no direct bearing on its outcome. If Hanscom wished to keep himself out of the limelight, this was the proper moment for him to make his revelations; for his story failed to arouse contemporary comments, and has not been alluded to by historians even down to the present day.

To believe that the unanimous change in the testimony of all key witnesses was a chance affair is to believe in an absurdity. That these respectable people could have been influenced by anyone but a person in high authority is also incredible; and in placing the responsibility for this attempt at perverting history one must look for some one who had both the power and the motive to carry it out.

Some one who had the power—

All the power at that time was concentrated in the War Department, where Stanton's reign was autocratic. Major Rathbone and Captain McGowan were officers of the army. Would they have taken orders to suppress evidence from any one of less exalted standing?

And some one who had the motive—

The only possible motive for veiling the events at the theatre could have been the wish to keep Parker out of the picture; and the only one who would have an interest in doing so is the person charged with the responsibility for Lincoln's safety.

Who, then, was responsible—legally responsible—for Lincoln's safety?

The answer to this is furnished by James Speed, attorney-general in Lincoln's Cabinet. In a letter to President Johnson, dated July 1865, he declared that:

'At the time of the assassination a civil war was flagrant . . . the principal police of the city was by Federal soldiers . . . and the President's House and person were, or should have been, under the guard of soldiers.'[1]

And so, with a sly dig at the delinquency of his colleague in the War Department, the attorney-general of the United States placed the responsibility for guarding Lincoln—and, by inference, the failure to protect him adequately—squarely on the shoulders of Secretary of War Edwin M. Stanton.

[1] Pitman, op. cit., p. 403.

CHAPTER V

The President is Refused Protection

There is some reason to believe that Lincoln himself doubted the reliability of the new guard who was to accompany him to the performance of *Our American Cousin*. Lincoln was a shrewd judge of human nature and well acquainted with the personnel of the White House. At any rate, when the President paid one of his usual visits to the War Department on 14 April, he asked Stanton to let him have his chief aide, Major Thomas T. Eckert, as escort for himself and his guests.

'I have seen Eckert break five pokers, one after the other, over his arm,' Lincoln declared, 'and I am thinking he would be the kind of man to go with me this evening. May I take him?'[1]

This request Stanton refused point-blank; he had some important work for Eckert that night, he said, and could not spare him. But Lincoln was not so easily rebuffed. He went into the cipher room, over which Eckert presided, and told the latter of his plans for the evening. He also repeated his request that this strong-armed assistant of Stanton's become one of the theatre party, coaxing him good-naturedly to come along, as both he and Mrs. Lincoln wanted him. So far as the work was concerned, the President suggested that it could be done the next day as well. Eckert also very decidedly refused to go, however, pleading work that could not be put off; and so Lincoln reluctantly left. 'I shall take Major Rathbone along,' he said in parting, '. . . but I should much rather have you, Major [Eckert], since I know you can break a poker over your arm.'[2]

[1] David Homer Bates, *Lincoln in the Telegraph Office* (Century Co. (D. Appleton-Century Co.), New York, 1907), p. 367.
[2] Ibid., p. 368.

This event was written up by one of Stanton's telegraph operators who was his fellow townsman and whose loyalty and affection for his superior have never been questioned. It must have left a deep impression on both the Secretary of War and his assistant, in view of the tragic consequences which their refusal brought about; but, so far as is known, neither of them ever mentioned it. Eckert's reticence was almost proverbial, so much so that he had earned the sobriquet of 'Silent Eckert'; no enlightenment regarding this incident could, therefore, be expected from him.[1]

Stanton did make one reference to Lincoln's last visit to him, but he presented a totally different version of it. The Secretary of War, in a detailed account he gave to General James B. Fry a few days after the tragedy, said '. . . that he had never felt so sensible of his deep affection for Lincoln as he did during their final interview. At last they could see the end of bloody fratricidal war. . . . As they exchanged congratulations, Lincoln, from his greater height, dropped his long arm upon Stanton's shoulders, and a hearty embrace terminated their rejoicings over the close of the mighty struggle. Stanton went home happy. That night Lincoln was assassinated. . . .'[2] This is Stanton's best recollection of what took place. Not a word about Lincoln's request for Eckert's services, nor about his obvious disappointment in having been refused so cavalierly. On the other hand, the operator, David Bates, who was such a keen observer, must have entirely missed the touching episode that filled Stanton's mind to the exclusion of everything else when he remembered Lincoln's call. Of course, it is possible that both these happenings took place and, having no other witnesses to fall back upon, this is the only conclusion that one can reach under the circumstances. Strange though, that if it had not been for Bates's memoirs, the story of this unusual occurrence would never have become known, in spite of the momentous importance that attaches to it.

[1] David Homer Bates, *Lincoln in the Telegraph Office*, p. 323.
[2] Allen T. Rice (Ed.), *Reminiscences of Abraham Lincoln by Distinguished Men of His Time* (North American Publishing Co., New York, 1886), p. 404; see also supplementary note to chapter v, 'The Story Told by David Homer Bates'.

The President is Refused Protection

What can it mean that Stanton, during a congressional investigation, testified under oath that Lincoln did not visit the War Department at all after 13 April? 'The order of Mr. Lincoln, of 12 April, is on file in the War Department,' he stated, 'and was the last order he ever made, of which I have any knowledge. It was made the last time he was in the War Department.'[1]

In his eagerness to put himself on record regarding this matter, Stanton stumbled. He actually contradicted himself a moment later, admitting that the President had come to the War Department again a day later, on 13 April, during the middle of the afternoon. There, according to Stanton, he wrote out a telegram; it '. . . was the last act that was ever performed by Mr. Lincoln in the War Department'.[2] But William Crook, Lincoln's bodyguard, is as positive as David Bates in his assertion that he accompanied the President to the War Department in the afternoon of 14 April.

Which one of these two accounts is one to believe? The story of Bates, confirmed by Crook, which places Lincoln in the War Office a few hours before his death, or the one of Stanton which denies it, but is inconsistent in its dates?

As the conversation regarding Eckert's services could not have taken place on any other day but 14 April, after General Grant's positive cancellation of his proposed visit to the theatre, Stanton's sworn statement to the contrary assumes a peculiar significance; the more so, as there was no necessity for the Secretary to refer at all to Lincoln's visits. The questions asked of him by the congressional committee merely related to the proposed meeting of the Virginia legislators in early April 1865. Lincoln's presence in the War Office was not under investigation; yet, Stanton twice went out of his way to emphasize that the President had not visited him on the day of the assassination.

It may have been just boorishness on the part of Stanton to refuse Lincoln's request for an escort of his own choosing, but it was almost insubordination on the part of Major Eckert. The President could easily have turned his request into a command, or have taken serious offence at the attitude of both the secretary

[1] *Impeachment Investigation* (Government Printing Office, Washington, D.C., 1868), p. 400.
[2] Ibid.

43

and his aide. That any really important work for Stanton and Eckert was in prospect for that evening was quite improbable. The war was practically over, and Lincoln's suggestion that whatever tasks were to be done could just as well be put off until another day bore the mark of his habitual good sense. It becomes of interest, therefore, to investigate what actually transpired at the War Department while the performance at Ford's Theatre was proceeding. What were Stanton and Eckert doing during these fateful hours and what important activity developed for them and for their office?

Only three telegrams addressed to either Lincoln or Stanton are officially on record as having arrived at the War Department during the evening of 14 April. There is some doubt as to the time when the second dispatch was received, but it presumably reached Washington before midnight.

(No. 1)
                                              Richmond, Va.
                                        14 *April* 1865—11 a.m.
                                           (Received 9.30 p.m.)

PRESIDENT OF THE UNITED STATES:

Mr. R. M. T. Hunter has just arrived under the invitation signed by General Weitzel. He and Judge J. A. Campbell wish a permit for their visit to you at Washington, I think, with important communications.

                                              E. O. C. ORD,
                                                Major-General.[1]

(No. 2)
                                              Richmond, Va.
                                         14 *April* 1865—4 p.m.
HON. E. M. STANTON,
Secretary of War:

Several applicants are here, some by General Shepley's invitation, to start a newspaper with the type and press of the *Sentinel.* I have declined to grant their application. Can you not send a reliable gentleman to attend to this matter? I am, where I can do so consistent with the interest of the service, kind to the submissive, and I am trying to make the military rule acceptable. In order to supply food and fuel and enable the poor or needy

---

[1] *Official Records,* I, vol. 46, part 3, p. 748.

to get home, I am about to let the coal, canal, and Fredericksburg railroad companies open their communications with the city, and am granting passes home to civilians on the same terms Grant gave to Lee's army. Please correct me when this course may require it.

E. O. C. ORD,
Major-General.[1]

(No. 3)

City Point, Va.
14 *April* 1865
(Received 8.30 p.m.)

HON. E. M. STANTON:

I send you the farewell address of Lee to his army, which I obtained a copy of at Appomattox Court-House just as I left there day before yesterday....

E. B. WASHBURNE.[2]

The few other messages that were filed that night were only of routine character and were not addressed either to the President or to Stanton.

The second and third dispatches are of no consequence, but the first telegram probably clears up the mystery of the message that Hanscom took to the presidential loge. Yet if the dispatch he transmitted was from Major-General Ord there must have been an almost unbelievable state of laxity in discipline both at the War Department and at the White House. The message was addressed to the President personally, and would, therefore, be sent to the White House as soon as received—and perused— by Stanton's satellites. The time, 9.30 p.m., at which it reached Washington checks fairly well with the time at which the editor of the *National Republican* appeared at Ford's Theatre, which was about ten minutes before ten, according to Lieutenant Crawford's testimony. What remains inscrutable is why, if the dispatch was considered important, its delivery was entrusted to a newspaperman who happened to be available at the moment; or, if it was regarded as unimportant, why it was delivered at all. Lincoln could hardly have acted on General Ord's message while attending a play. Nevertheless, it is quite possible that the

---

[1] *Official Records*, I, vol. 46, part 3, p. 749.
[2] Ibid., p. 744.

message went from the War Department to the White House marked 'For the President—Important', and that Hanscom volunteered to take it to Lincoln. The contents of the dispatch would, of course, be unknown both to him and to the White House attendants who so readily accepted the editor's services.

All that is of no great moment, however. What is more to the point is this: if the message presented to Lincoln was Ord's telegram, the handling of that dispatch proves that neither Stanton nor Eckert was on duty at the War Department at 9.30 p.m. when the wire from Richmond came in. If either of them had been at his desk the dispatch never would have been sent to the White House, since both the Secretary and his chief cipher operator knew that Lincoln was at the theatre that evening. They would naturally, therefore, have sent the telegram straight to the playhouse and not to the Executive Mansion. Everything considered, they probably would not have sent it at all, as its contents were not of a nature to require immediate action.

Apparently, neither Stanton nor Eckert, in spite of their assurances to Lincoln that they expected a busy evening, even put in an appearance at the War Department that night. Not a single wire went out from there signed by either of the men, and only two were received that were personally addressed to Stanton. But there is also direct evidence to show that Stanton, at least, did not even make a pretence of showing up at his office. According to the Secretary's own account of his experiences on the evening of 14 April, he went home and dined as usual. He then went to see Secretary of State Seward, who was sick in bed due to the effects of his recent accident. There he found six or eight people and stayed chatting with them till he heard the music of a procession which had notified him that it would call on him. Thereupon he went home, made the serenaders a little speech, and, shortly after ten o'clock, locked up the house and went to his bedroom. He was nearly undressed when the news of the assault on Seward was conveyed to him. Of the attack on Lincoln he was not apprised until later.[1]

When Stanton told the President that he expected to do a lot of work that night, he seems to have evaded the truth. In the

[1] Moorfield Storey, 'Dickens, Stanton, Sumner, and Storey' in *Atlantic Monthly*, Apr. 1930, p. 464.

light of his own statements it looks as if he had no intention of doing any work at all in the evening.

Now as to Eckert. Was he at his post during the hours when Lincoln had requested his protection against a possible assassin?

He was not. The cipher department was left in charge of Mr. Bates; Eckert was not anywhere near there. Bates confirmed the report of a quiet evening, for he remembered nothing in particular that occurred prior to the assassination. He made no mention of the message which went to the White House, probably thinking it of no consequence.

The War Department was pretty well deserted. Two of Bates's comrades were in the audience at Ford's Theatre.[1] They, too, could hardly have expected a great rush of work, and appeared to have had no difficulty in obtaining permission to absent themselves during the time when, according to Stanton's statement to the President, a great deal of work would have to be done.

So far as Eckert is concerned we have no record of his doings that night, either from his mouth or his pen. It is only known that he left the cipher room in charge of a subordinate and that at half-past ten he was found at home shaving, when one of the telegraphers came running from the theatre to his house to advise him of the catastrophe.[2]

David Homer Bates's charge that Stanton and Eckert brusquely refused Lincoln's request to give him the protection he desired for the evening of 14 April is so serious that a confirmation of his story from other sources would be desirable. Unfortunately, no corroborating witnesses have been found, and it is improbable that any existed. Bates did not publish his account until 1907—forty-two years after the event. Is it possible that the incident never happened, and was only the product of an elderly man's imagination?

Did Lincoln visit the telegraph office at all on his last day on earth, or was Stanton right in his claim to the contrary?

If Lincoln had not made his usual calls at the War Department, it would have been the subject of comment from many

[1] *Boston Sunday Post*, 11 Apr. 1915
[2] Ibid.

quarters. Moreover, it is known that the President was then particularly anxious about news from Sherman and, as Stanton never sent dispatches to the White House, Lincoln hardly would have omitted his daily inquiries at the fountainhead of all military information. That he did call on this occasion is averred by Bates not only in his book but also in a previous paper, read in 1900, and in an article published by him five years before that time. It is further supported by William Crook, the White House guard, who emphasized the incident in his recollections, and is known to have mentioned it also in at least one private letter.[1]

It may therefore be accepted as an historical fact that, Stanton's sworn testimony notwithstanding, Lincoln did visit the War Department on the day of his death and, what is still more noteworthy, it was Stanton who caused Grant to decline the President's invitation.

That Bates, who was a great admirer of the War Minister and a life-long friend of Eckert, invented the remainder of the picturesque story is highly improbable.

[1] David Homer Bates, 'Some Recollections of Abraham Lincoln', *History of the Ohio Society of New York* (The Grafton Press, New York, 1906), p. 635, and letter in Hannah Collection, Chicago, by courtesy of Mr. Alexander Hannah, *New York Independent*, 4 Apr. 1895.

CHAPTER VI

Premonitions v. Secret Service Reports

Was it a premonition of the approaching tragedy that prompted Lincoln to ask Stanton for a suitable guard on the eve of his assassination? Lincoln had brought with him to Washington all the mysticism and superstitions of his backwoods environment; only a few days prior to his death he had told his friend Ward Lamon of a pitiful dream he had had, in which he saw himself on a bier in the East Room of the White House, the victim of an assassin. William Crook, the President's bodyguard during the afternoon of the last day, remembered that Lincoln had said 'good-bye' to him instead of 'good-night'.[1] But if Lincoln had evil forebodings at that time they were not necessarily the vague feelings of a psychic mind. There were numerous tangible reasons why imminent danger to the President's life should have been anticipated and provided against. If Lincoln knew of these dangers, he only knew what was bruited about the Capital and what was generally accepted as true in all informed circles.

Over and above the threatening letters which Lincoln, like other prominent persons, was constantly receiving, reports had reached Washington that a serious attempt would be made toward the end of the war either to kidnap or murder the President. As early as 19 March 1864 the *New York Tribune* had printed a letter believed to have originated in the South. In this letter the possibilities for the success of such an enterprise were discussed at length.

'One hundred and fifty picked men were to go secretly North and take quarters in Washington, Georgetown, Baltimore, and

---

[1] Crook, *Through Five Administrations*, pp. 67–8.

Alexandria, so as to be able to communicate daily with each other, and, upon a day fixed by their leader, were to assemble in Washington for the purpose of making the seizure. The President, it was claimed, could be easily seized at a private hour, at the White House, or in going to or returning from church, or on some other favourable occasion, and thrust into a carriage and driven off. The carriage was to be joined a few miles out of the city by twenty-five or thirty armed men on horseback. It was proposed to drive to Indian Point, about twenty-five miles south of Washington, on the Potomac—two or three relays of fleet horses being stationed on the way—where a boat was to be waiting to cross the river, and land the captive a few miles south of Occoquan, when it would be an easy matter for his captors to work their way with him through the woods by night into the Rebel lines. To prevent pursuit, every bridge between Washington and Indian Point was to be mined beforehand, and blown up as soon as the captive and his captors had crossed. Huge trees were also to be ready cut and thrown across the road in various places, as soon as they had passed, by men stationed along for the purpose, who were afterward to separate and escape as best they could. ...

'But this is not the only scheme by any means that has been devised for kidnapping our President. Last summer a club or society of wealthy citizens of Richmond was formed for the purpose of raising a fund for this object. Circulars were sent to trustworthy citizens in every other city and town in the Confederacy, inviting co-operation in the grand undertaking, and an immense sum of money was subscribed. ...

'Whether these schemes have been abandoned, or whether the kidnappers are only awaiting a favourable opportunity to execute them, remains to be seen; but certain it is that too much caution can not be observed by the President, or the military commanders stationed at the capital.'[1]

On 17 April 1864 the *Tribune* had followed this with what it considered further evidence of the existence of such a plot, quoting one of the conspirators as exclaiming that he would willingly sell his soul to the devil for the honour of playing

---

[1] *Assassination and History of the Conspiracy* (J. R. Hawley & Co., Cincinnati), pp. 56–8.

a conspicuous part in 'the destruction of the Great Hydra'.

It does not matter whether the letters were genuine or spurious. The plans, as outlined in detail, were entirely feasible, and called for measures to guard against their execution.

Some such measures actually were put into effect, much against Lincoln's fatalistic wish to be left alone. A troop of Ohio light cavalry of picked men, mounted on the best black horses to be found, was detailed to act as the President's escort, and was quartered near the White House, ready for instant duty, and under orders to accompany its commander-in-chief on his frequent trips through the surrounding country.[1]

In order to safeguard the President on his walks and while at home, the four special bodyguards previously referred to were selected from Washington's Metropolitan Police Force; so that it can be said that reasonable precautions had been taken to protect him against such attacks as could be foreseen.

During the last few weeks of Lincoln's life the vague rumours which had caused all this anxiety began to assume more concrete shape, and some of his advisers were moved to issue new warnings to him. Ward Lamon, prior to leaving for Richmond on a special mission a few days before Lincoln's death, begged his friend and master not to visit any theatre during the marshal's absence and, although Lincoln did not actually promise this, he seemed to be greatly impressed by Lamon's insistent pleadings.[2]

'The Marshal W. H. Lamon has several times within the last two months told me that he believed the President would be assassinated . . .', Orville H. Browning wrote in his diary on 14 April.[3]

Lieutenant David D. Dana, a lesser provost-marshal in Washington, and one who was to play an important part in the pursuit of Booth, declared many years afterward that the Government had tangible information of a plot against Lincoln which was to mature at that time.[4] The Booth group of conspirators,

[1] Robert McBride, *Some Personal Recollections of Abraham Lincoln* (Bobbs-Merrill Co., Indianapolis, 1926), pp. 16, 17.

[2] Ward H. Lamon, *Recollections of Abraham Lincoln* (A. C. McClurg & Co., Chicago, 1895), p. 275.

[3] Orville H. Browning, *Diary* (Illinois State Historical Society, Springfield, 1933), II, 18, 19.

[4] *Boston Sunday Globe*, 12 Dec. 1897; also quoted in Finis L. Bates, *Escape and Suicide of John Wilkes Booth* (Memphis, Tenn., 1907), p. 95.

according to later confessions, was actually embarrassed in its movements, owing to the many rumours afloat in the Capital.[1] Sam Arnold, one of its members, was afraid that the authorities were well informed, for in his fatal letter to Booth, he said:

'You know full well that the G——t suspicions something is going on there; therefore, the undertaking is becoming more complicated. Why not, for the present, desist . . . ?'[2]

In this Arnold probably was right, for Grant's cipher operator, Captain S. H. Beckwith, had heard of the threats against Lincoln's life. He wrote subsequently: 'Secret service agents in Washington and elsewhere had got wind of several suspicious plots that foreboded ill to our eminent officials.'[3]

Even members of the Cabinet were aware of some definite danger. After the tragedy John P. Usher, Secretary of the Interior, reported that when he visited Mr. Seward, the Secretary of State remarked 'that if he had been able to be out . . . Mr. Lincoln would not have gone to the theatre that night'. From which it may be assumed that the State Department knew of, or anticipated, some serious design against the President's life.[4]

Neither Seward nor Lamon nor any one else ever found it expedient to disclose what information they possessed. The reason for this secretiveness is another matter left to the whims of speculation.

Lincoln himself apparently had either a premonition or a warning from an unknown source that an attempt on his life would be made on the night of the fourteenth. This extraordinary fact is attested by William Crook, one of the President's bodyguards, who, many years later, wrote that when he accompanied Lincoln to the War Department late in the afternoon of 14 April, the Chief Executive suddenly turned to him and said: 'Crook, do you know, I believe there are men who want to take my life?' After a pause, he added, as if to himself, 'And I have no doubt they will do it.'

The President's calm and sure tone so disconcerted the guard

---

[1] Laughlin, op. cit., p. 228; see also supplementary note to chapter vi, 'The Plot to Kidnap Lincoln'.

[2] Pitman, op. cit., p. 236.

[3] *New York Sun*, 27 Apr. 1913.

[4] John P. Usher, *President Lincoln's Cabinet* (1925), p. 12.

that he could only stammer: 'Why do you think so, Mr. President?'

'Other men have been assassinated . . .', was the reply. 'I have perfect confidence in those who are around me. . . . I know no one could do it and escape alive. But if it is to be done, it is impossible to prevent it.'[1]

A fairly good guess can be made as to at least one cause of the general alarm, by drawing on some official information which, shortly after the death of the President, found its way into print. It relates to an event which deserves much greater attention than has been given it by most students.

Some time about the middle of March, probably on the twentieth of the month, an actual attempt was made to kidnap the President of the United States. It was on this day that Booth and his little band of conspirators assembled for real action; it was their first and last mobilization. An announcement had been made that Lincoln was to attend a performance of *Still Waters Run Deep* at the Soldiers' Home, three miles from the city, and Booth decided that the proper time for the execution of the plot had at last arrived. Surratt was there to take the reins and drive the carriage across Benning's bridge into Maryland. Lewis Paine was there to match his herculean strength against the physical prowess of the man they hoped to capture. Arnold and O'Laughlin acted as look-outs, while the boyish Herold waited for the party at Surrattsville, with supplies of ropes, rifles, and repair tools. The ropes were to be stretched across the roads to delay pursuing cavalry until Port Tobacco could be reached. This place was some thirty-six miles south of Washington. There Atzerodt was ready with his boat to carry the party across to the shores of Virginia.[2]

It was early afternoon when the presidential carriage came into view. What happened then has never been clearly told. It is only known that the conspirators quickly discovered that the person inside the carriage was not the President. Who took his

---

[1] Crook, *Through Five Administrations*, p. 66.
[2] Pitman, op. cit., p. 118; see also supplementary note to chapter vi, 'The Spelling of the Names of Paine and Wiechmann'.
Laughlin, op. cit., pp. 45, 288 ff.

place that day the authorities have never disclosed. Surratt thought he recognized Chase, but he was probably in error. No matter who the occupant of the conveyance was, it is almost certain that he and the coachman sensed their peril when they observed the suspicious actions of the plotters. The chances are that the horses were whirled around and driven at top speed back to Washington, where the adventure must have been reported to the secret service with telling effect.

It is significant that Colonel Burnett, who conducted some of the investigations in regard to the assassination and who later assisted the judge-advocate in the trial, stated that the attempt to abduct the President was made about 20 March.[1] During the trial all the testimony indicated 16 March as the date of that enterprise. Where did Burnett get this date, if not from reports that had been made to the authorities by those who were in the presidential coach?

That Booth's band thought its intentions had been correctly interpreted is plainly shown by the haste with which its members scattered in all directions—to Baltimore, to Richmond, to New York. 'The guilty flee when no man pursueth,' a commentator remarked when he reviewed this event.[2] But Booth and his army could hardly have done anything but flee. They naturally expected that the returning carriage would give the alarm and that thereafter the President would be carefully guarded against all possible danger.

Did Stanton and his staff know of this attempt to attack Lincoln within the limits of his capital? It is almost impossible to think otherwise. Nothing that pertained to such matters could be kept from the Secretary of War; and no step of importance could be taken without his consent. If there had been any hope in the secretary's mind that the numerous whispers of plots were idle rumours, here was tangible evidence that Lincoln's enemies were able and ready to strike.

But there are more direct indications that the War Depart-

[1] Henry L. Burnett, *Assassination of President Lincoln and the Trial of the Assassins* (Ohio Society of New York, 1906), p. 601; Pitman, op. cit., p. 120.
[2] *Surratt Trial* (Government Printing Office, Washington, D.C., 1867), II, p. 1139.

ment—charged with the responsibility of protecting the President—knew about this bold attempt to kidnap him. The conspirators happened to have in their midst an eavesdropper who betrayed to the authorities what he knew of this enterprise long before it had culminated in action. This man, Louis J. Wiechmann, confided in a fellow clerk, one Captain Gleason, in the office of the commissary general of prisoners, where both of them were employed. Gleason undertook to see that Stanton was informed through Lieutenant Sharp, an assistant provost-marshal on the staff of General Augur, while Wiechmann unburdened himself to a United States enrolling officer, named McDavitt, who in turn notified his superiors.[1] Wiechmann first informed Gleason, on 20 February, that 'the time set was Inauguration Day'. Before that date the War Department had been fully advised.

Although Gleason's part in this matter was hushed up at the time and although one looks in vain for most of the names mentioned by him, either among the witnesses in the conspiracy trial or in contemporary newspapers, a part of the truth seeped through two years later, when Wiechmann was being grilled by a hard cross-examiner. For once he lost his bland equanimity and went a little beyond his carefully rehearsed testimony.

Q. Do you recollect of stating ... that if Captain Gleason had not betrayed you, you never would have said a word about this matter?
A. No, sir. ... Mr. Gleason never went to the War Department until about ten days after I had first given the information.[2]

Inasmuch as Gleason admittedly went to the War Department —it does not matter when—it is inconceivable that its officials did not know that Lincoln was in imminent bodily danger. More than that, it is practically certain that they also knew the identity of the entire group which had participated in the kidnapping venture. When Surratt, a few days later, passed through Washington on his way from Richmond to Canada he did not dare sleep at home because detectives had been looking for him

[1] D. H. L. Gleason, 'Conspiracy Against Lincoln' in *Magazine of History*, Feb. 1911.
[2] *Surratt Trial*, I, 454.

there; and, after the assassination had taken place, O'Laughlin was arrested in Baltimore before there was any chance for the War Department detectives to do more than learn how the crime had been committed, and before any possible connection could have been established between the deed at Ford's Theatre and this young man of Baltimore. Neither Gleason, Sharp, nor McDavitt was ever asked to testify, and the names of the two last men were not even divulged to the public.

Clara E. Laughlin, with keen insight, felt that this apparently trifling incident called for further elucidation. 'On what information Arnold and O'Laughlin were arrested so promptly the records do not tell us,' she wrote in *The Death of Lincoln*, 'but John Surratt's explanation makes it clear; he said, in his Rockville lecture of 8 December 1870, that the abduction plot was known to the Government detectives, who quite naturally jumped to the conclusion that the men involved in it were those implicated in the President's murder'.[1]

The Government evidently wanted it understood that it was shrewd detective work, based on the 'Sam' letter found in Booth's trunk, that led to the arrest of its author, Sam Arnold, and to that of Michael O'Laughlin. General Harris, in his book on the assassination, remarked: 'In Booth's trunk a letter was found from Samuel Arnold to Booth, dated at Hookstown, Md., 27 March 1865. This letter was signed simply "Sam", but was proved to be in Arnold's handwriting, and led not only to his own arrest, but also to that of his friend and fellow conspirator, Michael O'Laughlin.'[2]

This is exactly the impression the prosecuting attorney desired to create in the mind of the military judges, whose reasoning power probably did not rise above the level of modest mediocrity. As a matter of fact, the author of the 'Sam' letter was not identified until 17 April. A man named Robert G. Mowry, employed in the ambulance department, appeared before the authorities on that day and made this statement:

[1] Laughlin, op. cit., pp. 165–6, 232.
[2] T. M. Harris, *Assassination of Lincoln* (American Citizen Co., Boston, 1892), p. 71.

'There was a notice in the paper yesterday [16 April] giving some description of the writing of a man who passed by the name of 'Sam', and from the description I thought it might possibly be the writing of a man I knew. It occurred to me that it might be the writing of a man named Samuel Arnold.'

On his being shown the letter, his suspicions were verified.

'I believe that is the man's handwriting. To the best of my knowledge it is the handwriting of Samuel Arnold.'[1]

This was on 17 April; but it had been two days earlier that detectives had looked for O'Laughlin in his Baltimore home. William Wallace, the Government agent in charge, testified at the conspiracy trial to that effect. 'O'Laughlin', he stated, '. . . said that when he got to his brother-in-law's house, on Saturday afternoon, he heard that the detectives had been there.'[2] Saturday had been 15 April.

The actual arrest of O'Laughlin took place on the seventeenth, long before Arnold's identity could have been connected with that of his Baltimore companion. The problem of this connection is an interesting one in itself, and there is nothing to show how it was solved. If Harris's brilliant deductions be followed, the 'Sam' letter led to the discovery of Arnold, and the discovery of Arnold was followed, as a logical sequence, by the arrest of O'Laughlin; but matters worked out in just the opposite way. O'Laughlin was arrested first, not Arnold.[3]

Furthermore, if Arnold's identity was really established by Mr. Mowry's statement, it would hardly have been possible to arrest him so quickly. It was first necessary to trace him to Hookstown and then to obtain the information there that the suspect had accepted work in Fort Monroe, all of which would have taken considerable time. But Arnold's arrest was ordered by Assistant-Secretary of War C. A. Dana in a wire to Provost-Marshal McPhail of Maryland, on 16 April at 2.55 p.m., and was made by two men from McPhail's office, fully a day before the handwriting of the accused was identified.[4]

---

[1] War Department Archives, Washington, D.C.
[2] Pitman, op. cit., p. 222.
[3] Ibid., p. 234.
[4] *Official Records*, Series I, vol. 46, part III, p. 806.

On what information could O'Laughlin and Arnold possibly have been suspected, unless their names had been known to the Washington authorities through Wiechmann's disclosure of the attempted abduction?

In arresting these two men so quickly, the War Department erred, just as Stanton had blundered when announcing that the assassination had been planned prior to 4 March. Both were slips that passed unnoticed. They point, however, to some secret knowledge possessed by the Secretary of War and his department.

Perhaps it was at the time of the kidnapping attempt that some precautionary measures were adopted to prevent the easy passage of vehicles over the bridges across the Potomac.

'. . . We had understood', said John Surratt, one of the plotters, a few years later, 'that the Government had received information that there was a plot of some kind on hand. They had even commenced to build a stockade on the Navy Yard bridge, gates opening toward the south, as though they expected danger from within, and not from without.'[1]

With Wiechmann's confession in hand, and proof that an actual assault on Lincoln had only been prevented by his sudden change of plans, could the War Department have done less than barricade the bridges that led toward the Confederate States?

According to Sam Arnold, several splendid opportunities to kidnap Lincoln had from time to time presented themselves. The President on two different occasions had passed over the Eastern Branch bridge, accompanied only by his coachmen and a single guard within the carriage. 'Information was immediately conveyed to Booth', reports Arnold, 'of these occurrences. He paid but slight attention to the matter, on account, as he said, of the pressure of business at the time, and thus the only favourable opportunities were permitted to pass by without the slightest notice being taken. . . .'

Booth, so Arnold concluded, had become a monomaniac on the plan of abducting Lincoln from the midst of a theatrical audience. Anything less spectacular than that had ceased to

[1] Laughlin, op. cit., p. 227.

58

appeal to his imagination. The President was to be seized in his box by the actor himself, possibly with the aid of the redoubtable Paine; Arnold's part was to help lower the trussed-up Chief Magistrate to the stage, whence the captive would have to be carried to a waiting conveyance. It was in vain that Arnold combatted the utter impracticability of this plan. Booth was obstinate, and sulked when outvoted by his less romantically inclined comrades. He would play the game according to the rules laid down by himself, or else he would not play at all.[1]

Arnold's story is supported by Booth's proven attempt to engage an actor, named Samuel Chester, to take part in the enterprise. In furtherance of the project, the gas in the playhouse was to be turned off and, as the main regulating valve was located near the prompter's desk, the presence on the stage of an actor-conspirator was necessary. Chester, however, was obdurate, and rejected Booth's offer. His sworn testimony in the conspiracy trial puts the time of the attempted kidnapping as January 1865. He was under the impression that, besides turning off the lights, he was also expected to open the back door of the theatre.[2] In this he was probably mistaken.

Other indications that preparations were being made at that time to execute the kidnapping venture came from a man named Eddy Martin, who told of his visit to Atzerodt about 10 January 1865. He had made arrangements with him to cross the Potomac, but could get no action. 'I was losing confidence in Atzerodt. ...' he testified. 'He came to the hotel about 11 o'clock. I accused him of intending to cross over that night with other parties; told him I had been paying him all that he asked, and that I must cross by the first boat. He denied that anybody was going to cross that night. ... He then made this explanation: He said ... on Wednesday night a large party would cross of ten or twelve persons; that he had been engaged that day in buying boats; that they were going to have relays of horses on the road between Port Tobacco and Washington.'[3]

Booth's insistence on making a theatre in Washington the scene of his daring attempt gives a possible key to the much debated question of why he undertook the assassination at all. The

[1] Samuel B. Arnold, 'The Lincoln Plot', *Baltimore American*, 1902.
[2] Pitman, op. cit., p. 44.
[3] *Surratt Trial*, I, 215.

conception of a heroic deed to be performed in a large Washington theatre may have taken such a strong hold on his imagination that he felt bound to carry out the plan, even though nothing was to be gained by it; for with the surrender of Lee, the capture of the Northern chief had lost all practical value. There remained only one move—assassination.

Chester testified that the actor had described to him several good opportunities to shoot Lincoln. 'What an excellent chance I had to kill the President, if I had wished, on inauguration day!' Booth had exclaimed.[1] But evidently neither kidnapping nor killing was as important to the scion of Junius Brutus Booth as the proper stage setting for his part.

Stanton seems to have taken it for granted that Lincoln had known of some definite threat against his life, for on the day after the tragedy he sent the following wire to General Sherman:

... I FIND EVIDENCE THAT AN ASSASSIN IS ALSO ON YOUR TRACK, AND I BESEECH YOU TO BE MORE HEEDFUL THAN MR. LINCOLN WAS OF SUCH KNOWLEDGE.[2]

This tell-tale message conveys three distinct and separate allegations: first, that evidence on hand showed an assassin to be on Sherman's trail; second, that Lincoln had possessed actual knowledge of his impending assassination; third, that he had taken no heed of this warning.

Now, if the President was loath to protect himself, it was Stanton's duty to guard him. But in this one instance, if David Homer Bates is a reliable witness, Lincoln had really tried to 'be more heedful of such knowledge' by asking for a bodyguard of his own choosing, and it was Stanton who had refused his request. Should the dead President have been blamed for his secretary's failure to act properly?

According to Bates, the *enfant terrible* of the otherwise reticent group with which Stanton had surrounded himself, 'extra precautions were taken by the authorities to protect the President and lieutenant-general against expected attempts to kidnap

[1] Pitman, op. cit., p. 45.
[2] *Official Records*, I, vol. 47, part III, p. 221.

or kill them, because of secret service reports that plans had been made to accomplish such evil designs during the excitement of that occasion'. What these extra precautions were Bates did not say.[1]

'It is idle to conjecture', he continued, 'what might have been the result if the alert and vigorous Eckert had accompanied Lincoln to Ford's Theatre that night. Had he done so the probabilities are that in view of Eckert's previous knowledge of the plot to kidnap or kill the President, Booth might have been prevented. . . .'[2]

Eckert then, so Bates recollected, had known of the plot to kidnap or kill the President. Stanton, of course, knew whatever Eckert knew. Possessed of this knowledge, should they not have warned Major Rathbone to be watchful, considering that the air was filled with ugly rumours? If they had done so, is it likely that Rathbone would have seated himself farthest away from the door to the box and, according to his sworn statement, been 'intently observing the proceedings upon the stage, with his back toward the door', without being aware of Booth's presence until he heard the discharge of the pistol behind him?[3] Should the War Department not have warned Parker that danger was lurking in the theatre, in the crowd, that any stranger who might try to enter the loge of the President was a putative murderer?

What Stanton did has already been stated. He went visiting, made a speech, and then retired to bed.

And while Stanton was undressing and Major Eckert stood shaving in his dressing-room, the unguarded President was put to death by the hand of an assassin.

[1] Bates, op. cit., p. 364.
[2] Ibid., p. 368.
[3] Laughlin, op. cit., p. 290.

CHAPTER VII

Grant Suddenly Leaves Washington

The President and Mrs. Lincoln had invited Mr. and Mrs. Grant to be their guests at Ford's Theatre on Friday night, and the general had accepted the invitation. But the Grants did not attend the performance; instead they left abruptly for the north to visit their children. This discourteous conduct cannot be passed over lightly. It would have been doubtful etiquette to decline such an invitation in the first place; but to accept and then to leave town, especially after public notice had been given that Grant would attend the performance, looks like a colossal *faux pas*. Or has the incident a deeper significance than appears on the surface?

Grant's life had been that of a soldier; strict obedience to the wishes of a superior must have been second nature to him. The invitation to a presidential party, given in honour of the victor of Appomattox Court House, implied a command. Ordinarily in such circumstances Grant would have gone to the theatre, regardless of his own wishes in the matter. More than a year later, long after he had become conscious of his power and popularity, he still meekly complied with similar requests of President Johnson, with whom he was never on as good terms as he had been with Lincoln. On 18 August 1866 an invitation was tendered to the general, through Johnson's secretary, to attend a reception given at the Executive Mansion. 'Grant was still unwilling to take any definite political position, such as his presence at this reception would indicate,' said Adam Badeau, Grant's biographer, who knew and loved his chief, 'but he felt himself obliged to obey the summons of the President. . . . Grant

thought that without positive rudeness he could not refuse.'
Again, when Johnson had finished the plans for his famous
swing around the circle, he asked Grant to accompany him.
'A subordinate', observed Badeau, 'can hardly decline such an
invitation from the Chief of the State. . . .'[1]

If Grant thought, as he must have done, that correct manners
for an army officer meant obedience to Johnson's summons—
regardless of his own inclinations—he certainly could not in
decency have snubbed President Lincoln, who had been his loyal
supporter and whose invitation was inspired by nothing but
goodwill and the desire to honour the hero of the day. Then why
Grant's sudden change of plans?

Some writers have attributed the general's reluctance to go to
the playhouse that night to his innate modesty. Maybe so. However, it is difficult for those who have studied Grant's character
to determine whether he was exceedingly shy or exceedingly
vain, or both. During his campaign in the field, when he was
taking his bath, he would not permit even a servant to enter the
tent; on the other hand, while in Washington during the early
part of 1864, he let one of his admirers hoist him on to a sofa
so that the crowd could see him better. 'He would not be lion-
ized,' wrote Coolidge in his *Life of U. S. Grant*;[2] but it was
Badeau's opinion that his chief was not indifferent to the recognition of the world or to the praises of his friends. 'The attention
and consideration he received were far from disagreeable to him,'
says his biographer.[3] Horace Porter claims that Grant had been
so much an object of curiosity in Washington that it had become
irksome to him. 'I have become very tired of this show business,'
he quoted Grant as complaining;[4] but Jesse Grant wrote that his
father stood up with unflagging interest under a round of social
and civil ceremonies which the younger man could not endure.[5]

Grant was a queer mixture of human traits, and those who

[1] Adam Badeau, *Grant in Peace* (Hubbard Bros., Philadelphia, 1885),
p. 38.
[2] Louis A. Coolidge, *The Life of U. S. Grant* (Houghton Mifflin Co.,
Boston, 1922), p. 200.
[3] Badeau, op. cit., p. 82.
[4] Horace Porter, *Campaigning with Grant* (Century Co. (D. Appleton-
Century Co.), New York, 1897), p. 22.
[5] Jesse Grant, *In the Days of My Father, General Grant* (Harper & Bros.,
New York, 1925), p. 310.

ascribe his sudden turn-about on 14 April to his extreme modesty are basing their arguments on debatable ground.

In his memoirs Grant passed over this episode quickly and skilfully. He stated that he had accepted Lincoln's invitation conditionally; if able to finish his work early his intention was to join his children in Burlington, New Jersey, about an hour's train ride from Philadelphia.[1] But it is difficult to accept this explanation. People who are chosen for presidential invitations are not supposed to accept conditionally; and if Grant had committed this error Mrs. Lincoln would hardly have tolerated such ill manners on the part of a subordinate. Moreover, as a hostess at a public function she had the right to demand a clean-cut decision.

Can one really believe that Grant's longing for his children was so irresistible that it had to be gratified without delay? One of his sons, seven-year-old Jesse, had been with him at City Point and was with him in Washington. Mrs. Grant, Fred, and Jesse had come to visit the head of their family at Christmas time; and after all, Burlington was only a comparatively short distance from City Point. Besides, the evening train which the Grants took from Washington at 6 p.m. was not due in Burlington until early in the morning. All that they stood to gain by suffering the discomforts of a night ride in an ordinary coach, and making two transfers at very inconvenient hours, was that they would see their children in the forenoon. By travelling on the morning train they could have taken in the performance and still have arrived at Burlington in the early afternoon.

The following timetable illustrates the possible connections between Washington and Burlington at that time:

CAMDEN AND AMBOY RAILROAD
(The only line running from Washington to Burlington)

	Exp.	Mail	Mail	Exp.
Lv. Washington:	7.30 a.m.	11.15 a.m.	6.00 a.m.	7.30 p.m.
Arr. Baltimore:	8.55 a.m.	12.45 p.m.	7.25 p.m.	9.00 p.m.
Arr. Philadephia:	1.32 p.m.	5.32 p.m.	12.00 a.m.	1.55 a.m.

	Acc.	Exp.
Lv. Philadelphia:	6.00 a.m.	2.00 p.m.
Arr. Burlington:	7.00 a.m.	2.58 p.m.

[1] U. S. Grant, *Memoirs* (Charles L. Webster, New York, 1885), II, p. 508.

Due to the unusual circumstances, the railroad ran a special from Philadelphia to Burlington that night; but this hardly contributed to an early family reunion. If Grant had waited till morning a private carriage or even a special train might have been allotted to him to eliminate the strain of travel in a day-coach.

It is unlikely that Grant would have been guilty of ill manners. He had been educated at West Point and could be expected, therefore, to know his rules of etiquette. 'Grant was in reality one of the most sensitive of men. He regarded the feelings of others carefully . . .' wrote his biographer.[1] Nor is there anything in the story of his life that indicates an inclination toward rudeness. But even if such a tendency had existed, his wife was still to be reckoned with. She was included in the invitation to the theatre and certainly would have to be consulted on the question of acceptance.

Mrs. Grant was a woman of education and refinement. She came of a family that held itself as high as any in the old society of semi-southern St. Louis. Four years younger than her husband, she had been educated in her native city at Professor Moreau's finishing school, one of the finest institutions of its day. She was a woman of much general intelligence, and exceedingly well-informed on all public matters. She was noted for her amiability, her cheerful disposition, and her extreme cordiality of manner.[2] If it was Mrs. Grant who induced the general to decline the invitation, or if she concurred with him in refusing it, she must have had very sound reasons for her action.

What about Grant's work, which he was doubtful of finishing that day? The official records indicate that his activity consisted of sending a single telegram to General Meade at Burke's Station, Virginia. It conveyed an order to permit two Confederate messengers to return to Danville, and reserved an answer to a question propounded by Governor Smith of Virginia which related to administrative matters.[3] During most of the day the lieutenant-general was at the White House, first at the Cabinet meeting and later in conferences. How much time he spent at the War Department is a matter for conjecture, but as only one relatively unimportant telegram was sent out by him, it

---

[1] Badeau, op. cit., p. 81.
[2] Ibid., p. 170; Porter, op. cit., p. 284, quoted verbatim.
[3] *Official Records*, I, vol. 46, part III, p. 745.

is obvious that his work was already practically finished when he accepted Lincoln's invitation.

Grant himself admitted as much when he wrote that on 13 April—he had arrived in the morning—he was very busy for a time preparing orders. 'But by the 14th', he said, 'I was pretty well through with this work. . . .' [1] As a matter of fact Grant must have been at leisure in the late afternoon of the thirteenth, or he would not have spent the evening visiting Secretary of War Stanton.

If Grant hesitated to tell the whole story in his memoirs it was perhaps due to a chivalrous impulse; for the truth would have cast a reflection on an unfortunate woman who, at the time of his writing, had been dead only a few years.

It so happened that a few weeks previously Mrs. Grant had been hostess to Mrs. Lincoln at City Point. An excursion was arranged to the front lines of the army, and both ladies were part of the company, riding together in an ambulance. All other ladies had been ordered to the rear, with the exception of Mrs. Griffin, the wife of one of the generals, who was on horseback and had joined Lincoln and a group of his staff. When Mrs. Lincoln heard of this, she flew into a rage. 'Do you know', she exclaimed angrily, 'that I never allow the President to see any woman alone?' In her excitement she tried to stop the carriage by throwing her arms around the driver, and could be pacified only with difficulty. Mrs. Grant was mortified and begged that news of the incident be suppressed. But worse was yet to come. On the next day it was the wife of General Ord who aroused Mrs. Lincoln's uncontrollable jealousy. In the presence of a crowd of officers Mrs. Lincoln insulted the poor woman, calling her vile names, and accusing her of trying to flirt with the President. When Mrs. Grant sought to interfere the First Lady of the Land snapped at her the accusation of having aspirations to the White House herself, which brutal attack Mrs. Grant parried neatly by saying she was quite satisfied with her present position, a better one by far than she had ever hoped to attain. But nothing would calm Mrs. Lincoln's fury, and the accompanying officer trembled lest she should jump out of the carriage. [2]

[1] Grant, *Memoirs*, II, p. 508.   [2] Badeau, op. cit., p. 357.

Taking all this into consideration, it is no wonder that Mrs. Grant did not enjoy the prospect of an evening in the same loge with the Lincolns. Even a harmless exchange of remarks between her and the President might have provoked a humiliating scandal. At any rate, she could scarcely have accepted, especially as she had again been rudely insulted the evening before when Washington was illuminated in honour of the recent victories. Mrs. Lincoln had invited General Grant to drive about the streets with her to watch the demonstration; but Mrs. Grant had not been included in the invitation.[1]

Under these circumstances no one could have expected Mrs. Grant to become a guest at the party that night; but this by no means settled the matter for her husband. General Grant must have been in a very trying predicament; he was the highest officer in the army, and what was merely a social affair for his wife took on the character of an official function for him.

Grant's final decision was made still more difficult by the publicity given to his proposed visit to the theatre. It is significant that the advertisements inserted in the *Washington Evening Star* centred around the appearance of Grant, barely mentioning the fact that the President and his wife also were expected at the performance. A Chief Executive of greater sensitiveness might even have taken offence at the way in which the announcements were worded.[2]

Lincoln was not an unusual sight in his own capital, but Grant was sure to arouse the curiosity of the crowds. For the leader of the Northern armies, whatever his faults, had never been a parlour-general. With the exception of a few rare and hurried trips to Washington, he had spent his time in the midst of his troops. The Northern population knew him only from pictures. It is, therefore, not surprising that Ford's Theatre was almost sold out that night. The people wanted to see Grant, not Lincoln. As to *Our American Cousin*, that comedy was no longer a glamorous attraction. The testimony of many witnesses shows that it was solely the expected appearance of Grant that turned this Good Friday, a notoriously bad night from the box-office point of view, into a well-attended gala affair.[3]

[1] Badeau, op. cit., p. 362.
[2] *Washington Evening Star*, 14 Apr. 1865.
[3] Pitman, op. cit., p. 76.

67

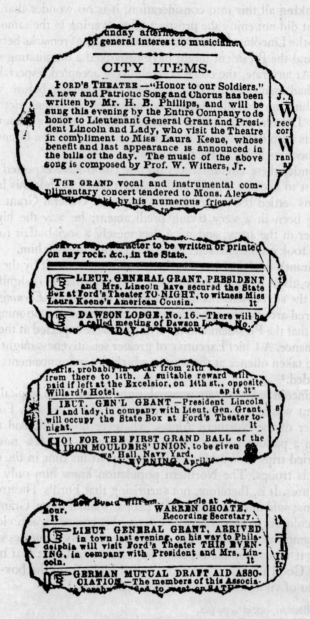

CITY ITEMS.

Ford's Theatre—"Honor to our Soldiers."
A new and Patriotic Song and Chorus has been
written by Mr. H. B. Phillips, and will be
sung this evening by the Entire Company to do
honor to Lieutenant General Grant and President Lincoln and Lady, who visit the Theatre
in compliment to Miss Laura Keene, whose
benefit and last appearance is announced in
the bills of the day. The music of the above
song is composed by Prof. W. Withers, Jr.

The grand vocal and instrumental complimentary concert tendered to Mons. Alexa
ki by his numerous friend

character to be written or printed
on any rock. &c., in the State.

☞ **LIEUT. GENERAL GRANT, PRESIDENT**
and Mrs. Lincoln have secured the State
Box at Ford's Theater TO-NIGHT, to witness Miss
Laura Keene's American Cousin. 1t

☞ **DAWSON LODGE, No. 16.**—There will be
a called meeting of Dawson Lodge, No. 1

afls, probably in a car from 2th
from there to 14th. A suitable reward will
paid if left at the Excelsior, on 14th st., opposite
Willard's Hotel. ap 14 3t*

LIEUT. GEN'L GRANT—President Lincoln
and lady, in company with Lieut. Gen. Grant,
will occupy the State Box at Ford's Theater to-
night. 1t

HO! FOR THE FIRST GRAND BALL of the
IRON MOULDERS' UNION, to be given
's Hall, Navy Yard,
EVENING, April 1

The New Board will   at
hour. **WARREN CHOATE,**
1t   Recording Secretary.

☞ **LIEUT GENERAL GRANT, ARRIVED**
in town last evening, on his way to Philadelphia will visit Ford's Theater THIS EVEN-
ING, in company with President and Mrs. Lincoln. 1t

☞ **GERMAN MUTUAL DRAFT AID ASSO-**
CIATION.—The members of this Associa-

From the Washington Evening Star, *14 April 1865.*

Whether or not Grant cared about the disappointment his absence would cause to the audience is not known. There is no question that Lincoln felt the affront keenly. He hinted at it rather strongly as Grant took his leave. But apparently his plea fell on deaf ears.[1]

Mrs. Grant had learned, about three o'clock in the afternoon, that Secretary and Mrs. Stanton, who were also to have been guests at the theatre, had definitely refused the invitation, and thereupon she sent a note to her husband which was handed him at the White House.[2] What this note contained one can only surmise; it very likely announced her unequivocal decision to leave Washington that evening. She probably left it to the judgement of her husband whether he would go with her or stay for the President's party, thus putting him more than ever into an unhappy and embarrassed frame of mind.

In his perplexity Grant went to the War Office, possibly only to gain time. He was received there by the Secretary of War, in whom he may have confided. All that is positively known is that Stanton immediately told him the presence of both the President and the lieutenant-general at a public function would invite disaster. He urged Grant not to go to Ford's Theatre that night, and easily obtained his acquiescence.[3] By this time the general must have been more than half inclined to leave Washington with his wife and was probably looking for an excuse to do so. He used the desire to see his family as a fairly plausible pretext, and shortly afterwards bade the President a final adieu.

Lincoln undoubtedly resented Grant's action; but his only known remark relative to it expressed his redoubled determination to attend the theatre regardless of the general's absence. He felt that the people who had been led to visit the performance of *Our American Cousin* in the hope of seeing the illustrious victor deserved some consideration and should not be disappointed altogether.[4]

After the announcements in the Press had done their work of drawing an unusual number of people into the theatre and the streets leading to it, it did not matter, of course, whether Grant

[1] Porter, 'Campaigning with Grant', in *Century Magazine*, Oct. 1897, p. 891.
[2] Storey, op. cit.   [3] D. H. Bates, op. cit., p. 366.
[4] Crook, op. cit., p. 67.

actually attended the play or not. The dangerous situation pictured by Stanton had been created, and Grant's absence would only remove the risk for himself, without preventing what the Secretary of War had deemed an open invitation for attack. If such an assault were planned, the plotters, who could not know far in advance of Grant's sudden change of mind, would find only Lincoln there to wreak their vengeance on. But this idea does not seem to have occurred either to Grant or to Stanton. Grant stolidly boarded his train to Philadelphia, leaving his host to face the situation as best he could; and Stanton, who had professed such anxiety, did nothing to protect Lincoln against the very dangers that had made him so apprehensive for the life of his lieutenant-general.

If Grant had been in the theatre that night it is more than likely that the attempt on Lincoln's life would not have been made. Not that Grant was a dangerous antagonist in a physical encounter. The general was scarcely a match for the young and athletic Booth; nor was he particularly alert. It is quite possible that the assassin could have entered the loge unhindered and unobserved, so far as Grant was concerned. His presence would have been fatal to the plans of an assassin for quite a different reason. With Grant in the box hundreds of eager eyes would have been turned in his direction every minute of the time, and Booth's entry and exit could not have escaped detection. His murderous bullet might not have been stopped, but he could not have escaped.

Moreover, it is almost a certainty that Grant's presence in the box would have led to a more efficient guarding of the door through which Booth entered with such ridiculous ease. Even the neglectful Parker, who had once been a soldier, would have hesitated to leave his post when standing sentry for the lieutenant-general. One could take liberties with Lincoln, but hardly with Grant. It is also possible that Captain McGowan and Lieutenant Crawford, as a result of their soldierly training, would have planted themselves in Booth's path on his way to the President's box if they had known that their leader was a guest there. Strangers may not enter the tent of the commanding general without sharp scrutiny.

From the point of view of the assassin, it was absolutely essential to have Grant absent from the theatre that night; and whoever induced the lieutenant-general to turn his back on Washington, played—knowingly or unknowingly—straight into the hands of the conspirators.

Verification of Bates's statement that it was Stanton who helped bring about Grant's departure is furnished by Samuel Beckwith, his cipher operator, who accompanied the general to Philadelphia on 14 April. In an account written many years after the event he stated that Stanton had urged the general-in-chief not to accept Lincoln's invitation.

'General Grant', Beckwith wrote in the *New York Sun* of 27 April 1913, 'was easily persuaded of the indiscretion of such an exposure. As a matter of fact he didn't want to go at all but he yielded to the President's request. . . . When he learned at the War Department of the fears of Stanton he acquiesced at once in his suggestion that the visit to the playhouse be abandoned.'

It is interesting to note that Stanton, in his first official telegram pertaining to the Lincoln assassination, simply stated that 'General Grant and wife were advertised to be at the theatre this evening, but he started to Burlington at 6 o'clock this evening', while next morning, in his lengthy letter to the American minister at London, he elaborated on this announcement. 'Public notice had been given', he wrote, 'that . . . General Grant would be present at the theatre, and the opportunity of adding the lieutenant-general to the number of victims to be murdered was no doubt seized for the fitting occasion of executing plans. . . . But General Grant was compelled to be absent. . . .'[1]

If Lincoln's murder had been investigated by ordinary criminologists, they would have been curious to know what *compelled* Grant to be absent or else who influenced him to leave town, thereby making it easier for the assassins to accomplish their purpose. They would have interrogated the unimaginative general, absolving him at once of anything worse than tactlessness; but they might have, had they gone far enough, given Stanton an extremely uncomfortable quarter of an hour.

[1] *Official Records*, I, vol. 46, part 3, pp. 780, 785.

CHAPTER VIII

How the News of the Tragedy was Handled

Stanton had appropriated the role of distributor of all important Washington news items, and it was therefore his duty to acquaint the country as quickly as possible with the story of Lincoln's death. If the chief assassin were to be caught it was extremely important that his name and description be instantly flashed as far as the powers of the Washington Government extended. With this in mind it is difficult to understand why the first dispatch of the Secretary of War was not written out until 1.30 a.m., more than three hours after Booth's murderous deed; it actually did not leave Washington until fifteen minutes past two. Stanton had then been at Lincoln's bedside for at least three hours.

The early morning editions of the metropolitan papers and practically all smaller dailies would go to press between two and two-thirty in the morning, and every minute's delay might defer or prevent the printing of the news. The Associated Press, of course, could be expected to supply the information to its members, regardless of Stanton's actions; besides, some of the papers in the large centres of population had their own correspondents in the nation's capital. The bulk of the daily journals, however, depended on the War Department's official messages for their Washington news. Even those who had independent service probably were apprehensive when they used their special telegrams without official endorsement. Stanton's censorship was strict and merciless, and the printing of so sensational a story as that of Lincoln's assassination, if the report had been proved untrue, would have led unfailingly to a suspension of the guilty paper and the most severe punishment for its editors. The hoax of Lincoln's bogus proclamation and its disastrous consequences to some of the newspapermen of New York had not been forgotten by their fraternity in what was then less than a year's time.[1]

What is still stranger and more difficult to explain than the belated sending of the first dispatch is the fact that it failed to mention Booth's name. If there was to be a successful hunt for the murderer it was imperative that both his identity and his description should promptly be made public. But not until two hours later did Booth's name appear in the telegrams, and by that time it was too late for some of the morning papers to print it. The first edition of a journal as prominent as the *New York Tribune*, for instance, had not received official information of the assassination up to the time of going to press and, had it relied on Stanton, would not have mentioned the crime at all in its early edition. The forms had already been set up when private and Associated Press wires on Lincoln's murder came ticking in, and what was printed about it had to be put on the editorial page. This shows how narrowly the *Tribune* missed printing the news altogether. It was not until a later edition, printed at 4.30 a.m., that the story was complete, and Booth's name was given to the public.

Stanton's 1.30 a.m. dispatch did not reach the *New York Times* in time to appear in its first issue, which carried only the earliest advice from the Associated Press agent, besides a hasty account from its own correspondent. The latter message was put on the wires as early as 11.15 p.m., and was one of the first to go out of Washington. It preceded Stanton's telegram by two hours, yet it contained substantially the same information. A later edition of this morning journal gave a more detailed account of the assassination and contained also a telegram filed as late as 2.12 a.m.; but still Booth's name did not appear within its black-bordered columns. A private dispatch declared that 'the person who shot the President is represented as about thirty years of age, five feet nine inches in height, sparely built, of light complexion, dressed in dark clothing, and having a genteel appearance.'

The *New York Daily News* received the first two short Asso-

[1] See supplementary note to chapter viii, 'The Bogus Proclamation'.

ciated Press messages and also all of its lengthier report. The latter probably was sent about 2 a.m. It had Stanton's wire of 1.30 a.m., and three reports from its own representative, bringing the news up to at least 1.30 a.m., Washington time. Its special correspondent in his midnight dispatch said: 'I have heard several names mentioned, but as the murderer is not positively known, I refrain from giving them.' Later on, in a wire sent at 1.15 a.m., he ventured a little farther: 'Some of the witnesses say they are certain Wilkes Booth is the assassin.' The *News*, lacking official confirmation, quickly set up an editorial and, boxing it in mourning fashion, demanded in bold type: 'WHO WAS THE ASSASSIN?' This is a question that must have been on many lips when the shocked readers perused the account of the catastrophe. For next to the query as to whether the President would live, it was the most natural question that every person would ask.

Not until three o'clock in the morning did Stanton finally disclose the name of the assassin. But this dispatch did not leave Washington until 3.20 a.m., and therefore benefited only those papers which were able to set up extra editions. The *New York Herald* was one journal that changed its forms continuously, and its readers, thanks to a private dispatch, were advised from the very beginning that Booth was the murderer. But in the leading editorial the sentence: 'Who he [the assassin] is is not positively known, tho' suspicion points strongly to a certain individual,' remained unchanged even in the 8.10 and 10 a.m. issues.

If Stanton wanted Booth caught it was important to broadcast his name all over the country as soon as the actor's part in the crime had been ascertained. It is, therefore, of interest to determine just when the Secretary learned who had killed the President.

Major A. C. Richards, the superintendent of the Metropolitan Police, had been in Ford's Theatre when Lincoln was shot and, together with many others in the audience, had recognized Booth with certainty. There can be but little doubt that Richards immediately got in touch with General Christopher C. Augur, who was in charge of the troops in Washington, and advised him of this identification. In fact, Richards applied to Augur for horses to mount his police,[1] so that contact between these two men in authority is positively established. Augur, in turn, was in and out of the Petersen house—where Stanton held forth—all night long, and could hardly have failed to acquaint Stanton with his own knowledge of the facts. But, Richards had plenty of other evidence that it was Booth who had committed the deed. The police blotter of Washington for that night shows the arrival of not less than seventeen persons at Richards's headquarters between eleven and twelve o'clock, some of whom were people of prominence and all of whom knew who the murderer was. The notation that follows the entry of eleven o'clock reads:

'At this hour the melancholy intelligence of the assassination of Mr. Lincoln, President of the United States, at Ford's Theatre was brought to this office, and the information obtained from the following persons goes to show that the assassin is a man named John Wilkes Booth.

NAMES OF THE WITNESSES:

E. D. Wray—Surgeon-General's Office
J. S. Knox—No. 25 Indiana Avenue
Joseph B. Stewart—349 K. Street
Capt. G. S. Shaw—on General Augur's staff
C. W. Gilbert—92 and 94 Louisiana Avenue
James B. Cutler—New Jersey Ave.
Jacob G. Larner—441 F. Street
James Maddox—at Ford's Theatre
Anthony Lully—406 K. Street, between 9 and 10
W. S. Burch—333 F. Street
John Deveny—[an ex-army officer]
Harry Hawk—[the actor who was on the stage when the assassination occurred]
John Fletcher—299 E. Street—Nailor's Stables
Andrew C. Mainwaring—Soldiers' Home
William Brown—
John Gratton—at Record Hospital
J. L. Debony—at Ford's Theatre—Boards next door to Callans Drug Store.

[1] Osborn H. Oldroyd, *Assassination of Abraham Lincoln* (Washington, D.C., 1901), p. 66.

After this no further entry was made on the blotter until morning.[1]

Leaving aside all circumstantial evidence, there is more direct proof that Stanton had full knowledge of the assassin's identity long before he sent his first official telegram to General Dix, at 1.30 a.m. In the back parlour of the Petersen house he and Chief-Justice Carter of the District of Columbia (a close friend of Stanton's) had established a preliminary court of inquiry, and several persons, who had been either on the stage or in the audience when the fatal shot was fired, appeared there as witnesses.[2]

One man so interrogated was Lieutenant Crawford, the same officer to whom we are indebted for his recognition of Hanscom. 'I saw him [the murderer] as he ran across the stage . . .', he declared. 'He very strongly resembled the *Booths*.'

Harry Hawk, the actor who had been the sole occupant of the stage when the assassin jumped down from the box, was another witness. '. . . I believe to the best of my knowledge that it was *John Wilkes Booth*,' he testified. But the horror of accusing a brother actor of such a crime made him waver. 'Still I am not positive that it was him,' he continued. 'I only had one glance at him as he was rushing towards me with a dagger and I turned and ran and after I ran up a flight of stairs I turned and exclaimed "My God, that's *John Booth*".' After a few more remarks he concluded sadly, 'In my own mind I do not have any doubt but that it was *Booth*.'

Henry B. Phillips, an actor who was to have sung a patriotic song that night, was in his dressing-room when he heard the shot. He rushed down in his shirt-sleeves and heard some one on the stage say that it was Booth who had shot the President. When he saw Harry Hawk a little while later there seemed to be little doubt in the latter's mind.

'Are you certain it was Wilkes Booth?' Phillips asked, as Hawk was telling him how Booth had rushed by him, a dagger in his hand and a wild glare in his eyes.

'I could say it if I was on my deathbed,' replied Hawk.[3]

---

[1] Records of Metropolitan Police Department, Washington, D.C.

[2] Tanner papers; see also supplementary note to chapter viii, 'Flower and Pitman Re-edit History'.   [3] Tanner papers.

James C. Ferguson, a restaurant keeper of the neighbour-hood, was another witness who came before the investigators. He knew Booth well, had talked to him that very afternoon, and had identified him without a doubt. He even reported that he had left the theatre as quickly as he could and had gone to the police station on D Street. Ferguson told more than that. After he left the police station he ran up Tenth Street to the house where the President lay dying, and told Colonel Wells that he had witnessed the murder and knew the name of the assassin. Colonel Wells, who was standing on the steps of the Petersen house, ordered the guard to let Mr. Ferguson pass through, and the latter then went in and made his statement.[1] Unless Colonel Wells was very remiss in his duty, Stanton must have been advised of Booth's identity right then, which was long before midnight.

William Withers, Jr., orchestra leader at the theatre, who stood in Booth's path, and whose coat was slashed by a vicious stab of the murderer's knife, also recognized the assassin. It is not known whether he was called on by Stanton and Carter for his version of the occurrence, but he did not hesitate to make a positive statement about it when called to give testimony in the conspiracy trial.[2]

Inasmuch as Withers must have talked freely to the other employees of the playhouse, none of whom was permitted to leave the building, it is hard to believe that his testimony failed to reach the ears of the investigators across the street at the Petersen house.

John Deveny, a former army officer, testified that he knew Booth at once, just as soon as he landed on the stage. 'I said, "He is John Wilkes Booth, and he has shot the President." I made that remark right there.'[3] He might have added that he rushed over to the police station to record that information on the blotter, but for some reason or other he forebore mentioning this on the witness stand a few weeks later.

It is not surprising that Corporal James Tanner, who took the shorthand notes at the Petersen house, in a letter written two

[1] Pitman, op. cit., p. 77.   [2] Ibid., p. 79.
[3] Ibid., p. 39.

77

days after this unforgettable experience should have said, 'In fifteen minutes I had testimony enough down to hang Wilkes Booth . . . higher than ever Haman hung.'[1] In fifteen minutes, Tanner says. He had commenced writing about midnight, according to his own statement, so that it is safe to say that by 12.15, or by half-past twelve at the latest, Stanton could have sounded the general alarm for Booth's capture. Instead of doing this he waited three hours before disclosing the name of the assassin, and for two hours he did not send out any news at all.

But even if the out-of-town papers were late in mentioning Booth through Stanton's inexplicable tardiness, this normally should not have been of any particular benefit to the murderer. It was the Washington Press that chiefly endangered his chances of escape. In the few hours between the attack on Lincoln and the appearance of the capital's morning papers he could not travel far from the seat of his crime. If the Richmond papers were to join in the hue and cry for Booth, his progress would be further imperilled, especially if they offered rewards for his capture. The Washington papers, of course, did not have to depend on any telegraphic dispatches and would, therefore, blazon Booth's name on their front pages as soon as it could be rushed on to the sheet.

Strange to say, the Washington papers did nothing of the kind. Instead, they dealt with the crime in a wriggling, embarrassed manner, as if they were bursting with desire to communicate to their patrons all they knew, but were being held in leash by something, or somebody, that they did not dare disobey.

'Rumours are so thick and contradictory', wrote the harassed editor of the *National Intelligencer* at two o'clock on the morning of 15 April, '. . . that we rely entirely upon our reporters to advise the public of the details and result of this night of horrors.' And after a few more editorial remarks about the then known incidents of the crime, he continued: 'We forbear to give the name of one of the supposed murderers, about whom great suspicion gathers. . . . At the police headquarters it is understood that Mr. Hawk, of Laura Keene's troupe, has been held to bail to

[1] William E. Barton, *The Life of Abraham Lincoln* (copyright, 1925, used by special permission of the publishers, The Bobbs-Merrill Co.), II, p. 472.

testify to the identity of the suspected assassin of the President, whom he is said to have recognized as a person well known to him.'

The editor ventured one step farther. 'Some evidence', he quoted from the Associated Press report, 'of the guilt of the party who attacked the President are [is] in possession of the police.' And with this scant information the anxious public who read the *National Intelligencer* in the morning had to be satisfied.

The star reporter for the *Washington Chronicle* went even farther afield in his attempt to withhold the truth as long as possible. 'We then ascertained', he wrote in the leading column of his paper, 'that the police were on the track of the President's assassin, and found that a variety of evidences, all pointing one way, would in all probability justify the arrest of a character well known throughout the cities of the United States. Evidence taken amid such excitement would, perhaps, not justify us in naming the suspected man, nor could it aid in his apprehension.'[1]

Here the unbiased observer must pause to catch his breath. There may be no justification for the suspicion that some one was holding back the eager newspapermen of Washington from shouting aloud the greatest news story that would ever come to them; but who can follow this reporter in his assertion that the name of the assassin would not aid in the apprehension of the murderer? What, one must ask, would have aided in his capture, if not his name and his description? Or, inversely, how could his apprehension have been accomplished without his name or description being known?

The actions of L. A. Gobright, agent of the Associated Press in the capital, add to the strangeness of the situation. He was about to close his office, after having filed what he thought was his last dispatch for the evening, when he was informed of the tragedy. Rushing to the telegraph office, he sent a short special.[2]

THE PRESIDENT WAS SHOT IN A THEATER TONIGHT AND PERHAPS MORTALLY WOUNDED.

[1] *Washington Daily Morning Chronicle*, 15 Apr. 1865, 5 a.m. edition, col. 3, p. 1.

[2] L. A. Gobright, *Recollections of Men and Things in Washington During Half a Century* (Philadelphia, 1869), p. 348.

79

Although Gobright was in Lincoln's box before eleven o'clock, his telegram apparently reached only a few papers before midnight. Among these was the *New York Tribune*. Others received it later—probably due to an interruption in the wire service—and their columns indicate that it left Washington at 12.30 a.m., although Gobright must have filed his dispatch much earlier. Emerging from the telegraph office, he tore over to Ford's Theatre in a hack and was fortunate enough to find Booth's derringer on the floor of the presidential box. He was still more fortunate in meeting Superintendent of Police Richards, to whom he entrusted the weapon and from whom he could have obtained, and probably did obtain, complete information in regard to the chief conspirator. But if he knew this secret he was careful not to disclose it. All the news about Booth which he vouchsafed to his papers came in a telegram sent considerably later. 'Some evidence of the guilt of the party who attacked the President is in possession of the police,' he wired. This little item came at the very end of a long dispatch sent from Washington at 1.30 a.m. The result was that most papers went to press before the crux of the message reached them.

'Some few persons', this representative of the Associated Press wrote four years later, 'said he [the assassin] resembled Booth, while others appeared to be confident as to the identity.'[1] What more did a reporter need to make at least reference to the name of the murderer when announcing an assassination to an astonished world?

Gobright seemed to have been more proud than ashamed of his delinquency. When called upon to testify at the conspiracy trial a few weeks afterward, he not only defended his action, but tried to denounce those who had given Booth's name to the public.

'I was not perfectly satisfied that night that it was J. Wilkes Booth who had killed the President,' he maintained. 'It was telegraphed over the country that he was the assassin, but not by me; I could tell by whom, if necessary.' But no one was interested in pursuing this line of inquiry.[2]

When asked point-blank whether he became satisfied during

[1] Gobright, op. cit., p. 350.
[2] Pitman, op. cit., p. 213.

the night that Booth was the assassin, he sidestepped the question. 'I did not so telegraph that night,' is all that he said. 'After I saw the official bulletin the next morning, I came to the conclusion that J. Wilkes Booth was the man,' he concluded.[1]

Which last sentence is perhaps the most astounding statement ever made by the representative of a prominent Press association.

If it was a significant feature of Gobright's early telegrams that he did not divulge Booth's name, it was still more remarkable that he did not refer to the question of who the assassin was. As an experienced news reporter he should have at least stated at once that the name of the murderer was as yet unknown, and that every effort was being made to ascertain it.

Even in his long telegram of 1.30 a.m., when he summed up the facts which he was then willing to reveal, he kept this point till the last. It was perhaps his journalistic conscience asserting itself that made him write all night long of the tremendous excitement prevailing in Washington. In one dispatch he mentioned it not less than four times—the excitement is of the wildest possible description—the shock to the community is terrible —everybody there is so excited—the entire city to-night presents a scene of wild excitement. Would the veteran agent of the Associated Press have blundered so amateurishly without an urge to fill space that should have been devoted to news and not to platitudes?

There is one thing Gobright did do that night to which he never referred later. He sent a peculiar wire to the papers that subscribed to his services. This followed closely on the heels of the special he had dispatched at eleven o'clock, and appeared in the *New York Tribune* as 'Second Telegram' in this form:[2]

OUR WASHINGTON AGENT ORDERS THE DISPATCH ABOUT THE PRESIDENT 'STOPPED'. NOTHING IS SAID ABOUT THE TRUTH OR FALSITY OF THAT DISPATCH.

The correct interpretation of this wire would make fascinating reading. Perhaps if Gobright had written his reminiscences

---

[1] *Trial of the Assassins and Conspirators at Washington, May and June, 1865, for the Murder of President Lincoln* (T. B. Peterson & Bros., Philadelphia, 1865), p. 153; also Pitman, op. cit., p. 213.

[2] *New York Tribune*, 15 Apr. 1865, early edition, col. 3, p. 4.

a year later he might have thrown some light on it. But in 1868, when his book appeared, Stanton still was a power that a Washington journalist had to reckon with.

In spite of all these remarkable delays and hindrances, some newspapers did, after all, receive news of Booth's identity before Stanton's official release. The evidence which had accumulated at police headquarters before midnight could not be denied. And so, while one reporter assured the readers of the *Washington Chronicle* in the first column that disclosure of the assassin's name would not aid in his apprehension, another reporter, shielded by the authority of the police superintendent, blurted out the truth in the second column of the page.

'A preliminary examination was made by Mr. Richards and his assistants,' he announced. 'Several persons were called upon to testify, and the evidence, as elicited before an informal tribunal, and not under oath, was conclusive to this point: the murderer of President Lincoln was John Wilkes Booth.'[1]

The *New York Tribune* had Booth's name from its Washington reporters in private wires sent out as early as 1.30 a.m., or perhaps a little sooner.[2] The *New York Herald's* staff man sent this telegram as early as 1 a.m.: 'Popular report points to a somewhat celebrated actor of known secession proclivities as the assassin; but it would be unjust to name him until some further evidence of his guilt is obtained.'

The two o'clock edition of the *New York Herald*, which gave the earliest account published on the morning after the crime, also carried another dispatch which contained this statement: 'Laura Keene and the leader of the orchestra declare that they recognized him [the person who fired the pistol] as J. Wilkes Booth, the actor.' As a result this paper, throughout all its issues, carried Booth's name as the alleged assassin among the subheads in the first column of its first page.

There was no mystery about Booth's identity in the streets of the capital immediately after the assassination. Two soldiers,

---

[1] *Washington Chronicle*, 15 Apr. 1865, p. 1.
[2] *New York Tribune*, 15 Apr. 1865, col. 2, p. 1.

Sergeants Dye and Cooper, who had been waiting in front of Ford's Theatre for an opportunity to see Grant, but who had left a few moments before the murder, gave proof of this in the form of sworn statements. Their testimony, unconsciously humorous in part, was called for in the Surratt trial in 1867.[1]

Sergeant Dye's testimony:

Q. You went, as you have stated, to the oyster-house; what did you do after you went there?

A. Ordered oysters.

Q. What next?

A. We sat down to eat them. I do not recollect whether we ate all of them or not; I do not think we did. A man came rushing in and said the President was shot. . . .

Q. How came you to tell this lady at the window on H street that Booth had shot the President?

A. The man who came into the saloon said it was Booth. . . .

Sergeant Cooper's testimony:

Q. Just after you had ordered your oysters some one came in and said the President was shot. Tell us what was said at that time.

A. . . . He said J. Wilkes Booth had shot him . . . it was just a few minutes after we had left the front of the theatre.

Nor was the audience in Ford's Theatre in doubt regarding the assassin's name. 'Then some one said: "Booth!",' reported one of the actors, 'and the cry was taken up, louder, and still louder: "Booth!" "*Booth!*" "Booth!"'[2]

Even Colonel John A. Foster, investigator for the War Department, said in an official report dated 23 April 1865: 'He [Booth] was recognized by at least a hundred men, some of whom were on the most intimate relations with him.'[3]

Stanton was in no hurry to inform the country that it was Booth who had shot the President; and, since the great majority of papers depended upon the War Department or the Associated

---

[1] *Surratt Trial*, I, pp. 155, 187.

[2] *Abraham Lincoln—Tributes from His Associates* (Thomas Y. Crowell & Co., New York, 1895), p. 13.

[3] War Department Archives.

Press for their Washington news, the bulk of the population did not learn the name of the murderer until the afternoon papers made their appearance.

The Secretary of War himself seems to have felt that his first dispatch from Lincoln's death-bed lacked something vital. He started his telegram to General Dix in masterly newspaper style. 'Last evening . . . the President . . . was shot by an assassin . . . the pistol-ball entered the back of the President's head. . . . The wound is mortal. . . . The recovery of Frederick Seward is doubtful.' All this is fine reporting; but suddenly, just when the question *Who is the murderer?* called for an answer, Stanton faltered. 'At a Cabinet meeting yesterday . . . the President was very cheerful and hopeful; spoke very kindly of General Lee and others of the Confederacy, and the establishment of govern-ment in Virginia.'[1]

There is something in this message that does not ring true. Why this sudden change from the announcement of historical events to mere gossip—and sentimental gossip at that? A Stanton who suddenly turned sentimentalist was not Stanton at all. In-tentionally or not, the Secretary of War, with his allusion to irrelevant matters, diverted the attention of his audience from the all-important question: Who shot the President?

A bizarre incident on the night of 14 April was an interrup-tion of all telegraphic communication between Washington and the outside world, lasting about two hours. 'Within fifteen minutes after the murder', wrote Townsend in the *New York World* on 2 May, 'the wires were severed entirely around the city, excepting only a secret wire for Government uses, which leads to Old Point. I am told that by this wire the Government reached the fortifications around Washington, first telegraphing all the way to Old Point, and then back to the outlying forts. This information comes to me from so many creditable channels that I must concede it.'[2]

Townsend's story was not written on the spur of the moment, and is entitled to serious consideration. If the conspirators were

[1] *Official Records*, I, vol. 46, part 3, p. 780.
[2] George Alfred Townsend, *Life, Crime and Capture of John Wilkes Booth* (Dick & Fitzgerald, New York, 1865), p. 46.

able to isolate the capital by cutting off its wire communications, there must have been many of them. But wire service was resumed early in the morning of the fifteenth, which would indicate that an actual severance of the wires, such as Townsend suspected, never took place; for the repair of the system, if actually destroyed, could not have been accomplished at night in so short a time. The impression the correspondent of the *New York World* leaves with the reader is, of course, that a cutting of the lines would have been of benefit to the conspirators by shielding them in their flight; 'they had evaded the pursuit of lightning', he expressed it, 'by snapping the telegraph wires'.[1] The inference, it must be admitted, is reasonable.

No official mention of this break in the wire system was ever made; yet, the report would not down. Finally, during the so-called impeachment investigation of the House of Representatives' judiciary committee in 1867, this matter was brought to the fore, and Major Eckert, who by that time had resigned as Assistant Secretary of War, was put on the witness stand. The questions and answers that followed are not without interest:[2]

Q. Did you have knowledge of the telegraph lines at or about the time of the assassination of President Lincoln?
A. I did.
Q. Was there any interruption of the lines that night?
A. Yes, sir.
Q. What was it?
A. It was my impression at the time they were cut, but we got circuit again very early the next morning. The manager of the Commercial office reported the cause to have been crossing of wires in main batteries. Throwing a ground wire over the main wires would have caused the same trouble, and taking it off would have put it in ordinary working condition.
Q. Was there an investigation into what was the real cause of the difficulty?
A. No, sir. It did not at the time seem to be sufficiently important, as the interruption only continued about two hours. I was so full of business of almost every character that I could not give it my personal attention. The interruption was only

---

[1] Ibid., p. 49.   [2] *Impeachment Investigation*, p. 673.

of a portion of the lines between Washington and Baltimore. We worked our City Point line all the time.

Q. Do you know whether the Commercial lines were interrupted at that time?

A. Yes, sir. It was only the Commercial lines that were interrupted; it was in the Commercial office and not in the War Department office. I could not ascertain with certainty what the facts were without making a personal investigation, and I had not the time to do that.

This matter should have been thoroughly looked into, in spite of Mr. Eckert's opinion to the contrary; the more so as, in the light of his disclosures, the interruption of the lines looked like an inside job. If an outsider had disrupted the telegraph service he would have cut the wires; but an outsider could not approach the main batteries undetected. Had he been able to do so, he would probably have destroyed them instead of causing a short circuit. The mere suspicion that there might be a traitor within the ranks of the telegraphic corps should have been enough to warrant a painstaking inquiry. But evidently no alarm was felt by Eckert or by Stanton, and no investigation was ever made.

Once before Eckert had pleaded an excessive amount of work; that was when Lincoln had asked him to act as his protector on the night of the assassination. Now again Stanton's former confidant took this tack in disavowing responsibility, and again it behoves the student to check up on Eckert's activities.

So far as the official records shed any light on Eckert's work at this time, he seems merely to have followed his routine duties at the War Office. His signature appears at rare intervals and under telegrams of no particular importance. On 15 April he endorsed a message of Stanton's demanding that all roads to Baltimore should be guarded; on 16 April he personally addressed Generals Meade and Sheridan as follows:[1]

Washington
16 April 1865.

MAJOR-GENERAL MEADE:

The President died at 7.22 yesterday morning. J. Wilkes Booth was the assassin of the President. Secretary Seward passed

[1] *Official Records*, I, vol. 46, part 3, pp. 786, 895, 952.

a bad night, but is much better this morning and probably out of danger. His son Frederick will not live, although he still lingers with wonderful tenacity.

THOS. T. ECKERT.

(Same to General Sheridan.)

On 22 April, Eckert's signature is found under a simple acknowledgement of an order to send a dispatch to General Grant:

Have sent the above as directed.

THOS. T. ECKERT,
Major, etc.

On 25 April, Stanton asked Eckert to be sure to deliver a telegram, regarding a photograph that had been taken of Lincoln's corpse, to General Townsend in New York.

This concludes the story of Eckert's work, so far as the records show. All of it could have been taken care of by any ordinary telegrapher.

Eckert, however, spent a great deal of time in an effort to clear up the great crime of the day.

'Once I made an examination of the register of the National Hotel,' he testified before the judiciary committee of the House in 1867, 'to see if I could get some trace of Booth's movements in this city. I found three or four entries of his name. I went to the court room at the arsenal and gave Judge Holt the dates.'[1] This work was not exactly within Eckert's province and scarcely required the services of his highly specialized talents.

But Eckert wasted many hours in a manner he did not mention at the congressional investigation. This assistant of Stanton seemed to be bent on getting some sort of confession out of the conspirator Lewis Paine, and spent much time on the gunboat in the Potomac River, where the suspects were being held prisoners. Paine told his inquisitor a great deal that was immaterial and much that was untrue.[2] Eckert again did no better there than a professional detective could have done, and probably did worse. He also busied himself in examining witnesses who were to appear at the conspiracy trial, and particularly those who had

---

[1] *Impeachment Investigation*, p. 672.
[2] Bates, op. cit., p. 380.

information against Jefferson Davis. But while the future Assistant Secretary of War ran errands to the National Hotel to look up names and dates, and employed his days examining political prisoners, the mystery of the interrupted wire connection, which he was best fitted to disentangle, remained uninvestigated.

Four years earlier, while Lincoln was on his first trip to Washington, severed wires had played a part in a possible conspiracy against the President's life. At that time news that the presidential party had secretly left Harrisburg was to be kept from the public, and to this end telegraphic connections out of the Pennsylvania capital were deliberately interrupted. All accounts of this incident state that the wires were cut; this seems to be the only method known to the average reporter. However, the wires on that occasion were not cut but grounded, which, of course, is the procedure any expert would follow. One cuts wires in the enemy's country, never at home.

Fortunately, we have a vivid description of how this grounding was accomplished in 1861. Allan Pinkerton, the detective in charge of these operations, wrote:[1]

'To effectually prevent this [use of the telegraph] I determined that the telegraph wires which connected Harrisburg with her neighboring cities should be so "fixed" as to render communication impossible.

'To arrange this matter Capt. Burns was sent to the office of the American Telegraph Company, and obtaining from . . . the manager of the company, a competent and trustworthy man for the purpose, departed for Harrisburg in order to carry out the proposed measures. . . . Walking out of the city nearly two miles, . . . [the linesman] climbed the poles and placing fine copper ground wires upon the regular lines, the city was soon entirely isolated from her neighbours. No message could possibly be sent from Harrisburg, and the capital of Pennsylvania was cut off temporarily from the rest of the world.

There is hardly room for doubt that this same method was used when Washington was telegraphically isolated on the night of Lincoln's death. If it had been part of the assassin's plot to interrupt the telegraphic service radically, the wires would have

[1] Allan Pinkerton, *Spy of the Rebellion* (A. G. Nettleton & Co., Chicago, 1883, used by courtesy of Mrs. W. J. Chalmers), pp. 89–93.

been cut. The fact that they were merely grounded shows either that the interruption was a strange coincidence or else that the task was performed by experts who had due regard for the interests of the Government.

Garbled versions of this incident found their way into contemporary print. In Hawley's *History of the Conspiracy*, for instance, one may read the following:[1]

'It appears that at precisely ten minutes past ten there were twenty-two wires leading from the War Office in different directions, and connecting with the fortifications and out-posts cut. These wires having been cut at a considerable distance from each other, together with the simultaneousness of this work, shows very plainly that a number of men were engaged in it, and it is now believed that there were twenty-two men appointed to do this work. The time at which this was accomplished furnishes beyond a doubt, the hour which the President was assassinated. . . .'

Whatever, or whoever, was at the bottom of the interrupted wire service, its effect was that, for two critical hours, few telegrams pertaining to Lincoln's death left Washington. But when Stanton got ready to send out the first of his dispatches, the telegraph was functioning again. The Secretary of War had therefore no cause for complaint, which is perhaps the reason why Eckert did not 'have the time for a personal investigation'.

While the news of Lincoln's assassination was known to the people of the Northern states on the morning of 15 April, it took much more time to spread this information throughout the South. The *Savannah Republican* and the *Charleston Courier*, for example, did not print the first official telegrams until 19 and 20 April, respectively. New Orleans did not know before 19 April that the President had been shot. News of the tragedy travelled slowly down the Mississippi River through St. Louis newspapers, and it was only at Baton Rouge that the telegraph was used for quicker transmission of the story. It seems odd that five days had to elapse after such a national calamity before it

---

[1] *Assassination and History of the Conspiracy* (J. R. Hawley & Co., Cincinnati, 1865), p. 63.

was possible to communicate the news to a city that had been in Federal possession since 1862. But this was actually the case; even Allan Pinkerton, who happened to be in New Orleans at the time, had no inkling of the event until he read of it in the papers; for on 19 April he sent the following wire to Washington:[1]

New Orleans, La.
19 April 1865.

HON. EDWIN M. STANTON,
Secretary of War:

This morning's papers contain the deplorable intelligence of the assassination of President Lincoln and Secretary Seward. Under the providence of God, in February, 1861, I was enabled to save him from the fate he has now met. How I regret that I had not been near him previous to this fatal act. I might have been the means to arrest it. If I can be of any service please let me know. The service of my whole force, or life itself, is at your disposal, and I trust you will excuse me for impressing upon you the necessity of great personal caution on your part. At this time the nation cannot spare you.

E. J. ALLEN (ALLAN PINKERTON).

The last paper to announce Lincoln's death, so far as is known, was the *Macon Daily Evening News*, which did not receive Stanton's dispatches until 26 April, and then by way of the *Atlanta Intelligencer* of 20 April and the *Chattanooga Gazette* of 16 April.

It is not surprising that the Southern papers were unable to obtain news from Washington until after a considerable interval. Wire communication was at its worst in the days following Lee's surrender, and even military dispatches to the Federal commanders were delayed. Stanton's telegram to Sherman, dated 15 April, advising him of an alleged assassination plot against his person, did not reach Raleigh, North Carolina, until 17 April, and Sherman did not acknowledge it until the next day.[2] Charleston and Savannah had to be supplied with the New York newspapers of 15 April by mail boats, as the Confederate telegraph system was in a hopeless condition of disrepair.

[1] *Official Records*, I, vol. 46, part 3, p. 845.
[2] Ibid., vol. 47, part 3, pp. 220, 245.

First announcement of Lincoln's assassination in the *Charleston Courier* on 20 April and in the *Macon Daily Evening News* on 26 April

Originals in the collection of the Chicago Historical Society

Such a state of affairs was bound to work in favour of the assassins. Booth and his accomplices could have reached any of the Southern ports at least as rapidly as the news of their bloody deed. But under the circumstances this could not have been helped.

There was one point in the South where an early publication of the news was important. This was Richmond. The chances were ten to one that Booth's flight would take him through the territory covered by the Richmond papers.

If possible, the *Whig*, the one newspaper then appearing in Richmond, should have been speedily supplied with full information and with instructions to publish it forthwith. Wire service with Richmond was open. An official telegram, announcing the assassination, was sent to Generals Ord and Patrick at the former Confederate capital about midnight of 14 April. The dispatch still bears the date of that day and refers to the event as having occurred 'to-night'.[1] The time when the message arrived is not stated in the official records, but it is probable that the transmission was accomplished in less than two hours. For on the fifteenth Grant wired General Ord at 4 p.m. and received a code reply in time to respond to it by 8 p.m., which shows that the exchange of communications took about four hours.[2] General Ord was in command of the troops that held Richmond for the Federal Government, and General Patrick was provost-marshal-general of the Virginia district. It would have been easy for these two officers to instruct the *Richmond Whig* to circulate the description of Booth, who was well known in the city and was virtually certain to pass near it in his flight. But the *Whig* did not print the news of the assault on Lincoln until Monday morning, 17 April. Neither the Saturday nor the Sunday issues contained any reference to the catastrophe that had struck Washington, a hundred miles away.

That the *Whig* failed in its duty to the public was probably no fault of the editors. Strange as it may seem, the news of Lincoln's death was not generally known in Richmond until Sunday night. Vague whispers had preceded by a few hours the receipt of concrete reports, but these rumours were not credited. John T. Ford, the owner of Ford's Theatre, had arrived in Richmond

[1] *Official Records*, I, vol. 46, part 3, p. 745.
[2] Ibid., pp. 762, 763.

on the day of the assassination. Not until three days later did he know positively what had transpired.

'It was on Monday morning', Ford testified, 'that I had the first positive information of the assassination. I went to the boat at six o'clock in the morning . . . and saw the *Richmond Whig* in heavy mourning.' Ford added that he had heard about the tragedy on Sunday afternoon, but had not believed it. In fact, he had laughed off the rumour as not deserving the slightest credence.[1] If Ford did not know what had happened in his own theatre, it is safe to assume that the public at large was equally ignorant.

Astonishing as it is that Richmond was unaware of Lincoln's assassination for more than two days, it is still more puzzling how it was possible to keep the news from reaching there. Officially, travel was open between the two capitals which so recently had been rivals. Lincoln himself, on the day of his death, had given orders to that effect, declaring that passports were no longer necessary. Of course, after the murder all traffic was restricted by the authorities; but communication between Washington and Richmond could not be completely stopped, although no passes to Richmond were honoured until the sixteenth.

Ford reported that on Sunday, 16 April, he met Forney, the publisher of the *Washington Chronicle*, at the Spottswood House, the most prominent hotel in Richmond, but that the Washington editor, who was close to the administration, 'said nothing . . . about it [the assassination], although he knew it'.[2] Why this attempt to keep the assassination a secret?

That the news of Lincoln's death actually reached Richmond during the night of Friday, 14 April, is confirmed by Colonel D. C. Forney, brother of the J. W. Forney referred to by Mr. Ford. In an interview granted to the *Washington Star*, and published on 27 June 1891, Forney tells of his experiences:

'I was in Richmond on that terrible night with a party of gentlemen who arrived there the afternoon of that day with the intention of spending a few days there and then going further south. How well I recollect that evening at the Spottswood Hotel. Col. J. W. Forney, Hon. Samuel J. Randall and Hon.

[1] *Impeachment Investigation*, pp. 534, 535.
[2] Ibid., p. 535.

Report of Lincoln's assassination in Richmond, Savannah, and New Orleans

Originals in the collection of the Chicago Historical Society and of the author

E. B. Hart of New York were of the party, numbering about twelve in all. We were all assembled in one of the public parlours of the hotel, entertaining, with a well-supplied commissary we brought with us, quite a number of prominent confederates who had called to pay their respects as well as to share in the luxuries we had brought with us and of which they had been deprived during the war. In the midst of our festivities a mounted orderly arrived at the hotel, very much excited, with an important dispatch, as he said, from the Union general still in command of Richmond, for Col. John W. Forney. I remember being outside on the pavement in front of the hotel walking up and down . . . and noticing the unusual excitement of this orderly I approached him for the purpose of receiving the dispatch, but he refused to deliver it to any one but Col. Forney himself. We then went upstairs, and when the dispatch was read it stated that President Lincoln with several members of his cabinet had been assassinated. . . .'

The party then left abruptly on a special train, accompanied part of the way by their Confederate friends. These gentlemen from Richmond, by the way, having learned the contents of the dispatch, were unanimous in condemning Booth's act. Hence some people in Richmond had news on Saturday morning of Lincoln's assassination, and it may be assumed that the *Whig* did not remain entirely ignorant of it until Sunday night.

The Richmond paper was then practically under military control. 'The publication of *The Whig* is resumed this afternoon, with the consent of the military authorities,' the publisher had announced after the evacuation of the city. 'The proprietor . . . has had a conference with . . . the Military Governor, who has assented to the publication of the paper on conditions which will be cheerfully and faithfully complied with.'[1]

If the editors of the *Whig* did not print the story until Monday morning, it was hardly a matter of their own choice. Most likely it was a matter of cheerful compliance—more or less.

On 17 April the morning edition of the *Petersburg* (Virginia)

[1] James Melvin Lee, *History of American Journalism* (The Garden City Publishing Co., Inc., New York, 1923, used by permission of, and by arrangement with Houghton Mifflin Co.), p. 290.

Express had the headline 'PAINFUL RUMOR', on its third page, with this information beneath it:

'. . . the assassination . . . is said to have occurred on Friday night last at 40 minutes past 10 o'clock. The version which seemed to gain most credence is, that while the President was retiring from Ford's Theatre, he was fired upon from a crowd. . . . At the time of this writing, we have no means of ascertaining the truth. . . .'

At eight o'clock, as the paper went to press, 'parties from City Point confirm[ed] the melancholy intelligence'. Booth's name was then put before the readers for the first time.

The generals in command of the Richmond district were not alone in their anxiety to suppress the news of the tragedy. On the seventeenth, immediately after receiving the official dispatches announcing Lincoln's assassination, General Howard, at Raleigh, advised General Logan at Morrisville of the event.[1]

> *Headquarters Army of the Tennessee*
> *Raleigh, N.C.*
> 17 *April* 1865

MAJ. GEN. JOHN A. LOGAN,
Commanding Fifteenth Army Corps:

GENERAL: Our noble President has been assassinated and is dead. Seward also, and his son. It is thought that Seward will live, but his son cannot. The assassins are said to have attempted Grant, but failed. They are reported on the track of Sherman, and the Secretary puts him on his guard. My heart is filled with gloom and sorrow. We have lost our noble head.

> Respectfully,
> O. O. HOWARD,
> *Major-General.*

(Same to General Blair.)

But only a few hours later he followed his first telegram with another, the purport of which must have proved a surprise to the recipient.

---

[1] *Official Records* I, vol. 47, part 3, p. 239.

RICHMOND WHIG, MONDAY
MORNING, APRIL 17, 1865.

Assassination of President Lincoln!

The heaviest blow which has ever fallen upon the people of the South has descended. Abraham Lincoln, the President of the United States, has been assassinated! The decease of the Chief Magistrate of the nation, at any period, is an event which profoundly affects the public mind, but the time, manner, and circumstances of President Lin-

Earliest notice of Lincoln's assassination in the *Richmond Whig* on 17 April

Original in the collection of the Chicago Historical Society

> *Headquarters Army of the Tennessee*
> 17 *April* 1865.

MAJ. GEN. J. A. LOGAN,
Commanding Fifteenth Army Corps, Morrisville:

GENERAL: If you have received a dispatch from me this a.m. with reference to one received from Washington, please not to publish it.

> O. O. HOWARD,
> *Major-General.*

General Blair was advised in still stronger terms to keep the matter strictly under cover.

> *Headquarters Army of the Tennessee*
> *Raleigh, N.C.*
> 17 *April* 1865.
> (Received 4 p.m.)

MAJ. GEN. F. P. BLAIR,
Commanding Seventeenth Army Corps:

GENERAL: The general commanding desires that the communication sent you announcing the assassination of the President be kept as secret as possible. You will please not publish it to your command.

> Very respectfully, your obedient servant,
> A. M. VAN DYKE,
> *Assistant Adjutant-General.*

Perhaps it was feared that the announcement to the troops would create a delicate situation and lead to excesses toward the civilian population. But this argument is not convincing, for sooner or later the soldiers had to learn the news of the crime, and the outburst, if one were to occur, could only be postponed. As matters turned out, the Federal troops held themselves thoroughly in hand when they finally heard of Lincoln's death; and the Southern population, equally stunned by the import of the news, gave no offence that led to friction with the invaders.

As no other motive seems to present itself, it must be assumed that an imaginary danger was bought off at a tremendous price— at the risk of giving the fugitive assassins a start of several days in territory that should have been aroused to a superlative degree of watchfulness.

How groundless all fears were that the soldiery would get beyond control is demonstrated by the fact, printed in the *Richmond Whig* on 18 April, that all the flags in Richmond and in its harbour were at half-mast as early as Sunday. The army evidently took official notice of Lincoln's death before the populace was apprised of it; yet no hostile acts of any kind were reported. In other places the troops behaved with equal self-restraint. On 18 April, for instance, Sherman wired Halleck: 'The news of Mr. Lincoln's death produced a most intense effect on our troops. At first I feared it would lead to excesses, but now it has softened down and can easily be guided.'[1]

One cannot state definitely whether the commanding generals in Richmond, Raleigh, and other cities in the South acted on their own initiative in exercising such a fateful censorship, or whether they had been ordered to do so. The official records contain no dispatches bearing on this riddle. On the surface, this would indicate that no instructions on how to handle the intelligence were received from Washington; but it is inconceivable that these subordinates would have shouldered such responsibility without even asking for advice. General Howard's follow-up telegram asking General Logan to make no reference to a message sent to him several hours before, and the fact that other generals, though independent of each other, followed similar courses of action, leads one to believe that they were guided by secret orders sent to them by the War Department.

[1] *Official Records*, I, vol 47, part 3, p. 245.

CHAPTER IX

Every Avenue of Escape Blocked—
Save One

The measures taken by the authorities to close in on Lincoln's murderer were, to all appearances, very thorough ones. A general alarm was sounded urging the commanders of troops in and around Washington to find and arrest the assassin at all hazards. Secretary Welles mobilized many naval vessels with the same object in view. In the early morning hours after the murder scores of military dispatches left the War Department, each one designed to close some possible avenue of escape to the conspirators.

For unfathomable reasons it was deemed advisable to arouse first the northern and north-western environs of the capital. It was a direction the assassins could hardly be expected to take. The roads toward the north led into Union territories, where neither shelter nor aid would be available. Nevertheless, Colonel Thompson, commanding at Darnestown, was probably the first to be instructed; he was ordered to scout north of Washington. The telegram left Washington so early that the colonel was able to reply half an hour before midnight. His zeal was spurred on by an official intimation that 'THE ASSASSINS ARE SUPPOSED TO HAVE ESCAPED TOWARD MARYLAND'.[1] By twelve o'clock three squadrons were out, scouring the roads parallel with the Potomac and covering those toward Tenellytown, Barnesville, and even as far as Frederick. It is certain that Booth could not have passed through this area without immediate detection and capture.

[1] *Official Records*, I, vol. 46, part 3, p. 752.

The next dispatch, sent just at midnight, went to General
Slough, military governor of Alexandria, south-west of Wash-
ington. To him the information was conveyed that 'IT IS NOT
KNOWN IN WHICH DIRECTION THE ASSASSIN HAS ESCAPED'.[1]

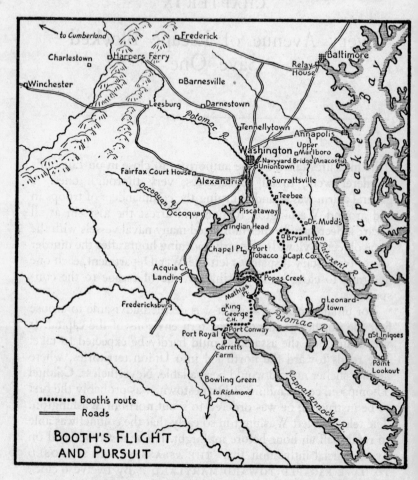

But he was told to order out his entire police force and to prevent any one from leaving the city. There was no possible escape
for Booth through Alexandria; neither was there any great
chance that he would choose this route, as it led to a district
fairly swarming with Federal troops. But to insure more than

[1] *Official Records*, I, vol. 46, part 3, p. 752.

ordinary watchfulness, General Hardie wired the railroad agent at Alexandria that the assassin was headed his way, thereby probably driving the poor man into a frenzy of fruitless activity.[1]

If the fugitive had tried to flee straight west, circling Alexandria to the north, he would have been trapped at Fairfax Court House, where General Gamble was ordered, shortly after midnight, to scatter his mounted troops along the river roads between Washington and Leesburg. As morning dawned 800 of his cavalrymen were out scouting; any one caught in this territory would have been faced with immediate seizure. But, lest Gamble should fail in his duties, a telegram was sent to Major Waite of the Eighth Illinois Cavalry at Fairfax Court House: 'ORDER GENERAL GAMBLE TO ALLOW NO ONE TO PASS HIS LINES. TO ARREST EVERY ONE WHO ATTEMPTS.'[2]

If Booth had penetrated through here it would have been a miracle; but it probably would have availed him nothing, for the alarm had been flashed as far ahead as Winchester and Harper's Ferry, as well as to Cumberland to the north-west.[3] No doubt the western and north-western gates of Washington were securely closed and bolted.

The next place warned was Baltimore. General Morris, commander of the district, was advised at three o'clock in the morning to guard thoroughly 'every avenue leading into Baltimore, and if possible arrest J. Wilkes Booth, the murderer of President Lincoln'.[4]

Within twenty minutes Morris replied that 'The most vigorous measures will be taken. Every avenue is guarded. No trains or boats will be permitted to leave this department for the present.'[5]

The district commander of Baltimore took his duties a trifle too seriously, for three trains on the Baltimore and Ohio were held up at the Relay House until Stanton admonished his subaltern to temper his zeal with reason. Nevertheless, a keen eye was kept on all passengers, and the highways to the capital were patrolled with care.

The authorities also arranged to watch their own end of the lines leading north. The commander of the veteran reserve corps, Colonel Gile, received on 14 April the following instructions:

---

[1] *Official Records*, I, vol. 46, part 3, p. 773.   [2] Ibid.   [3] Ibid., p. 775.
[4] Ibid.   [5] Ibid., p. 776.

'The major-general commanding directs that you detail a commissioned officer and ten enlisted men to accompany train which leaves this city for Baltimore 15 April. Shortly after leaving the city the officer in charge will search every car in the train and arrest, if found, J. Wilkes Booth, and other parties whom you may deem it for the interest of the service to apprehend. At each stopping place or station this search will be made. The party will in each case return to Washington by the train leaving Baltimore first after its arrival there, and carry out the same instructions on the return trip.'[1]

The roads leading from Washington directly into Virginia had been closed immediately after Lincoln's assassination. Before morning on 15 April, all these south-western exits were barred by Stanton's orders, and it was only on the sixteenth that General Ord was allowed to respect passes issued by General Meade.[2] This precaution on the part of the War Department would have been effective provided Booth had remained in Washington. As it happened, he was thirty miles out of Washington by four o'clock in the morning, and the precautions taken proved no handicap to him. Indeed their only effect was to impede any would-be pursuers who desired to leave the capital.

If the assassins had intended to use the Potomac for their flight their plans would likewise have been frustrated. Before midnight a wire had been dispatched to Saint Inigoes near the mouth of the river urging Commander Parker of the navy to guard this outlet.[3] To Point Lookout, at the southern tip of the Maryland peninsula, word was sent to stop all vessels going down the river and to hold all persons on them until further orders. Even Annapolis had its instructions to let no boats depart.[4]

South-eastern Maryland was taken in hand by Provost-Marshall McPhail of Baltimore, who boldly claimed that Booth had fled in that direction.[5]

There still remained a chance for the fugitives to evade capture by crossing the Patuxent River and boarding a vessel on Chesapeake Bay. Again Washington used the ruse of terrifying

---

[1] *Official Records*, I, vol. 46, part 3, p. 751.
[2] Ibid., p. 787; also de Russy's dispatch, loc. cit., p. 773.
[3] Ibid., p. 754.   [4] Ibid., p. 756.   [5] Ibid., p. 773.

the commanders of these districts by intimating that the murderers had gone into their territory; but more tangible measures were not neglected. By the sixteenth the mouth of the Patuxent was closed, and the whole western shore of the Chesapeake was under the guard of six patrol vessels. To what lengths the authorities went in their efforts to block all possible routes of escape by water is depicted by a telegram sent by an officer in charge of the coast patrol to his superior.

> *Depot Quartermaster's Office*
> *Baltimore Md.*
> 17 *April* 1865—1 p.m.

Brevet-Maj. Gen. M. C. Meigs,
Quartermaster-General, U.S. Army, Washington, D.C.:

I have the honor to report the following arrangements as having been made for patrolling and guarding the western shore of the Chesapeake Bay to Point Lookout, in accord with your orders. On receipt of your dispatch every vessel in this department fit for service was immediately put in readiness, each one furnished with a military guard of four men, except the dispatch boat, which is provided with a sergeant and ten men, and ordered down the bay with the following instructions to their respective captains, viz.: To cruise back and forth constantly between certain points named until further orders, keeping as near shore as is consistent with safety to their vessels; taking on board all persons desiring to come off from the shore, and detaining them; overhauling all small vessels or boats, and holding every one found thereon until further orders for their disposition, the guards to be concealed on approaching the shore or any boat or vessel. Vigilance, activity, and a prompt compliance with the foregoing instructions were enjoined upon all. . . . I will report promptly any intelligence that reaches me from these steamers.

> R. M. Newport,
> *Colonel and Quartermaster.*[1]

Booth had caused a virtual blockade of the whole Atlantic coast from Baltimore to Hampton Roads.[2]

---

[1] *Official Records*, I, vol. 46, part 3, p. 819.
[2] Ibid., p. 806; see also supplementary note to chapter ix, 'How Atzerodt left Washington'.

Only one hole was left in the network that Stanton had spun around the nation's capital. This was the road that pointed straight south from Washington to Port Tobacco. It was the road Booth was most likely to use; for it led toward the Confederacy, the only place where the assassin could hope to find protection. In all the wires sent out from the War Department during the night of 14 April, this route was not mentioned once and no precautions were taken to guard it.

The only road that Stanton failed to bar was the one by which Booth escaped from Washington; and there never should have been the slightest doubt that he would use it.

CHAPTER X

The Man-Hunt is On

When Lincoln's assassin had been swallowed up in the darkness of the night and the clatter of his horse's hoofs had died away, it seemed at first thought a hopeless task to divine his probable direction or to organize anything but a haphazard pursuit. On second consideration, however, the choice of possible routes of escape narrowed down perceptibly. Booth, who had been seen on the stage by thousands, could not risk passing through northern cities, where he might have been recognized by any chance passer-by. The country west of Washington was held by Federal troops; even if Booth was ignorant that the War Department had alarmed such far-away posts as Cumberland and Charlestown, he would have shied at the prospect of traversing these districts. Nor did the north-western roads lead to friendly territory. There remained Baltimore, a town in which Southern sentiment always ran high and where Booth had many friends; and finally, the South itself, where the assassin could hope for acclaim and assistance. But it is probable that Baltimore would have proved a *cul-de-sac* rather than a shelter; Booth was much more likely to strike for broader spaces in the hope of thus evading his pursuers.

The fact that no trains left Washington after 7.30 p.m. and the probability that all railroads would be kept under strict surveillance, should have been given serious thought by both the assassin and the authorities. Trains would certainly be closely watched, and Booth would have been insane to use them.

The only likely route for Booth to take was the one he actually followed. It was what was then known as the underground railway to Richmond and was travelled by spies and dispatch-

bearers, by Confederate mail-carriers and by dealers in contraband. There was no other section of the country that boasted of
more violent secessionist sympathies than the southern Maryland peninsula. A sparse population, an abundance of swamps,
and an intricate network of bad roads all contributed to make
this territory an ideal place for Booth to select. That the assassin,
contrary to his original plans, stayed in concealment there for a
week without being detected is ample evidence that he chose
wisely.

To assume that the Government in Washington was not
aware of this well-travelled route to Richmond would be to impute to it an incredible degree of imbecility. This was the route
by which the conspirators had agreed to carry the captive Lincoln into the country of his enemies if their kidnapping scheme
had been successful, and Stanton had been so advised through
information furnished by both Wiechmann and Gleason. Besides, nearly every one along the roads leading to Port Tobacco
had heard of this plot. It seems to have been discussed so openly
that it must have reached the ears of the Federal spies with which
the countryside was filled. Some of the most prominent men
living in southern Maryland were cognizant of the scheme to
kidnap Lincoln, or were implicated in it.[1]

A glance at a map must have shown Stanton that here was a
line of possible flight which should be blocked more carefully
than any other. Yet not a single message in the official archives
of the War Department shows that this section was given even
momentary consideration.

The authorities in Richmond were not the only ones who
habitually used this backdoor line of communication between
the two capitals. The Federal Government often found it advisable to have its own emissaries pass that way. The head of the
secret service of the United States, Colonel Lafayette C. Baker,
had himself adopted this route when he had entered Richmond
as a spy in the early days of his career;[2] others, no doubt, had
followed in his footsteps. That Washington did nothing to close
this underground railway was perhaps due to its usefulness in the
system of counter-espionage practised by the War Department.

[1] Oldroyd, op. cit., pp. 267, 269.
[2] Lafayette C. Baker, *History of the U.S. Secret Service* (Philadelphia,
1867), p. 48.

Many a spy took money from both the North and the South, and not a few secret dispatches sent by Jefferson Davis to his Canadian Cabinet were conveniently opened and copied in Washington before being forwarded to their destination.[1] To close this round-about way of communication would have been easy; so easy, in fact, that the unwillingness of the Federal Government to take this step should have aroused the suspicions of the Southern leaders.

It is probably because the use of this route helped the Government, on the whole, that no action was taken in January 1865, when an official missive was received at the State Department in Washington from the United States consul at Toronto, giving a minute description of how the messengers of the Confederacy proceeded in their transportation of contraband correspondence.

'The messenger arriving at Baltimore [so the letter read] receives additional instructions . . . and proceeds to Washington, here he undergoes a thorough examination, is searched and permitted to pass—he takes a south-easterly direction to "Port Tobacco", where he is sheltered . . . and at dead of night crosses in an india rubber boat to the south side of the Potomac, thence he goes to "Bowling Green" . . . he returns by the same route. The last trip was made in fourteen days—(Dec. 14–28) . . .'[2]

A notation made in pencil on the margin of this document stated that a copy was sent to the War Department. Here is, then, official confirmation that the War Department was aware of this clandestine route to Richmond. Hence, its failure to close it after Lincoln's death is not easily explained.

A document has come to light showing that General Augur, late on the night of 14 April, asked Stanton for further instructions as to the guarding of roads, all previous orders having evidently been carried out. The paper is in C. C. Augur's own writing, very hurriedly penned. There is no indication of the hour when it was written.[4]

[1] Pitman, op. cit., p. 26.
[2] War Department Archives.
[4] Ibid.

Headquarters Department of Washington
22nd Army Corps.
Washington D.C.
14 April 1865.

COLONEL NICHOLS:

I have sent to arrest all persons attempting to leave the city by all approaches. Have telegraphed to troops on the upper Potomac to arrest all suspicious persons—also to Gnl. Slough at Alexandria and Gnl. Morris at Baltimore—All our own police and detectives are out. No clew has yet been found by which I can judge what further steps to take. Can you suggest any?

Respectfully,
C. C. AUGUR

The following endorsement is on the back of the paper:

Respectfully submitted to the Hon. Secretary of War—Gen. Augur has been advised to search and patrol the roads leading from Washington particularly in the direction of the Occoquan. The telegraph line to Baltimore was broken at 11.45 p.m., supposed to have been cut—It is now working to Philadelphia.

R. WILLIAMS
Asst. Adjt.-Genl.

Augur's request was an open, though unintentional, challenge to the Secretary of War to point out the necessity of protecting the Maryland peninsula, hitherto so completely ignored. But Stanton did not rise to the occasion.

The Occoquan route had received a great deal of publicity in the *New York Tribune* correspondence of 1864, and for this reason Booth was almost certain to avoid it, even had he been willing to expose himself to the soldiery which filled the country between Alexandria and Fredericksburg. Nevertheless, orders had been sent to Alexandria to cover this ground; and now, following Stanton's urging, an attempt was made to prevent a crossing of the Potomac from the Washington side opposite the mouth of the Occoquan. This was the signal for the first Federal cavalry troops to venture out on the road Booth had taken. But while at all other places colonels and generals were marshalling regiments and brigades, here a mere handful of horsemen under a lieutenant were following Booth's trail. This young officer was a brother of Charles A. Dana, Assistant Secretary of War, a man whom Stanton had made and on whom he could absolutely depend. The name of the lieutenant was David D. Dana.

Just at what time Lieutenant Dana was sent out on this highly important errand does not appear on the records. It is probable that it was about four o'clock in the morning, as this would coincide with General Augur's orders to General Slough at Alexandria and also with Lieutenant Dana's time of arrival at Piscataway. From there he sent the following telegram to Washington.[1]

Piscataway
15 April 1865.

CAPT. R. CHANDLER,
Assistant Adjutant-General:

SIR: I have the honor to report that I arrived in this place at 7 a.m., and at once sent a man to Chapel Hill to notify the cavalry at that point of the murder of the President, with description of the parties who committed the deed. With the arrangements which have been made it is impossible for them to get across the river in this direction.

Very respectfully, your obedient servant,

DAVID D. DANA,
First Lieutenant and Provost-Marshal, Third Brigade.

I have reliable information that the person who murdered Secretary Seward is Boyce or Boyd [Boyle], the man who killed Captain Watkins in Maryland, I think it without doubt true.

D. D. DANA

To what arrangements the young officer refers, he does not say. They could hardly have been of his own making, as he probably had no more than a dozen men with him. He may have meant the arrangements made by General Slough, who by that time presumably had his patrols in open sight on the right bank of the Potomac, opposite Piscataway, thus preventing a crossing of the river there. At any rate, Lieutenant Dana concluded that his presence in that vicinity was useless, and therefore took it upon himself to make two decisions that were so pregnant with possibilities that they could easily have changed the course of

[1] *Official Records,* I, vol. 46, part 3, p. 767.

history. First he decided to send a message to Chapel Point (he mistakenly called it Chapel Hill) to notify the cavalry there of the murder of the President. Chapel Point is a little slope of ground near Port Tobacco and was occupied at that time by comparatively few soldiers. It lay on, or near, the direct route Booth was preparing to take, and to arouse the garrison there to action was a matter of the greatest import. It should have been done hours sooner, and certainly ought not to have been left to the chance whim of a junior officer. There were no telegraph stations at Port Tobacco or Chapel Point, which explains the necessity of dispatching a messenger.

Instead of confining his message, however, to the conveying of the news that Lincoln had been murdered and that the troops at Chapel Point should keep a sharp look-out, he ordered the men to leave their post and scatter along the shores of the Patuxent River. Instead of concentrating them at the only point where they might have halted Booth's flight, he sent them on a wild-goose chase to a place where the fugitive was not and had no intention of going.[1] Whether Dana did this on his own initiative has not been ascertained. It certainly was a tremendous responsibility to shoulder.

The second step the young officer took was to leave Piscataway, where nothing could be accomplished, and proceed to Bryantown. This brought Dana within four miles of the house in which Booth and his dog-like follower, Herold, were sleeping at that moment. The actor, having injured his leg by jumping to the stage, had been forced to change his original plans of crossing the Potomac early in the morning at Port Tobacco and had detoured to Dr. Mudd's house near Bryantown to have his foot bandaged and to rest from his painful exertions. If Lieutenant Dana had searched the district without delay it is possible that he would have caught the assassin. But he did nothing at all. Perhaps he did not have enough soldiers; perhaps he thought he had already done his share of the day's work.

But the great opportunity which he had once missed came to the young officer a second time. On Sunday morning, 16 April, Dr. Samuel A. Mudd told his cousin, Dr. George Mudd, that he had extended hospitality to two strangers, one of whom had

---

[1] *Boston Sunday Globe*, 12 Dec. 1897; see also supplementary note to chapter x, 'Lieutenant Dana Scatters the Chapel Point Garrison'.

required medical help, and that the recent events at Washington had made him suspicious of them. He begged his cousin to bring this matter immediately to the attention of Lieutenant Dana. Dr. George Mudd complied, at his leisure.[1] It is not apparent that Dana took any measures to follow up this promising clue until the next day, when several detectives arrived, sent by Provost-Marshal James R. O'Beirne, with orders to scour the neighbourhood. To them Dana related Dr. Mudd's story. Its importance was not understood, however, and it was not until Tuesday, the eighteenth, that these officers found it worth their while to ride out to Dr. Samuel Mudd's house to interrogate him.[2] They did not search his house until Friday, the twenty-first. Then they found Booth's name inscribed in the boot the doctor had cut from the assassin's foot. Thereupon they arrested the ill-fated physician.

'It was in great part by reason of Dr. Mudd's having delayed from Saturday night until Sunday noon to send to the authorities at Bryantown information as to the suspected persons who had been at his house', remarked General Thomas Ewing, Jr., counsel for Dr. Mudd at the conspiracy trial, 'that he was arrested and charged as a conspirator; and yet I assert this record shows *he* moved more promptly in communicating his information than *they* [the detectives] did in acting on it.'[3] And in this it is difficult to disagree with General Ewing.

If Booth had not hurt his leg he should have reached Port Tobacco at four o'clock in the morning, allowing about six hours for a trip of thirty-six miles. By early forenoon he would have been near King George Court House, Virginia, and out of immediate reach of all organized pursuit. It would not have mattered, therefore, that the Government had blocked the road behind him. This, however, does not excuse Stanton and his group of advisers for leaving out of consideration Booth's logical route, and the one he actually did follow. In view of all the events that took place, Booth most likely would have been captured before leaving southern Maryland if the pursuit had been conducted there with forces and commanders at least on a parity

[1] Pitman, op. cit., pp. 206–11.
[2] Ibid., p. 87.　　　　　[3] Ibid., pp. 329–30.

with those in charge of it in other sections of the country. Elsewhere telegraphic communications were available and troops in large numbers were on hand to throw a cordon across the culprit's path. Southern Maryland had no such facilities; why, then, were the troops from Washington not thrown into the breach and put into motion at once?

The very fact that no large body of soldiers was garrisoned along Booth's way on the peninsula should have prompted the Government to make unusual exertions there. Instead, a mere lieutenant was sent out, not with instructions to pursue the murderer, but to see that the crossing of the Potomac at Piscataway was as well guarded on the Maryland side as it was on the western shore. That the young officer followed Booth's route as far as he did seemed to have been due to accident, or to the prosaic fact that Bryantown boasted the best hotel in the district.

When Lieutenant Dana crossed the Navy Yard Bridge he did not know that Booth and Herold had preceded him. He was not even inquisitive enough to ask if any men answering their description had been noticed by the guards; for when he arrived at Bryantown the next noon he was still under the impression that Booth had not yet left Washington. He made this statement to Dr. George Mudd, who so testified later under oath.[1]

The negligence displayed by this young officer on the track of a criminal is matched only by his heedlessness in asserting to the populace that the assassin was still behind him. Instead of pushing the pursuit, he blocked the road he was travelling on, never figuring that closed exits would hinder the conspirators only if they were still within the city, but would actually be of help to them if they had already made their escape. More than that— by giving his uncalled-for opinion to the inhabitants of southern Maryland, he turned their attention in the wrong direction. Even if some one had seen the wounded assassin at Dr. Mudd's house that day, Dana's rash statements would have lulled suspicion to rest; and if Herold had been recognized during his search for a wagon with which to continue his flight, he would not have been stopped; for Dana had announced that Booth's travelling companion was not Herold, but a notorious desperado named Boyle, who was known in that region and who had pillaged there three or four weeks before.[2]

---

[1] Pitman, op. cit., pp. 206–11.   [2] Ibid., p. 327.

Did the War Department really make possible Booth's flight by ignoring the Port Tobacco road?

The Official Records, it is true, contain no reference to this avenue of escape; but orders concerning it may have existed at the time and been lost later. It is also possible that they were not included in the final compilation which was, to a certain extent, left to the discretion of the editors. Augur's private note to Stanton, in which he tells of his orders to arrest persons leaving by all exits from the city, may indicate that due consideration was given to every existing road.

On the other hand, the Official Records are unusually complete in regard to the happenings at the time following Lincoln's assassination. Dispatches are extant covering every other road leading out of Washington, and in many cases both the outgoing and incoming messages were duly chronicled. In addition, the compilation of the Official Records was originally in the hands of Stanton's most intimate friends, and the material was jealously guarded by the Secretary of War. That the most interesting telegrams of all—the ones relating to the route Booth actually took —should have been deliberately omitted is therefore improbable.

Augur's private note may convey the impression that all roads were being watched and patrolled, but this is not the only possible interpretation. Augur, in fact, mentions specifically all the points the War Department had aroused, and mentions them almost in the order in which they appear in print. There are even grounds for the contention that Augur was aware of the opening in the net around the capital and subtly brought his observation to Stanton's attention, either to have the error corrected or to protect himself against future accusations.

According to Lieutenant Dana's reports it must be assumed that no soldiers had arrived at Piscataway before he reached there at seven o'clock in the morning of 15 April. The testimony of people then living at Surrattsville and Bryantown showed that not until the forenoon were there troops in that part of the Peninsula through which Booth was travelling.

Thus it would appear—although the evidence is primarily negative—that the Port Tobacco road was left unguarded during the entire night of Lincoln's assassination.

CHAPTER XI

John Fletcher Tells His Story

Although the assassins' plans for their flight were shrouded in mystery immediately after the murder, the direction which they had taken should have been known by midnight, if not sooner. By then the disclosure of the route they were following ceased to depend on reasoning; it was laid bare by the adventures of a simple stableman named John Fletcher. This hostler had become suspicious of David Herold, Booth's companion, who was riding a horse from the livery stable for which Fletcher worked, and had stayed out beyond the time that had been agreed upon. The suspicion, to be sure, concerned only Herold's honesty; but when Fletcher happened to see his animal being spurred on toward the Navy Yard Bridge at a time when it should have been returned, he saddled a horse for himself and followed Herold to the bridge over the east branch of the Potomac. There he arrived a few minutes after Booth and Herold had crossed.

A Sergeant Cobb, who was in charge at the north end of the bridge, had questioned Booth and, after a brief conversation, had let him pass. Herold, also finding the guard easy to deal with, had followed his master at an interval of not more than ten minutes. But Fletcher was not so gently handled. He was told that if he followed Herold, in an attempt to recover his horse, he could not re-cross the bridge until the next morning. Under these circumstances, he decided to turn back and get a good night's rest.[1]

It is characteristic of Booth that he did not hesitate to give his true name to the sentinel at the bridge, for, in the fantastic mind of the assassin, his act was to be the perfect crime of the ages,

[1] Pitman, op. cit., p. 84.

and he the most heroic assassin of all time. It might even have hurt his vanity had he known that it was only a major and not a colonel that was Lincoln's companion at the theatre. 'I walked with a firm step through a thousand of his friends,' he wrote in his diary; 'was stopped, but pushed on; a colonel was at his side.'[1] No disguise of his face then, though nothing could have been easier for an actor; no disguise of his name now. A fair fight between the fox and the hounds! Probably he had also deliberately accosted the delinquent Parker, too proud to take advantage of an error on the part of his quarry. Perhaps he had even given the bodyguard his own card. There was to be no possibility of retreat; only a jump on to the stage could save him. He had calculated to a nicety that part of the play when only one actor would be out in front, only a woman and a boy in the wings. A laugh from the crowd which usually followed the exit of two ladies in the comedy would drown out any commotion in the box.[2] The audience could be depended on to remain inactive, stunned, for the fraction of a minute he needed to traverse the stage and reach his horse. Everything had been figured out with meticulous care. Booth was no half-crazed criminal, fired by alcoholic spirits, as so many writers have professed to believe. The man who had plotted this act had plotted it with the brains of a psychologist who knew his theatrical crowds and with the mathematical accuracy of a general charting a well-laid campaign.

But in spite of all his care, the presence of mind of a quick-witted lawyer, Colonel Stewart, almost thwarted him, for Stewart in his pursuit failed to reach him by only a few feet.[3] There was one contingency, however, the actor could not foresee. As he jumped on to the stage his spur caught on the flag decorating the presidential box. He fell, and broke a small bone in his leg. It was one chance in a thousand—but it upset all his plans for escape.

To return to Sergeant Cobb; one can understand his decision to let Booth and Herold pass unconditionally, although he refused Fletcher the same privilege. He had to make his decisions, and he made them according to his best judgement. On what

[1] Booth, *Diary*; also *Impeachment Investigation*, pp. 286 ff.
[2] Laughlin, op. cit., pp. 95, 281.
[3] Pitman, op. cit., p. 79.

grounds can it be explained, however, that having heard Booth's name from his own lips, this soldier did not give the alarm as soon as the news of Lincoln's assassination reached him? If all the avenues leading out of Washington were as closely watched as the great ado at headquarters would lead one to believe, how was it that not a single detective or officer thought it worth while to approach the Anacostia Bridge and inquire if any suspicious horsemen had crossed there?

What time did the news of the tragedy at Ford's Theatre reach the guard at the bridge? No one seems to know, and no one has ever seemed to care. The distance from the bridgehead to the playhouse was three miles. It is barely possible, though extremely improbable, that when Cobb was relieved at one o'clock in the morning—as the military records show—he was still in ignorance of what had transpired. This fact would not explain, of course, why no one had arrived by that time to ask questions; the Anacostia Bridge was one of the main arteries of traffic out of Washington, and one would certainly expect some inquiry to be made there as to whether or not Booth had crossed it. At the trial of the conspirators Cobb made no reference to any such inquiry, and none of the lawyers or journalists was curious enough to find out if he had been questioned by any one. But even if no probe had been made until Cobb had retired for the night, was his sleep held so sacred that he could not be disturbed in his barracks to give information to one of the pursuing squads. The answer to this is that there was no pursuing squad to which to give information. That night the span across the east branch of the Potomac that had carried Booth to safety seems to have been the loneliest spot in the capital.

After John Fletcher, foreman of Nailor's livery stable, had been turned back by Sergeant Cobb, he rode slowly homeward. When he came to Third Street, as he later testified, it was ten minutes before midnight, and he was still worrying about the horse which Herold had failed to return. Inquiring of another stableman if the roan had been put up there, he received no news of the animal, but was informed instead that Lincoln had been shot and that Seward was dying.

'I then returned to the stable,' swore Fletcher in court, 'put up the horse, came outside of the office window, and sat down there; it was half-past one o'clock.'[1] That was all.

A remarkable hostler, this John Fletcher. A horse is stolen from under his eyes, a stupid sergeant forbids him to follow the thief, and in his fury he rides back so slowly that more than an hour elapses before he covers the two and a half miles to Third Street. He does not report his loss to the police; he hears of Lincoln's assassination, but does not connect the two fleeing horsemen with this calamity. If Pitman's official report of the trial is correct, Fletcher was indeed a noteworthy character.

If Pitman's report is correct. Curiosity has led to a comparison of Fletcher's testimony, as officially given, with the transcriptions of the trial found in the archives at Washington; and the shocking discovery is made that the liveryman did not conclude his testimony the way Pitman would have it appear. On the contrary, the interesting part of his story begins where Pitman's report leaves off. Fletcher continued his testimony by stating that he overheard people on the sidewalk saying 'that it was men riding on horseback that had shot President Lincoln'. Then the liveryman became suspicious. 'I . . . asked a cavalry sergeant if they had picked up any horses. He told me that they had . . . and for me to go down to the police-office on Tenth Street.'[2]

Here is a chance to check up on Fletcher's story. Did he really go to the police station, as he stated? There is undeniable evidence that he did, for his name appears on the blotter among those who called there between eleven and twelve o'clock. There can be no mistake about this, for the entry reads: 'John Fletcher 299 E. St., Nailors Stable.'

According to this hostler's testimony at the conspiracy trial, he did not go to the police station until after 1.30 a.m., while the police records mark the time of his appearance at headquarters before midnight. On the face of it, other parts of Fletcher's story, as told in court, do not ring quite true either. It is more than likely that he was infuriated when Sergeant Cobb turned him back at the bridge, and infuriated people do not, as a rule, ride slowly. He got to the police station at Tenth Street before midnight, which would have been impossible had he reached

---

[1] Pitman, op. cit., p. 84.
[2] Benjamin P. Poore, *Conspiracy Trial* (J. E. Tilton & Co., Boston, 1865), I, pp. 329, 330.

Third Street at ten minutes before twelve and meandered
through the town in the manner he described.

In a hearing before the judge-advocate-general on 23 April
Fletcher's statement was given as follows:

'... At the Navy Yard Bridge the guard halted me, and I gave
the description of the horse to the guard and he told me such a
horse had crossed there. I asked him if I could cross the Bridge
after him and he said yes, but I could not return. So I concluded
to go no farther. When I got back to 14th Street again I went
around to Dorsey's stables and inquired if the horse had got
back, and he said no. I went down to 10th Street to the police
office, by the direction of a Sergeant, I went up to Gen. Augur's
office and identified the saddle and bridle which they had
found....'[1]

Nothing is said here about riding slowly back to town, about
looking at the watch or about sitting down at a window at half-
past one. If this statement of Fletcher, given before Judge Holt,
is correct, the stableman acted quite sensibly. But what—or who
—caused him to insert all those misleading statements into his
testimony at the conspiracy trial?

It is a safe wager that Fletcher, who seemed a conscientious
employee, wanted to report the loss of his horse as quickly as he
could; but if he was at the police station before midnight, as undoubtedly he was, he must have heard there the story of Lincoln's assassination. His name is listed among those persons
whose information 'goes to show that the assassin is a man
named John Wilkes Booth'. It is therefore more than probable
that the foreman of Nailor's stable did connect the tragedy at
Ford's Theatre with the loss of his animal, and that he gave
Booth's name as that of one of the men who had escaped over
the east branch of the Potomac. Evidently he had heard the
name mentioned while conversing with the soldiers at the bridgehead.

Certain it is that Superintendent Richards connected these
two events, for he immediately sent a request to General Augur
for horses to mount his police.[2] What the chief of police would
have done had his request been granted is not known; but next

[1] War Department Archives.
[2] Oldroyd, op. cit., p. 66.

John Fletcher Tells His Story

hcacu if a could cross the bridge after them. He said, "Yes, you can cross, but you can not return." I said, "If that is so, I will not go." So I turned around and came back to the city again. When I came to Third Street, I looked at my watch, and it wanted ten minutes to 12. I rode pretty fast going down to the Navy Yard, but I rode slowly coming back. I went along E Street until I got to Fourteenth Street, and inquired of the foreman at Murphy's stable, by the name of Dorsey, whether this roan horse had been put up there. He said, "No; but," said he, "you had better keep in, for President Lincoln is shot and Secretary Seward is almost dead." I then returned to the stable, put up the horse, came outside of the office

window, and sat down there; it was half-past 1 o'clock.

Cross-examined by MR. STONE.

When I caught sight of Herold on the horse, near Willard's, the horse seemed somewhat tired, and as if he wanted to go to the stable, and appeared as if he had been ridden a right smart distance. He was then going an easy kind of pace. I am quite satisfied that it was Herold I saw on my horse.

I became acquainted with Herold by his calling at our stable, about the 5th or 6th of April, inquiring for the man Atzerodt,.but he did not inquire for him by name; he wanted to know if the man that kept the horse in the side stable had been there that day. He came to our stable every day, from about the 5th or 6th of April until the 12th, inquiring for Atzerodt, and I saw him ride with him. One day Atzerodt went out riding, and sent the horse back by Herold, and the next day Atzerodt asked, "How did he bring the horse back?" and if he rode him fast.

SERGEANT SILAS T. COBB.

For the Prosecution.—May 16.

On the night of the 14th of April, I was on duty at the Navy Yard bridge. At about

outside of the office window and sat down there; it was half past one o'clock. There were people passing on the sidewalk, and they were saying that it was men riding on horseback that had shot President Lincoln. Then on account of Atzerodt leaving the stable so late at night and Herold having the horse, I had a suspicion of the party. I went across E St again into 14th St and asked a cavalry sergeant if they had picked up any horses. He told me that they had picked up some horses

(TOP) John Fletcher's testimony as it appears in Pitman's official report, p. 84.

(BOTTOM) John Fletcher's testimony as it appears in the transcript of the court stenographer's notes.

Original in the Archives of the War Department

his name?" — "Yes, said he: he said his name was Smith.

I asked the sergeant if I could cross the bridge after them. He said, "Yes: you can cross the bridge; but you cannot return back." I said, "If that is so, I will not go." So I turned around, and came back to the city again. When I came to Third Street, I looked at my watch, and it wanted ten minutes to twelve. I rode pretty fast going down to the Navy Yard; but I rode slow coming back. I went along E Street until I got to Fourteenth Street, and inquired of the foreman at Murphy's stable, by the name of Dorsey, whether this roan horse had been put up there. He said, "No." But said he, "You had better keep in; for President Lincoln is shot, and Secretary Seward is almost dead." I then returned to the stable, put up the horse, came outside of the office-window, and sat down there: it was half-past one o'clock. There were people passing on the sidewalk, and they were saying that it was men riding on horseback that had shot President Lincoln. Then, on account of Atzerodt leaving the stable so late at night, and Herold having the horse, I had a suspicion of the party. I went across E Street, again into Fourteenth Street, and asked a cavalry sergeant if they had picked up any horses. He told me that they had picked up some horses, and for me to go down to the police-office on Tenth Street. So I went down Tenth Street to the police-office, and met with a detective there by the name of Charley Stone, and called him to one side, and asked him if they had picked up any horses of such a description. He told me there were some horses up at General Augur's headquarters, and asked me who I hired the horse to; and I told him. I told him the time he left the stable. He then asked me to go along with him to General Augur's office. We went there together; and, when we went into the office, General Augur asked me if I knew the man that I hired the horse to. I told him I did. I gave him the name of Herold, his description, and his age, as far as I could judge, and told him that I had pursued him to the Navy-Yard Bridge. There was a saddle and bridle lying right close to his desk in the office, and that was Atzerodt's saddle and bridle; for he came for his horse many days while the colored boys were at dinner, and I would saddle and bridle the horse for him. General Augur asked what kind of a horse had that saddle and bridle on. I told him a big, brown horse, blind of one eye; a heavy horse, with a heavy tail; a kind of a pacing horse. He asked me did I know that man's [Atzerodt's] name. I told him that I did not know his name, but I had it at the office. He sent the detective, Charley Stone, with me down to the office; and I went into the office, and got his name right upon one of our cards, and brought it up, and gave it to the general.

Q. [Exhibiting saddle and bridle to the witness.] Will

saddle, and close on fifteen hands high.

Q. When did you say you saw that saddle and bridle at General Augur's office?

A. At two o'clock on the night of the 14th of April.

Q. You mean the morning of the 15th?

A. Yes, sir: I count that the night

Fletcher's testimony as it appears in Poore's report, I, pp. 329, 333.

day, when he did get his horses, he rode straight to Surrattsville, following the exact road Booth had taken. No horses were granted to Richards on Friday night, however, and the best opportunity to catch the fugitive murderers was thereby thrown away. The reasons for Augur's refusal are not apparent. There was plenty of cavalry around the capital that night.

Fletcher then continued his testimony, saying that he went in company with a city detective named Stone to General Augur's headquarters.

'General Augur asked me if I knew the man I hired the horse to. I gave him the name of Herold, his description and his age, as far as I could judge, *and told him that I had pursued him to the Navy Yard bridge.*' Fletcher stated on further examination that '*it was then two o'clock on the night of the* 14th *of April*'.[1] Now, of course, General Augur would surely move every man at his command to follow the culprits. But not a single soldier was dispatched to the Anacostia Bridge for hours afterward, even to investigate this obvious trail, and of an actual pursuit there was none at all.

It could not have been much later when Captain Gleason put in an appearance at Augur's office. Gleason was the man to whom Wiechmann had confided the story of the attempted kidnapping, and he knew that the conspirators would take the road to Port Tobacco. He begged to be given a mounted squad, knowing exactly which way to go; but he, too, was flatly refused. Gleason was told that his services were of more value in Washington; the reason for this is not clear, for he was not assigned to any duty, but kept idling at headquarters until morning, when he was allowed to go home.[2] Thus another chance was lost of catching Booth before he had time to cross the Potomac.

There is no explanation for General Augur's odd conduct. That he was in constant contact with Stanton has already been pointed out. If the road to Port Tobacco, which many—but not those in authority—felt sure Booth would follow, had been left open through oversight, now was the opportunity to correct this

---

[1] Poore, I, p. 330. Italics are the author's.
[2] D. H. L. Gleason, 'Conspiracy Against Lincoln' in *Magazine of History*, Feb. 1911.

stupendous error. But nothing at all was done about it. Colonel Baker, who did not come to the scene until two days later, offered a lame excuse; he said it was too improbable that Booth would be so careless as to give his true name to the sentinel,[1] and that the Government therefore expected a ruse and went to look for him everywhere else except on the road he had taken. This is rather twisted logic; but even if its validity be admitted, does it explain why no effort was made to send at least a few officers to the bridge, if for no other purpose than to bury the false lead once and for ever?

If all the delinquencies in connection with Fletcher's story be excused, there still remains the fact of Pitman's mutilated official report. In the foreword to this document it is plainly stated that the publication was made with the approval of the Secretary of War, and that Colonel Burnett of the Bureau of Military Justice, one of Stanton's subordinates, would be *responsible for its strict accuracy*. Colonel Burnett himself certified its faithfulness and accuracy, and Pitman, the official compiler, emphasized that '*the entire testimony adduced at the trial . . . is contained in the following pages*'.[2]

The deleted testimony of Fletcher's visit to the police and to Augur's headquarters possibly throws unexpected light on the blunders of the authorities in their pursuit of Booth; and if Pitman deliberately re-edited Fletcher's story—and there can be no doubt of that—he hardly did so on his own initiative and responsibility.

[1] L. C. Baker, op. cit., p. 487.
[2] Pitman, op. cit., preface. Italics are the author's.

CHAPTER XII

Baker Directs the Pursuit

The story John Fletcher told should have caused all pursuit of Booth to converge on the roads through the Maryland peninsula; but this was not the immediate result. It was eight o'clock on the morning of 15 April when the first squad, dispatched by the indefatigable Major Richards of the Washington police, appeared at Lloyd's tavern in Surrattsville on the route of Booth's flight. Lloyd, who was well acquainted with all the leading conspirators, had once been a policeman in the capital and knew some of Richards's men; yet he failed to mention to them that Booth and Herold had passed his house and had spoken to him during the preceding night. Worse than that, he deliberately sent his former colleagues off on the wrong road, so that they travelled to Piscataway instead of keeping in a southerly direction.[1] No soldiers followed Richards's troop for quite some time; Lieutenant Dana, at 11 a.m., was the first to reach Bryantown, where he camped at his leisure all day Saturday, Sunday, and Monday. It was not until Monday the seventeenth that the real pursuit of Booth and Herold started.

The squad that came closest to capturing the fugitives was sent out by Provost-Marshal O'Beirne and led by Lieutenant Lovett. Major O'Beirne was one of several who had been told by Stanton to use his own discretion in hunting down the assassins. He immediately moved some of his detectives along the route Booth had taken. One of these officers has left a vivid description of the incident.

[1] *Surratt Trial*, I, p. 701.

'About daylight [of 17 April] the cavalry, under the command of Lieutenant Lovett, dashed up to the front of the hotel, and General [then Major] O'Beirne commanded Captain Williams to take the cavalry and hunt for Booth.

' "Where must I go?" asked the captain.

' "How do I know?" replied the General. "Go, and don't return to Washington until you find Booth; but mind—don't harm a hair on his head.

'Mounting a magnificent charger the captain clapped spurs and with a "Come, boys!" the cavalry were soon going at a rapid speed toward the Eastern Branch Bridge, which was successfully crossed by the captain knocking the sentry down by running over him with his horse.

' "There was no time to stand and explain to the sentry," said the captain; "time was precious." '[1]

Time was precious indeed; but Booth and Herold had by then a start of two and a half days; and so it seems that the upsetting of a sentry was more spectacular than useful.

It may or may not have been merely a lapse of memory which made Lieutenant Lovett swear during the conspiracy trial that he had started in pursuit of the fugitives on the day after the assassination. It was really three days after the event when he led his troops out of Washington. This fact is positively established through the official records of the expedition on file in the archives of the War Department.

Lieutenant Lovett was influenced to give the wrong date through a leading question on the part of the judge-advocate, who asked him whether, on the day after the assassination, he and others were engaged in the pursuit of the murderers. The natural answer to this question was an affirmative; yet, the impression created by Pitman's wording is that the expedition was started instantaneously, and not after three days' delay.[2]

From the Navy Yard Bridge Lieutenant Lovett's men proceeded to Surrattsville, where they arrested the tavern keeper Lloyd. They then rode on till they reached Bryantown, where they fell in with Lieutenant Dana, who put them on the track of

---

[1] J. E. Buckingham, *Reminiscences and Souvenirs of the Assassination of Abraham Lincoln* (Rufus H. Darby, Washington, 1894), p. 63.

[2] Pitman, op. cit., p. 87.

Dr. Samuel Mudd. By this time it was 18 April; Booth had left Dr. Mudd's house on the fifteenth and was then lying concealed in a tobacco patch on Cox's farm, about ten miles distant.

While O'Beirne's men, under Lieutenant Lovett, were watching the movements of Dr. Mudd and examining him with indifferent success, another pursuit was being organized by Colonel [later General] Lafayette C. Baker, 'who', as Milton remarked in *The Age of Hate*, 'glorified in his title of general but was really one of the worst rapscallions of an age in which rascality paid high dividends'.[1] Yet, cruel though he was, and entirely devoid of scruples, he was head of Stanton's secret service, and a capable man. Baker had been hastily summoned from New York and arrived in Washington on Sunday morning, 16 April. He immediately ordered additional rewards proclaimed and photographs of the fugitives distributed. Thus armed, some of his detectives spread through lower Maryland to pick up what information they could. But, according to Baker, they soon returned to Washington and reported utter failure.[2]

Besides the squads of O'Beirne, Baker, and Dana, the following contingents were now in the field: Captain John Kennedy, chief of police of New York, and his detectives; Colonel H. S. Olcott of the secret service with his New York squad; Colonel Wells, at the head of the forces of General Augur; and Superintendent of Police Richards of Washington. They were assisted by an unknown number of soldiers, estimated by different writers all the way from 700 to 10,000.[3] But instead of improving the chances of Booth's capture, this multiplication of efforts actually made them worse; for there was no co-operation between the pursuing parties. Avarice, jealousy, and ambition soon overcame patriotism, and each group kept to itself whatever facts it was able to gather.

Major Richards, for example, had corralled Louis Wiechmann, the intimate of the conspirators and hence a most valuable aid, and practically made him his personal prisoner. Keeping

[1] George Fort Milton, *The Age of Hate* (Coward-McCann, Inc., New York, 1930), p. 193.

[2] L. C. Baker, op. cit., p. 526.

[3] Townsend, op. cit., p. 50 ff.; see also supplementary note to chapter xii, 'Booth's Pursuers'.

his prize captive from contact with other Government agencies, he arranged a private trip with him to lower Maryland on Saturday, one to Baltimore on Sunday, and a jaunt to Canada on Monday. He had Wiechmann sleep in a police station to keep him out of reach of other detectives, and freely admitted his motives two years later on the witness stand in the Surratt trial, when he stated:

> . . . we wanted to use him [Wiechmann] to pursue the suspected assassins of the President. . . .
>
> Q. You had him in charge?
>
> A. Yes, sir; but not to his knowledge. It was our intention to hold him as a witness, for the reason that certain other parties were monopolizing all the information, and we wanted to hold him, as we thought we had not been treated altogether proper.[1]

Richards's grammar may have been faulty, but he managed to make himself thoroughly understood.

The apparent inactivity of Lovett's men around Dr. Mudd's house is also difficult to account for, unless they wanted to catch the assassin without outside help and pocket the entire reward themselves. According to statements they made later in Washington—statements that were never given to the public—they watched the dwelling of the country physician for four days without taking action, although convinced that it was Booth whom the doctor had treated. They thought the assassin was hiding in the swamps of the neighbourhood and that he would eventually have to emerge for food and further medical aid. Then they would entrap both him and Dr. Mudd.

'Dr. Mudd seemed to be very much reserved,' wrote Lieutenant Lovett in his official report, 'and did not care to give much information. I was then satisfied . . . and made up my mind to arrest Doctor Mudd when the proper time came. I was under the impression that Booth and Herold were in the neighbourhood and that Dr. Mudd knew where they were and was secretly giving Booth medical attendance. After arranging things so that if Booth and Herold were in the neighbourhood and the Doctor go to them we would get the whole of them. . . .'[2]

[1] *Surratt Trial*, II, p. 988.
[2] War Department Archives; see supplementary note to chapter xii, 'Lieutenant Lovett's Report'.

If Lovett had searched the physician's house immediately Booth's riding-boot would have been discovered three days sooner, and the story of his injury would then have become known. A definite clue to his wanderings on the first night after the murder would thus have been obtained. But the plan of O'Beirne's subordinates was to lull Dr. Mudd's suspicions, and they therefore held their hand. It was one of the most glaring errors in the story of the great man-hunt, for it was due to Lovett's secretiveness that Washington did not know until 22 April where Booth had been, or that he was crippled—points that were of the greatest importance in shaping an intelligent campaign of pursuit.

In the meantime O'Beirne himself had gone farther south and was scouring the shores of the Potomac for traces of the assassin. Booth may have thought himself secure in the thickets of Cox's farm, but he never knew how near O'Beirne came to capturing him. In a diary, which this provost-marshal kept at that time, there is an entry showing that the chase might have ended right then and there.

'Sam[ue]l Cox (at Scotia Swamp). His mill servant states to another colored man that Cox had been cooking provisions lately & carrying it to persons down in the swamp, & he judged from the amt Etc that it was a person of some importance from the provision that was made for them.'[1]

That close O'Beirne came to getting his man.

It is quite plain that the major did not have enough men with him to investigate all the reports he received from his operatives; yet, rather than call for additional men, he let slip what was the only real clue ever found that would have led to Booth's discovery and capture on Maryland soil.

Colonel Baker had been summoned to Washington by a direct telegraphic appeal from Stanton.[2]

[1] O'Beirne papers.
[2] L. C. Baker, op. cit., p. 525.

Washington
15 *April* 1865

COLONEL L. C. BAKER:

Come here immediately and see if you can find the murderer of the President.

EDWIN M. STANTON,
Secretary of War.

Nevertheless, he seems to have been anything but welcome after his arrival. When he tried to possess himself of the little information the War Department had, he was told, at General Augur's headquarters, that neither his services nor the services of his force were required. To further inquiries he received equally evasive or insulting replies.[1]

The large rewards offered, totalling over $100,000, were working out better for Booth than they were for the nation.

General Augur and his staff were very careful not to hand out information promiscuously, lest it fall into the hands of Baker or other competing pursuers. For example, Colonel Wells had flashed word from Bryantown to General Augur, on the twenty-first or twenty-second, that Booth had crippled his leg, and on the twenty-second this vital piece of news was wired to Major Waite at Leonardtown.[2] Waite was on Augur's staff, had been sent out on special duty, and was, in a manner of speaking, his personal representative. This information about Booth was given him now for exclusive use in his territory, while such a trusted Government employee as Captain Beckwith, Grant's cipher operator, was kept in ignorance of the fugitive's injury.

'I well remember the Sunday morning of 23 April 1865,' wrote Beckwith, 'when I was summoned by Major Eckert to the telegraph office in the old War Department building at Washington to engage in the pursuit of Lincoln's fugitive assassins.

'Promptly returning to General Grant's Headquarters I donned full riding dress, and received Secretary Stanton's *carte blanche* order for myself and escort of soldiers to proceed to Port Tobacco, Maryland.'[3]

[1] L. C. Baker, op. cit., p. 529.
[2] *Official Records*, I, vol. 46, part 3, p. 899.
[3] O'Beirne papers.

Arriving at his destination Captain Beckwith met Major O'Beirne there and was informed by him that Booth had broken a bone in his leg. Beckwith immediately recognized the import of this fact, and on the twenty-fourth wired it to Major Eckert. This shows that a day after General Augur had advised his own searching party of Booth's crippled condition, others in Washington were still unaware of it; even Major Eckert, Stanton's right-hand man, had not been informed by General Augur. For if he had, the only possible inference would be that he wilfully withheld this knowledge from his own squad.

It is plain that by this time the lure of fame and money had overcome all sense of duty and decency; it overshadowed even the desire for Booth's seizure, unless this could be accomplished with a cash profit to the captors.

In the meantime Lincoln's murderer had crossed the Potomac to the Virginia side. His first attempt on the twenty-first had not been successful, but on the following day he and Herold managed to reach the opposite shore, and by the twenty-fourth they were again under shelter at the Garrett Farm, about three miles south of Port Royal, Virginia.

When Major O'Beirne fell in with Captain Beckwith at Port Tobacco, he gave Grant's telegraph operator a summary of his achievements and plans. It appeared that on 16 April two labourers had left Dent's Farm, on the banks of the Potomac, not far from where the two officers were then conferring, and had crossed the river in a small boat. O'Beirne was convinced that these two farm-hands were in reality Booth and Herold, and he had picked up their trail on the way to King George Court House on the previous day. As a matter of fact, the suspected persons were what they purported to be. They had left the neighbourhood several days before. But Booth and Herold, a week later, crossed the Potomac at a near-by point and took the same road south. O'Beirne, following the wrong men, stumbled on the track of the assassins by accident, and had he held to it for a few more hours would probably have captured them. But the forces of the vigorous provost-marshal had been too tired to keep up with him on the trail, and were lying scattered behind him. O'Beirne had crossed back to Port

Tobacco to find them. It was at this moment that an unlucky star led Captain Beckwith into his path. This officer was so much impressed with the tale unfolded to him, that he cut into the telegraph lines leading to Washington and gave to the War Department the gist of the information he had received. O'Beirne was anxious to be on his way again, but was requested to linger. One can imagine his surprise and despair when orders came over the wire from Washington to discontinue his expedition and remain on the Maryland side of the Potomac.[1] But orders were orders, and there was nothing left for O'Beirne to do but obey. Had he been less free with his information to Captain Beckwith, it is probable that he would have captured Booth.

Perhaps O'Beirne thought at that time that his recall had its compensations. Through one of the many queer coincidences with which the history of Lincoln's assassination seems to abound, a new and promising clue had been discovered near Bryantown. A hired girl at the house of a Mr. Turner reported that two men, one of them on crutches, had stepped out of an adjoining swamp and beckoned to her to bring them food. The poor girl, almost scared into hysterics, immediately informed her master, with the result that a new man-hunt through the swamps began under O'Beirne's leadership. It was conducted with more vigour than had been shown in any previous efforts. The two men were never found, however, nor has their identity ever been established.[2]

Beckwith's telegram arrived in Washington at 11 a.m., and orders to have him abandon the pursuit of Booth were immediately sent to O'Beirne. Very shortly afterward Colonel L. C. Baker dispatched the following note to Major-General Hancock, U.S. Army:[3]

[1] O'Beirne papers; also in *Official Records*, I, vol. 46, part 3, p. 937; L. C. Baker, op. cit., p. 494.
[2] O'Beirne papers; also War Department Archives.
[3] Baker, op. cit., pp. 530–1.

War Department
Washington City
24 April 1865.

MAJOR-GENERAL HANCOCK,
United States Army:

GENERAL: I am directed by the Secretary of War to apply to you for a small cavalry force of twenty-five (25) men, well mounted, to be commanded by a reliable and discreet commissioned officer.

Can you furnish them? and if so, will you please direct the officer commanding the squad to report to me with the men at No. 217 Pennsylvania Avenue, opposite Willard's Hotel, at once?

I am, Sir, your obedient servant,
L. C. BAKER,
Colonel, and Agent War Department.

In response to this communication, Lieutenant Doherty, with twenty-five men from the Sixteenth New York cavalry, reported for duty and was put under the orders of Lieutenant Luther B. Baker, a cousin of the colonel. Former Lieutenant-Colonel Conger accompanied the troops and, by courtesy, was conceded the command. At four o'clock in the afternoon a boat was ready to take these pursuers down the Potomac.

'You are going after Booth,' Colonel Baker said to his cousin, as they parted. 'Lieutenant, we have got a sure thing,' he added significantly.[1]

What information was it that Colonel Baker had received to make him so supremely confident? Could he have known of Booth's hiding-place even while the soldiers were looking for him? It is quite possible that he did. His detectives were scouting continually through the Maryland peninsula, a fact which the chief of the secret service never mentioned but which leaked out when Lieutenant Baker was being examined at the Surratt trial two years later. He was requested to tell the history of his pursuit. 'Will it be necessary to commence from my first search?' he asked. 'I went on three distinct trips.'[2] If Major O'Beirne's

---

[1] *Impeachment Investigation*, p. 487.
[2] *Surratt Trial*, I, p. 316.

men had reports about a prominent stranger being fed surreptitiously near Cox's farm, why could not Baker's men have had them too? The peculiar reluctance of the War Department to dwell on this part of Booth's flight would thus be accounted for. Such secret knowledge of the fugitive's movements would also have made it easy for Baker to time Conger's pursuit to a nicety.

Nevertheless, in the absence of positive evidence, this assumption is no more than an intriguing hypothesis. It is safer to presume that Baker based the trip of Conger's squad on Major O'Beirne's disclosures to Captain Beckwith, appropriating them for his own benefit.

There is nothing in the Official Records that would throw any light on this question. With the exception of Beckwith's wire, there were no dispatches relating to Booth's whereabouts received at the War Department on 24 April. Baker explained in his own fashion what had prompted his actions:

'There was brought to my headquarters a colored man, who I was informed had important information respecting the assassins. On questioning the colored man, I found he had seen two men, answering the description of Booth and Harrold, entering a small boat in the vicinity of Swan's Point. . . . This information, with my preconceived theory as to the movements of the assassins, decided my course.'[1]

This sounds plausible enough. Two of Baker's detectives, Hubbard and Woodall, had left by boat for Port Tobacco with Captain Beckwith on Sunday, the twenty-third. They arrived on Monday morning, and obtained this valuable information there. In his official report to the Secretary of War, on 24 December 1865, Lieutenant Baker went into detail.

'On Monday, the 24th, General Baker . . . sent one of his men, Theodore Woodall . . . into Lower Maryland . . . Woodall, while on this duty, fell in with ——, an old negro, whose statements so impressed him, that, instead of sending it by telegraph to Washington, he took and delivered him bodily to his superior. 'The examination of the colored man satisfied General Baker that he had at last struck the trail of the fleeing murderers.'[2]

[1] L. C. Baker, op. cit., p. 527.
[2] Ibid., p. 533.

All of this is simple and reasonable; but on closer analysis the truth of the story becomes doubtful. For one thing, Detective Woodall did not react like an ordinary man. Hardly had he landed near Port Tobacco, a district which by that time was overrun with professional and amateur sleuths, when he, of all people, was vouchsafed the discovery of a negro who had seen the escaping assassins. What an unheard-of stroke of good luck! And then, with a fortune awaiting him if he followed the hot trail, he preferred to take his precious witness back to Washington. By using Beckwith's wire connection with the War Department, over which he could have notified headquarters of his find, there would have been no sharing of the reward with any one else. But Woodall chose otherwise. He lost a full day coming and going, just to let Baker confirm his own suspicions, and then without a murmur he relinquished his rights of pursuit to a squad of cavalry men.

The improbability of his story is further enhanced by the time factor in the case. It took the tug *Keyport*, running downstream, from four o'clock in the afternoon till midnight to reach Port Tobacco; the landing was not effected until morning.[1] Even if Woodall had caught his negro and had examined him, all within five minutes of his arrival, he still could not have returned by boat, as reported, in time for Baker to arrange his expedition by noon or shortly thereafter.

The importance of this matter entitles it to closer scrutiny. Both Woodall and the negro would surely be taken care of in the distribution of the final rewards. But one looks in vain for the name of either the one or the other. Perhaps the congressional awarders would not recognize the rights of coloured men. But no. One negro woman received $250 for information that was practically useless. Still, perusing the lists of those who shared in the distribution of the rewards, every name is accounted for; there is no mention anywhere of this mysterious coloured informant.[2]

At this point the search might well have come to a dead end, had there not lived in Washington at that time a lawyer and former congressman by the name of Albert Gallatin Riddle who

[1] L. C. Baker, op cit., p. 527.
[2] Oldroyd, op. cit., p. 88.

was intimately connected with these events and who enlarged upon them in his *Recollections*. A prominent member of the Bar, he aided the Government in its preparation of the Surratt case in 1867, and counted among his clients Lafayette C. Baker, whom he defended in a rather unsavoury case involving charges of false imprisonment and robbery. Riddle defended Baker successfully, limiting his penalty to a fine of one dollar, and continued to represent him in litigation against the city of Washington to recover a reward that had not been paid. In his memoirs Riddle expressed the opinion that the conception and successful execution of Baker's scheme to arrest Booth and Herold must rank with the most famous exploits in the wide field of detection. But he added:

'The old negro informant is to be relegated to the realm of myth; all the means taken to reproduce him were futile; *he was never again heard of or found*, and became the theme of the unsparing gibes and sarcasms of Baker's rivals and enemies.

'He was a pure creation of the genius of L. C. Baker. . . .

'The old negro was a necessary creation, to *give color* as a real informant, and to make seeming ground on which the expedition could rest; and those who derided the invention unconsciously did homage to the genius of the inventor.'[1]

Which disclosure, incidentally, explains why, in Lieutenant Baker's official report, the name of the negro is marked only by a dash.

Riddle's oratory was evidently better than his logic. Why did the expedition need any 'ground on which to rest'? One would infer from Riddle's account that every move made by the pursuers had to be justified in a public forum. In reality, the public never knew of this elusive negro until Baker saw fit to give out his story, and the colonel was the last man in Washington to care about public sentiment.

There is more to the story than this. If Riddle considered Baker a genius for planning and executing the only successful pursuit, basing it on the mere word of a darky, how much more of a miracle-worker he would have appeared if he had not invented this informant. By introducing the negro Baker was

[1] Albert G. Riddle, *Recollections of War Times* (G. P. Putnam's Sons, New York, 1895), pp. 334–5.

really belittling his own achievement and giving the lie to the power of intuition attributed to him by his admirer. The truth is, of course, that when the chief of the secret service detracted from his own fame he did so for a good reason: he did not care to state how he came into possession of the knowledge which enabled him to send his own cousin out at the head of the searching party that had 'the latest reliable information concerning them [the fugitives]'.[1]

Did Stanton believe that Baker used O'Beirne's revelation to send his cousin to catch Booth? Apparently he did. In an official communication from O'Beirne dated 27 December 1865, setting forth his claims for the reward, one reads this:

'In obedience to orders subsequently asked by me from the Secretary of War, I returned to Washington after Booth and Harold had been discovered a short distance beyond where I pursued them. I repaired at once in person to the Honorable Secretary of War. I was by him warmly congratulated and complimented during my interview with him in the hallway of the 1st floor War Department Building. He spoke in words and substance as follows: "You have done your duty nobly and you have the satisfaction of knowing that if you did not succeed in capturing Booth, *it was, at all events, certainly the information which you gave that led to it.*" This was said in the presence of Mr. Murray, U.S. Marshall for the Southern District of New York'.[2]

In an affidavit attached to O'Beirne's letter Marshal Murray confirms the fact that Stanton made this remark. Other witnesses also testified that it was the telegram that O'Beirne had sent to the War Department which led the pursuit to a successful ending.

Because of an odd set of circumstances O'Beirne, following a false clue, almost caught up with the fleeing assassins. Returning part of the way to reorganize his forces, he met and confided in Beckwith, a telegraph operator from Washington. This operator wired to Washington, and as a result the ambitious major was restrained from further pursuit. It is significant that of all the telegrams pertaining to this matter, this one in particular is not on file in the War Department. But O'Beirne proclaimed its exis-

[1] L. C. Baker, op. cit., p. 531.
[2] O'Beirne papers. Italics are the author's.

tence—which no one denied—even in official letters to Stanton himself, written in May 1865, and claimed for ever after that he would have captured Booth if he had not been interfered with.

That Baker did all in his power to retain the glory and money for his own family is understandable; Stanton's part in the matter is not so clear. Did he give due consideration to the fact that O'Beirne was already within striking distance of Booth and had the start of Baker's party by at least twenty-four hours?

CHAPTER XIII

The End of the Trail

The hunt for Booth and his accomplice was, according to all reports, conducted with a zeal unsurpassed in the annals of crime. The swamps of Maryland had never witnessed such scenes as were described by George Alfred Townsend in the *New York World*:

'Here the soldiers prepared to seek for the President's assassin, and no search of the kind has ever been so thorough and patient. . . .

'The military forces deputed to pursue the fugitives were seven hundred men of the Eighth Illinois Cavalry, six hundred men of the Twenty-second Colored Troops, and one hundred men of the Sixteenth New York. These swept the swamps by detachments, the mass of them dismounted, with cavalry at the belts of clearings, interspersed with detectives at frequent intervals in the rear. They first formed a strong picket cordon entirely around the swamps, and then, drawn up in two orders of battle, advanced boldly into the bog by two lines of march. One party swept the swamps longitudinally, the other pushed straight across their smallest diameter.'[1]

Dr. Abner Hard, writing the history of the Eighth Illinois Cavalry Regiment, was also much impressed with the measures taken and the manner in which they were carried out.

'. . . the country [was] so thoroughly picketed and searched', said he, 'that a rabbit could have hardly made his escape through

[1] L. C. Baker, op. cit., pp. 492, 493.

our lines without being discovered . . . [the pursuers] leaving no nook or corner in which the assassin could be secreted.'[1]

But perhaps the hunt was not, after all, quite as thorough-going as would appear from these descriptions. When, on 26 April, Major O'Beirne and Captain Beckwith descended upon this territory after having been recalled from Port Tobacco, they found much to criticize.

'It appears to us from all we can learn,' reads their official telegram to Major Eckert, 'that troops have not been pushed through with much system. The colored troops, while deployed and advancing, upon hearing shout[s] on one part [of the] line, made [a] rush in that direction, leaving considerable space un-covered.'[2] O'Beirne was particularly wrathful because the cripple and his companion, whose discovery had been used to draw him away from his promising trail in Virginia, had proved to be mythical. Together with Beckwith he immediately repaired to Turner's house, 'where Booth and Herold were seen by two servants to inquire for food, then enter a pine thicket about twenty rods distant from [the] house, and two miles north from Bryantown'. Parties on the ground, he reported to Washington, had been through there, losing the track and accomplishing nothing.

'. . . I struck the crutch track and we followed it in a direction circling around toward the piece of timber from which they first issued far enough to justify the belief [that] they are still in [the] same vicinity from which they started, and that while the troops were searching the thicket where they were last seen, they, by taking course above described, gained time enough to tem-porarily conceal themselves again.'[3]

Major O'Beirne had every right in the world to be indignant. He had been forced to abandon a pursuit which, as later events showed, would have brought him up with Booth; instead, he had to follow an apparently promising clue which led him nowhere. He must also have been mystified by his inability to find the cripple who had so obligingly left crutch tracks all through the

---

[1] Abner Hard, *History of the Eighth Cavalry Regiment, Illinois Volunteers, During the Great Rebellion* (Aurora, Illinois, 1868), pp. 320–1.
[2] *Official Records*, I, vol. 46, part 3, p. 964.
[3] Ibid.

neighbourhood; and, while he literally walked around in circles, looking for these two phantoms who never materialized, Lieutenant Baker's troops took up the trail where he had left it and came home with the Big Prize.

How it was possible for these two strangers, one of them crippled, to escape this combing of the entire district is an enigma. One would almost think that they had never existed and that they were, like Baker's negro, the convenient product of a conjurer's hat. But before letting this suspicion grow into conviction, it is well to remember the curious and far more important fact that Booth and Herold also remained for six days undiscovered in their tobacco patch. This hiding-place was only a short distance from a public road.[1] The soldiers were at times so close to them that the fugitives could hear the hoof-beats of the horses and the rattling of the accoutrements. If the Maryland peninsula had been searched as thoroughly as it should have been, Booth and Herold could never have eluded their pursuers for such a length of time.

The man-hunt through lower Maryland was replete with sins of omission and commission; but a worse blunder was the inexplicable failure to extend the search at once over the neighbouring counties of Virginia. Through Wiechmann and Gleason the authorities had learned of the route the conspirators were most likely to follow. Captain Gleason was on the spot to repeat his story, yet his urgent plea for troops with which to pursue the murderer was totally ignored.

'It took a long time to reach General Augur's,' he recalled later, 'and when we arrived we found everybody excited. . . . I went at once into a small room where several officers were holding some sort of [a] conference, told them all I knew about the persons suspected . . . [and] *also asked for a cavalry squad to go with me to the Surratt place in Maryland, as I thought the assassin would escape that way.*'[2] Even disregarding this source of intelligence, the secret service, as has been pointed out before, must have known of the probable course of Booth. On 17 April, for

[1] Oldroyd, op. cit., p. 270.
[2] Gleason, op. cit. Italics are the author's.

instance, a Philadelphia paper received the following from its Washington correspondent:

'There was, for a long while, a very efficiently worked underground railway system between the Rebel capital and the vicinity of Port Tobacco and Leonardtown, Maryland, and not only correspondence but light freight and passengers were transferred over the secret route.'[1]

If newspapermen spoke openly of this route as having been used for a long time, one certainly would expect that the importance of investigating it would have occurred to the secret service.

Booth left the place of his crime at about twenty minutes after ten and passed over the Anacostia Bridge some fifteen minutes later. This much was known immediately, or at least within a few hours of the crime. The likely points at which he could have crossed into the Confederacy were about thirty-odd miles away. If Booth had not injured his leg, a circumstance that could not have been suspected in Washington at the time, he probably would have reached the lower Potomac not later than five o'clock in the morning. As it was, he arrived at Dr. Mudd's house, thirty miles distant, about four o'clock, 'with the bone of my leg tearing the flesh at every jump', as Booth himself put it.[2] If the pursuers had subjected their problem to an intelligent analysis, they must have surmised that Booth would be in Virginia by the early morning of 15 April. The proper thing, therefore, would have been to mobilize the Richmond troops at once and then to order out additional cavalry to the south as fast as news of the assassination could be spread. If soldiers from Richmond had been thrown into action as quickly, for example, as were the useless troops of Colonel Thompson to the north of Washington, they could have arrived at Fredericksburg by dawn, and within a few hours would have been in a position to guard all crossings of the Rappahannock River. This would have bottled Booth up, no matter how fast he travelled. But no pursuers at all went south of the Potomac, let alone as far as the Rappahannock, until 23 April, when Major O'Beirne penetrated to King George Court House, only to be recalled. Lieutenant

[1] Barclay, *Terrible Tragedy*, p. 30.
[2] Booth, *Diary*.

Doherty stated that when he started out on 24 April, he was told by Colonel Baker that no troops had yet been in Fredericksburg but that he 'must reach that vicinity with all dispatch'.[1]

That Booth was compelled to remain in southern Maryland all this time was solely due to his accident. Had he proceeded as he had planned, he would have found that no troops or detectives were barring his way to the deep south and to eventual freedom.

A great deal of mystery surrounds the expedition that finally overtook the fugitives at Garrett's barn on 26 April. Beckwith's wire containing O'Beirne's report may have led Colonel Baker to direct the successful pursuing party, but there is a question of whether this theory is tenable. Doubts must also have assailed the members of the House committee who were called upon to distribute the rewards which had been offered by the Government. The report reads in part as follows:

'In the first place, upon what information Colonel Baker proceeded in sending out the expedition which, on April 26, overtook and seized the two fugitives, is in no manner disclosed or intimated in his official report.

'In a paper, however, filed by Messrs. Conger and Baker, and indorsed and commended to the attention of the Secretary by General Baker, it is stated that the information in question was derived, on 24 April, from 'an old negro', from whom it was obtained and reported on the same day to General Baker by Theodore Woodall, 'one of his men'; and that this information was to the effect that Booth and Herold had crossed the Potomac near Mathias Point on the night of Saturday, 22 April. *But the name of this negro is not made known, nor has any claim whatever been filed by such a person.* Whether or not, therefore, any one might be deemed entitled to a compensation for this information cannot be determined.

'In the next place, the item of intelligence furnished through Major J. R. O'Beirne, and regarded both by him, Colonel Wells, and the telegrapher who transmitted it to Washington, S. H. Beckwith, as having directly conduced to the arrest, cannot, it is

[1] Edward P. Doherty, 'Narrative' in *Century Magazine*, Jan. 1890, p. 447.

conceived, be properly so considered. This information, which had been gathered by employés of Major O'Beirne, was contained in a telegram of 24 April, from Port Tobacco, to the Assistant Secretary of War, in which it was set forth that two persons, believed to be Booth and Herold, had crossed the Potomac on the morning of 16 April, from Swan Point, in Maryland, to White's Point, in Virginia. But it is made very clear from the testimony adduced in connexion with the late conspiracy trial that Booth and Herold actually crossed the river on or about 21 or 22 April, and from the mouth of Pope's creek, below Allen's Fresh, in Maryland, to Mathias Point, in Virginia—a quite different time and locality from those specified in the telegram. The persons therein alluded to, therefore, must, it is believed, have been quite other than the fugitives; and information in regard to the crossing of such persons can hardly be considered as conducing to the arrest of Booth and his companion.'[1]

If Baker, therefore, did not get his clue from Major O'Beirne, from whom did he get it? The mystery is intensified, rather than penetrated, by Baker's lawyer, Albert Gallatin Riddle.

'Before the starting of the party', Riddle related, 'the Chief spread out a map of Virginia and designated the crossing-place of the fugitives and the place where they had probably landed; then, taking a compass, he placed one point at Port Conway, where a road crossed the Rappahannock, and drew a circle, which he said included a space of ten miles around that point, and within that territory they would find the fugitives. . . . The *fugitives . . . were captured . . . within Baker's circle.*'[2]

Riddle says further that Baker's achievement ranks with the most famous exploits in the wide field of detection. 'His intuitive grasp of the conditions of the case made it certain that the assassins would seek cover in Virginia.'[3]

Unfortunately, this intuition came to Baker a little late. He had been wrestling with the question of Booth's whereabouts for a week or more when this brilliant thought flashed through his mind. Perhaps he just happened to take a look at a map. But

---

[1] House of Representatives, 39th Congress, First Session, Executive Document No. 90, p. 6. Italics are the author's.

[2] Riddle, op. cit., p. 334. Author's italics.

[3] Ibid., p. 335.

Riddle's story is partly corroborated by Lieutenant Baker, who, in a private paper written many years afterwards, stated that the 'old general', his cousin, gave the party a 'general detailed idea' where they would find Booth.[1] A picture showing Colonel Baker and his two leaders in conference around a table, with a map spread between them, appeared in his *History of the Secret Service*, and in a current magazine. It was reprinted many times afterwards.

Another bizarre feature in the story of Booth's pursuit is the failure of the War Department to prosecute some people who had sheltered Booth and helped him in his flight. Again the House committee, debating the distribution of rewards, was puzzled. In a proclamation dated 20 April, Stanton had declared that 'all persons harboring or secreting the said persons [the conspirators] . . . or aiding . . . their concealment or escape, will be treated as accomplices in the murder of the President . . . and shall be subject to trial before a military commission, and the punishment of death'.[2]

Now the committee found this to worry about:

'But although several parties were arrested in both Maryland and Virginia upon strong suspicion of having thus given aid and comfort to these criminals, yet none of them have been proceeded against by the government or otherwise. . . .'[3]

The persons alluded to in particular must have been Captain Samuel Cox, on whose property Booth and Herold had been secreted for almost a week, and Thomas A. Jones, his half-brother, who had guided the assassins and furnished them a boat for their escape across the Potomac. Both these men had been arrested, but were released after a few weeks. The evidence against them was overwhelming, yet they were not prosecuted. Furthermore, their names were carefully kept under cover; and

[1] Luther B. Baker, private statement to his son, L. H. Baker, Lansing, Michigan.
[2] House of Representatives, 39th Congress, First Session, Exec. Doc. No. 90, p. 7.
[3] Ibid.

although they appear frequently enough in the private records of the bureau of military justice, they were hardly mentioned in the public prints of that time. At the conspiracy trial, it would be thought, unwelcome prominence for them could scarcely have been avoided; but the judge-advocate got around that by the simple, though drastic, stratagem of skipping the entire period of Booth's flight from the moment he left Dr. Mudd's house on 15 April until his arrival at the Rappahannock on 24 April. It was a bold thing to do, and there must have been weighty reasons for such an unusual procedure. What these reasons were has never been divulged. Benn Pitman, the official recorder of the conspiracy trial, was well aware of this gap in his report of the famous case. On 14 August he wrote from Cincinnati to the War Department that he needed a map of Booth's route to make his book complete.

'The testimony', he said, 'relates to Booth and Herold at Dr. Mudd's on the 15th and at the ferry on the Rappahannock on the 24th and contains no word relating to the flight of the conscience stricken fugitives in the interval. I think the Appendix ought to supply this in the way of a good map, showing the ground over wh.[ich] they travelled.'[1]

This suggestion was quickly accepted by the War Department and the map was supplied within five days, thus closing the breach for the cursory reader.

Whatever the explanation of these singular doings might be, they all worked out to Booth's advantage. It was almost as if an invisible guardian angel were watching over his every step and shaping fortune in his favour. First he meets the complaisant sergeant at the bridge who turned back the first pursuer; then the dangerous statement of a hostler is ignored, and later suppressed; the road the assassin was bound to take is left unpatrolled; the only troops across his path at Chapel Point are removed. The newspapers are tardy in announcing his name; the state of Virginia is left unguarded and his course through it is unobstructed; an ardent officer who gets on his trail by accident is recalled. When final capture, due to an injury, is inevitable, the task is entrusted to Secretary Stanton's most confidential lieutenants. Once more the Fates are kind to the fugitive; for, in spite of all

[1] War Department Archives.

orders to the contrary, the man whom the soldiers believed to be
Booth is shot dead.

Thus Booth's vow that he would never be taken alive was
apparently fulfilled; all that Washington could gloat over was
a corpse whose very identity proved difficult to establish.

The man who died at Garrett's Farm was stripped of his belongings before he was dead. The things that were taken from
him were of no great consequence, with the sole exception of a
diary in which he had written some declamatory descriptions of
his experiences and sentiments. This diary was subsequently to
become the centre of a fiery controversy, not so much because of
its contents as because it had been kept hidden from the public.
When it was finally discovered two years after the drama at
Garrett's barn, one sentence in it aroused curiosity. Booth had
written:

'I have almost a mind to return to Washington and . . . clear
my name, which I feel I can do.'[1]

No one knows just what the assassin meant by these words;
but General Ben Butler, then a member of Congress, chose to
give it an ominous interpretation. 'How clear himself?' he
shouted. 'By disclosing his accomplices? Who were they? . . .
If we had only the advantage of all the testimony, we might have
been able . . . to find who, indeed, were all the accomplices of
Booth.'[2]

The House of Representatives shortly afterward appointed a
special commission to investigate ' "all the facts and circumstances connected with the assassination tending to show who
were the persons engaged in the conspiracy," many of whom . . .
"holding high positions of power and authority . . ." acted
"through inferior persons who were their tools and instruments" '.[3]

The unearthing of the diary was entirely due to Baker. He
had already disclosed the fact of its existence to a correspondent
of the *New York World*, who had casually mentioned it as early

---

[1] Booth, *Diary*.
[2] David M. DeWitt, *Assassination of Abraham Lincoln* (Macmillan & Co.,
New York, 1909), p. 180.
[3] Ibid.

as 28 April 1865; but the news item had evidently been overlooked on its first appearance. At the conspiracy trial a great deal might have been uncovered had the lawyers for the defence handled their cases with more skill. When Colonel Conger was on the witness stand on 17 May he told, under direct examination what he had taken from the pockets of the dying man.

Q. (Exhibiting to the witness a knife numbered 28.) State if that is the weapon you took from him.
A. I did not take it from him myself; but that is the knife. I saw it taken. . . .
Q. (Exhibiting to the witness a pair of pistols.) Do you recognize these pistols as having been taken from him?
A. . . . they were similar to these.
Q. (Exhibiting to the witness a belt, a holster, and a knife.) Do you recognize these?
A. That is the belt and holster, and that is the knife taken from Booth.[1]

In a similar manner a file, a spur, a pipe, and some cartridges were identified by the witness. A Spencer rifle and a Canadian bill of exchange followed. Then the line of interrogation turned to other matters. If only at this time one of the lawyers for the accused had asked the simple question: *What else was taken from the body?* the truth would have been out. But the great opportunity passed unheeded and was lost for the accused. Thus both the prisoners and the world at large were robbed of a vital piece of evidence. Conger was telling the truth and nothing but the truth, but he did not tell the whole truth; he and the bureau of military justice stand guilty of having withheld a fact that would, in all likelihood, have saved human lives. For Booth's notebook showed plainly that, up to the last day, kidnapping and not murder had been the goal of the conspirators. Some of the defendants would have been greatly benefited by this revelation.

For two years the little volume lay locked up in the archives of the War Office. In the meantime Baker had been dismissed and had written his book, *The History of the Secret Service.*

[1] Poore, *Conspiracy Trial*, I, p. 318; see also supplementary note to chapter xiii, 'Booth's Diary'.

Therein repeated references were made to Booth's diary, creating a sensation in all circles. The judiciary committee of the House, then in session, seized upon the item with alacrity, and bade Baker take the stand and repeat his statements under oath. There the detective exploded another bombshell: *the diary had been mutilated since it had been taken from the body at Garrett's Farm.* Again Butler's voice was heard in Congress, denouncing this tampering with important evidence.

'That diary, as now produced,' he thundered, 'has eighteen pages cut out, the pages prior to the time when Abraham Lincoln was massacred, although the edges as yet show they had all been written over. Now, what I want to know, was that diary whole? . . . Who spoliated that book?'[1]

On 7 February Baker took the stand. He asserted that he had read portions of Booth's memorandum book in the afternoon of the day the assassin was shot, and that he thought there had been a great deal more to the original volume at that time.

'. . . in my opinion', he testified, 'there have been leaves torn out of that book since I saw it'. He particularly seemed to remember a sheet with the pencil sketch of a house on it which should have been in the book. Baker had intended to find the location of that house and its connection with the conspiracy and had, therefore, taken particular notice of it.[2]

On the same day Judge-Advocate-General Holt declared as a witness before the House committee that the diary was in the same condition as when he had received it. But when Holt was first shown the little red book which was the centre of all this excitement it had already passed through many hands and had been in the possession of his superiors in the War Department for some time. On 2 April, feeling that a mutilation of the diary was imputed to Stanton, he came valiantly to the assistance of his chief by developing before his audience two theories that could account for the loss of the missing leaves. He pointed out that the volume was an old one, and had seen much use. It appeared likely to him that the removed pages concerned personal matters which the owner did not choose to have exposed; or else the entries might have compromised his friends and co-conspirators. In either case it would be rational to assume that it had

[1] DeWitt, *Assassination*, p. 179.
[2] *Impeachment Investigation*, p. 33.

been Booth who had cut out the leaves. The latter theory seemed more probable to Holt, as the deleted portion preceded the entries made on 13 April and on the following days.[1]

On 1 April Stanton gave his version. There was no doubt in his mind that the leaves had been gone when the relic was brought to him.

Q. When you saw the diary in the room of the Committee on the Judiciary, was your attention called to the circumstance that certain leaves had been cut or torn from it?

A. My attention was called to it at that time. I had observed the fact at the time on which I first saw the diary. I examined it then with great care; read over all the entries in it, and noticed that leaves had been cut or torn from it at the time.

Q. According to your recollection, was the diary, when you saw it in the committee-room, in the same condition it was when you first saw it?

A. It was precisely in the same condition. . . .[2]

So far it was Baker's word against Stanton's, for besides these two men only Lieutenant-Colonel Conger, Lieutenant Baker, and possibly Major Eckert, had seen the diary before any one else had had an opportunity to tamper with it. On 13 May the committee heard Conger, but Baker's former aide was not at all sure of his facts. To a direct question of whether the book was in the same condition as when he had delivered it to Mr. Stanton, he answered that he thought it was. When pressed further, he would only say that he thought the same leaves were then missing. He remained uncertain to the end. He thought the diary had read a little differently when he went through it two years previously, but it was so long ago, he added, that his memory could not be trusted. When asked whether he could swear with definiteness that all these leaves had been torn out when he first saw the book, he answered that this was his impression.[3] After receiving unsatisfactory replies of this kind for some time, the investigators gave up and turned back to Stanton. On 18 May the secretary appeared again as a witness and stated that he had noticed the absence of the missing leaves when the book was given to him.

[1] *Impeachment Investigation*, pp. 28, 285.
[2] Ibid., p. 281.
[3] Ibid., pp. 324, 330.

He thought that he had even counted the pages, but could not recollect the number.[1]

Three days later the War Minister was followed again by Baker, who was then at outs with the War Department. The detective, as an opening thrust, reported that some of the men had taken copies of the diary but had been forced to give them up on orders from Stanton, who decreed that not even extracts should be retained by any one. What was left of the diary had been read before the committee by Holt on 2 April, and it was plain that there was nothing in it that would have called for such precautions. The point Baker was trying to drive home now became fully apparent. In answer to a direct question, he claimed to be still of the opinion that the book had been mutilated. One of the examining congressmen tried to trip him by asking whether Baker had counted the stubs at the time of Booth's capture. But Baker was positive that he had never seen any stubs until he examined the book in the committee room.

Q. Do you mean to say that at the time you gave the book to the Secretary of War there were no leaves gone?
A. I do.
Q. That is still your opinion?
A. That is still my opinion.
Q. Did you examine it pretty carefully?
A. I examined the book, and I am very sure that if any leaves had been gone I should have noticed it.
Q. Did you examine it carefully?
A. It did not require careful examination to discover the absence of so many leaves.[2]

Baker claimed that Stanton had promised to permit him to incorporate the contents of Booth's memorandum book in his forthcoming *History of the Secret Service*, but when the publishers came down from New York to get the copy the Secretary of War told them that conditions had changed and that he was not disposed to let the book go out of his possession.

When asked if he had seen Stanton count the stubs of the missing pages, as the secretary had testified under oath, Baker gave his former chief the lie direct. But he scored his best point

[1] *Impeachment Investigation*, p. 408.
[2] Ibid., p. 458.

at the last. Upon being asked whether any observations were made on the subject of the stubs when Stanton looked over the relic, he answered: 'No, sir; that is the reason I think the leaves were not gone. I think Mr. Stanton would have asked me what had become of the missing leaves, if any had been missing.'[1]

This shot must have told, for the investigators quickly abandoned the subject. To those who knew Stanton's character and training it must have appeared very improbable that he would have accepted a mutilated piece of evidence without severe cross-examination. That Stanton really had taken over the diary without comments had been corroborated by Lieutenant-Colonel Conger, and was not denied by the secretary himself. All in all, Baker had decidedly the better of the argument.

The diary even became the subject of a Cabinet discussion. Should the contents of the little volume be published? Stanton was violently opposed to such a procedure, but Welles calmly asked what possible objection he could have. It is not known what Stanton replied, or if he replied at all.

But on 22 May Lieutenant L. B. Baker introduced a new element into the controversy. He also had handled the diary, and he thought that some leaves were gone when he first saw it. He disclosed the fact, however, that he found one of the torn leaves in Virginia a few days later. Booth had sent two notes to a Dr. Stewart, from whom he had expected hospitality on his flight, and had torn or cut sheets from this notebook to convey his messages.[2] This new discovery may have accounted for some of the uncertainty displayed by several of the witnesses. New doubts were raised, and the truth became even more uncertain than before. Many months later, on 22 November 1867, the committee again tried to get to the bottom of the problem. It was recalled that Conger had made a copy of the famous diary, and it was hoped that this copy would disclose the contents of the missing portion. Colonel Baker came forth to declare positively that he had surrendered the copy either to Stanton or to Eckert. To the question: 'How do you explain the fact that neither General Eckert nor Mr. Stanton could produce it?' he had no answer, for it was a question that really should have been pro-

---

[1] *Impeachment Investigation*, loc. cit.
[2] Ibid., p. 484.

pounded to them rather than to Baker.[1] It never was, however, and no further testimony on the subject was forthcoming.

This closes all the available evidence in regard to Booth's diary and the riddle of its missing pages. It is difficult to arrive at a verdict. On one hand there stands a disgruntled ex-secret service man whose love of veracity is not of the highest rating; with some of the members of the House judicial committee he left the impression that '. . . it is doubtful whether he has in any one thing told the truth, even by accident'.[2] Against him was pitted Edwin M. Stanton, who, as a young man in Cadiz, Ohio, during the presidential campaign of 1840, had once cited the Constitution and deliberately deleted one line, thereby distorting the entire meaning;[3] as Secretary of War he was responsible for the actions of the Bureau of Military Justice, which had not hesitated to mutilate the official report of the conspiracy trial.

It is impossible to glean the truth from the contradictory statements of two such men.

When Colonel Lafayette C. Baker was released from the United States Army on 8 February 1866, and thereby ceased to be the head of the secret service, he must have felt a bitter resentment against his erstwhile chief, the Secretary of War. He had been the latter's faithful and trusted servant, and his discharge had, for the most part, been the result of his overzealous endeavours to spy on President Johnson in the interests of Stanton. Baker had gone so far as to plant one of his operatives in front of the White House in order to get evidence against the President in connection with some pardon brokers who were then doing a thriving business in the capital. Andrew Johnson finally forbade Baker to enter the Executive Mansion.

'You can go and tell your friend Stanton all I have said,' the President is reported to have shouted at the detective.[4]

Baker found himself out of work and immediately started to

[1] *Impeachment Investigation*, p. 1192.

[2] House of Representatives, 40th Congress, First Session, Rep. Com. No. 7, *Impeachment of the President*, p. 111.

[3] Walter G. Shotwell, *Driftwood* (Longmans, Green & Co., London, 1927), pp. 81, 82; see also supplementary note to chapter xiii, 'Stanton Quotes'.

[4] L. C. Baker, op. cit., p. 604.

write a book on the history of the secret service. He engaged a New York journalist named Headley to do the literary work, while he furnished the necessary data. The volume was put on the market during the early months of the year 1867. It makes good reading, and has been liberally quoted by almost every writer who has dealt with the assassination. Careful scrutiny, however, will show that some queer things, which seemingly have escaped observation, can be read between the lines.

The chapters of Baker's book dealing with the assassination are divided into two parts. The first is merely an extended quotation from the *New York World*; the second part is his own narrative.

'I shall freely quote from sketches written . . . chiefly at my headquarters,' Baker acknowledged. 'One of the writers . . . sat in my office under unusual nervous excitement.'[1] But Baker was not honest enough to copy everything the correspondent had written; nor did he state when and why such omissions were made. He does not mention, for example, that Mr. Townsend, the *New York World* reporter, began by saying, 'A hard and grizzly face overlooks me as I write. Its inconsiderable forehead is crowned with turning sandy hair, and the deep concave of its long insatiate jaws is almost hidden by a dense red beard, which cannot still abate the terrible decision of the large mouth, so well sustained by searching eyes of spotted gray, which roll and rivet one.'[2]

Next, a flattering description of Conger and young Baker is deleted, and perhaps it is not surprising that the following is also left out:

'It could not but have struck Booth that this isolated part of Maryland ignorant and rebel to the brim, without telegraph or railways, or direct stage routes, belted with swamps and broken by dense timber, afforded extraordinary opportunities for shelter and escape.'[3]

It was not in Baker's heart to copy the generous praise which Townsend bestowed on all the other police officers who had taken part in the Great Man-Hunt.

[1] L. C. Baker, op. cit., p. 476.
[2] Townsend, op. cit., p. 28.
[3] Ibid., p. 43.

'In the crowning success of Doherty, Conger, and Baker on the Virginia side of the water we have forgotten the as vigorous and better sustained pursuit on the Maryland side.'[1]

But the most interesting part of Baker's book lies in the intimations contained, half-hidden, within its lines. Facts which the Government had striven carefully to keep in the background were being brought forth in a way that could not but attract attention. There is, for instance, the incident of the interrupted wire service, mention of which had been made in the *New York World*, but which had failed to arouse proper attention. Now Baker trotted out this story by quoting the metropolitan paper, but he quoted it in such a way that most readers took the excerpts for original material. The resurrection of this episode found an immediate repercussion in a congressional investigating committee then in session, and must have proved extremely embarrassing to the powers in Washington.

Then, of course, there was Booth's diary. Clumsily, Baker tried to convey the impression in his own portion of the narrative that he had read some of its missing pages:

'The diary kept by Booth after the murder of the President, to which I referred in connection with the giving of the personal effects of Booth to the Secretary of War, recorded the adventures of the fugitive; one of these was the killing of his horse in the tangled forest to avoid detection, and then sleeping between the animal's legs to get the warmth while it remained in the dead body, during the long hours of the horrible night.'[2]

No such experience as this is described in the preserved portion of Booth's diary. General Holt had read the entire memorandum book to the committee investigating the matter, and there was no reference to a horse in it. This, of course, seemed to substantiate Baker's claim that an essential part of Booth's writings had been destroyed. When driven into a corner, the ex-detective shied off and asserted that he had really not read the little volume; he had picked up an idea of its contents from gossip floating around his office and from other persons who had actually perused it.[3] Baker evidently overlooked the fact that the

[1] Townsend, op. cit., p. 49.
[2] L. C. Baker, op. cit., p. 508.
[3] *Impeachment Investigation*, pp. 286, 450, 451.

missing leaves preceded those which had been preserved; therefore they could not allude to events that transpired after 13 and 14 April, the dates of the first undisputed entries. No matter what was written on the lost pages, it is safe to say that they did not refer to the fugitive's horse. The committee took no notice of this fatal error on Baker's part, and it is difficult to say whether the reading public fully appreciated his subtle insinuation.

The next thing to which Baker turned in his book was another incident that the War Department would most likely have preferred to leave in the limbo of forgotten things. This was Major O'Beirne's recall when he was close on Booth's heels. Again Townsend had referred to this in the *New York World*, and again the public had paid but little attention to the story.

'. . . Major O'Beirne, with a single man [Baker reminded his readers], pushed all night to King George's Court-House, and next day, Sunday, re-embarked for Chappell's Point. Hence he telegraphed his information, and asked permission to pursue, promising to catch the assassins before they reached Port Royal.

'This the department refused. Colonel Baker's men were delegated to make the pursuit with the able Lieutenant Doherty; and O'Beirne, who was the most active and successful spirit in the chase, returned to Washington, cheerful and contented.'[1]

Baker's favourable mention of O'Beirne is in itself strange and quite in contrast to the egotistical spirit that otherwise pervades his book. But the ludicrous addendum wherein the baffled provost-marshal is pictured as returning from the chase *cheerful and contented* must have a deeper meaning. Originally the remark may have been dictated by Baker to the correspondent of the *World* as a sneer toward an unsuccessful competitor. Its repetition here was bound to have a startling effect; for even a hasty reader would probably wonder at this peculiar phrasing. Return to Washington after almost coming in contact with the conspirators—yes; but happy and contented? Never.

Clara E. Laughlin, that fine observer, in her book, *The Death of Lincoln*, remarks doubtfully: 'We are glad to have Baker's assurance about the cheer and content, but O'Beirne's would be more convincing.'[2] Is it not possible that this is an example of

[1] L. C. Baker, op. cit., p. 494.
[2] Laughlin, op. cit., footnote, p. 143.

the very effect which Baker tried to produce by the reiteration of this anomalous statement?

If the judiciary committee of the House had chosen to give this chapter of Baker's book sufficient attention, it would have proved somewhat embarrassing to the War Department.

When Baker stopped quoting Townsend and proceeded with what he called 'a brief official history' of his own connection with the arrest of Lincoln's assassins,[1] he brought more discomfort to Stanton. After describing how he hastened to Washington from New York, he wrote:

'As I entered the Secretary's office, and he recognized me, he turned away to hide his tears. He remarked—"Well, Baker, they have now performed what they have long threatened to do; they have killed the President."'[2]

Therewith one of Stanton's secrets was a secret no longer. Baker's indiscretion suddenly disclosed that Stanton had been aware of threats against Lincoln's life. This must have been annoying to the Secretary of War, to say the least. The committee of the House could well have asked who 'they' were and what threats had come to the knowledge of the War Minister. It was fortunate for Stanton that they failed to do so.

There were other insidious attacks. The Bureau of Military Justice had made most strenuous efforts to bury the testimony of the livery foreman, John Fletcher, going so far as to falsify public records. Again Baker ruthlessly tore the veil from the hidden chapter:

'He [Fletcher] learned that two suspicious characters had just crossed [the Navy Yard Bridge] on horseback. He returned to General Augur's headquarters about one o'clock on Saturday morning, and reported the fact. Here begins the first series of blunders in this attempted search for the assassins. Fletcher's statement was entirely disregarded. No steps were taken by those in possession of this information to follow up the clue thus given until sixteen hours afterward. This delay enabled the assassins to get entirely beyond the reach of those sent in pursuit.'[3]

[1] L. C. Baker, op. cit., p. 524.
[2] Ibid., p. 525.
[3] Ibid., p. 529.

153

Baker gave the hour of Fletcher's appearance at Augur's head-quarters as one o'clock in the morning. According to Fletcher's testimony at the conspiracy trial, he was still at his stable at 1.30, unaware of the great tragedy. Evidently the former secret service man was bound to wreck the entire fabric the judge-advocate's office had so carefully woven in its effort toward concealment.

Next the ex-detective quoted another disconcerting paragraph from Townsend:

'. . . Booth gave his proper name to the officer at the bridge. This, which would seem to have been foolish, was, in reality, very shrewd. The officers believed that one of Booth's accomplices had given his name in order to put them out of the real Booth's tracks. So they made efforts elsewhere, and Booth got a start.'[1]

Baker must have recognized the glaring incongruity of this explanation, which explained nothing and raised only new and more serious doubts instead; but he could afford to be frank, because the incident had happened before he was called in on the case. He might have ridiculed his rivals and let it go at that; but he chose to build for them a defence that would focus suspicion on a blunder which was so incredible that it could easily have been something worse.

Baker's final stroke came in his recital of how he and Conger had brought to Stanton's knowledge the news of the drama at Garrett's barn. By way of contrast, and as a fitting introduction, he gave an account of his own feelings when he heard of the capture:

'It is not often that I am unbalanced by tidings of any sort; but I sprang to my feet, and across the room, and felt like raising a shout of joy over the triumph of justice. . . .'[2]

A carriage was ordered immediately and, in company with Lieutenant-Colonel Conger, Baker hurried to the Stanton residence.

'When I entered the room he was lying upon a sofa. . . . I rushed into the room, and said, "We have got Booth." Secretary

[1] L. C. Baker, op. cit., pp. 486–87.
[2] Ibid., p. 540.

Stanton was distinguished during the whole war for his coolness, but I had never seen such an exhibition of it in my life as at that time. He put his hands over his eyes, and lay for nearly a moment without saying a word. Then he got up and put on his coat very coolly.'[1]

Stanton, impetuous and impulsive and anything but cool at critical moments, should logically have reacted explosively, regardless of the nature of the news. But when he put his hands over his eyes *for nearly a moment* while lying on a sofa, and continued to lie there without saying a word, he exhibited all the symptoms of a person who dreaded a deadly blow. Baker exclaimed, 'We have got Booth', when he entered Stanton's rooms. What did Stanton expect to hear next? What did Baker strive so hard to intimate? Were his lines intended to convey the thought that Stanton was obsessed with a ghastly fear—a fear that did not subside until a more detailed account of the capture convinced him that the detectives did not have Booth, but had only his dead body?

Before the judiciary committee Baker tried to create the impression that efforts had been made to keep his book from being published.

'Was there any effort made on the part of any member of the Executive Department to suppress the publication of your book?' Baker was asked on 7 February 1867, even before the final proof sheets were in his hands.[2]

'Yes, I think there was,' he replied; but when pinned down to facts the author of *The History of the Secret Service* became evasive. His testimony, as well as that of Secretary Seward, shows that Baker had selected as his publisher a man named Derby who once had been a member of a firm of booksellers in Auburn, New York, Seward's home town. The firm had failed after moving to New York, whereupon Derby had obtained a position as dispatch-agent in the State Department. Seward thought it quite likely that Derby still continued 'some connection with bookmaking', as he phrased it.[3] Riddle, Baker's attorney, happened to live next door to the chief clerk of the

[1] L. C. Baker, op. cit., p. 540.
[2] *Impeachment Investigation*, p. 13.
[3] Ibid., pp. 13, 372.

State Department, and in this manner Baker had heard that proof sheets of his book were before Seward and had been read by him. Objection was offered to some of Baker's chapters, and the work was suspended for several months.

Baker admitted that he had never talked about the book directly to either Mr. Seward or Mr. Stanton. Eventually he became his own publisher, but it looks as though he had made extraordinary efforts to bring the manuscript to the attention of Seward through the selection of Derby. Baker's finances had experienced some reverses through an unfortunate investment in a Michigan hotel enterprise, and it is not improbable that the story about an attempted suppression of his forthcoming book was something of a publicity stunt.

General Baker died on 3 July 1868, only a year after his examination before the House judiciary committee. He left no papers, so far as is known, and whatever additional data he had, or whatever suspicions he harboured, were buried with him. According to a notice in the *Philadelphia Press* on 4 July 1868 he died in his forty-fourth year, and 'although he had been ill for several months, the disease that proved fatal was a recent attack of typhoid fever'. His death certificate, however, signed by a Dr. Owen L. Richards, and filed in the Philadelphia city hall, states that he died of meningitis.

CHAPTER XIV

Death Visits Garrett's Farm

When Lieutenant Doherty's detachment of twenty-five men under the leadership of ex-Lieutenant-Colonel Conger and ex-Lieutenant Baker surrounded the tobacco shed at Garrett's Farm shortly after midnight on 26 April they found it occupied by two men. One of them proved to be Herold; about the identity of the other the soldiers did not bother, for they had every reason to believe that he was Booth.

Young William Garrett, a paroled Confederate cavalryman, was sent into the barn to obtain the weapons of the besieged men, but in this mission he was unsuccessful. After a short parley, during which one of the men inside proposed to shoot it out with Doherty's troopers, Herold surrendered, and shortly afterward the shed was set on fire. The other man, now plainly visible through the cracks in the wooden structure, started to move toward the door; at this moment there was a shot and he fell to the ground. A bullet had entered his neck on the right side and paralysed his spinal cord. He died on the porch of the Garrett house just as the sun rose, on 27 April.

This, in bare outline, is what happened at Garrett's Farm that night. It leaves at least two questions unanswered: First—who shot the man in the barn? Second—why was he not taken alive?

Tradition has it that the killing was done by Boston Corbett, a somewhat eccentric sergeant, who claimed that Providence had directed him to do it. At any rate, this is what he told Colonel Conger at the time. When under oath in the conspiracy trial, he contented himself by making the less dramatic statement that 'one of the men, who was watching him [Booth], told me that he aimed the carbine at me. He was taking aim with the carbine, but at whom I could not say. My mind was upon him attentively to see that he did no harm, and when I became impressed that it was time I shot him. . . .'[1]

No other soldier has ever come forward to say that he witnessed Corbett's deed. There were men all around him; they had been placed at a distance of about thirty feet from the barn with strict instructions not to move from the lines laid out for them. If Boston Corbett fired the shot, as he said he did, he must have left his post and crawled up close to the shed to place the muzzle of his pistol—or carbine—in the proper position. With the blaze gaining headway inside, Corbett's figure should have been plainly visible to his comrades; but not one of them ever confirmed his story.

Only one witness has been found to corroborate Corbett's account partially; he was Garrett's younger son, Robert, then twelve years old, who gave his recollection of the affair in a Baltimore paper some twenty-two years afterward.

'Through the cracks [he reported] could be seen the form of Booth standing in the middle of the building, supported by his crutch. In his hands he held a carbine. . . . At this instant, Sergeant Corbet . . . fired through a crack in the wall. . . . He said afterward that Booth had his gun to his shoulder and was about to kill one of the officers. This is not so, as I was standing within six feet of Corbet when he fired the shot, and Booth never made a motion to shoot.'[2]

The chairman of the congressional committee which undertook to divide the reward, stated that Corbett was 'an insane man' who 'forsook his place, thrust a pistol through a crack and fired it without knowing where the ball was going'.[3]

Others took a less charitable view of the matter. A quarter of a century later Lieutenant Ruggles, one of the Confederate officers who had recommended Booth to Garrett's hospitality, felt 'convinced that Sergeant Boston Corbett has a reputation undeserved as the slayer of Mr. Lincoln's assassin. From the spot where Sergeant Corbett was he could not have seen Booth where

[1] Pitman, op. cit., p. 94.
[2] H. G. Howard, *Civil War Echoes* (Howard Publishing Co., Washington, 1907), p. 98.
[3] DeWitt, *Assassination*, p. 277.

he stood, and certainly could not have been able to shoot him in the back of the head.'[1] Unfortunately, Ruggles was not an eye-witness, and did not even cite the source of his information. Nevertheless, his testimony is corroborated, in a measure, by the evidence of Lieutenant Baker.

'Booth was just between Corbett and me,' this young officer declared in 1867; 'and it was remarked afterwards that if he had missed Booth, he might have shot me.'[2] Now, Lieutenant Baker was in front of the shed, so it may be safely assumed that Corbett was behind it. As the man in the shed was moving toward the door—that is, toward the front side of the building—it is difficult to see how Corbett could have thought that he was menaced at the moment when he fired.

The bullet that killed the man inside the barn entered his neck on the right side and, taking an oblique downward course at an angle of about twenty degrees, penetrated three vertebrae and passed out on the left side.[3] Such a wound might possibly have been inflicted from a distance, but the probabilities are strongly against it. If this had been the case, one would have to assume that when the man in the barn was hit he was standing with his head bent sharply to the left and with his profile toward the right wall and parallel to the door. While such a possibility must be conceded, the only argument which apparently can be put forth in its favour is that, at times, truth is stranger than fiction.

Was it Colonel Conger who killed the crippled visitor of the Garrett household? Lieutenant Baker thought so at one time, for when on the witness stand before a congressional investigating committee he testified as follows:

'I supposed, at the time, that Conger shot him, and I said, "What on earth did you shoot him for?" Said he, "I did not shoot him." Then the idea flashed on my mind that if he did, it had better not be known.'[4]

[1] M. B. Ruggles, 'Narrative' in *Century Magazine* (Jan. 1890), p. 446; see also supplementary note to chapter xiv, 'Who Shot the Man in Garrett's Barn?'

[2] *Impeachment Investigation*, p. 481.

[3] Records of the Smithsonian Institution, Washington, D.C.

[4] *Impeachment Investigation*, p. 481.

Conger, according to his own sworn statement, was by the side of the tobacco house, while Corbett was on the other side around the corner of the building.[1] Conger was, therefore, in a position to fire a bullet entering at the side of the neck. But why should its course have been downward? It is unfortunate that we do not know the exact position of Conger at this juncture. After the shooting he immediately rushed into the barn, a natural impulse, if he had been the slayer. This is not conclusive evidence, however, for, as one of the commanders of the party, it would be the normal thing for him to do. It is far more significant that Corbett showed no interest whatever in the injured man.

Conger was well aware of the suspicion that his fellow detective harboured. When examined at the Surratt trial, he testified as follows:

'He [the man in the tobacco house] then turned his eye on the fire, to see . . . whether he could put it out. He satisfied himself by a glance at it that he could not. . . . He dropped his carbine . . . and . . . came towards the front door.'[2]

Hurrying to meet him there, Conger heard the report of what he judged to be a pistol shot.

'I supposed he had shot himself. I went around to the front door, and found it open. Baker had gone in, and when I went to him stood partly bent down, looking at Booth, who lay on the floor, to all appearance dead. I stooped over, looked down at him, and said he had shot himself. Baker said, "No, he did not. . . ." He had the appearance of a man who had put a pistol to his head and shot himself, shooting a little too low; and I said again, "He shot himself." Baker said, "No, he did not." He spoke very positive about it. I thought it a little strange, rather, as if he doubted my word when he said so.'[3]

DeWitt, the careful historian, was sorely puzzled about the manner of Booth's death. 'Who fired the shot . . . ?' he asked. 'This question, to settle which beyond controversy the authorities were in possession of evidence abundant and conclusive, they preferred to let rest upon testimony inconclusive, impeachable and contradictory.'[4]

[1] *Impeachment Investigation*, p. 325.   [2]*Surratt Trial*, I, p. 307.
[3] Ibid., p. 308.   [4] DeWitt, *Assassination*, p. 87.

THE MURDERERS DOOM. MISERABLE DEATH OF J. WILKES BOOTH, THE ASSASSIN OF PRESIDENT LINCOLN.

Shot through the head by Sergeant Boston Corbett in a barn on Garrett's Farm, near Port Royal, near the Rappahannock, April 25, 1865.

There are a number of historical inaccuracies in this contemporary print of the drama at Garrett's barn. Herold was out of the barn and not on the point of surrendering. The structure had no openings except the front door; the shooting was done through a crack in the wall. The building was filled with furniture, not with hay.

Original print in possession of author

He then continued:

'The autopsy should have disclosed the calibre of the pistol and the size of the ball with which the wound was inflicted; the War Department having possession of Booth's weapons might easily have shown whether or not one chamber of the revolver was empty . . . and it does not appear that the pistol, with which the assassin might have carried out his resolve never to be taken alive, was ever examined.'[1]

It is interesting to note that Conger received the lion's share of the final reward paid out—$15,000—while Lieutenant Baker was given only $3,000.[2]

Baker also could have been suspected of having fired the bullet. He had placed all available men on three sides of the building, remaining alone at the front where the door was— a singular disposition.[3] Yet, this arrangement was not one of his own choosing; it had been ordered by Colonel Conger, for reasons of his own. Baker testified that he was the first to enter the shed, and it is barely possible that, acting under secret orders, he might have held his opponent with his right arm while discharging the pistol with his left. This would conform with the direction taken by the ball. When Mr. Garrett had opened the door of his house Lieutenant Baker, threatening him with his pistol, had held the weapon in a similar position. 'I placed my hand on his shoulder, and, presenting my pistol, asked him where those two men were who were stopping with him,' he testified.[4] Garrett's boy also mentions that when his father opened the door 'a pistol was placed at his head and he was told to reveal the hiding-place . . .'.[5] Townsend, the reporter for the *New York World*, wrote that 'Baker seized him by the throat at once, and held a pistol to his ear'.[6]

On the other hand Lieutenant Baker was not the man to shoot an unresisting opponent; besides, he was being watched and closely followed by young Robert Garrett, who confirmed

[1] DeWitt, *Assassination*, p. 90.
[2] Laughlin, op. cit., p. 312.
[3] L. C. Baker, op. cit., p. 536.
[4] *Surratt Trial*, I, p. 318.
[5] Howard, *Civil War Echoes*, p. 98.
[6] Townsend, op. cit., p. 31.

the lieutenant's report that the cripple was already lying prostrate on the ground when they entered.[1]

Furthermore, William Garrett, an older brother, corroborated this version of the event. Writing in the *Confederate
Veteran* in 1921 he related that

'An officer, Lieutenant Baker, was standing near the front
door, and when the shot was heard he said to me: "Give me the
key; he has shot himself." I unlocked the door, and he and I ran
in and took hold of the man to lift him up.'[2]

William Garrett also had testified under oath in 1867 that
Baker and he were at the unlocked door when the shot was fired;
they entered the barn together immediately afterward.[3] Disregarding unimportant discrepancies, mostly in the form of em-
bellishments that exaggerate his own importance in the story,
William Garrett's two accounts tally well with each other and
definitely exonerate Lieutenant Baker.

Baker strongly suspected Colonel Conger; perhaps this is
why his first statement, made to Judge Holt in the cabin of a
gunboat on the night of his return to Washington, was misplaced.

'My testimony has never been taken, except before Judge
Holt,' he swore in 1867, 'and that has been disposed of.'

Q. What do you mean by that?
A. It cannot be found.[4]

When further pressed to state what he thought had become
of it, he said: 'My opinion is that there has been some foul play
about it.'

Q. What do you mean?
A. I think it has been destroyed.[5]

Lieutenant Baker was not called as a witness in the conspiracy
trial, and he was greatly surprised that no reason for this was
given him.

[1] Luther B. Baker, private statement.
[2] William Garrett, 'True Story of the Capture of John Wilkes Booth'.
Confederate Veteran Magazine (Apr. 1921), p. 130.
[3] *Surratt Trial*, I, p. 305. In the Surratt trial William Garrett is referred
to as John W. Garrett.
[4] *Impeachment Investigation*, p. 483.   [5] Ibid., p. 486.

As Conger intimated, the man in the barn may have committed suicide. If he had held a pistol to the right side of his head and shot low, the wound would have been like the one inflicted. Considering that the man was a cripple who had just thrown away his crutch, and that he was acting under great excitement, this argument has something in its favour. Lieutenant Ruggles felt sure that this was what had happened.

'No one saw Corbett fire,' he wrote, 'and one chamber of Booth's revolver held in his hand was empty, and I am by no means alone in the belief that he killed himself.'[1]

Unfortunately, Ruggles again fails to bring forth the facts on which his belief is based, nor does he say how he knew that one chamber of the dead man's revolver was empty. It was within the power of any of the three leaders of the expedition—Conger, Baker, or Doherty—to have ordered an immediate examination of all firearms on the place, thereby establishing the truth beyond all controversy. That this was not done does not necessarily imply bad faith; for it must be remembered that all the men were dog-tired, so tired in fact, that some of the soldiers had fallen asleep on their horses as they rode to the Garrett farm, and had to be kicked into action. It may be surmised that the leaders were equally fatigued and incapable of doing what they would not have neglected under ordinary conditions.

Far more blame attaches to Conger and Baker for their failure to capture alive the fugitive in the shed. They had two dozen men, trained soldiers all, against one cripple, and the task was by no means impossible. Boston Corbett expressed his ideas about this in plain language:

'. . . I twice offered to my commanding officer, Lieutenant Doherty, and once to Mr. Conger, to go into the barn and take the man, saying that I was not afraid to go in and take him; it was less dangerous to go in and fight him than to stand before a crack exposed to his fire, where I could not see him, although he could see me; but I was not sent in.'[2]

For a man suspected of insanity, who was subsequently committed to an asylum, Sergeant Corbett seems to have possessed an astounding amount of good judgement.

[1] Ruggles's 'Narrative' in *Century Magazine* (Jan. 1890), p. 446.
[2] Pitman, op. cit., p. 95.

A contemporary newspaper agreed with Corbett's views, stating editorially that 'there were few . . . able to understand how, after an assassin had been tracked to a barn and there surrounded by a squad of cavalry numbering twenty-eight men, he could not be taken alive, even if he had been maimed and rendered powerless by sundry shots before his capture. . . . The public will ask . . . for a thorough inquest into the circumstances of the capture.'[1]

It would also have been easy to surround the structure, wait until daylight, and then either take it by storm or else starve its inmates into submission. Was it fear that the rewards would have to be shared with reinforcements, which might arrive, that made the two detectives take such precipitate action? Or did Conger have secret orders to kill the fugitive? Did Lieutenant Baker suspect something of this sort when he said that if Conger shot the man in the barn it had better not be known? What else could he have meant by his enigmatic remark?

Shortly after the events in the Virginia barn Beverly Tucker, a prominent Confederate, expressed an opinion probably shared by many others when he penned the following:

'The valorous twenty-six . . . knights, who failed to capture alive . . . one poor crippled youth, have sealed the only lips that could unravel this dark and mighty mystery [of Lincoln's assassination]. Did they, it has been more than once pertinently asked, act in this respect under instructions; and if not, why have they so promptly received the plaudit, 'Well done, good and faithful servants?' *Would it have been inconvenient to any one to have taken him with the power to speak?* Alas! we can never know all that died with this daring, yet misguided young man. . . .'[2]

If the cripple in the barn had been taken alive his pursuers would have escaped all criticism, and one of the riddles of history would have been answered: Who was shot at Garrett's Farm on the night of 26 April 1865?

No attempt to answer this query will be made within the confines of this volume.

[1] Newspaper clipping, believed to be from the *New York Herald*.
[2] Howard, *Civil War Echoes*, p. 104.

CHAPTER XV

The Plots against Grant, Stanton, and Johnson

On 16 April the *Washington National Intelligencer* wrote: 'We can state on the highest authority that it has been ascertained that there was a regular conspiracy to assassinate every member of the Cabinet, together with the Vice-President.' Considering the fact that Secretary of State Seward had been assaulted and badly wounded, this statement seemed probable enough. No traces of a plot against the lives of the other secretaries have ever been found, but the Government prosecuted Michael O'Laughlin for attempted assassination of General Grant, and George Atzerodt for planning the murder of Vice-President Johnson. It was claimed that, but for a lucky stroke of fate, Stanton also would have fallen victim to a murderous assault; he generously abstained from pressing the case, however. He was the moving spirit of the prosecution; to have taken such an action—as his supporters were eager to point out—would have placed him in a delicate position.

Practically every writer on Lincoln's death has subscribed to the story that the lives of Grant, Stanton, and Johnson actually were threatened on the night of the tragedy. Nevertheless, a careful examination of the evidence leaves some doubt about the soundness of this assumption.

It was Michael O'Laughlin's task, according to his indictment, to 'lie in wait [during the nights of 13 and 14 April] for Ulysses S. Grant . . . with intent, then and there, to kill and murder the said Ulysses S. Grant'.[1] The evidence against him

[1] Pitman, op. cit., p. 20.

was this: on the evening of 13 April Grant had accepted an invitation to be Stanton's guest, and a great crowd had assembled in front of the house on K Street. At half-past ten a stranger stepped forth and inquired for the secretary. Stanton's son at first thought that the man was intoxicated, but changed his opinion after talking to him. The stranger did not ask for General Grant at all, and left quietly and of his own accord. Young Stanton had never seen the man before, and did not set eyes on him again until asked to identify him among the prisoners on the monitor; there it was dark, and he could obtain only an indistinct view of the accused. A Major Knox corroborated David Stanton's statement. He confirmed the fact that O'Laughlin, if O'Laughlin it was, did not even ask to see General Grant. Knox did not identify the prisoner positively, but merely felt 'pretty certain' that the prisoner was the man he had seen.[1]

It is astounding that the Bureau of Military Justice dared to put forth such evidence in court without fear of exposing itself to public ridicule; for the third and last witness against O'Laughlin, a Sergeant Hatter, did not help the case much. He claimed to have seen the stranger at nine o'clock, not at half-past ten, as the others had. O'Laughlin, he said, simply asked the whereabouts of Grant and did not even attempt to enter Stanton's house.[2]

Against these flimsy accusations the defence could muster half a dozen reputable witnesses, among them an ensign in the United States Navy, who had been with O'Laughlin all the time, day and night, on 14 April, and whose alibis for their companion make it certain that O'Laughlin was, to put it mildly, a victim of mistaken identity. Their testimony goes to show that he never was within a mile of Stanton's house. Walter Cox, the attorney for the defendant, inquired quite pertinently why the Government, with all this information, did not charge that the intended victim was Secretary Stanton instead of General Grant.[3] There was no more sense in one assertion than in the other, and of course, there was no answer to his question.

In his argument for the prosecution, the assistant judge-advocate, John A. Bingham, thought it best not to go into the core

---

[1] Pitman, op. cit., pp. 226, 227.
[2] Ibid., p. 227.
[3] Ibid., p. 344.

of this matter at all; instead, he tried to have O'Laughlin convicted on the vague grounds of conspiracy; and 'After mature consideration of the evidence . . . the [military] Commission find the said accused—Of the Specification . . . GUILTY. Except [that] ". . . *the said Michael O'Laughlin did there and then lie in wait for Ulysses S. Grant, . . . with intent then and there to kill and murder the said Ulysses S. Grant"; of said words* NOT GUILTY. . . .'[1] Evidently even the military commission could not see that the life of the general—or that of any one else, for that matter— had been put into jeopardy by O'Laughlin.

So much for the alleged attempt on the part of the conspirators to murder the leading general of the Federal army.

There may have been danger for Grant, on 14 April, from an entirely different quarter. When he returned to his hotel, preparatory to leaving Washington, Mrs. Grant told him that a man with a wild look had followed her into the dining-room at lunch-time and had stared at her continually from a seat opposite her table. The general made light of this incident; but when the carriage which was taking the Grants to the depot was proceeding along Pennsylvania Avenue, a horseman who was riding in the same direction passed them and peered inside. Mrs. Grant recognized him as the same man who had annoyed her at the lunch-table. Before they reached the station the rider turned and again gazed intently at the occupants of the carriage. When the photograph of Booth appeared in the public prints the Grants found that he closely resembled the man who had attracted their attention by his rudeness.[2]

Later General Grant received an anonymous letter saying that its author had been designated by the conspirators to assassinate him, and had been ordered to board the train and commit the deed there; that he had attempted to enter Grant's car for this purpose, but had been baffled by a locked door; and that he thanked God he had thus providentially been prevented from staining his hands with the blood of his intended victim.[3] This singular story was not given to the public until many years after the event, and did not appear at all in the newspapers of the day.

---

[1] Pitman, op. cit., pp. 248, 390; italics are the author's.
[2] Jesse Grant, *In the Days of My Father*, pp. 36–40; also in Porter, 'Campaigning with Grant' in *Century Magazine* (Oct. 1897), p. 892.
[3] Porter, op. cit., p. 892.

No efforts were made to trace the unknown man with the wild looks, nor the anonymous correspondent. That some horseman followed Grant's carriage and gazed at its occupants is undoubtedly true; what his purpose was cannot be stated at this late day. He may have been Booth or merely a particularly tactless admirer of the General, and the anonymous epistle may have been nothing more serious than the work of a crank.

The story of an attempt on Stanton's life is based on a report that some persons, hastening to his house with the news of the shambles at Seward's home, had seen a man shrink into the shadows at their approach. According to an account by Stanton himself, as cited by one of his biographers, his life was saved because of a broken doorbell.

'I was tired out and went home early,' the account reads, 'and was in the back room playing with the children when the man came to my steps. If the door-bell had rung it would have been answered and the man admitted . . . but the bell-wire was broken a day or two before, and though we had endeavoured to have it repaired, the bell-hanger had put it off because of a pressure of orders.'[1]

A likely tale, this. It would be exceedingly interesting to have the name of the bell-hanger who was so busy with other orders that he had the audacity to incur the ire of the all-powerful Secretary of War by postponing the repairs on what was then perhaps the most important doorbell in Washington.

On one other occasion Stanton declared himself an intended victim of the conspiracy. On 12 May 1865 he wired to Edward Pierrepont of New York, an attorney who two years later was to figure prominently in the Surratt trial:

'I have written to-night to retain you . . . to prosecute Horace Greeley and the owners of the *Tribune* for Greeley's persistent effort the last four weeks to incite assassins to finish their work by murdering me. . . . I shall not allow them to have me murdered and escape responsibility without a struggle for life on my part.[2]

[1] Frank A. Flower, *Edwin McMasters Stanton* (Saalfield Publishing Co., Akron, 1905), p. 279.
[2] *Official Records*, I, vol. 46, part 3, pp. 1141–42.

And on the following day he continued:

'I have proof of express personal malice against me by Greeley, and believe that I can establish a combination between him and others which may end in accomplishing my death, as it did against Mr. Lincoln and Mr. Seward. . . .'[1]

If Stanton wished to be considered a martyr his efforts fell flat; for his ravings against the *Tribune* received scant publicity.

There remains for examination the reported attempt to kill Vice-President Johnson. Amplified as it is with many circumstantial details, its truth has never been questioned.

On the day preceding Lincoln's assassination a rough-looking stranger had entered the Kirkwood House, a Washington hostelry at Twelfth Street and Pennsylvania Avenue, and had registered there under his true name, G. A. Atzerodt. He never occupied the room he had rented.[2] Vice-President Johnson also had his living quarters at this hotel, and hence a detective of Major O'Beirne's squad, John Lee, was sent there as a guard, after the assault on Lincoln, on the night of 14 April. A bartender by the name of Michael Henry told the detective of his suspicions regarding an odd-looking stranger who had behaved queerly.[3] With permission of the hotel owners, the door to Atzerodt's room was thereupon broken open. Inside was found an array of things which Lee inventoried for his superiors. The list comprised:

One Colt revolver with six chambers, loaded and capped.

Three boxes of Colt's pistol cartridges, calibre 0.44.

One bowie knife, blade 12 inches long, 1½ inches wide, ⅛-inch thick, somewhat stained. This knife had been clumsily hidden underneath the sheets of the bed; the revolver had been laid under the pillow.

Hanging in full view was a black coat which, as later investigation proved, did not belong to Atzerodt, but to Herold. In its pockets were found a bank book with J. W. Booth's name written both outside and inside, and a war map of the Southern states.

---

[1] *Official Records*, I, vol. 46, part 3, p. 1149.   [2] Pitman, op. cit., p. 144.
[3] O'Beirne papers.

A further search of the room disclosed:

One handkerchief, marked Mary R. E. Booth.

One handkerchief, marked F. M. Nelson.

One handkerchief, marked H.

One brass spur.

Some toilet articles, a pair of gauntlets, a plain envelope franked 'Hon. John Conness',[1] and other trifles made up the remainder of the list.[2]

From these premisses the obvious conclusion was drawn that Atzerodt had intended to murder Vice-President Johnson. His failure to do so has been ascribed to his cowardice, a quality for which this German carriage-painter was well known in his home town of Port Tobacco.

That Atzerodt really was assigned the part of assassinating Johnson has been accepted as an historical fact. 'His aimless movements [during the evening] lend a touch of the comic to the horrors of the night . . .' said DeWitt. 'At ten he . . . rode to the Kirkwood [House], but went no nearer his prey than the bar. . . . Poor, pitiable caricature of an assassin!'[3]

Oldroyd wrote that 'Atzerodt made no attempt upon the life of Vice-President Johnson, although he had been assigned by Booth to perform that act, but probably through cowardice he failed to make the attempt.'[4] No one seems to have harboured the slightest doubt that the murder of the Vice-President was one of the objects which the conspirators endeavoured to attain.

Yet there are certain points in this general fabric of circumstances that look incongruous. To start with, no real effort was made by Atzerodt to come even within striking distance of Johnson at any time in the evening; further, the man supposed to have been selected by Booth was notoriously unfit for the task allotted to him. Such flaws in the plans of this brilliant plotter are unlikely; they become unbelievable on a closer examination of the clues left in Atzerodt's room for the benefit of the police.

On 14 April this German, whose queer looks made him the cynosure of curious eyes wherever he went, rented a room at the

[1] Conness was a senator from California.

[2] War Department Archives; also Pitman, op. cit., p. 144; also Poore, op. cit., I, pp. 64, 65.

[3] DeWitt, *Assassination*, pp. 52, 53.

[4] Oldroyd, op. cit., p. 48.

Kirkwood House. He behaved so strangely that the detectives, sent there to guard the Vice-President, were immediately warned against him and hastened to make an investigation; but Atzerodt had left his room, taking the key with him, thereby confirming and accentuating the previous suspicions. The door to his room was forced, and the searchers found a coat belonging not to him but to Herold. In its pockets were two handkerchiefs, one marked 'H' and another marked 'F. M. Nelson', which was the name of one of Herold's sisters. They also contained one of Booth's bankbooks inscribed with his name.[1] If the detective who made these startling discoveries had ever hoped some day to find the visiting card of a murderer lying next to his victim, he must have felt that the dream of his life had at last come true.

The entry in the register gave Atzerodt's true name; a coat and a bankbook showed the identity of his co-plotters; and, lest there should be any question as to the nature of the conspiracy, there was, barely covered by the bed-sheet and pillow, a small arsenal of arms and ammunition. But Booth, in his contempt for the intelligence of the police, and perhaps in a spirit of bravado, went one step farther. To show his pursuers where he had gone, he left behind him a map of the Southern states; and for fear someone might think that he had made his getaway on foot, or by train, there was a spur in the room to indicate that he had fled on horseback. The very obviousness of all this should have aroused the suspicion of the detectives; everything bore so plainly the earmarks of a stage melodrama. But again Booth proved himself the eminent psychologist who always knew how far he could go with his audience. The excitement he left in his wake precluded clear thinking, and the ambition of the sleuths blinded them to the unusual nature of the evidence.

That the conspirator really created the desired impression is proved by the inferences universally drawn and well expressed by General Harris, one of the judges at the forthcoming trial, who wrote:

'This coat evidently belonged to Booth, and its being thus found in Atzerodt's room showed that Booth had visited him there during the day; and that he had spent some time with him schooling him in his part was shown by the fact that he had

---

[1] Pitman, op. cit., pp. 144 ff.

taken off his light overcoat and hung it up against the wall, and had evidently become so much absorbed in mind with the purpose of his visit that he forgot to take his coat when he left. The revolver loaded and capped, and the huge bowie-knife hidden in the bed, serve to explain the nature of the interview between Booth and Atzerodt. . . .'[1]

No doubt General Harris thought himself a great detective.

If the assassins had done no more than put the pursuers on their track by leaving behind a map and a spur, and divulged their identities through items marked with their names, it would be possible to assume that the fox was just indulging in a little fun with the hounds. It would be in harmony with Booth's disdain of all disguise at the theatre and with his audacity in giving his real name to the sentinel at the bridge. But the actor had not yet finished his programme.

Two days before the assassination Atzerodt had called at the Kirkwood House and had asked a passing colonel where the Vice-President's room was; he had also requested that this army officer point out Johnson to him.[2] Now, Johnson's face was one that was known to every one in Washington, his features were plainly recognizable and not easily forgotten. If Booth had wanted his assistant to familiarize himself with them, he could have chosen methods far less conspicuous. Had Johnson been found murdered on the fourteenth the questions asked by Atzerodt would have been remembered and would have proved his undoing. That Booth would allow his subordinate to commit so flagrant a mistake is highly improbable, for where he really expected to strike he adopted quite different tactics. At Seward's house, for instance, Lewis Paine, big, powerful, and fearless as he was, used great caution in making his approach.

'A man came to the window of the dining room of the Sewards' house on the morning of the 13th and 14th of April,' Private Robinson, the male nurse employed by the Sewards, told the authorities, 'and enquired each day about the Health of the Secretary. . . . When I first saw the man . . . at the time he

---

[1] Harris, op. cit., p. 69.
[2] Pitman, op. cit., p. 144.

made the attack, I thought I recognized him to be the same person. . . .'[1]

In his own attack Booth gave no warning of the impending blow, no hint of his intentions. And so the investigator is confronted, on one side, with the curious spectacle of a man fleeing from Stanton's house in the dark, for no apparent cause; of a horseman gazing intently at Grant and making himself conspicuous, but committing no hostile act; and of a great commotion around Johnson's hotel, but no attempt at assassination. On the other side, he finds sly inquiries or no inquiries at all, but quick and murderous action.

Still, Booth was apparently not quite satisfied that his intentions against Johnson had been revealed with sufficient clearness. His scorn for the stupidity of the authorities must have been boundless; for as an afterthought he sent to the Vice-President a card, on which he had written:

> Don't wish to disturb you Are you at home?
> J WILKES BOOTH[2]

With this evidence before them, the authorities were almost forced to believe that Booth was concerned in a plot to murder Johnson. The Vice-President could be congratulated on his narrow escape, due to his absence from his rooms. It probably would not occur to the secret service that his absence might have been known to the caller and had been calculated upon, and that Booth was throwing dust in their eyes. Would any one be sharp-witted enough to realize that if Lincoln were to be done away with at ten o'clock Johnson was as safe at four o'clock as if he had been a thousand miles away? In all the historical documents of these turbulent times only one voice ever uttered a suspicion that the ostensible plot against Johnson was nothing but a sham. This voice belonged to a convicted perjurer who was then languishing in prison, and to whom no one paid the slightest attention.[3]

Even during the conspiracy trial some inkling of the truth began to be discernible, had any one chosen to be discerning. When John M. Lloyd, the tavern-keeper at Surrattsville, de-

[1] War Department Archives.
[2] Ibid.
[3] DeWitt, *Assassination*, p. 175; refers to Sandford Conover.

scribed his midnight conversation with the assassins, he quoted one of them as saying: 'I am pretty certain that we have assassinated the President and Secretary Seward.'[1] Not one word about Johnson. If the latter's death had been included in the murderers' plans, how could they be so sure, two hours after the proposed attempts at assassination, that Johnson was unharmed? Yet, this impediment to the accepted theory of the projected wholesale slaughter was entirely disregarded, as if by unanimous consent.

Booth, talking freely about himself to some Confederate officers a few days afterward, said that he had left the note at Johnson's hotel to compromise him, in the hope that Lincoln's successor might appear to be implicated in the plot.[2] This is an astounding revelation; for what sense was there in Booth's trying to throw suspicion on a dead Johnson? The assassin showed neither surprise nor disappointment on hearing that Johnson had escaped Atzerodt's clutches; instead, he tried to explain away the card, therefore, the memory of this card must have worried him. The sending of the message was a false move, and Booth began to see it. After going through all the trouble of arranging Atzerodt's room, this piece of pasteboard, if properly interpreted, might completely ruin the effect of the decoy arsenal. For if Johnson had been killed in the afternoon, Lincoln and Seward would have been guarded so well in the evening that no assassin could have reached them. Instead of emphasizing the plot against Johnson, this card was liable to give away the whole show. That is why Booth kept talking about it to people who knew nothing of the episode, and at a time when one would have expected that his mind would be occupied with the pressing problem of his escape.

In 1890 Lieutenant Ruggles, one of the three Confederates who assisted Booth to reach Garrett's Farm, came forward with a story published by the *Century Magazine*, in which he said that

---

[1] Pitman, op. cit., p. 86.
[2] M. B. Ruggles and Edward P. Doherty, 'Pursuit and Death of John Wilkes Booth' in *Century Magazine* (Jan. 1890, D. Appleton-Century Co.), p. 445; see also supplementary note to chapter xv, 'The Mystery of Booth's Note to Johnson'.

Booth had told them, in his own account of the conspiracy, that deadly blows were to be struck at Lincoln and Seward. Again there was no mention of Johnson.

It is also significant that Booth, in his conversation with these three Southerners, absolved Atzerodt of all intentions to commit murder.

'In the plot to kill', Ruggles quoted Booth as saying, 'Paine alone was implicated . . . not even Herold knowing what was to be done. Atzerodt knew nothing of the intended assassination.'[1] That Booth was telling the truth in this instance can hardly be doubted; there would have been no point in lying. Lieutenant Bainbridge, a comrade of Ruggles, in his account of the affair, said, 'When Booth realized that we were kindly disposed, he threw off all reserve and became quite communicative.'[2]

After due consideration of these facts, it may be taken as proved that neither Johnson, Grant, nor Stanton were in any danger on the night Lincoln and Seward were assaulted, but that enough clues were planted to mark these leaders as projected victims of attacks which were never contemplated.

Some slight evidence exists that Secretary of the Navy Welles was in danger, or else that an affair was staged to create that impression. Welles had retired about half-past ten and was just falling asleep when his messenger, James Smith, called to him that the President and Secretary Seward had been shot.

'I immediately dressed myself [one reads in Welles's diary], and . . . went directly to Mr. Seward's, whose residence was on the east side of the square, mine being on the north. James [Smith] accompanied me. As we were crossing 15th Street, I saw four or five men in earnest consultation, standing under the lamp on the corner by St. John's Church. Before I had got half across the street, the lamp was suddenly extinguished and the knot of persons rapidly dispersed. For a moment and but a moment I was disconcerted to find myself in darkness, but, recollecting that it was late and about time for the moon to rise,

---

[1] Ruggles and Doherty, op. cit., p. 445.
[2] Ibid., footnote 1, col. 1, p. 444.

I proceeded on, not having lost five steps, merely making a pause without stopping.'[1]

It is not on record that Welles ever made a report of this little adventure to the authorities, and the newspapers of that day made no mention of it.

The faked attempt on Johnson's life calls for an explanation. Who profited by it? Certainly not the assassins. The fury against them could only be further intensified by the belief that they had intended to spread terror in Washington by a carnival of murder. Then who could possibly wish to create the illusion of an organized wholesale massacre while singling out Lincoln and Seward as the only real victims?

The President and the Secretary of State were the two men in power whose programme of reconstruction chiefly stressed conciliation. Lincoln especially was willing, nay anxious, to have the South resume, unpenalized, its former role in the concert of all the states. Stanton and Johnson, on the contrary, were at that time the South's worst enemies. They were not only in favour of treating the Confederacy as conquered territory but even vowed that a traitor's death awaited the leaders of their enemies. Had Lincoln and Seward alone been attacked, it could have been suspected that the plot had its origin in the minds of Radical Republicans who hated Lincoln and Seward and what they stood for; but if both friends and enemies of the Southern people were the apparent victims in the murder plot, then—so it would be reasoned—it was the product of brains that tried to rob the North of its entire Government and thereby render it impotent. In other words, if Lincoln's assassination were only part of a plot to throw the North into anarchy, the inference would be justified that the murder was a last and despairing war move of the dying Confederacy. But if the existence of such a plot could not be proved, the South would be innocent, and suspicion would naturally fall on the Radicals of Lincoln's own party. They were the only ones who were benefited.

The grave question of who instigated Lincoln's assassination may hinge on the genuineness of the attempts on the lives of Grant, Stanton, and Johnson.

[1] Welles, *Diary*, II, p. 284.

CHAPTER XVI

Stanton Invents a Novel Torture

The conspirators—or those whom the Government chose to designate as such—were eight in number. Mrs. Mary E. Surratt, a boarding-house keeper of Washington, formerly of Surrattsville, Maryland, was the only woman among them. The remainder were: Lewis Paine, the young gladiator who had assaulted Seward; David E. Herold, Booth's companion during his flight; Dr. Samuel A. Mudd, who had set the assassin's broken leg and had harboured him for several hours; and George A. Atzerodt, whose room at the Kirkwood House had yielded such generous information. In addition to these there were Samuel B. Arnold and Michael O'Laughlin, friends of Booth and former Confederate soldiers, who admitted having participated in the plot to abduct Lincoln as a war measure; and, finally, Ed. Spangler, a scene-shifter at Ford's Theatre, who was accused of having facilitated the murderer's escape from the playhouse. For a few days these suspects were merely held in chains and in close confinement; but on 23 April a peculiar order was issued by Stanton, reading as follows:

'. . . that the prisoners on board iron-clads . . . for better security against conversation shall have a canvass bag put over the head of each and tied around the neck, with a hole for proper breathing and eating, but not seeing. . . .'[1]

The war that was just drawing to a close had produced a great many barbarities reminiscent of medieval tortures. Prisoners were shackled in various ways designed to produce pain; they

[1] DeWitt, *Judicial Murder of Mary E. Surratt* (John Murphy & Co., Baltimore, 1895), p. 13.

were starved, and often they had to carry heavy cannon balls until they fell from exhaustion. Stringing up by the thumbs, or even partial hanging to the point of death, were favourite methods of punishment or intimidation among the more brutal of the soldiery. But the war between the states does not reveal a single instance of hooding suspects; and a thorough search through all the refined processes of inflicting agony which were in vogue among Oriental or Spanish inquisitors has failed to disclose a single instance of this particular punishment. Stanton must have invented it specially for the occasion. The object of this departure from the recognized methods of torture—if there are such things—seems to be without rhyme or reason. Yet Stanton's actions were seldom without a definite purpose.

That the hooding of the prisoners really produced an exquisite form of suffering cannot be doubted. Sam Arnold, one of those upon whom Stanton's device was practised, bore witness in later days to the distress he and his companions had to endure, describing it in these words:

'The covering for the head was made of canvas, which covered the entire head and face, dropping down in front to the lower portion of the chest. It had cords attached, which were tied around the neck and body in such manner that to remove it was a physical impossibility . . . it being with the greatest difficulty, and frequently impossible, to place food in my mouth, a sentinel kindly volunteering his services to perform that office for me . . . daylight never lit upon the eye, they not even permitting the cap to be withdrawn for the purpose of washing the swollen, bloated and soiled visage.'[1]

When the trial of the conspirators began, a new and differently constructed hood was prepared for the prisoners. It was of a still more fiendish pattern than the one formerly used. It fitted the head tightly and contained cotton pads placed directly over the eyes and ears. These pads pushed the eyeballs far back into their sockets. One small aperture to breathe through, opposite the nose, and one other, to admit food, opposite the mouth, were the only openings provided.

The humane prison surgeon, Dr. George Loring Porter, intervened with Stanton to ease the brutality with which his

[1] Samuel A. Arnold, 'The Lincoln Plot', *Baltimore American*, 1902.

Sam Arnold.
(Arraigned.)

Sketch of Sam Arnold made by General Lew Wallace. The hood actually worn by the prisoners completely covered eyes, nose, and chin

By courtesy of General Lew Wallace Study, Crawfordsville, Indiana

charges were treated. He made it plain that in the hot summer days at Washington the constant pressure of these thickly padded hoods might bring about insanity. He was led to believe that he actually succeeded in having the padding reduced to less agonizing proportions.[1] It was not the intention of those in power, however, to give real heed to Dr. Porter's protests. According to Arnold's statement, the torture was actually increased.

The secretary's official order intimated that the hoods were to serve as 'better security against conversation' on the part of the prisoners. The question naturally arises why it was of such importance to keep these unfortunates from talking. What could they have gained by it? They might have consoled each other in their misery, but they would have wasted their time if they had planned an escape from their strongly guarded prison. On the other hand, their remarks might have brought out some information which the administration should have been anxious to acquire.

After the accused were taken from the gunboat in the river to the penitentiary on the old Arsenal grounds, they were lodged in solitary cells on different tiers and separated from each other as far as possible. But instead of loosening the bonds in which the prisoners were held, this change of location brought with it further restrictions. The captives' hands were secured in what was known as stiff shackles, so named because the handcuffs were fastened to each other by a bar of iron about fourteen inches long, which prevented the moving of one arm without a corresponding movement of the other.[2] Incidentally, this made it impossible for the prisoners, blinded as they were, to write out legible messages. Furthermore, each was attended by guards, who were not permitted to talk to him. Visitors had to present passes signed by Secretary of War Stanton and countersigned by the Secretary of the Navy. As it was almost impossible to obtain such passes, there were no visitors.

There was now no chance for the prisoners to communicate with the outside world in any manner. For all practical purposes, they were blind, deaf, dumb, and paralysed. Torture is usually

[1] George L. Porter, 'How Booth's Body Was Hidden', *Magazine of History*, vol. 38, No. 1, p. 30.
[2] Oldroyd, op. cit., pp. 120, 123.

employed to extort confessions from the accused; this mad invention of Stanton's made confessions impossible. Was there method in this madness?

'I was the only person permitted to converse with the conspirators without witnesses,' wrote Dr. Porter. But his official instructions forbade even him to answer any question or to make any remarks not connected with a physician's duties. 'To prevent all possible chance of communication,' the doctor continued, 'aside from being ironed . . . each of the prisoners virtually occupied three cells; that is, there was a vacant cell on each side of the one occupied by a prisoner. This was the method taken to prevent any attempt at communication by means of knocking or rapping, which is in vogue in so many of our prisons. . . . A company of infantry . . . was constantly on guard in the penitentiary room. Its members could see the guards standing on the different galleries in front of the cells.'[1]

Dr. Porter described the hoods as being padded an inch thick with cotton; they soon had their effect upon his charges, who were deprived of light and air.

'I was afraid that they would become mentally affected before their trial . . .' the physician reported to the Secretary of War. His judgement was confirmed by Dr. Gray, head of the Utica infirmary, a noted insanity expert of that time, who agreed that the hoods were likely to cause mental derangement. A joint representation was made to Stanton, and the two physicians were assured that the hoods would be removed, that daily exercise would be given the prisoners, and that they would be furnished with reading matter.[2] None of these promises was kept.

That the health of the conspirators was not of great moment to their jailors is also attested to by a story of Arnold's, regarding the only bath allowed him before the beginning of the trial. He was forced into a tub of ice-cold water and, shivering as with the ague, was made fun of by the detective who was watching him.[3]

There is no question that the hoods, in combination with the shackles and the solitary confinement, did prevent all com-

[1] George L. Porter, op. cit., pp. 30, 31.
[2] Ibid., p. 30.
[3] Arnold, 'The Lincoln Plot' in *Baltimore American*, 1902.

munication on the part of the prisoners, just as Stanton had commanded. It is far less plain why these unheard of efforts were made to prevent such intercourse. What the suspects may have said among themselves did not matter. Was it something these unfortunates could have made known to others that had to be suppressed by such desperate devices?

Of all the prisoners Mrs. Surratt alone escaped the ordeal of the hood and the stiff shackles. She was also allowed visits from her daughter and from two Catholic priests. Common prudence kept the War Department from hooding its only woman prisoner; the danger of public indignation, if it had become known that she had been so treated, was too great. To Mrs. Surratt, in all likelihood, a promise of clemency was held out.

'That Mrs. Surratt would be sentenced to imprisonment', wrote Wilson in *John Wilkes Booth*, 'few doubted, but that she would be hanged, few, if any, for one moment imagined. . . . All the assurances of her legal counsel, her friends, and her faithful daughter, were of a character to reconcile her to the thought of a prison sentence that might ultimately be commuted. . . .'[1]

'Her, too?' asked the executioner, Captain Rath, in astonishment on the day of the hanging. When General Hancock, in command of the proceedings, had failed to appear at the expected hour, Rath, like every one in Washington, had felt sure that Mrs. Surratt would be saved.[2]

General Hancock himself entertained secret hopes that the hanging would not take place. He had stationed cavalrymen at points between the White House and the Arsenal to speed the tidings, should the President relent and grant a pardon.[3]

'She had all along been encouraged to hope,' commented DeWitt. 'She, herself, had never been able to realize the possibility of a capital condemnation in her own case.'

When Mrs. Surratt realized that her hopes had been in vain, it was too late to talk, even had she intended to do so. She col-

[1] Francis Wilson, *John Wilkes Booth* (Houghton Mifflin, Boston, 1911), p. 101.

[2] John A. Gray, 'Fate of the Lincoln Conspirators' in *McClure's Magazine* (Oct. 1911), p. 636.

[3] John W. Clampitt, 'Trial of Mrs. Surratt' in *North American Review* (Sept. 1880), p. 238.

lapsed and remained in a semi-delirious condition until the end.

'During the remainder of the day and throughout the night, she was so prostrated by physical weakness and mental derangement as to necessitate medical aid to keep her alive and sane.'[1]

Thus, even without hoods, means were found to silence Mrs. Surratt.

If it be true that the extraordinary method of hooding and shackling the male conspirators was a measure taken to insure their silence—and no direct proof for this assumption exists—it was imperative that they all should suffer the penalty of death; for their gagging could not be continued indefinitely. Although Judge-Advocate Holt and his assistant, Bingham, tried vigorously to have the death-sentence passed on all the defendants, the military commission balked at this wholesale hanging. The lives of Dr. Mudd, O'Laughlin, Arnold, and Spangler were spared, and they were sentenced to prison at Albany, New York. Delivered from the clutches of military discipline, and confined in a state jail, the victims of Stanton's wrath would soon have been at liberty to talk. But this was not allowed to happen. On 5 July Andrew Johnson decreed that the survivors of the trial should be sent to the penitentiary at Albany; on the fifteenth this order was suddenly altered 'so as to direct that the said Arnold, Mudd, Spangler, and O'Laughlin, be confined at hard labor in the military prison at Dry Tortugas, Florida. . . .'[2] No reason for this alteration was given to the public. According to Welles, it was Stanton who had mentioned to the President the desirability of having the unfortunate victims sent to the far-off southern island.[3]

The Dry Tortugas was a military prison and it was a long way off; no fear need be entertained that curious newspaper correspondents would get from the prisoners whatever secrets they may have been suspected of possessing. But even this removal to the distant fort, surrounded by vast stretches of tropical seas, could not be considered a constant barrier to communication. The prisoners would naturally talk to each other and to the

[1] DeWitt, *Mary E. Surratt*, p. 120.
[2] Pitman, op. cit., pp. 249–50.
[3] Welles, *Diary*, II, p. 334.

guards. The garrisons would be exchanged, and the soldiers, returning to their firesides, might disseminate whatever tales they had heard. Removing the conspirators from New York state to Fort Jefferson in Florida would only postpone the day of reckoning. Hence, more interference with their liberty of speech could be expected. It was not long in coming.

The prisoners reached the Tortugas Islands on 24 July 1865. On 17 August the sinister shadow of General L. C. Baker crept into the comparative peace and quiet of the fortress, and brought new misery to the condemned men. On that day the chief of the secret service dispatched a message saying that he had discovered a conspiracy to liberate the state prisoners, the term by which they were known in their new surroundings.

Louisville, Ky.
17 *August* 1865.
9 a.m.

HON. T. T. ECKERT,
Acting Assistant Secretary of War:

I have important papers. I think the commanding officer at Dry Tortugas should be put on guard against an attempt to rescue the State prisoners in his charge. A company is organizing in New Orleans for that purpose. I have all the facts from a reliable source.

[signed] L. C. BAKER,
Brig.-Gen., Pro. Mar., War Dep't.[1]

Louisville was not a particularly likely spot in which to pick up information regarding a plot for a Florida jail delivery, and neither Baker nor any one else ever volunteered further information regarding it. Nevertheless, severe counter measures were immediately taken.

New Orleans
20 *August* 1865.

COMMANDING OFFICER, *Tortugas:*

The enclosed telegram is forwarded for your information. You will at once take measures to prevent the accomplishment

---

[1] Arnold, op. cit.

of such purpose as the surprise of your post and the release of the prisoners therein.

Report by return of the bearer the strength of your garrison.

Very respectfully, . . .

P. H. SHERIDAN,

Maj.-Gen.[1]

Soon afterward a swift steamer arrived from Fort Monroe with another staff officer, bearing a letter of the same import from the adjutant-general of the army, and explicit in its instructions. '. . . you will place the four state prisoners', so the communication read, '. . . under such restraint . . . as shall make abortive any attempt at escape or rescue.'[2]

'At that time', wrote Captain W. R. Prentice, who was then in charge of the prisoners, 'Dr. Mudd was quietly pursuing his duties as day nurse among the sick prisoners; Arnold was writing in the provost-marshal's office; Spangler was enjoying life and whistling away the days as he wielded hammer and saw and plane; and O'Laughlin was pining to his death. Looking back to those days, I am certain that some one played a practical joke on General Baker, the Secretary of War, and General Sheridan. . . .'[3]

One wonders.

A little later Dr. Mudd and his comrades were put to hard labour and were confined in a small damp room. They were at a loss to account for this harsh treatment.

'We were', wrote Arnold, *'denied all intercourse with everyone* upon the desolate island, and our footsteps were always accompanied by an armed guard. . . .'[4]

After the lapse of a year matters had gone from bad to worse. 'By January 1867', so Arnold wrote, 'the system . . . of confinement remained unchanged.' The objects of Baker's and Stanton's solicitude were still forbidden to hold conversation with any one but their own cellmates. The enlisted men treated the unfortunate state prisoners with kindness, and some of the officers even apologized for the severity of their treatment;

[1] W. R. Prentice, 'On the Dry Tortugas' in *McClure's Magazine* (Apr. 1902), p. 570.

[2] Arnold, op. cit.

[3] Prentice, loc. cit.

[4] Arnold, op. cit.; author's italics.

it was, they declared, the result of orders 'from higher authority'.[1]

Dr. Mudd, writing to his wife, confirmed these statements. 'We can't move five steps', he reported, 'without permission of the sergeant of the guard. . . . *This . . . has been brought about by no word or act of ours.* All the rest of the prisoners . . . are allowed the freedom of the island. . . .' The only information granted the condemned men was that *orders for this treatment emanated from the War Department.*[2]

'. . . no such conspiracy as detailed by Gen. Baker ever existed . . .' protested Arnold. 'We were made the leaders so that further persecution and tortures could be heaped upon us.'[3] Perhaps Arnold was wrong; the tortures and the persecution may have been only incidental and unavoidable. What evidently was required was *silence*. If silence could have been produced again by hoods and manacled hands, who knows but what the unfortunates would have been spared the other tortures?

At one time smallpox broke out on the island, and the patient was placed in such close proximity to the dungeon of the state prisoners that they expected to fall victims to this dread disease. 'The action of the authorities in this affair was so pointed', Arnold continued, '. . . that it was done for the express purpose of inoculating us with this fearful and loathsome malady. . . . What mind among those mazy windings can unearth the cause of all these secret machinations?'[4]

Sometimes—not often—an opportunity is given the student of history to check his inferences as a mathematician does. The supposition that Stanton and his satellites were afraid of some knowledge which the conspirators possessed is simply an unpleasant thought; it may appear probable from the events as they unfold themselves; but it cannot be proved.

Nevertheless, it is tempting to follow an hypothesis purely as a speculation when it can be substantiated by independent evidence, as in this case. If the Government really was anxious to

[1] Arnold, op. cit.
[2] Nettie Mudd, *The Life of Dr. Samuel A. Mudd* (Neale Publishing Co., New York, 1906), pp. 204–5, 139, 143, 227, 244. Author's italics.
[3] Arnold, op. cit.
[4] Ibid.

prevent Booth's associates from disclosing anything they knew, then the tactics it employed would have to be changed as circumstances demanded. With those plotters who were under arrest physical means to enforce silence could be employed; these were unusual and brutal, but undoubtedly effective. With Mrs. Surratt a more conciliatory attitude would have to be adopted.

'It was not really believed, however, that any extreme sentence would be pronounced upon Mrs. Surratt in view of her age, her sex, her previous reputation, and the character of the evidence against her,' wrote Clara E. Laughlin in *The Death of Lincoln*.[1]

As a matter of fact gossip in Washington had it that she would be pardoned at the last moment,[2] and there is every reason to think that the poor woman herself believed in her last-minute deliverance, even as she was carried to the gallows.

Fugitives who had been away from the seat of the conspiracy for some time would present an entirely different problem. If they already had been given an opportunity to converse freely with others, imparting to them whatever secrets they knew, then their return for prosecution would be fraught with danger to the accusers. Death, or else permanent banishment, would answer in their cases better than vigorous pursuit.

Well, Booth himself did not come back alive. Stanton's most trustworthy lieutenants had been sent out to capture him and not a hair of his head was to be harmed; but all they brought back was a body.

If Booth possessed some dangerous knowledge the question of whether he would return a live prisoner or whether death would have sealed his lips forever must have weighed heavily on Stanton's mind. Was it a hint of this that Baker was trying to convey in his description of his chief's strange behaviour when advised of Booth's capture?

Baker had exclaimed, 'We have got Booth', when he stormed into Stanton's room; but he had failed to state whether they had 'got Booth' dead or alive. The tale of the capture proceeded, however, and the dead man's effects were laid on the table. 'Then he [Stanton] got up and put on his coat very coolly.'[3] Booth was

---

[1] Laughlin, op. cit., p. 189.
[2] DeWitt, *Assassination*, pp. 137, 139.
[3] L. C. Baker, op. cit., p. 540.

dead and had failed to talk. There was no further ground for apprehension.

Boston Corbett, who claimed to have fired the shot that killed the assassin, never was punished for disobedience of orders. Conger charged him with breach of military discipline and returned him to Washington for court-martial. When the matter was brought before Stanton, he relented. He praised Conger for leaving the culprit to the discretion of his superiors and dismissed the complaint against Corbett. 'The rebel is dead—the patriot lives,' he said; 'he has saved us continued excitement, delay and expense—the patriot is released.'[1]

Stanton's reference to the continued excitement from which he was saved is interesting. Yet, there is nothing conclusive in all this. Baker is an unreliable witness; his insinuations may have been prompted by motives of his own, and the shooting of Booth could have been an accident.

The War Department had insistently demanded that Booth should be brought back alive. It is remarkable, therefore, that there is at least one instance known where positive orders were given to kill him if he were found. This happened at the house of Dr. Mudd, shortly after his arrest. The authorities were then still uncertain of Booth's whereabouts and suspected that he was hiding in the near-by swamps. It was hoped that a trap could be laid for the assassin by permitting Mrs. Mudd to take food to him. One day a relative came over to get some garden seeds. To procure them, Mrs. Mudd took a basket, and the two ladies proceeded to see the gardener.

'A few moments after we entered the garden we were surrounded by soldiers,' related Mrs. Mudd. 'One officer came over and demanded to know what we had in the basket. The little packages of seeds were unwrapped, the contents examined. With a crestfallen look he remarked, "I thought you were carrying food to Booth." '[2]

Dr. Mudd's house was guarded by three young detectives, Wallace Kirby, Aquilla Allen, and Bernard Adamson, under direction of William P. Wood, superintendent of the Old Capitol Prison in Washington. *These young men were instructed to*

[1] Byron Berkeley Johnson, *Abraham Lincoln and Boston Corbett* (Waltham, Mass., 1914), pp. 37, 38.
[2] Mudd, op. cit., p. 35.

shoot any one who dared to enter the garden. They did not even take precautions to keep these orders secret, for their intentions were fully known in the Mudd household.[1] Captain Wood also made his headquarters in the physician's house, but went out during the day in search of Booth. What he would have done if he had encountered the fugitive can only be surmised.

The indications multiply that the man who was shot at Garrett's Farm was not killed unintentionally.

[1] Mudd, op. cit., pp. 35, 36.

CHAPTER XVII

Stanton's Inner Council

Stanton had few friends, and even fewer employees in whom he could absolutely trust. In the emergency following Lincoln's death he carefully placed his most loyal assistants where they could aid him best.

One of these men was Major Thomas T. Eckert, whom he had promoted from captain to brigadier-general and on whose devotion he could depend. Eckert was the man who had refused to accompany Lincoln to the theatre. Now there was plenty of confidential work for him in the capital. It was in his custody, for instance, that Lewis Paine was placed until the day of his execution. With this conspirator, who probably knew more than any other, Eckert kept vigil for days, remaining with him almost constantly.[1] One would think that an ordinary detective should have been able to fill this post of observation. Why an assistant secretary of war was assigned to it remains unexplained.

Another man on whose blind allegiance Stanton could count was Charles A. Dana. On 1 April 1862 Dana had resigned his position as an editor of the *New York Tribune*.[2] Stanton, who was then laying the foundation for his censorship of the Press, perceived the value of having a trained journalist on his secretarial staff, and immediately engaged his services. That Dana was on bad terms with Stanton's untiring critic Greeley, and that he belonged to a faction opposed to Seward, may have had some

---

[1] Bates, *Lincoln in the Telegraph Office*, p. 380.
[2] *Appleton's Cyclopædia of American Biography* (D. Appleton & Co. (D. Appleton-Century Co.), New York, 1892 ed.), II, p. 64.

influence in his selection.[1] Dana's powers of observation were appreciated by the War Secretary, who used him quite openly to pry into the affairs of his generals. He was sent to spy out the Western armies, as Coolidge expressed it.[2] The ostensible function with which Dana was entrusted was that of special commissioner to investigate the pay service; 'but your real duty', the secretary reminded him, 'will be to report to me every day what you see'.[3]

In 1863 Dana was appointed Assistant Secretary of War, and in this capacity he spent months at a time in the military zones, exchanging confidential reports with his chief. Some of these dispatches, taken from the records of the last part of the war, illustrate the part Dana played in Stanton's entourage.

On 5 April 1865 he telegraphed:

GENERAL GRANT HAS COMMANDED ARMIES IN PERSON SINCE BEGINNING OF OPERATIONS, HAVING GOT DISGUSTED WITH GENERAL MEADE'S STICKLING ABOUT HIS OWN DIGNITY.[4]

On 10 April, Stanton wired the following significant message to Dana at Richmond:

YOU WILL PROCEED IMMEDIATELY TO GENERAL GRANT'S HEADQUARTERS. REPORT YOUR ARRIVAL THERE AND FURNISH SUCH DETAILS AS MAY BE OF INTEREST OR USE TO THE DEPARTMENT.[5]

Only a few lines, but pregnant with meaning.

Even Lincoln's actions were included in Dana's espionage. On 5 April, Stanton's aide reported:

JUDGE CAMPBELL AND MR. MEYER HAD AN INTERVIEW WITH THE PRESIDENT HERE THIS MORNING. . . . GENERAL WEITZEL, WHO WAS PRESENT, TELLS ME THAT THE PRESIDENT DID NOT PROMISE THE AMNESTY, BUT TOLD THEM HE HAD THE PARDONING POWER, AND WOULD SAVE ANY REPENTANT

---

[1] Charles A. Dana, *Recollections of the Civil War* (D. Appleton & Co. (D. Appleton-Century Co.), New York, 1902), pp. 1, 2.
[2] Coolidge, op. cit., p. 126.
[3] Dana, op. cit., p. 21.
[4] *Official Records*, I, vol. 46, part 3, p. 574.
[5] Ibid., p. 684.

SINNER FROM HANGING. . . . THE PRESIDENT WENT TO CITY
POINT THIS MORNING. . . .[1]

Two days later he added:

MEETING OF FIVE MEMBERS OF THE VIRGINIA LEGISLATURE
HELD HERE TO-DAY UPON THE PRESIDENT'S PROPOSITIONS
TO JUDGE CAMPBELL. THE PRESIDENT SHOWED ME THE
PAPERS CONFIDENTIALLY TO-DAY.[2]

This meeting was one which Lincoln was particularly anxious
to keep secret; that he told Dana about it in confidence did not
seem to deter Stanton's secretary from giving his chief the news
as quickly as he could.

Stanton had good reasons to consider Charles A. Dana a
trustworthy servant and a deserving member of his coterie.

Colonel Baker was another of Stanton's confidants. He was
busy in Washington mapping out the plans for Booth's pursuit,
and it was left to his cousin to lead the successful expedition to
Garrett's Farm. One may read something of interest about
Baker in the *Recollections* of Chittenden, Lincoln's Registrar of
the Treasury and, incidentally, a great admirer of Stanton:

'Baker wore the uniform, and probably had authority to assume the rank, of a colonel in the army. He took into his service
. . . men who claimed to have any aptitude for detective work,
without recommendation, investigation, or any inquiry, beyond
his own inspection. . . . How large his regiment ultimately grew
is uncertain, but at one time he asserted that it exceeded two
thousand men.

'With this force at his command, protected against interference from the judicial authorities, Baker became a law unto
himself. He instituted a veritable Reign of Terror. He dealt with
every accused person in the same manner; with a reputable
citizen as with a deserter or petty thief. He did not require the
formality of a written charge; it was quite sufficient for any
person to suggest to Baker that a citizen might be doing something that was against law. He was immediately arrested, hand-
cuffed, and brought to Baker's office, at that time in the base-

[1] *Official Records*, I, vol. 46, part 3, p. 575.
[2] Ibid., p. 619.

ment of the Treasury. There he was subjected to a brow-beating examination, in which Baker was said to rival in impudence some heads of the criminal bar. This examination was repeated as often as he chose. Men were kept in his rooms for weeks, without warrant, affidavit, or other semblance of authority. If the accused took any measures for his own protection, he was hurried into the Old Capitol Prison, where he was beyond the reach of the civil authorities. . . .

'Corruption spread like a contagious disease, wherever the operations of these detectives extended. . . . Honest manufacturers and dealers, who paid their taxes, were pursued without mercy for the most technical breaches of the law, and were quickly driven out of business. The dishonest rapidly accumulated wealth, which they could well afford to share with their protectors.'[1]

Chittenden once caught Colonel Baker committing a forgery. 'Perfectly unabashed, without a blush,' the Registrar reported, 'the fellow smiled as he looked me in the face and said, "That game didn't work, did it?"'[2]

It was this same Colonel Baker about whom the minority report of the judiciary committees in 1867 contemptuously stated:

'And there can be no doubt that to his many previous outrages, entitling him to an unenviable immortality, he has added that of wilful and deliberate perjury; and we are glad to know that no one member of the committee deems any statement made by him as worthy of the slightest credit. What a blush of shame will tinge the cheek of the American student in future ages, when he reads that this miserable wretch for years held, as it were, in the hollow of his hand, the liberties of the American people.'[3]

There remained William P. Wood, another of Stanton's intimates, who owed to the War Minister his appointment as warden of the Old Capitol Prison, an appointment involving great

[1] L. E. Chittenden, *Recollections of President Lincoln* (Harper & Bros., New York, 1891), pp. 345–6.

[2] Ibid., p. 349.

[3] *Impeachment Investigation*, p. 111 (40th Congress, First Session, Rep. Com. No. 7).

privileges. Originally a maker of models and patterns, Wood was made superintendent of the Old Capitol Prison on 13 February 1862, and became one of Stanton's most devoted aides. His position was one that the Secretary of War never would have given to any one he could not fully trust.

The story of Wood's life contains a chapter that does not make pleasant reading.[1] In 1854 Stanton had been engaged in the famous McCormick-Manny reaper case. Helping him defend Manny against a patent infringement suit brought by Cyrus H. McCormick were Abraham Lincoln and Peter H. Watson, the latter then a patent attorney in Washington. McCormick claimed that a curved divider, separating the standing from the falling grain—an essential feature of a successful harvesting machine—was his invention, fully covered by patents, but boldly copied by Manny in the construction of his reapers. Stripped of all technicalities, the whole case hinged on this point. If McCormick had emphasized the curved blade in his original conception, he would win the decision; if he had used a straight divider, he would lose it.

McCormick, represented among others by Reverdy Johnson —who a few years later was to defend Mrs. Surratt—felt secure on this point. He was dumbfounded, therefore, when Stanton's client exhibited to the court one of the early McCormick models, showing a straight blade. The old machine had been obtained from a man named Sampson, who had bought it from the inventor himself in 1840, and who testified particularly that its condition when he sold it was exactly the same as when bought by him fifteen years previously. All cross-examination of the witness proved fruitless; he clung tenaciously to his statement. As a result McCormick lost the case.

Forty-two years later, on 16 December 1897, there appeared before a notary-public in Washington William P. Wood, then a sick old man, who, at the request of Frank A. Flower, Stanton's biographer, made a sworn statement for the purpose of awarding to Cyrus H. McCormick the justice which a misled court of law had withheld from him.

It appears that after the old reaper had been bought from

---

[1] Flower, op. cit., pp. 63–5; also McCormick Historical Association, Chicago.

Mr. Sampson, then a man eighty-two years of age and almost blind, Wood secretly changed the curved piece on the divider into a straight one, and by the use of vinegar, rust, and dirt hid his handiwork so well that no traces of the fraud were detected or even suspected. Wood himself was not known in the case and consequently was not put on the stand. Peter H. Watson, who aided Stanton as a patent attorney, had previously secured for his client a patent which necessitated the reversal of a previous decision on the part of the patent office. Finally, Watson secured expert witnesses who testified that the altered machine was substantially in accord with McCormick's claims. This was contrary to the truth, so Wood now declared on his oath.

The drawings necessary for Wood to make his models were furnished him by Albert E. H. Johnson, at that time a clerk in Watson's office.

Mr. Wood took pains to state in his affidavit that no one else but himself had any knowledge of what had been done. Even Manny's attorneys were not let in on the secret, and Stanton, while welcoming the reaper with the straight divider, which helped him win his case, had no idea whence it had so providentially appeared.

A. E. H. Johnson told Stanton's biographer that when the models were placed under protection of the court, Watson gave the old janitor who had charge of the rooms the sum of twenty-five dollars.

'Manny had the two ablest managers in America in charge of his case—Edwin M. Stanton and Peter H. Watson,' Johnson declared. 'If they had been on the other side McCormick would have won, as he deserved. . . .'[1]

It is worthy of note that Stanton's associates in the reaper case did not fare badly in later years. But inasmuch as Wood swore that the attorneys in the case knew nothing about his operations, it must be presumed that Stanton made Watson Assistant Secretary of War because he was a good patent attorney; that he gave Johnson the rank of major and attached him to his office as confidential secretary because he was an excellent draftsman; and that he appointed Wood superintendent of the Old Capitol Prison because he was an experienced pattern-maker.

[1] Flower, op. cit., p. 65 (footnote); McCormick Historical Association, Chicago.

It was to this Captain Wood that the promising task of lying in wait for Booth at Dr. Mudd's house was delegated, and it was he who had given orders to shoot on sight any one who dared enter the premises. The only person of interest who could have entered was Booth, provided that he was concealed in the swamps and would be driven by hunger to approach the house. Was Wood acting on secret orders from Stanton, or did he take it upon himself to have the assassin shot against his master's command? And if Dr. Mudd's home was considered a crucial point, why was it assigned to the keeper of a prison in Washington? With a multitude of detectives at the command of the War Department, why was it necessary to remove a jail warden from his post, at a time when suspects were being delivered to his prison by the hundreds and his duties at home should have absorbed his entire attention?

CHAPTER XVIII

The Odyssey of John Harrison Surratt

John Surratt, the next in rank to Booth among the conspirators —at least he was so considered by the authorities—had escaped to Canada. No great efforts appear to have been made by Stanton's various departments to intercept his flight. At 9.40 on the morning of 15 April the provost-marshal's office in Washington wired the following circular to the border stations:[1]

'It is believed that the assassins of the President and Secretary Seward are attempting to escape to Canada.

'You will make a careful and thorough examination of all persons attempting to cross from the United States into Canada, and will arrest all suspicious persons. The most vigilant scrutiny on your part, and the force at your disposal, is demanded.

'A description of the parties supposed to be implicated in the murder will be telegraphed you to-day. But in the meantime be active in preventing the crossing of any suspicious persons.

By orders of the *Secretary of War*

N. L. JEFFERS,

Brevet Brigadier-General.'

Booth's description could have been sent out immediately but it was not. *In fact, so far as the Official Records show, it was never sent out at all.* To E. G. Spaulding at Buffalo, a former Congressman, C. A. Dana sent a wire at 8.40 in the evening, picturing Booth as 'five feet six inches tall; of a slight graceful figure; black hair, and eyes rather close together, and pale complexion; about twenty-six years old';[2] but to the chiefs of police of the

---

[1] *New York Evening Post*, 15 Apr. 1865, second edition, p. 3, col. 6.
[2] *Official Records*, I, vol. 46, part 3, p. 782.

northern cities a telegram went out that did not even mention Booth; *and instead of giving a description of Surratt, it described Atzerodt.*

> Washington, D. C.
> 15 April 1865.
> (Sent 9 p.m.)

CHIEF OF POLICE,
Baltimore:

The following is a description of G. A. Atzerodt, the assassin of Mr. Seward. He is twenty-six or twenty-eight years old, five feet eight inches high; light complexion, but browned from exposure; brown hair; long and rather curly mustache and goatee, dark from being dyed; wore dark pants, vest, and coat, and long gray overcoat; was rather round-shouldered and stooping position; was in company with a man giving his name as S. Thomas, about thirty years of age; poorly clad in dark suit, low slouch hat; wore a mustache and heavy beard; was a rough and weather-beaten looking man.

> C. A. DANA,
> *Assistant Secretary of War.*

(Same to chiefs of police Philadelphia, New York, &c.)[1]

It is not known if and when the War Department corrected its gross error and substituted Surratt's name and picture for that of Atzerodt. According to the official records on file no such correction was ever made.

It will be remembered that between two and half-past two in the morning of 15 April, Superintendent of Police Richards had made up his mind that Surratt was implicated in the crime and had entered his house in order to apprehend him. The War Department was in possession of the same information and knew that Surratt was involved in the kidnapping scheme.

And so, equipped with a false signalment, and further burdened with the thought of the man Thomas who did not figure in this story at all, the police looked in vain for an Atzerodt who never appeared. In the meantime Surratt slipped into Canada without difficulty.

[1] *Official Records*, I, vol. 46, part 3, p. 783.

'When I stepped on the platform at the depot at St. Albans [the border station],' Surratt related in a lecture given five years later, 'I noticed that one of the detectives scanned every one, head and foot, myself as well as the rest. . . . I had provided myself with an Oxford-cut jacket and round-top hat peculiar to Canada at that time. . . . I believe that costume guarded me safely through St. Albans. I went in with others and moved around, with the detectives standing there most of the time looking at us. . . . One of the detectives approached me, stared me directly in the face, and I looked him quietly back. In a few moments I was speeding on my way to Montreal. . . .'[1]

Perhaps it was not altogether the Canadian make-up that was responsible for Surratt's lucky escape. With a description of Atzerodt in his hands the detective could hardly have been expected to arrest some one else.

At that it seems that Surratt, through one of the queerest of coincidences, had an extremely narrow escape at St. Albans. The *Burlington Times* on 18 April had finally brought a description of Booth, and a saloon-keeper there, eagerly watching all strangers in town, thought that Surratt somehow could be made to fit it. When asked in court, during the Surratt trial in 1867, if he recognized the defendant, he stated that the nose, eyes, forehead, height and actions of the accused appeared to be those of the man he had seen at St. Albans. At any rate, he had endeavoured at that time to have the suspicious stranger arrested.

'I followed him to the depot and tried to find an officer there. From that I started up town to find an officer,' he testified. Meeting an acquaintance, the cashier of a local bank, he went with him as far as the jail to find a policeman or detective, but failed to do so. 'The last I saw of him was at the depot, when I returned back there,' he added.

Q. How did he escape you?
A. I could not say. I could get no officer.[2]

When the bank official and his brother were examined, they

---

[1] Laughlin, op. cit., pp. 243–4.
[2] *Surratt Trial*, I, p. 358.

added the information that a photograph of Booth had arrived at the St. Albans hotel on the eighteenth. They calculated that the mail could have brought it there if it had been dispatched from Washington as late as the seventeenth. It was also disclosed that a train was standing on the tracks ready to leave for Montreal when they saw the last of the suspect. The cashier of the bank was quite certain that the man they had followed was identical with the defendant in the courtroom.

If Surratt had been stopped at St. Albans it would have been due to an odd mistake; but the facts that stand out as significant are: first, that no officers could be found in an important border town or at its depot to arrest a man supposed to be one of the assassins, although a train for Montreal was on the point of departing, and Montreal was one of the most likely havens for conspirators of Southern sympathies; further, that Booth's description did not reach the papers in St. Albans until the morning of the eighteenth, after an unexplained delay of three days; and lastly, that a photograph, purporting to be that of Booth, was such that some observers made it fit John Surratt, who did not resemble the assassin in any way.

There was one man who was in dead earnest about capturing Booth and every one else connected with the conspiracy. This man was Richards, chief of the Metropolitan Police Force. It was he who had given Booth's name to the Press and who had collected names of witnesses at his headquarters. The detectives who invaded Mrs. Surratt's house at two o'clock in the morning were city policemen, not Government agents. It was Richards who had vainly requested horses to lead his men over the Anacostia Bridge; and it was Richards again who had organized the first intelligent pursuit of Booth in southern Maryland, taking Wiechmann along to identify the fugitive, and had followed it up with a search in Baltimore on the next day.

It was this energetic police officer who, playing a lone hand, had tracked Surratt into Canada. His party left Washington on 17 April and, accompanied by Wiechmann, who knew Surratt's every thought, came very close to capturing him.

'One day', reported Surratt, 'I walked out and saw Weichmann on the lookout for me. He had little idea that I was so near. . . . I was told that they were going to search the house, and that I must leave immediately, which I did. They searched it before morning.'[1]

When Richards's men got back to Washington, and the Government heard of the unsuccessful exploit, the chief of police received scant praise for his efforts. The intra-departmental correspondence of the War Office contains in its file a curious letter bearing on this matter:

> *Headquarters Department of Washington*
> *Office Provost-Marshal General*
> *Defenses North of Potomac*
> *Washington, D.C. . . . 1865.*

Dear Col.

Richards the Supt. of Metrop. Police was here last evening to answer Foster's[2] querie about the sending of Weichmann and Holahan to Canada *on a wild chase after Surratt.* F. was ordered by the Secy. to find out all about the matter and therefore the above interview. *Richards said he had been at the Secy.'s office just before, and been severely reprimanded for sending the two men off.* . . .

> Yrs. truly
> H. S. O[LCOTT].

COL. BURNETT
(Rec'd. Apr. 25, 1865)[3]

Possibly Richards's ardour cooled after this experience. Having been taken to task for a 'wild chase' which had almost succeeded, it would have been a dense police chief who would not have felt that the hunt for the murderers and their accomplices was a personally conducted affair, and that his help was neither wanted nor appreciated. In a note Richards sent to Colonel H. L. Burnett on 4 May he wrote contritely:

'I have the honor to report that I have no testimony in my possession, nor have I taken any, relative to the assassination of the late President.

---

[1] Laughlin, op. cit., pp. 244–5.
[2] This was Colonel John A. Foster, one of Stanton's chief investigators. Holahan was, like Wiechmann, an inmate of Mrs. Surratt's boarding-house.
[3] War Department Archives. Author's italics.

'I have a hat which is supposed to have belonged to the late President, also a hat supposed to have been worn by the assassin, Booth, also a spur supposed to have been worn by Booth. These articles are subject to your order and can be delivered at any time, upon your receipt for them for my own protection.'[1]

This ends Richards' part in the pursuit of Booth and his accomplices. Although the police superintendent was put on the carpet for arranging the expedition to Canada in search of John Surratt the War Department afterwards claimed all the credit for the enterprise. Colonel Burnett, an assistant judge-advocate at the conspiracy trial, declared later that Wiechmann and Holahan had been sent to Montreal by Secretary Stanton's orders. He made this assertion with great positiveness before the Ohio Society of New York on 18 April 1892, in spite of the fact that the letters of Olcott and Richards had been addressed to him, and he knew that no one but Richards deserved credit for the Canadian expedition.[2]

The best test of whether the Government was anxious to bring back a conspirator who had been at large for some time and who could not be gagged, isolated, or put to death, was furnished by the case of John Surratt a few months later.

Surratt had continued his flight, and in September 1865, turned up in Liverpool, where his presence was made known immediately to the American authorities. He had then been absent for five months. Would Stanton's efforts now be directed toward keeping him out of his own country for much longer—for ever if possible?

Excerpts from the official correspondence relating to this matter speak for themselves.[3]

[1] War Department Archives.
[2] H. L. Burnett, *Assassination of President Lincoln and the Trial of the Assassins* (Ohio Society of New York, 1906), p. 596.
[3] House of Representatives, 39th Congress, Second Session, Exec. Doc. No. 9. Author's italics.

No. 538.   *United States Consulate*
                                              Liverpool
                                     27 September 1865.

SIR:

Yesterday, information was given me that—Surratt, one of
the persons implicated in the conspiracy to murder Mr. Lincoln,
was in Liverpool, or expected there within a day or two. I took
the affidavit of the person who gave me the information....

                              A. WILDING,
                                        Vice-Consul.

HON. WILLIAM H. SEWARD.

No. 539.   *United States Consulate*
                                              Liverpool
                                     30 September 1865.

SIR:

Since my dispatch No. 538, the supposed Surratt has arrived
in Liverpool, and is now staying at the oratory of the Roman
Catholic church of the Holy Cross....

I can, of course, do nothing further in the matter without Mr.
Adams's [U.S. minister to England] instructions and a warrant.
If it be Surratt, such a wretch ought not to escape....

                              H. [?] WILDING.

But the vice-consul at Liverpool probably got the shock of
his life when he received the reply of his superiors:

No. 476.   *Department of State*
                                              Washington
                                     13 October 1865.

SIR:

Your dispatches . . . have been received. In reply to your
No. 538 I have to inform you that, upon a consultation with the
Secretary of War and the Judge-Advocate-General, it is thought
advisable *that no action be taken in regard to the arrest of the
supposed John Surratt at present.*

                              W. HUNTER,
                                        Acting Secretary.

When the ship's surgeon, who had been Mr. Wilding's informant and who was so anxious to earn the reward of $25,000

for Surratt's capture, found himself baffled at Liverpool, he took up the thread of his endeavours upon his return to Canada.

Appearing before the United States consul at Montreal he volunteered additional information that would lead to the capture of Booth's accomplice. On 25 October 1865 the consul wrote to the State Department:[1]

No. 236.
It is Surratt's intention to go to Rome. . . .

I requested instructions in my telegram, *but hearing nothing yet*, I scarcely know what course to take. If an officer could proceed to England . . . I have no doubt but that Surratt's arrest might be effected, and thus the last of the conspirators against the lives of the President and Secretary of State be brought to justice. . . .

The Montreal consul was left waiting another two weeks before he heard anything from the State Department. Finally, on 11 November, he received the following cool reply:[2]

No. 164.
Your dispatches . . . have been received. The information communicated . . . has been properly availed of.

F. W. SEWARD,
Assistant Secretary.

On 13 November, the Secretary of State requested the attorney-general to 'procure an indictment against the said John H. Surratt as soon as convenient, with the view to demand his surrender'.[3]

This attempted interference of Seward with the work of Stanton's bureau must have been highly unwelcome. The blow was somehow averted, however, for congressional investigators of this episode reported later:

Whether an indictment was procured does not appear from the testimony, but it does appear that no demand for the surrender of Surratt was ever made upon the English government.'[4]

[1] House of Representatives, 39th Congress, Second Session, Exec. Doc. No. 9. Author's italics.
[2] Ibid.   [3] Ibid.
[4] House of Representatives, 39th Congress, Second Session, Report No. 33.

One would like to know more about the fate of Seward's request for the indictment and more of the reasons why no request was made upon the English Government; also why the available Government files in this matter are incomplete. But the spearhead of the congressional investigation was at that time pointed at President Johnson, and all matters not pertaining directly to him were considered extraneous.

The ship's surgeon, who could see the reward for Surratt's capture almost within his reach, kept pushing the case with undiminished vigour. In his statements to the United States consul at Montreal he did all he could to arouse the Government to immediate action. 'I hoped that an officer might have been sent out in the Nova Scotian, which sails tomorrow . . .' he complained; and to create further antagonism against the man whom he seemed to consider his private prey, he added, 'Surratt manifested no signs of penitence, but justified his action, and was bold and defiant . . . Surratt remarked repeatedly that he only desired to live two years longer, in which time he would serve President Johnson as Booth did Mr. Lincoln.'[1]

The last threat, so the worthy doctor must have felt, could not fail to bring quick action. It did. But the action was different from what he expected, for on 24 November Stanton issued his order No. 164, decreeing in substance that *the reward offered for the arrest of . . . John H. Surratt is revoked.*[2]

The committee on the judiciary, a short time later, suspecting that President Johnson was implicated in the murder of his predecessor, tried to fasten upon him the responsibility for this unexpected cancellation. The congressmen probably reasoned that such a step could not have been taken without a deep-seated motive. That Stanton, who had issued the order, might also have such a motive did not enter their minds. But the secretary took on himself whatever blame was attached to the move. 'It was done on my own responsibility,' he declared; 'the President left it at my discretion to do as I thought best in the matter.'[3]

Upon closer examination Stanton gave as his first reason for revoking the reward 'that many months had elapsed without

[1] House of Representatives, 39th Congress, Second Session, Exec. Doc. No. 9.
[2] Ibid. Report No. 33. Author's italics.
[3] Ibid.

accomplishing the arrest of these parties'. Considering that Surratt had come out of hiding only because many months had elapsed, such a statement, made under oath to a congressional committee, was most remarkable; moreover, the cancellation of the reward came only a month after the urgings from Montreal, and only eleven days after Seward had asked for Surratt's indictment.

The apathy of the Washington authorites enabled Surratt to travel unmolested through Europe. In April 1866 he arrived in Rome and, presumably for pecuniary reasons, enlisted as a Zouave in the Pope's service under the name of John Watson. Here he met a former schoolmate, named Sainte-Marie, to whom he confessed his identity, throwing himself on his mercy. Probably unaware that no further cash rewards awaited informers, Sainte-Marie hastened to the United States legation to betray his friend. On 23 April the American minister in Rome transmitted the whole story to Washington. Stanton had Surratt back on his hands again.

Perhaps by this time Sainte-Marie had been made acquainted with the revocation of the reward, but he remained steadfast in his denunciation. Sanctimoniously he hoped that 'justice to the ever lamented memory of President Lincoln will [would] be made'. Besides, he longed, as he added in his letter, 'to revisit my native land, and the grey hair of my father and mother, and wish to make of the United States my last and permanent home'.[1]

On 17 May 1866 Stanton was officially advised of the unwelcome news. The Secretary of War passed the matter on to his judge-advocate-general, who in turn demanded that Sainte-Marie furnish, together with certain data about himself, a full and sworn statement of Surratt's confession to him. Action was thus delayed for several weeks, as mail was slow, and efficient telegraphic connections with Europe were not established until July 1866.

Seward suggested to Stanton on 28 May that a special agent be sent to Rome to demand the surrender of John Surratt. Significantly Stanton did not reply at all to this letter.

By 20 July 1866 Stanton had the desired affidavits in his possession; but he did nothing further in the matter. In the mean-

[1] House of Representatives, 39th Congress, Second Session, Exec. Doc. No. 9.

time the American minister at Rome had been working on the case, and on 7 August was able to report that if the American Government desired the surrender of Surratt there would be no difficulty in the way. When this dispatch reached Washington Mr. Seward was on the point of leaving with President Johnson on the 'swing around the circle'. In the absence of the Secretary of State the matter was taken up with Stanton on 28 August by Under-Secretary Hunter.

'I will thank you to acquaint this department with your views . . . relative to the information communicated to Mr. King by Sainte-Marie concerning John H. Surratt,' he wrote.[1] No answer to this request was received from the Secretary of War.

On 16 October Seward finally bethought himself of something that evidently had not occurred to any one before. He suggested that some one be sent to visit Surratt to compare his features 'with a photograph herewith sent'. But the photograph was not enclosed; in a postscript it was promised for transmittal in the next letter. By this time, however, it was too late. The Pope's chancellor had ordered Surratt's arrest of his own accord; but Surratt escaped, and, 'incredible as the details of the story appear', to use the American minister's official words, no trace of him was found within the Pope's domain. 'I am assured', remarked the commanding papal officer cryptically, 'that the escape of Watson [Surratt] savors of a prodigy.'[2]

It may be of passing interest that the long-delayed photograph of Surratt apparently did not look a great deal like him. When the marshal of the District of Columbia was asked to look at it in the presence of the judiciary committee, he became somewhat embarrassed. At first he protested that he was not very good in determining the likenesses of persons. But finally he made this admission:

'I could not say that was the photograph of John H. Surratt whom I had in custody. It resembles him somewhat, but I could not say positively.'[3]

The suspicions of the chairman of the committee, Congress-

---

[1] House of Representatives, Report No. 33.
[2] Ibid., Exec. Doc. No. 9, pp. 20, 28.
[3] Ibid., Report No. 33.

man Boutwell, were evidently not allayed by this reply; for he continued his interrogation along the same lines:

Q. Is this so perfect a representation of Surratt, that with its aid you could have picked him from a crowd of men as John H. Surratt?

A. When he was delivered to me it was in a different costume. I am not prepared to say that, in the dress he wore when this photograph was taken, I would not have known him. There is some resemblance to him in my judgment.

Q. Suppose you had been sent out to arrest John H. Surratt, and the only description of him given to you was that photograph; would you have been able to recognize him?

A. I would not have been certain that it was the same person.[1]

This ends the story of Surratt's flight and pursuit, so far as Stanton is concerned. The judiciary committee, friendly to the secretary, found:

'The testimony . . . explaining and tending to justify the acts of the government in the premises, does not, in the opinion of your committee, excuse the great delay in arresting a person charged with complicity in the assassination of the late President of the United States; and while your committee do not charge improper motives upon any of the officers of the government, they are constrained from the testimony to report that, in their opinion, due diligence in the arrest of John H. Surratt was not exercised by the executive department of the government.'[2]

When Surratt was finally brought back by force to his native shores the old fear that the prisoner might talk seemed to take hold of the authorities. The President instructed the Secretary of the Navy to take proper precautions against such a contingency. Johnson felt that Surratt might make almost any statement and that no good could result from communication with him. Hooding the returned fugitive, like the unfortunate prisoners of 1865, was evidently not considered safe in view of a more tolerant public opinion. But it was agreed that he should not be allowed to come into contact with others, nor should unauthorized persons be permitted to see him.[3] The spirit of muzzling pri-

[1] House of Representatives, Report No. 33.
[2] Ibid.   [3] Welles, *Diary*, III, p. 31.

soners was the same as during the days of the conspiracy trial, even though the methods had to be changed.

Extraordinary efforts were made to bring about Surratt's conviction. Secretary of State Seward, prompted by unknown motives, employed A. G. Riddle—who once had acted as Colonel Baker's attorney—to hunt up or, if necessary, *manufacture* evidence against the prisoner.[1] Through some misadventure this scandalous move was disclosed to Johnson's Cabinet, but it is doubtful that its true significance was understood even there.

This time there could be no trial by a military commission, since the decision of the Supreme Court in the Milligan case prevented such an iniquity; but the Government did the best it could under the circumstances. The case was put in charge of a certain Judge Fisher, who was completely under the control of his associate, Judge Cartter, 'a coarse, vulgar Radical in the hands of Stanton', according to Welles.[2] Fisher did not disappoint his friends higher up. The trial was a mockery, as far as he could make it so. Welles wrote, 'The judge was disgracefully partial and unjust . . . and his charge highly improper.'[3] Nevertheless, the jury failed to agree, and the charges against Surratt were eventually dropped.

[1] Welles, *Diary*, p. 170.
[2] Ibid., p. 160.
[3] Ibid., p. 167.

CHAPTER XIX

The Case against Jefferson Davis

From the very first it was apparently Stanton's intention to saddle the guilt for Lincoln's assassination on Jefferson Davis and other Southern leaders. What his motives were there is no certain way of knowing; what their effect was soon became evident. The eyes of the public were diverted from many events that would not have stood close scrutiny, events that were intimately connected with the mishandling of the news dispatches during the night of the murder, the inadequate pursuit and other curious activities and derelictions of the War Department. Incidentally, all hopes of establishing a friendly reunion of the South and the North were frustrated. By accusing the erstwhile Confederate Chief of having caused Lincoln's death, the hatreds of war were to be continued *ad infinitum*.

Stanton's first message to General Dix, as has been pointed out before, contained a germ of mischief. To emphasize Lincoln's kindly feelings toward Lee and others of the Confederacy was strange, to say the least, especially as the secretary himself did not share these sentiments and never had made any pretence of doing so. In his third telegram the germ began to sprout:

THE MURDER WAS PLANNED BEFORE THE 4TH OF MARCH, BUT FELL THROUGH THEN BECAUSE THE ACCOMPLICE BACKED OUT UNTIL 'RICHMOND COULD BE HEARD FROM'.

In his letter to the United States minister at London, Stanton was still more outspoken: 'evidence [has been] obtained, that these horrible crimes were committed in execution of a conspiracy deliberately planned and set on foot by rebels, under pretense of avenging the South and aiding the rebel cause'.

What evidence did Stanton possess that emboldened him to make such an astounding public accusation?

In the early morning hours 'following the tragedy at Ford's Theatre a detective of the War Department had gone to the National Hotel, and had found in Booth's trunk a letter addressed to the actor and signed 'Sam'. In this letter there appeared the following passage: 'Time more propitious will arrive yet. Do not act rashly or in haste. I would prefer your first query, "go and see how it will be taken at R——d", and ere long I shall be better prepared to again be with you.'[1] That was all.

The phrasing used by Samuel Arnold, who was later identified as the author of this missive, was open to various interpretations. The simplest one, perhaps, is that Confederate authorities in Richmond should be approached to endorse the plan of procedure. Booth asked his co-conspirators for their opinions on this point. This indicates rather clearly that the Confederate authorities had not been previously consulted; otherwise Booth's query would have been meaningless. To conclude that advice from Richmond should be sought once more, is certainly not justified by the wording; and only through such a conclusion could Stanton have built a case against the South on the basis of Arnold's letter.

And where did the Secretary of War get his information that the conspiracy began prior to 4 March? Arnold's letter is dated 27 March, and nothing in it indicates the day of his withdrawal from the plot, or points in any way to the fourth of March. In fact, nothing in it indicates that the conspiracy was one to assassinate the President. Stanton must have known that the conspirators had tried to abduct Lincoln on 20 March, and that it was their failure which had led Arnold to withdraw from the conspiracy. In mentioning the date of 4 March Stanton made a bad slip, for nothing was then known to the public, or was ever brought to light later, to show that the conspirators intended to strike on that calendar day. Stanton was very careful never to mention that date again, and it was not alluded to in the proceedings of the trial. If the secretary had been asked to substantiate his official letter to Mr. Adams in London he would have been in a difficult position. But no one ever dared to ask Stanton anything.

[1] Pitman, op. cit., p. 236. War Department Archives.

Was there some other secret information in the hands of the authorities about an assassination plot that was to mature on 4 March? If so, the facts have never been laid bare. When Colonel Burnett, who belonged to the innermost Government circles so far as this affair is concerned, lectured many years later on the subject, he referred to it in this manner:

'It is part of the unwritten history of the time that on the day of President Lincoln's second inauguration, and while he was delivering his inaugural address, Booth sat near and just behind him with the purpose to stab him to death then and there if any fit opportunity should occur in the press and confusion of the crowd, for him to do the deed and make his escape. . . . Another curious fact connected with this event is that Booth secured his ticket of admission to these ceremonies through a United States senator, one of the most faithful and earnest of the Union republican group, and that it was procured through the inter-cession of his daughter, who, although she had only a casual acquaintance with Booth, had often seen him on the stage, and, like many of the romantic young ladies of our own time, had caught the fever of stage-hero worship.'[1]

The lady in question was the daughter of Senator Hale of New Hampshire, and what Burnett refers to as a casual acquaintance was an infatuation that had led to an actual engagement between the two young people. The matter was hushed up after Booth had shot Lincoln, but evidence of his courtship is preserved in a letter found in the actor's trunk and now in possession of the War Department. Its contents must have been well known to Colonel Burnett. The note was written to Booth by his mother, and read in part as follows:

'The secret you have told me is not exactly a secret, as Edwin was told by some one, you were paying great attention to a young lady in Washington—Now my dear boy I cannot advise you how to act—you have so often been dead in love . . . if the Lady in question is all you desire—I see no cause why you should not try to secure her—her Father I see has his appointment—would he give his consent? you can but ask, just be well assured she is really and truly devoted to you—then obtain his

[1] Burnett, op. cit., pp. 600–1.

consent, you know in my partial eyes—you are a fit match for any woman, no matter who she may be—but some Fathers may have higher notions—God grant if it is to be so, it will prove a source of happiness to you both——'[1]

It is probable that Miss Hale came forward after the assassination and acquainted the Government with all the facts in her possession, which could relate only to the procuring of the tickets and to the actor's presence at the inauguration. Booth's intentions on that occasion are mere guesswork on Burnett's part; but that Booth was really close to Lincoln on 4 March is also indicated by the testimony of an actor named Chester, to whom Booth confided that he had had an excellent chance to kill the President that day.

What the War Department did have knowledge of was Wiechmann's report of the abduction plot, which originally was to have culminated on 4 March. Stanton could not speak of this in public without explaining why Booth and his band of followers had not been promptly arrested.

Vague stories of a murder conspiracy planned for the day of the inauguration found their way into print. They rested on nothing more substantial than the threats of a madman named Clements. These the police did not take seriously, though they arrested the lunatic.[2] In the course of time these wild tales grew. When Oldroyd wrote his book on Lincoln's assassination he connected Booth with the plot of 4 March. According to his account the assassin tried to break through a police cordon on that day, and it was only the vigilance of a police officer named Westfall that saved Lincoln's life.[3]

The police records of Washington do not contain the name of Westfall, and Oldroyd's story is supported by relatively few other sources.[4]

If Colonel Burnett was so sure in later years that Booth had planned this crime for 4 March why did he not bring this out during the conspiracy trial? It would have had an important

[1] War Department Archives.
[2] *Washington Chronicle*, 6 Mar. 1865; see also supplementary note to chapter xix, 'A Plot to Kill Lincoln on 4 March'.
[3] Oldroyd, op. cit., p. 216.
[4] Lamon, *Recollections of Abraham Lincoln*, p. 267.

bearing on the issue. The authorities seemed to be of that opinion also, but instead of eliciting the facts through sworn testimony they preferred the medium of a whispering campaign, which evidently created the desired impression. Certainly General Wallace, one of the members of the military commission, was affected by it. In his former home at Crawfordsville, Indiana, there hangs a picture painted by him, which shows all the so-called conspirators assembled in Washington listening to Lincoln's inaugural address. Yet, no evidence had been brought before Wallace to indicate that they had actually been among the auditors.

What Arnold really had intended to convey is fairly plain, not only in the light of later events, but from the letter itself. He had told his family that he was definitely out of the kidnapping affair; he was thoroughly disgusted with Booth's methods of procedure, had quarrelled with him, but did not dare risk an open break with a man on whom he was financially dependent—hence his idea to procrastinate by invoking counsel from Richmond.

Booth's room was searched between two and three o'clock in the morning. The 'Sam' letter could not, therefore, have been in Stanton's possession at 1.30 a.m. when he discussed Lincoln's kindliness in his message to General Dix. Obviously Jefferson Davis was to be made the scapegoat, no matter how the evidence had to be procured. The finding of Arnold's imprudent letter was only a lucky development which Stanton was quick to turn to his advantage.

During the two weeks following the assassination the nation was given time to digest the suspicion so invitingly held out to it. Much editorial ink was spilled in its exploitation, and Jefferson Davis's flight and disappearance from his former haunts added fuel to the flames. On 2 May the country was startled still further by a presidential proclamation, signed by Johnson, and reading as follows:

'It appears from evidence in the Bureau of Military Justice that the atrocious murder of the late . . . Abraham Lincoln and the attempted assassination of . . . William H. Seward . . . were incited, concerted, and procured by and between Jefferson Davis

... Jacob Thompson, Clement C. Clay, Beverly Tucker, George N. Sanders, William C. Cleary, and other rebels and traitors against the Government of the United States. . . .'

At the same time a reward of $100,000 was offered for the capture of the fugitive ex-President of the Confederacy.[1]

Such an open denunciation of the Southern leaders could not fail to produce the greatest excitement and fury. Many doubters swung into line, believing that the War Department would not dare to make such sensational charges without being sure of its facts.

On 25 April the *New York Herald*, for example, referred editorially to the official announcement that the assassination was the result of a plot approved at Richmond. 'There was great probability', the paper commented, 'that all the other offenses and outrages of the chief traitors would have been forgiven and forgotten by the generous Northern people in the glad welcome extended to peace, and in the general joy of a restored Union . . . but the deliberately planned assassination . . . has caused a sudden revulsion in public sentiment. . . .'

On what grounds the Bureau of Military Justice based its accusation was not made known at the time, interesting as this information would have been. But shortly after this events transpired which forced the War Department to show its hand. It was a very poor hand indeed.

After the country had been advised that Jefferson Davis was one of Booth's accomplices, it became necessary to include him in the indictment against all the conspirators. To prove the charges before a military commission was not considered a difficult task.

The first witness for the Government was one Richard Montgomery, a professional spy who was in the habit of taking money from both the Confederate and the Federal Governments. The gist of his testimony was that he had frequently conferred with Jacob Thompson, the Canadian agent for Jefferson Davis, and that he had heard of a proposition to assassinate Lincoln, Stanton, Grant, and others, but that Thompson had deferred his approval

[1] DeWitt, *Assassination*, pp. 100, 101; also *Official Records*, II, vol. 8, p. 899.

until he had consulted his superiors at Richmond. The witness admitted that he did not know whether Jefferson Davis had ever answered or not, but he was under the impression that he had.[1]

Montgomery had been convicted of robbery in the New York courts and had frequently graced the prisons there with his presence.[2] It was shown later that at the time when he was supposed to have had these conversations with Thompson at Montreal the latter was not within three hundred miles of that city.

When Montgomery had arrived in Toronto during August 1864 he had been quickly recognized as a spy from Marshal Murray's office in New York and consequently had left abruptly.[3] That Thompson ever had any conversation at all with him after that is highly improbable.

The second witness against the deposed Southern president was a certain Dr. James B. Merritt, a physician who had lived many years at Windsor, Canada, where he was known as a disreputable citizen, a common liar, and a quack. Three justices of the peace gave sworn testimony to that effect, and their opinions were printed in the *Toronto Globe*, a paper friendly to the Northern cause.[4] On 20 April 1865 General Fry, provost marshal-general of the United States had written to him:

'The Secretary of War authorizes me to pledge your pro tection and security, and to pay all expenses connected with your journey both ways, *and in addition to promise a suitable reward if reliable and useful information is furnished.*'[5]

Five days later a Dr. G. W. Bingham furnished the Government some interesting information regarding this witness. 'Dr. Merritt', he wrote, '[is] an escaped secessionist . . . who has always, when speaking of your . . . Chief Magistrate, expressed himself in terms of unrelenting bitterness and hostility. . . . when the news of the assassination . . . came in, he fairly danced with joy upon the street.' Mr. Stanton was also advised that at the time of Merritt's arrival at Ayr in November 1864 he had claimed to have in his possession a recommendation which read:

[1] Pitman, op. cit., p. 26.
[2] Laughlin, op. cit., p. 208.
[3] Stuart Robinson, *Infamous Perjuries of the Bureau of Military Justice Exposed*, p. 6.
[4] Laughlin, op. cit., p. 209.
[5] Pitman, op. cit., p. 36. Author's italics.

'I have been intimately acquainted with Dr. J. B. Merritt for a long time, he having been my family physician for a number of years. It affords me great pleasure to commend him as a first-class physician, and as a gentleman entitled to every degree of public confidence.

(signed) ANDREW JOHNSON, Governor.'[1]

This recommendation was most likely a fraud.

That the authorities proceeded to use such a man, in spite of these facts in their possession, is almost beyond belief.

Merritt's testimony was that, according to a conversation he had overheard, 'Old Abe should never be inaugurated'; that Lincoln was called a 'damned old tyrant' who would never 'serve another term if . . . elected'. He claimed that he had given advance information of Lincoln's assassination to Squire Davidson, a justice of the peace at Galt, Canada, but that this information was ridiculed.[2]

Before the trial was over Merritt's testimony was shown to be a fabrication. Official proof of this was furnished in an unexpected manner.[3]

When the British minister in Washington read about the strange tale unfolded by the Canadian physician he considered it his duty to investigate it; for if advance information of Lincoln's assassination really had been brought to the attention of a Canadian official and had been withheld by him there might have been danger of international complications.

On 13 June the British legation therefore addressed a letter to the county attorney's office in Berlin, Canada, to which, a few days later, the following reply was received:

County Attorney's Office
Berlin, 19 June 1865.

SIR:

In answer to your communication of the 13th instant as to the truth of the statements made by James B. Merritt, a medical practitioner residing at Ayr, on the conspiracy trial at Washington to the effect that he, Merritt, on the 10th of April prior to the assassination of the late president, went before a Mr.

---

[1] L. C. Baker, op. cit., p. 551.
[2] Pitman, op. cit., p. 35.
[3] War Department Archives.

Davidson, J.P., at Galt to give information of the conspiracy. That the justice refused to act; that he then went before the judge of assize who told him to go before the grand jury, etc.

I have the honor to report that on the receipt of your letter I forwarded it with a communication from myself to Mr. Davidson and requested him to write me on the subject. I now enclose Mr. Davidson's letter for your information, simply adding that Mr. Davidson is a gentleman of first rate standing whose character is above reproach and whose statement in his letter is as undoubtedly true as if it were sworn to. As to Merritt having gone before the judge of assize (Mr. Justice Hagerty) I believe the statement to be utterly false. I acted as crown prosecutor at the spring assizes for this county and should most certainly have heard of it had such information as the intended assassination of the late president been given to the judge. I can say positively that Merritt did not go before the grand jury.

I may say, further, that there is no person of the name of Davidson in the commission of the peace for this county except the writer of the enclosed letter.

On inquiry I find Merritt has left Ayr for parts unknown.

I have, etc.

THOS. MILLER, *Co. Attorney*
County Waterloo.

The Solicitor General

Galt, 17 *June* 1865

THOMAS MILLER, *Esquire*
Co. Attorney, Berlin

DEAR SIR,

I have to acknowledge the receipt of your favor of the 16th inst., enclosing a letter from the Solicitor General beginning, 'as to the truth of certain statements sworn to by one James B. Merritt at the conspiracy trials at Washington, who there said that in April last he went before a Mr. Davidson, a J.P. at Galt and gave information of the conspiracy to kill President Lincoln.' It is needless for me to say that more than that the whole story is a miserable fabrication containing not a particle of truth.

I know nothing about the man personally but from inquiry

I find that his character stands very low in the neighborhood in which he lives.

I am, etc.

J. DAVIDSON.

I return to Solicitor General letter herewith.

The contents of these reports were communicated immediately to the State Department in Washington.

Private   *British Legation*
                                               Washington

MY DEAR SIR,

On reading Merritt's evidence I brought to Lord Monck's knowledge his statement that he had gone before Mr. Davidson in Canada to give information as to the plot to assassinate the late president.

I enclose you the result of the examination ordered by Lord Monck with a view to your making such use of it as in the interests of justice you may think right.

Yours faithfully

FREDERICK W. A. BRUCE

Honorable W. HUNTER

On 27 June Acting Secretary of State Hunter made the judge-advocate-general acquainted with the queer antecedents of Dr. Merritt.

(Unofficial)   *Department of State, Washington*
                                       27 June 1865

To the HONORABLE JOSEPH HOLT
Judge-Advocate-General

DEAR SIR:

I enclose for your information a copy of a private note to me of yesterday from Sir F. W. A. Bruce and of the papers to which I referred relative to the testimony of James B. Merritt before the court martial for the trial of the assassins.

Very truly yours

W. HUNTER

These letters were found in the files of the judge-advocate's offices pertaining to the conspiracy trial, and *it is therefore an unquestionable fact that Holt, Bingham, and, presumably, their*

*commander-in-chief, Stanton, wilfully suppressed the truth and used
testimony which they knew to be perjured.*

How desperately this testimony was needed is shown by the
fact that for his fabrication Merritt received $6,000 from the
Government.[1]

Montgomery's and Merritt's allegations comprised all that
the Bureau of Military Justice had at its disposal on 2 May when
it advised President Johnson to issue the proclamation stamping
Jefferson Davis and his intimates as instigators of a murder.
When Holt reluctantly, upon a direct command from Johnson,
disclosed this fact, he even had to admit that technically no
evidence at all had been on file in his department at that time;
everything rested on verbal statements. Incidentally, the examination of the witnesses was conducted in part by Major Eckert,[2]
the same Eckert who said that he had been too busy to look into
the mystery of the interrupted telegraph service on the night
of the assassination.

Not until 8 December 1866, more than a year and a half after
the issuing of the proclamation, did President Johnson bethink
himself to ask for the data on which his own accusations were
founded.[3] By then both Montgomery and Merritt had been
unmasked, but the former President of the Confederacy was still
a prisoner at Fortress Monroe and was being treated like an
ordinary criminal.

Not all people were taken in as easily as the President of the
United States. In May 1866 Thaddeus Stevens, who hated
Jefferson Davis with deadly malignity, related to George Shea,
one of Davis's counsels, how Holt had shown him the 'evidence'
upon which the proclamation was issued. He remarked that such
evidence was insufficient and incredible. Stevens then said
earnestly to Shea: 'Those men are no friends of mine. They are
public enemies and I would treat the South as a conquered
country and settle it politically upon the policy best suited for
ourselves. But I know these men, sir. They are gentlemen and
incapable of being assassins.'[4]

[1] Laughlin, op. cit., p. 210.
[2] *Official Records*, II, vol. 8, p. 977.
[3] War Department Archives.
[4] James Ford Rhodes, *History of the United States, 1850–1896* (The
Macmillan Co., New York, 1919), V, p. 158 (footnote).

Even Colonel Burnett, the assistant-judge-advocate, did not seem greatly impressed with the testimony adduced at the trial. 'Let me say here personally,' he declared twenty-seven years later, '. . . that my own judgment upon the testimony was at the time that while the proposed enterprise of assassinating the president and vice-president, members of the cabinet and General Grant had been brought to the attention of the Richmond authorities and to Jefferson Davis, there was no conclusive evidence to show that Davis sanctioned or approved this undertaking.'[1]

After issuing the proclamation against Jefferson Davis on 2 May more testimony was procured by the War Department, and when the great conspiracy trial began on 10 May additional witnesses were on hand. The most interesting of them was a man named Sandford Conover. He ascribed to the Southern Government the planning of fearful atrocities, from kidnapping to the introduction of pestilence, from assassination to the wholesale poisoning of New York City. Conover had been a witness in Montreal against the St. Albans raiders on 11 February 1865. He had stated at that time that he was a native of Virginia, had never served in the Confederate army, and had left his residence in the South in October 1864. Three months later he swore at the conspiracy trial that he had been born in New York, had been conscripted into the Confederate army and had left for the North in December 1863.[2]

Conover's evidence was taken at the very beginning of the conspiracy trial, and comparison with the records of the St. Albans court proceedings would have been easy. The Reverend Stuart Robinson of Kentucky, whom Conover had impudently attacked from the witness stand, issued a pamphlet declaring it an abomination 'that the "Bureau of Military Justice" and the law adviser of the President should have called for such a Proclamation of infamy against such men, upon evidence which, if they did not know, *they ought to have known* to be the evidence of perjured witnesses.'[3] Robinson's denunciation

[1] Burnett, op. cit., p. 600.
[2] Robinson, op. cit.; Pitman, op. cit., p. 28.
[3] Robinson, op. cit., p. 5.

appeared in print on 10 June 1865, and Conover was recalled to the witness stand on 27 June; but the court paid no attention to his obvious perjury. If the attorneys for the defence had kept themselves properly posted and had used the weapons at their disposal, the case against Jefferson Davis would have broken down long before the court adjourned.

It is difficult to criticize the Reverend Robinson when he wrote that 'the "Bureau of military justice" accepted, without question, this [Conover's] oath of May 12th, in face of the contradictory oath of the same witness at a public trial in which the United States Government was a party at Montreal, Feb. 11th. Either Messrs. Holt and Speed knew of his previous oath —officially published as it had been—or they did not. If they were aware of it, then they advised the proclamation on the testimony of one whom they knew to be a perjured man. If they were not aware of it, then surely the law officers at Washington must be extremely negligent of the Government law business about which they advise!'[1]

Conover—or Dunham, to use his real name—was an amusing scoundrel. He lied fluently and plausibly. Among other things he made the interesting statement that he had, as regular correspondent of the *New York Tribune*, advised that journal of the assassination plot as early as February 1865.[2] No one found it worth while to investigate this sensational story involving Horace Greeley's paper. Small wonder. Delving into this matter would either have shown Conover to be a perjurer, or the *Tribune* to be guilty of criminal negligence; or else, if the Government had been duly informed, some one in Washington had been strangely inattentive to his duties.

Of all the witnesses who appeared against the former Southern leader only two others deserve special attention. One was a pedlar named Samuel Jones who claimed to have heard the assassination plot discussed by Confederate officers, as they sat around their tents. His testimony is noteworthy from one angle only; Jones was blind. This, of course, should have made his trashy gossip still less admissible as evidence; but the fact of his blindness is omitted from Pitman's record.[3]

[1] Robinson, op. cit., p. 6.
[2] Pitman, op. cit., p. 29.
[3] Ibid., p. 37; Poore, *Conspiracy Trial*, I, p. 42.

The second person who deserves mention is a man named Henry Von Steinacker. This witness swore that he was in the Confederate service as an engineer officer in the topographical department, on the staff of General Edward Johnson.[1] What story he told is of no consequence. The interest lies in the fact

GENERAL COURT MARTIAL ORDERS, No. 281.

WAR DEPARTMENT,
ADJUTANT GENERAL'S OFFICE,
Washington, September 2, 1864.

I.. Before a General Court Martial which convened at Washington. D. C., August 10, 1864, pursuant to Special Orders, No. 122, dated March 19, 1864; No. 129, dated March 28, 1864; No. 131, dated March 29, 1864; No. 145, dated April 12, 1864; No. 175, dated May 12, 1864; No. 178, dated May 16, 1864; No 181, dated May 19, 1864; No. 223, dated June 30, 1864; No. 226, dated July 2, 1864; No. 244, dated July 21, 1864, and No. 254, dated July 30, 1864, War Department, Adjutant General's Office, Washington, and of which Brigadier General HENRY S. BRIGGS, United States Volunteers, is President, was arraigned and tried —

Private *Henry Von Steineker*, alias *Hans H. Vonwinklestein*, Permanent Company "A," United States Army.

CHARGE.—" Desertion."

FINDING.—"Guilty."

SENTENCE.

And the Court does therefore sentence him, Private *Henry Von Steineker*, alias *Hans H. Vonwinklestein*, Permanent Company "A," United States Army, " *To be dishonorably discharged the service of the United States, and to be imprisoned at hard labor for the term of three years, at such place as the Secretary of War may direct. He, the said Henry Von Steineker, alias Hans H. Vonwinklestein, forfeiting all pay and allowances now due or falling due to him.*"

Facsimile of the court-martial sentence of Henry Von Steineker (Steinacker), which was found attached to the files of the judge-advocate in charge of the con-spiracy trial. Although this document proves Von Steineker a convicted deserter, the government used him as an important witness.

that he was a convicted deserter from the United States army who had been dishonourably discharged and sentenced to three years of hard labour, *and that the judge-advocate-general knew it at the time of the trial,* for the transcript of his case was found attached to the records of the conspiracy trial in the archives of the War Department. The judge-advocate further knew that Von

[1] Pitman, op. cit., p. 38.

Steinacker, or to call him by his own name, Hans H. Vonwinklestein, was a horse-thief who had been court-martialled by the
Confederates after he had fled to them for protection. The testimony relating thereto also was in the possession of Judge Holt
and his assistants.

The Reverend Robinson accused Mr. Holt, the head of the
Bureau of Military Justice, of being *particeps criminis* with the
men whose testimony he employed. To this open insult Holt
never offered any defence, except the wail that a conspiracy had
been formed to defame his character. Even this plea was not
made until fifteen months later, after the perjuries committed by
his witnesses had been proven through their own confessions.

Jefferson Davis was found guilty by the military commission,
and Holt had every reason to believe that the case was settled
and that the means employed to bring about the desired results
would remain buried in his secret files. But public sentiment,
which he had aroused by his own efforts to paint the fallen leader
of the South as a devil incarnate, was not willing to let matters
drop. Davis had been pronounced guilty of the assassination,
but he had not been hanged. If his alleged tools had paid the
penalty of death, why was the archfiend himself not dragged to
the gallows?

On 10 January 1866 the House of Representatives passed a
resolution requesting the President to communicate to it the
'grounds, facts, or accusations upon which Jefferson Davis,
Clement C. Clay, jr., ... [and others] are held in confinement'.[1]
This forced the judge-advocate to bare his evidence and to
marshal all the arguments he could muster to show Davis's
complicity in the crime.

Holt must have felt embarrassed at the inadequacy of his
case; he started his report by claiming that he understood now
that the former President of the Confederacy was being held in
prison upon a charge of treason only; this gave him a way out of
the conspiracy charge. But finally he proceeded with the inevitable exposure of his material and went on to enumerate 'such
points of the testimony in the possession of the Government as
will indicate truly its character. . . .'[2]

---

[1] *Official Records*, II, vol. 8, p. 848.   [2] Ibid.

There followed the citation of a newspaper advertisement, which was later proved a hoax, of anonymous and signed letters to Jefferson Davis suggesting violent deeds in the North, and of plans for the destruction of bridges and ships. Of course, the fact that the suggestions of violence had not been followed robbed the argument of much of its force, while the projects aiming at physical destruction of certain property were merely recognized measures of warfare. But Holt could not afford to pass over a single point in his favour. 'The unhesitating and confident manner in which proposals of this class are perceived to have been addressed to the head of the rebellion', he asserted, 'in connection with the absence of all discussions as to their criminality . . . while it evinces the fact that the idea of assassination as a mode of warfare was widespread in the South, indicates also the general conviction that . . . those thus advanced were favored by Davis.'[1] The laboured grammatical construction of this sentence is quite in line with the laboured conclusions the honourable judge-advocate was trying to extract from his premisses.

The House of Representatives, through its judiciary committee, took quick action on Holt's report. Trying desperately to connect President Johnson with the conspiracy, besides hoping to encompass Davis's quick death, the committee undertook to re-examine some of the most promising witnesses who had starred at the conspiracy trial. Everything might have gone well had it not been for the courage and inquisitiveness of the minority member, A. J. Rogers of New Jersey. If Holt had hoped that the proceedings would develop into a formal approval of his own actions he was sorely disappointed. The very first witness to wilt under Rogers's cross-examination was the notorious Dr. Merritt; he confessed that all his allegations were perjuries. In vain the majority members of the committee tried to cover up their discomfort by refusing to let the stenographers transcribe and publish his statements; moreover, under Rogers's merciless questioning one after another of Holt's witnesses broke down. One of them, a shining light at the conspiracy trial, proved to be a gambler and ex-prize-fighter who had entered the army service as a detective and had been discharged by General Banks

[1] *Official Records*, II, vol. 8, p. 850.

for several crimes. Others proved to be relatives of Conover. They stated that they had been told of fabulous rewards available because 'Judge Holt wanted to get witnesses to prove that Davis was interested in the assassination of Mr. Lincoln.'[1]

A humorous note crept into the sordid proceedings when it was disclosed that Conover had run a veritable school for perjured witnesses at the National Hotel. He first wrote out the desired testimony for his pupils and then rehearsed them. What he had overlooked was the possibility of cross-examination. No such thing had occurred at the conspiracy trial and none was expected before the judiciary committee. It was not even considered necessary that the students at this school should be especially brilliant.

'Not one of these witnesses,' said Rogers, 'nor the parties using and instructing them, if any besides Conover, possessed any peculiar talent for imposture other than impudence and military power to awe all questionings.'[2]

The panic-stricken advocate-general sent one of his assistants to New York to summon Campbell, one of his pet witnesses, to Washington. But Holt's aide only corroborated Rogers's opinion of the intellectual and moral qualities of the men Conover had been training.

'I talked with him [Campbell] . . . and he was a good deal embarrassed,' he wrote to his chief. ' "This is all false",' he finally blurted out. ' "I must make a clean breast of it; I can't stand it any longer".'[3] If the house of cards erected by Conover and Holt had stood upright for so long, it was evidently only due to the fact that no one had dared to touch it.

Conover remained as Holt's last hope. He could not be found in New York, but was finally brought to Washington by a ruse. Confronted with Campbell in the rooms of the judiciary committee, his *sangfroid* did not leave him for a minute. He indignantly declared that every one was out of step but himself; that his former friends had all been bought up by Davis's associates; if permitted to go to New York he would procure such additional evidence as would prove this. The embarrassed majority members of the committee acceded to his request, but

[1] House of Representatives, Report No. 104, p. 37.
[2] Ibid., p. 39.
[3] *Official Records*, II, vol. 8, p. 922.

insisted that he be accompanied by a deputy on his trip north. Arrived at the metropolis Conover slipped away from his guard and disappeared.[1] The astonished and abashed judge-advocate, shorn of his support, was left alone and a subject of ridicule. Rogers openly averred that Conover had been assisted in his flight by some one high in authority, in order to make impossible an investigation into the disgraceful culpability of this high Unknown. Stanton's friends on the judiciary committee were in a quandary about how to word their report. They clung to some irrelevant correspondence found in the captured Confederate archives and declared:

'These documents are conclusive upon the point that Davis, Benjamin, and Walker, in the years 1861, '62, '63, '64, and '65, received, entertained and considered propositions for the assassination of the chief members of the government of the United States, and thereupon a probability arises that they took steps to accomplish the purpose. . . .'[2]

More than a probability even the staunch partisans of Holt and Stanton could not wring from the testimony. The perjuries confessed to by the key witnesses had to be admitted, of course; but the chairman Boutwell and his henchmen professed their inability to decide which statements were the true ones; they artlessly remarked that the disgraced witnesses had failed to give to the committee a reasonable explanation for the sudden reversal of their testimony, and let it go at that.

Into this tissue of falsehoods and evasions the minority member Rogers, unhampered by party ties, tore with the fury of an avenging angel.

'For some reason or reasons not fully stated', he began, 'the majority of the committee determined to throw in my way every possible impediment. . . . The papers were put away from me, locked in boxes, hidden; and when I asked to see them, I was told . . . that I could not.' The speaker of the House, before whom Rogers brought the matter for rectification, decided that he was not entitled to see the papers on which his opinions must be based till such time as the other committee members chose; and it was not until a day before the report was to be written

[1] DeWitt, *Assassination*, p. 171.
[2] House of Representatives, Report No. 104, p. 25.

that such permission was granted. 'It was said', wrote Rogers, 'the interests of the Government required that none should see these papers save and only Mr. Boutwell . . . who was preparing the majority report. . . .

'Secrecy has surrounded and shrouded, not to say protected,' Rogers continued, 'every step of these examinations, and even in the committee-room I seemed to be acting with a sort of secret council of inquisition, itself directed by an absent vice-inquisitor, and grand inquisitor too.'[1]

No names were mentioned by this fighting congressman from New Jersey; but he made it fairly plain that Holt and Stanton, respectively, were in his mind. He also revealed the interesting fact that Stanton had written to President Johnson on 7 February 1866 that the publication of the reports of the judge-advocate-general on this matter was 'incompatible with the public interests'. But for once the efforts of the Secretary of War to cover up the secret activities of his department were to no avail, although James Speed, attorney-general in Johnson's Cabinet, joined in the protest against publication of the testimony pertaining to Davis.[2]

'Most of the evidence . . . was obtained *ex parte*, without notice to the accused,' Speed wrote, 'and while they were in custody in military prisons. Their publication might wrong the government.'[3] This is indeed a surprising allegation. The Government was having things its own way; the defendants were absent, the lying witnesses not subject to cross-examination. In spite of this the former attorney-general was in fear that publication of the proceedings might hurt—not Mr. Davis— no, the Government. What an interesting opinion Speed must have entertained of this evidence!

Mr. Rogers lashed out pitilessly against Holt, and the thong of his whip at times reached Stanton himself:

'I do not say that "Judge Holt" did himself originate the charges or organize the plot of the perjurers, because I do not know that he did; I merely say that a plot based on the assassination was formed against Davis, Clay, and others, and that the

[1] House of Representatives, Report No. 104, pp. 30, 31.
[2] Ibid., p. 31.
[3] Ibid.

plotters did, and even yet, operate through the Bureau of Military Justice, and that the argument forwarded by Mr. Holt to the Committee of the Judiciary looked to me like a shield extended over the plotters . . . may be, with a desire to save certain officers of the government from the charge of having been betrayed into the . . . blunders of an excitement, which it was their province to allay or control, not to increase. . . .'[1]

Finally the minority member voiced still more strongly his suspicions against Stanton and his aides:

'. . . I believe this was done to hide the disgraceful fact that the assassination of Mr. Lincoln was seized upon as a pretext to hatch charges against a number of historical personages, to blacken their private character, and afford excuse for their trial through the useless forms of a military commission. . . .'[2]

In closing his arraignment Rogers wanted to know who had originated the whole plot of perjury to alarm the nation; he earnestly urged the House of Representatives to delve more fully into it, wondering who had placed President Johnson in the undignified position of making charges in his proclamation which could not stand even a preliminary examination before a justice of the peace. Rogers's concluding sentences are vitriolic in their sting:

'Had more than twenty-four hours been allowed me [in the preparation of the report], or had those twenty-four hours been less burdened with other duties . . . I might have been able, in addition to exposing the perjury, to have told this house who concocted it, who screened it, (I do not mean the committee,) why it was concocted and screened, and finally, why a committee of Congress acted towards one of its own members like a Venetian council of ten . . . no time was left me to pursue to the head the villainies I detected in the hand, or I might have been able plainly to tell Congress and the country that if in this plot we had a Titus Oates in Conover, so also we had a Shaftesbury somewhere.'[3]

Against this broadside Holt tried to maintain silence for a

---

[1] House of Representatives, Report No. 104, p. 36.
[2] Ibid.
[3] Ibid., p. 40.

time, but by 4 September 1866 he thought that his attitude was being misunderstood, and he therefore published a *Vindication*. Kicking out blindly, he accused his opponents of having hired his own perjured witnesses to bring him shame and discomfiture. Admitting the falsity of all testimony furnished by Conover and his band, he insisted that enough evidence remained to convict Davis, and that any one doubting the guilt of the Southern chieftain was a traitor.[1]

In comparison with Rogers's direct thrusts Holt's *Vindication* sounds like the whimpering of a child who has suddenly been deprived of his nurse.

George S. Boutwell, in his *Reminiscences of Sixty Years in Public Affairs*, does not make any reference to the proceedings of this committee. He does mention, however, his leadership in an investigation into the circumstances of Lincoln's death in the ensuing year. His private conclusions at that time did not point to Jefferson Davis as an accomplice of Booth in the assassination plot, although he believed him to have been a party to the scheme of abduction. Mr. Boutwell then added a tantalizing note. At the end of the investigation he remarked, there remained in the possession of the judiciary committee a quantity of papers, affidavits, and memoranda 'of no value as evidence'. These were placed in a sealed package and deposited with the clerk of the House. 'The preservation of the papers may have been an error,' according to Boutwell's memoirs. 'They should have been destroyed by the committee. . . . I am the only person living who has knowledge of the papers. . . . It is not in the public interest that the papers should become the possession of the public.'[2]

Mr. Boutwell, it would seem, undertook a big task. He held counsel with himself alone to determine whether certain documents of which no one else had any knowledge were of value as evidence. He withheld these documents from his fellow members of the judiciary committee, and finally decided that it would not be in the public interest to have the contents of this suppressed evidence become known to the world.

Boutwell's book was published in 1902. One would think

[1] *Vindication of Judge-Advocate-General Holt* (Chronicle Press, Washington, Sept. 1866).
[2] George S. Boutwell, *Reminiscences of Sixty Years in Public Affairs* (McClure, Phillipps & Co., New York, 1902), II, p. 62.

that by that time he might have shared his secrets with the students of history, lest others might disagree with him as to the value of the unknown facts buried in the sealed package. As matters stand the mystery is only deepened, not dispelled. Efforts to locate the parcel left with the clerk of the House have been unsuccessful.

Boutwell was a close political friend of Stanton and completely under the latter's domination; so much so that he confessed later to having literally written down, in accordance with the War Minister's dictation, a piece of legislation that Stanton wanted enacted.

Under these circumstances Boutwell's conduct as the head of the judiciary committee becomes more readily understandable.

In the year following the *débâcle* of Boutwell's investigating committee, the arch-perjurer Conover was captured. He was tried, convicted, and sentenced to ten years in the Federal penitentiary at Albany.[1] This meant the final collapse of the case against Jefferson Davis, whose release on bond was arranged in the same year. The proclamation of Davis's guilt, initiated with such a blare of trumpets, had ended in disgrace. If his persecution had been started to cover up some of the secret machinations of the War Department, this purpose had been only partially successful, thanks to the efforts of Congressman Rogers. So far as stirring up new hatred between the South and the North went, those who had maligned Jefferson Davis had cause to congratulate themselves; for by the time the Southern ex-President was allowed to leave his cell, reconciliation of the North and South along the lines which Lincoln and the peace-loving public of the whole country had striven for had become impossible. Almost another decade had to elapse before the wavers of the bloody shirt—and with them the Radical Republicans—were deprived of their dictatorial political powers.[2]

[1] DeWitt, *Assassination*, p. 173.

[2] See supplementary note to chapter xix, 'Jefferson Davis's Attitude toward Lincoln's Assassination'.

CHAPTER XX

The Setting for the Conspiracy Trial

On 1 May 1865 President Johnson ordered the assistant adjutant-general to select nine high-ranking officers of the army to serve as a military commission to try all persons implicated in Lincoln's assassination. At the same time he requested his attorney-general to furnish him with an opinion on the jurisdiction of a military tribunal. Advance information on these proceedings came to the retired chief law officer of the Government, Edward Bates, then living in St. Louis.

'I am pained to be led to believe', he wrote in his diary on 25 May, 'that my successor, Atty. Genl. Speed, has been wheedled out of an *opinion*, to the effect that such a trial is lawful. If he be, in the lowest degree, qualified for his office, he must know better.'[1]

Speed's opinion was not given to the public until two months later, for reasons that were never explained but which are easy enough to guess; in fact, the paper bears no date except 'July — 1865'. When Bates finally read it, his disgust found vent in strong words.

'This is the most extraordinary document I ever read, under the name of a law opinion,' he declared. 'This opinion is . . . dated "*July* — 1865". *After* the sentence, and in fact, after the execution of the accused who were condemned to death! And thus, it is apparent that the opinion was gotten up (a mere fetch of the War Office) to bolster up a jurisdiction, *after the fact*, so generally denounced, by lawyers and by the respectable press. . . .'[2]

[1] Edward Bates, 'Diary' in Annual Report of American Historical Society, 1930, IV, p. 483.
[2] Ibid., pp. 498-9.

When the findings of the military commission were approved by President Johnson, on 5 July, Orville Browning, later Secretary of the Interior, was moved to a similar expression of utter condemnation: 'This commission was without authority,' he wrote, 'and its proceedings void. The execution of these persons will be murder.'[1]

The actual detailing of the military judges was made by the Secretary of War. The very names of some of the members selected boded ill for the defendants.

The presiding officer, Major-General David Hunter, had long been a friend of Lincoln; he had accompanied the President-elect on his first trip from Springfield to Washington, and had guarded the body of his chief on its last journey back to Illinois. In 1861 Hunter had suffered a dislocation of the collar-bone as he kept the crowd in Buffalo from getting too close to his charge; in 1865 he had witnessed the excessive demonstrations of sorrow at every place where the funeral train passed.[2] In his devotion to Lincoln, he had set up an unobtrusive guard of loyal volunteers in the White House during the early days of his friend's incumbency.[3] Later he was put on the black list of the Confederate Government for having organized negro regiments. It can hardly be presumed that General Hunter was in a judicial frame of mind as he sat at the head of the commission that was to try the alleged murderers of his idol. The relationship between him and Stanton was a close one. The secretary had once sent him on a confidential mission to report on Grant's rumoured inebriety.[4] No wonder it was said, according to whispers in the capital, that the military commission had been organized to convict.

Of the remaining members of the commission only General Lew Wallace was then well known; a few years later he was to become famous as the author of *Ben Hur*, but at this time there did not seem to be much brotherly love in his heart. His votes,

---

[1] Browning, *Diary*, II, p. 37; see supplementary note to chapter xx, 'The Legality of the Military Commission'.

[2] Lloyd Lewis, *Myths After Lincoln* (Harcourt, Brace & Co., New York, 1929), pp. 125–6.

[3] David Hunter, *Military Services During the War of the Rebellion* (D. Van Nostrand, New York, 1873), pp. 7, 29.

[4] Flower, op. cit.. p. 384.

in fact, were so consistently against all the accused that shortly afterward Stanton appointed him president of the military court which hanged Captain Wirz, the former commandant of the Andersonville Prison.

Perhaps the selection of General Wallace was prompted by a silly order promulgated by him in Baltimore on 2 May, stating that 'The sale of portraits of any rebel officer or soldier, or of J. Wilkes Booth . . . is forbidden hereafter. . . .'[1]

What Wirz's attorney wrote to President Johnson, after his client had been sentenced by General Wallace's court, might have applied with equal force to the trial of the prisoners accused of having conspired to assassinate Lincoln.

'If I have the Government's patronage,' this lawyer declared, 'and perhaps the prospect of an office or two (as actually has been the case with some of the witnesses for the prosecution in the Wirz trial), and can also give a promise of safe conduct and perhaps a reward, I do not doubt in the least that . . . [among those from whom the Government had drawn its witnesses] I shall within four weeks find enough testimony to try, condemn, and hang every member of the Wirz military commission on any charge whatever, provided it is done before such a military commission.'[2]

Another of the judges was General T. M. Harris of West Virginia. Almost thirty years later this officer wrote a book on the trial of the assassins, and through this source the historian is granted the unusual privilege of getting the first-hand views of at least one court member. General Harris's book shows an absolute lack of either fairness or understanding; it is full of inaccuracies and completely ignores the results of the various investigations during 1866 and 1867. In 1892 Harris still accepted Conover's testimony at its face value, and stated that the assassination of Lincoln had fallen to Paine by lot—something that had not even been hinted at during the trial. He called Booth and Surratt the agents of the Canadian cabinet at Washington,[3]

---

[1] *Official Records*, I, vol. 46, part 3, p. 1072.
[2] Ibid., II, vol. 8, p. 774.
[3] The Canadian cabinet, so-called, consisted of several prominent Southerners who acted for the Confederate Government; among them were Jacob Thompson, Clement C. Clay, Beverly Tucker, and George N. Sanders.

and asserted that large pecuniary rewards were awaiting the murderers; but he never gave any references for his statements. Harris repeated as gospel truth all the irresponsible talk that had been handed around during the excitement, and showed very little inclination to abide by historical facts. According to his story Grant had received a telegram which called him to Philadelphia on business; the frustration of Booth's kidnapping plan on 20 March he laid to the presence of an imaginary cavalry escort. The soldier-judge even placed Booth in front of Ford's Theatre, waiting to shoot the President as he came out. That the assassin's horse was in the back alley, where Booth could never have reached it in safety, evidently did not trouble Harris's mind. The good general not only accepted all the hearsay evidence, so far as it was damaging to the defendants, but added matters that are not in the evidence at all, and at times even recorded his own bias against the prisoners.[1]

Of Dr. Mudd, for example, he said: 'He might just as well have admitted his complicity in the conspiracy. Mudd's expression of countenance was that of a hypocrite. He had the bump of secretiveness largely developed; and it would have taken months of favorable acquaintanceship to have removed the unfavorable impression made by the first scanning of the man. He had the appearance of a natural born liar and deceiver.'

In his foreword Harris unknowingly bore testimony to the skill with which Stanton's aides had built up the stories of their perjured witnesses. The impression General Harris carried away from the trial is exactly what was needed to insure the proper state of mind among the judges; for, under the circumstances, conviction would seem to these soldiers almost a patriotic duty. Harris wrote:

'The object of the writer in this introductory chapter has been to place clearly before his readers the formidable character of the conspiracy, which, with the President of the Confederacy at its head, and organized by his Canada Cabinet, was intended to throw the loyal North into a state of chaotic confusion and bring to the aid of their sinking cause the disloyal element all over the North, by a series of assassinations which would leave the nation without a civil and military head and without any con-

[1] Harris, *Assassination*, pp. 22, 23, 80.

stitutional way of electing another President, and at the same time would deprive the armies of the United States of a lawful commander. . . . the evidence in the possession of the government and adduced before the Commission, it will be seen, fully justified the government in making this charge.'

This was written more than a quarter of a century after all charges against Jefferson Davis had been dropped, after the perjuries committed by the Government witnesses had been exposed, and after the trial of John Surratt had shown the one-sidedness of the testimony on which the judges at the conspiracy trial had acted.

General Harris was, perhaps, the most stubborn of all the judges in refusing to admit that the condemnation of some of the so-called conspirators might have been a miscarriage of justice. He seemed deaf and blind to all denouements during and after the trial; his knowledge of the matters pertaining to the conspiracy he confined to Pitman's records. He recognized later evidence only when it suited his purpose.

According to Harris, Dr. Mudd pledged to Booth both sympathy and assistance in his escape. Of course, he did not unveil the source of this information, for no such source existed. Even Wiechmann did not dare testify that he had heard anything that would bear out such an assertion; but such trifles did not deter the general. He stated as a fact that Mudd had visited Booth two or three times in Washington during the winter, something that was not brought out in the evidence at all. In this fashion inaccuracy followed inaccuracy, with insinuations directed alternately at Dr. Mudd, Mrs. Surratt, and Spangler.

Into the hands of judges such as Harris was placed the fate of seven men and one woman who were battling for their lives.

The nine army officers were guided by the judge-advocate-general, Joseph Holt, and his assistants, John A. Bingham and Colonel Henry L. Burnett. As a demonstration of the efficiency with which this guidance was effected, the records show that of fifty-four objections, as recorded by Pitman, only three made by the prosecution were overruled. The defence, on the other hand, made twelve objections, all of which were overruled.

Holt had gained some notoriety as an unyielding judge-advocate during the war. He had handled the Fitz-John–Porter case,[1] and had obtained a favourable decision, which, after the war psychosis had subsided, was upset by the adverse ruling of another court. Even then his methods had been of a questionable nature, according to Welles: 'The *Chronicle* contains the argument of Judge-Advocate Holt. . . .', he observed. 'It seems to have been made after the finding of the Court instead of before, and is sent out with it as if in defense of the decision. The proceeding is singular and will be likely to cause censure.'[2]

The argument of Holt's assistant in the conspiracy trial was not sent out before the case; it was sent out afterward, but apparently also in defence of the case, and so widely that objections were raised from some quarters. 'Do not, I pray you, flatter yourself', Representative Eldredge of Wisconsin wrote to Holt in September 1865, 'that you and the Secretary of War can, by the circulation of these documents at your own or the people's expense, convince your countrymen that arrests without warrant, imprisonment without trial . . . and the worse than mockery of your victims in military trials, are anything but crimes. . . .'[3]

Against their redoubtable opponents the accused could pit only such legal talent as they procured at the last moment and under the greatest difficulties. The files of the War Department contain mute evidence of the frantic search for counsel by the accused. Some of the lawyers were busy on other matters: others shuddered at the thought of becoming involved in a case that promised little money and less fame and meant almost certain Government persecution. In view of these conditions it is remarkable that such an imposing array of counsel could have been produced for the defence. At the head stood the name of Reverdy Johnson, one of the foremost legal lights of his day, formerly attorney-general of the United States and at this time senator from Maryland. Next to him the observer is impressed by the name of General Thomas Ewing, Jun., a Federal officer just back from active service, and a brother-in-law of General

[1] *Battles and Leaders of the Civil War* (Century Co., New York, 1884-7, used by courtesy of D. Appleton-Century Co.), II, p. 696.

[2] Welles, *Diary*, I, p. 229.

[3] Mudd, op. cit., p. 131.

Sherman. Of the remainder, Doster and Cox were good men in their line: Aiken and Clampitt were juniors of Reverdy Johnson, but soon had almost all the work to do in defending Mrs. Surratt, for the senior counsel was bitterly insulted before he had really opened the case, and the resulting passage of words eliminated him as a useful defender of his client.[1]

The arrangement of the court was such that the witnesses had their backs toward the defending lawyers and were not permitted by the court to turn their heads to them when under examination.[2] What a handicap this must have been is obvious. But counsel for the defence had worse than that to contend with.

'I can not forbear the remark', said Cox in his final plea before the court, 'that, upon this trial, both the accused and their counsel have labored under disadvantages not incident to the civil courts, and unusual even in military trials. In both the civil courts and courts-martial the accused receives not only a copy of the charge, or indictment, in time to prepare his defence, but also a list of the witnesses with whom he is to be confronted. And, in the civil courts, it is usual for the prosecutor to state in advance the general nature of the case he expects to establish, and the general scope of the evidence he expects to adduce. . . . In this case the accused were aroused from their slumbers on the night before their arraignment, and, for the first time, presented with a copy of the charge. For the most part, they were unable to procure counsel until the trial had commenced and, when counsel were admitted, they came to the discharge of their duties in utter ignorance of the whole case which they were to combat . . . as well as, for the most part, wholly unacquainted with the prisoners and their antecedents. . . .'[3]

Ed Spangler, one of the prisoners, was without counsel until three days after the commencement of the proceedings against him. General Ewing did not see the charges and specifications until his clients had pleaded, nor did he get a seat in the courtroom until evidence was being introduced. On the next day Ewing complained that he and the other lawyers for the accused were not getting official copies of the court record in time to re-examine witnesses in case an error was discovered. The

[1] DeWitt, *Assassination*, pp. 106–10.
[2] DeWitt, *Mary E. Surratt*, p. 39.
[3] Pitman, op. cit., p. 333.

president of the commission agreed that witnesses should be detained one day at least, but when the judge-advocate was asked his opinion, he objected, thereupon General Hunter changed his mind, and another feeble attempt at fair play was defeated.[1]

Compelled to produce their own witnesses, the lawyers for the defence frequently had to spend almost the entire night in obtaining them from remote points of the adjoining states. During the day their labours were severe. Usually the trial lasted from ten in the morning till six at night, and the impure air in the crowded courtroom during the hot summer days of Washington must have sapped the vitality of the small troup who had to fight against such heavy odds.[2]

On 26 May the correspondent of the *New York World* sketched some of the persons in the courtroom in the following manner:

'The counsel for the accused strike me as being commonplace lawyers. They either have no chance or no pluck to assert the dignity of their profession. Reverdy Johnson is not here. The first day disgusted him, as he is a practitioner of *law*. . . .

'The commission has collectively an imposing appearance: the face of Judge Holt is swarthy; he questions with slow utterance, holding the witness in his cold, measuring eye. Hunter, who sits at the opposite end of the table, shuts his eyes now and then, either to sleep or to think, or both, and the other generals . . . watch for occasions to distinguish themselves.

'Excepting Judge Holt, the court has shown as little ability as could be expected from soldiers, placed in unenviable publicity, and upon a duty for which they are disqualified, both by education and acumen. Witness the lack of dignity in Hunter, who opened the court by a coarse allusion to "humbug chivalry"; of Lew. Wallace, whose heat and intolerance were appropriately urged in the most exceptional English; of Howe, whose tirade against the rebel General Johnson was feeble as it was ungenerous! This court was needed to show us at least the petty tyranny of martial law and the pettiness of martial jurists. The

[1] Pitman, op. cit., pp. 242, 243.
[2] Clampitt, op. cit., p. 234.

counsel for the defense have just enough show to make the unfairness of the trial partake of hypocrisy. . . .'

Commenting on the variety of the evidence which the prosecution presented in order to charge the atmosphere with a background of hatred the *World* remarked sarcastically that 'the wideness of subjects discussed makes one imagine that the object of the commission is to write a cyclopedia, and not to hang or acquit six or eight miserable wretches'.

The reporter could not suppress a grim joke that came to his mind as the farce in the courtroom developed before his eyes. 'What rights do accused persons enjoy?' a boy was asked by his teacher. 'Death by hanging,' was the rejoinder.[1]

An illustration of the attitude the court was wont to take against the lawyers for the defence is furnished by a discussion which took place on 29 May. It showed how these men were manœuvred into difficult positions when they tried to protect the interests of their clients, and how the members of the commission abused their prerogatives.

When the court met on 29 May Mr. Clampitt rose and asked for the recall of Henry Von Steinacker, the deserter about whom the judge-advocate had such damning evidence in his secret records, but whom he had not hesitated to use as a witness. The defence now had unearthed some of the past of this double-deserter and wanted him back for the purpose of cross-examination.

THE JUDGE-ADVOCATE. If the Court please, although the testimony of Von Steinacker has no earthly connection with Mrs. Surratt's case, I am perfectly willing he shall be recalled, if he can be found. I do not know where he is.

This sneering remark might easily have closed the argument. When wanted as a witness for the Government Von Steinacker was brought from Fort Delaware, where he had been held prisoner. He had subsequently been released, and no one knew where he had gone. Holt could afford to be generous, knowing as he did that Von Steinacker, being under a three-year sentence and obviously freed in gratitude for his testimony, would not linger near the scene of his crimes. But such a tame ending did

---

[1] Townsend, op. cit., pp. 67, 68, 69.

not suit the court members, and they went about provoking further trouble.

GENERAL WALLACE. I should like to inquire if the Judge-Advocate has at any time declined to issue the proper summons for the witness whose presence is desired.

THE JUDGE-ADVOCATE. Not at all. On the contrary, I have offered to do so, and to use every effort in my power. I have no more knowledge of the whereabouts of that witness than the gentlemen themselves.

GENERAL WALLACE. I asked the question with the view of seeing what necessity there was for putting this paper on our record. As I understand it, the Judge-Advocate has never refused, and I know the Court has not, to issue a summons for the witness.

In such cunning fashion an altogether false issue was raised in a few moments' time. The discussion continued:

MR. CLAMPITT. Certainly not.

GENERAL WALLACE. Then why make such an application?

MR. CLAMPITT. Counsel for the defence have never stated that there was any delinquency, or any desire on the part of the prosecution to deny to the counsel for the accused any witness they may call for; but it was for another reason and for another purpose that this paper was presented.

THE JUDGE-ADVOCATE. . . . . this witness might be recalled if he could be found.

The matter seemed once more to have come to a fairly amicable close. But the court rekindled the dying flames.

THE PRESIDENT. The decision of the Commission last week was, that if the witness, Von Steinacker, was desired by the defence, every effort would be made to obtain his attendance.

MR. AIKEN. We stated, in reply to that, that we did not wish to have Von Steinacker called for the defence. The object of his recall is simply . . . to impeach him.

THE PRESIDENT. . . . . if you did not wish to call him for the defence, as you had a full opportunity of cross-examining him when he was on the stand before, the Commission would not send for him.

MR. AIKEN. But, at the time . . . [we] were not aware that it was the purpose of the Government to connect Mrs. Surratt years back with Mr. Booth as aiding . . . a conspiracy to assassinate the President; and not knowing any thing about the man at that time, and supposing what he stated to be true, he was not then cross-examined at all. These facts have since come to light; and it is as much for the benefit of the Government that a man of that description should be known.

GENERAL WALLACE. I should like to know for which one of the prisoners this paper is considered necessary.

MR. AIKEN. For Mrs. Surratt; but it has a bearing, in a degree, on all of them.

GENERAL WALLACE. Will the gentleman please state the connection of the paper with Mrs. Surratt's case?

Mr. Aiken was now in an embarrassing predicament. Denying on one hand that the perjured testimony regarding some alleged utterances of Booth in 1863 had anything to do with the lady under his charge, he was forced to argue that the matter did concern her, as otherwise he could not have asked for Von Steinacker's recall.

MR. AIKEN. We wish to prove that Mr. Booth was not in Virginia at the time stated by Von Steinacker. . . . I suppose we have the right to prove by the witnesses who are here that they would not believe Von Steinacker on his oath.

THE JUDGE-ADVOCATE. . . . I wish the Court not to consider the question whether such a paper as this, so extremely defamatory in its character, shall be allowed to go upon the record here . . . whether there is any legitimate object to be obtained by spreading upon the records a paper so full of bitter aspersion upon the character of a witness who is absent as this is.

GENERAL WALLACE. I, for my part, object . . . and wish to say now that I understand distinctly, and hold in supreme contempt, such practices as this. It is very discreditable to the parties concerned, to the attorneys, and, if permitted, in my judgment will be discreditable to the Court.

And so, instead of being allowed to impeach Von Steinacker's testimony, the defence was itself charged by a member of the court with discreditable practices deserving of supreme contempt.

All this time the judge-advocate knew that Von Steinacker had a criminal record, and the accounts thereof were then on file among his papers. Perhaps this explains the relative gentleness with which he handled his opponents; or maybe his courtesy was due to his knowledge that Von Steinacker was safely stowed away in distant lands. But the members of the court took the offensive where the prosecutor left off; the wonder is not that counsel for the defence lost heart; the wonder is that they kept on fighting. Even after being so roughly handled in the Von Steinacker matter Clampitt showed considerable courage in thus addressing the court:

'We are here standing within the portals of this constituted temple of justice; we are here for the purpose of defending the very citadel of life; and we have felt it to be our duty . . . to use every exertion that is in our power, and consistent with the forms that obtain before a court, to impeach or destroy the testimony of any witness that can properly be impeached; and it was for that purpose that we have made this application, and for the purpose of shielding the accused, if possible. It was at the same time our bounden duty, and an obligation that we owed to her, that we should spread before this Court the character of the witness that has been brought here on the part of the prosecution. I make this explanation, and I hope it will be satisfactory to the Court.'[1]

To this manly speech General Wallace replied curtly that it was not satisfactory to him. And it may safely be assumed that the remainder of the court agreed with him.

The story of this strange interlude was not allowed to be spread on the records and does not, therefore, appear in Pitman's official report of the conspiracy trial.

In commenting upon the proceedings of the military court a year later Congressman Rogers wrote:

'In the progress of that trial every precaution taught by ages of experience and sanctified by authority was set aside.

[1] Poore, op. cit., II, pp. 371–4.

'The prisoners, said to have been incited to murder, by bullet, by infection, by arson, and by poison, by Jefferson Davis, were brought to hear these charges and specifications with irons upon them, with irons, too, of an unusual construction, irritating and painful, well calculated to distract their attention from the sayings of the military prosecutor . . . since the trial of Cranbourne, in 1696 . . . no prisoner has ever been tried in irons before a legitimate court anywhere that English is spoken. The chief justice of England said:

' "Look you, keeper, you should take off the prisoners' irons when they are at the bar, for they should stand at their ease when they are tried."

'But the parties alleged to have been incited by Mr. Davis did not so stand, but stood in constrainment and in pain, with their heads buried in a sort of sack, devised to prevent their seeing! In this plight, from dark cells, they were brought to be charged with having been incited by Mr. Davis, and to it they pleaded not guilty.'[1]

This, then, was the setting of the court in which the so-called conspirators were forced to stand trial.

The charge against all prisoners was that of 'maliciously, unlawfully, and traitorously, and in aid of the existing armed rebellion against the United States of America . . . combining, confederating, and conspiring together with . . . Jefferson Davis . . . and others unknown, to kill and murder, within the Military Department of Washington, and within the fortified and entrenched lines thereof, Abraham Lincoln . . . and lying in wait with intent . . . to kill . . . Andrew Johnson . . . and . . . Ulysses S. Grant . . .'.[2]

In vain General Ewing endeavoured to show that such a combination of crimes as cited in the indictment was unknown to law; he wanted the judge-advocate to explain whether the prisoners were on trial for conspiracy, a known offence, or for four crimes in one—conspiracy, murder, attempt at murder, and lying-in-wait.

[1] House of Representatives, Report No. 104, p. 32.
[2] Pitman, op. cit., pp. 18, 19; see also supplementary note to chapter xx, 'Holt Shuns Publicity'.

He could not tell, he contended, with how many different crimes his clients were charged. 'The offenses enumerated . . . are separate and distinct, and we, therefore, ask that the Judge Advocate should state . . . of which of said offenses . . . he claims they should each be convicted.'[1]

Assistant-Judge-Advocate Bingham replied that it was all one transaction. Thereupon Ewing struck another blow in behalf of the accused. He wanted to know by what code the unheard-of crime of ' "traitorously" murdering, or . . . assaulting, or . . . lying in wait' was defined. To this the judge-advocate could only answer that the common law of war embraced all these crimes. Then Ewing gave up in dismay. 'I am as much in the dark now', he said as he sat down, '. . . as I was in reference to the other inquiry.'[2]

General Ewing, in his final argument, stated very succinctly the issue thus created by the ingenious judge-advocate:

'. . . it then becomes a question vitally important to some of these parties—a question of life and death—whether you will punish only offenses created and declared by *law*, or whether you will make and declare the past acts of the accused to be crimes, which acts the law never heretofore declared criminal: . . . adapt the evidence to the crime and the crime to the evidence, and thus convict and punish. This, I greatly fear may be the purpose, especially since the Judge Advocate said . . . that he would expect to convict '*under the common law of war*'. This is a term unknown to our language—a *quiddity*—wholly undefined and incapable of definition. It is, in short, just what the Judge Advocate chooses to make of it.'[3]

When former Attorney-General Bates, in his retirement at St. Louis, read the legal quibbling through which the judge-advocate had robbed the prisoners of a proper defence, his anger rose.

'*The Laws and usages of war!*' he exclaimed. 'What are they? Who knows them? Are they written in any book? Are they prescribed by any acknowledged authority? There is no such thing as the *Laws of War*. War is the very reverse of Law—and

---

[1] Pitman, op. cit., p. 245.
[2] Ibid., p. 247.
[3] Ibid., p. 318.

its existence always implies . . . the absence or disregard of all law.'[1]

Holt must have felt that his legal position was not tenable, but a chance remark during the trial gave him an opportunity to establish an entirely new basis for his attacks, and he was not slow to develop it. When the prisoner Arnold was shown to have been a Confederate soldier at one time, and the prosecution tried to construe his entering that army as a crime, Ewing said indignantly that his client had not entered the army to assassinate the President.

'Yes,' cried Bingham, 'he entered into it to assassinate the President; and everybody else that entered into the rebellion, entered it to assassinate everybody that represented this Government. . . .' Bingham still harped on this theme in his final argument before the commission, when he said: 'The rebellion, in aid of which this conspiracy was formed and this great public crime committed, was . . . itself . . . a criminal conspiracy and gigantic assassination.' In this fashion all prisoners who had been wearing Confederate uniforms were guilty of Lincoln's murder without specific evidence, which, as the *New York World* remarked, 'is like attributing the measles to the creation of man'.[2]

Jefferson Davis was at the head of this 'gigantic assassination', and if the military commission could be induced to follow this extraordinary reasoning, the Government could logically have dispensed with all its perjured testimony and still obtained a conviction. The judges, being soldiers who had just fought the South for several years, could be expected to abide by the judge-advocate's arguments. Apparently they did.

'Their [the judges'] position towards the government . . .', wrote one of them later, 'had placed them where they were, as officers in its military service, and they could not be served from the loyal discharge of their duty';[3] their duty being, evidently, to find all the prisoners guilty.

One of the most absurd features of the trial was the offering

[1] Bates, *Diary*, p. 501.
[2] Pitman, op. cit., pp. 239, 351; Townsend, op. cit., p. 42.
[3] Harris, *Assassination*, p. 111.

as evidence of a cipher letter, supposed to have been picked up at Morehead City, North Carolina, as it came floating in on the tides of the river. A pile-driving contractor named Duell and his assistant, James Ferguson, had made this unusual find. At first they thought the letter was written in a foreign language, but the cipher was so plain that even these working men had no trouble puzzling out its contents, which read in part as follows:

Washington, April the 15, '65.
DEAR JOHN: I am happy to inform you that Pet has done his work well. He is safe, and Old Abe is in hell. Now, sir, all eyes are on you. You must bring Sherman—Grant is in the hands of Old Gray ere this. Red Shoes showed lack of nerve in Seward's case, but fell back in good order. *Johnson* must come. Old Crook has him in charge. . . .

Now, I say again, the lives of our brave officers, and the life of the South depend upon the carrying this programme into effect. . . . It's ordered no more letters shall be sent by mail.[1]

Note the abrupt change in this communication, from a stilted melodramatic verbiage to the easy flowing style of the cultured writer. But more remarkable still is the fact that the letter, although ostensibly written on 15 April and not picked up until the beginning of May, bore no marks of having been in the water for any length of time.

'The letter is picked out of the water at Morehead City', mocked Mr. Cox, one of the lawyers for the defence, 'no more blurred, I think, than any paper on this table. It looks as if it had been written and dropped in the water immediately before it was found, for the very purpose of being picked up by the Government agents, to be used as evidence.'[2] Cox might have added that the puerile statement about avoiding the mail, which was supposed to make the appearance of this cipher communication more plausible, made it, instead, an object of increased suspicion.

But more extraordinary even than the origin of this letter was the question of its admissibility as evidence and the discussion which took place concerning that point. General Ewing pleaded earnestly that it be disregarded by the commission.

[1] Pitman, op. cit., p. 42.
[2] Ibid., p. 68.

'In the first place,' he said, 'I really believe the letter to be fictitious, and to bear upon its face the evidence that it is so. In the second place, it is testimony that is wholly inadmissible under the plainest rules of evidence. It is not signed; the handwriting was not proved; it was in cipher; it was not shown at all that it was traced to anybody proved or charged to be connected with this conspiracy. . . .'[1]

This argument Mr. Bingham met with a remarkable contention; the charge against the prisoners, he declared, was that they had entered into the conspiracy with certain parties named and with others unknown, and that, therefore, the letter should be accepted as evidence. Which singular reasoning Mr. Cox was not slow to hold up to ridicule.

'The logic of my learned friend on the other side seems to be this: It is sufficiently established . . . that Booth was engaged in a conspiracy with some unknown persons; this letter comes from an unknown person; *ergo*, it is a letter from somebody connected with Booth in this conspiracy . . . this letter comes from somebody unknown; therefore it is admissible in evidence. . . . I submit to the Court that this is chop-logic.'[2]

After this the commission ruled—without blushing, so far as is known—that the letter should be admitted as evidence.

There were other letters of similar character brought forth during the trial, among them one addressed to 'J.W.B.' at the National Hotel in Washington. Perhaps what Robert Purdy, one of the Government's own witnesses, testified in regard to it throws some light on the others.

'I am acting for the Government', he declared under cross-examination, 'as detective and scout. I have been charged with writing that letter myself.'[3]

The introduction of a witness from New York, a Mrs. Mary Hudspeth, provided a farcical byplay in the solemnities of the trial. This good lady was riding on a street car one day in November 1864 when she overheard two men in earnest conversation. After they had left the car she picked up two letters which they had dropped. One of them was addressed to 'Louis',

[1] Pitman, op. cit., p. 66.
[2] Ibid., p. 68.
[3] Ibid., p. 43.

threatening the life of Lincoln in a picturesque fashion—'*Abe* must *die*, and *now*. . . . The cup failed us once, and might again . . . strike for your home, strike for your country . . .' and similar drivel. The other was written to her 'Dearest Husband' in an unknown feminine hand.[1] These two notes, known as the 'Selby' and 'Leenea' letters, were destined to become prominent in the trial of the conspirators.

Mrs. Hudspeth took the letters to General Dix, who forwarded them to Washington with some short and contemptuous comments, as if obeying an embarrassing duty.

'I should have thought the whole thing got up for the Sunday Mercury,' he remarked, 'but for the genuine letter from St. Louis in a female hand. The Charles Selby is obviously a manufacture.'[2]

Why a 'genuine letter from St. Louis', written 'in a female hand', should be considered above suspicion the general did not say. He merely stated that without these two remarkable features he would have considered both letters a joke. Nevertheless, the Bureau of Military Justice laid great stress on these documents in order to prove the existence of a plot as early as 1864. There remained only the proof that this plot—if one may dignify it by that title—could be connected with Booth.

Mrs. Hudspeth was sure that one of the two gentlemen had been that famous person, because he had a very white hand that had never been soiled by hard work. In the Surratt trial two years later she emphasized this point by adding that 'it was quite a small hand', thereby ruining her testimony, for Booth was known to have had a large hand, so large, in fact, that it approached deformity. But the dear lady, who so obviously enjoyed the limelight, had also noticed a scar on the right cheek of the mysterious stranger. This was tantalizing, for Booth had carried a scar on his neck; but although gently coaxed to say that the blemish was on the neck, she stuck to her story that it was near the jawbone, looking like a bite. With this the assistant judge-advocate had to be satisfied. But if he was, Pitman was not; for he omitted this whole incident from his report.[3]

To make a confused story more confounded, it may be added

---

[1] Pitman, op. cit., p. 40.

[2] Dana, op. cit., p. 276; also War Department Archives.

[3] *Surratt Trial*, I, p. 353; Poore, op. cit., I, p. 26; Pitman, op. cit., p. 39.

Ex. No. 85.

Headquarters Department of the East,

New York City, 17. Nov, 1864.

C. A. Dana Esq,

My dear Sir,

The enclosed was picked up in a 3d Av. R.R. Car. I should have thought the whole thing got up for the Window Mercury, but for the genuine letter I have of this in a female hand. The Charles Selby is obviously a manufacture. The party, who dropped the letter was heard to say he should start for Washington ~~Thursday~~ Friday night. He is of medium size, has black hair & whiskers, but the latter are believed to be a disguise. He had disappeared before the letter was picked up & examined.

Very truly,

John A. Dix

Letter from General John A. Dix to C. A. Dana, forwarding the famous
Charles Selby and Leenea letters.

Original letter in the Archives of the War Department

that Major Eckert, while riding in a street car on 26 November 1864, picked up an unsealed envelope of similar import. The enclosures, which Major Eckert examined, included 'a letter giving directions, evidently referring to a kidnapping plot and also a picture of Lincoln with a rope around his neck. . . . These papers were afterward discovered to belong to Payne, the assassin.'[1]

Major Eckert did not testify to this, however, preferring to keep the matter from the court and from the public. Had he added this story to that of the two desperate conspirators who talked loudly of their plans in a crowded street car and then obligingly dropped some incriminating messages, even that jury of stern officers might have indulged in a smile.

[1] Bates, *Lincoln in the Telegraph Office*, p. 298.

CHAPTER XXI

The Prisoners at the Bar

Eight prisoners faced the military commission when the trial opened on 10 May 1865; all of them deserve at least passing consideration.

There was George A. Atzerodt, a shrinking little man of German ancestry and no breeding. His parents had emigrated from Seebach, a village near the Prussian town of Langensalza, in 1844, when the defendant was only eight years old; but although the boy had grown to maturity in the United States, he was still a Prussian subject and spoke English with a German accent.[1] Atzerodt was undoubtedly involved in the kidnapping plot, and his part would have been the transportation of Lincoln and his captors across the Potomac from Port Tobacco. In a confession made by him he admitted guilty knowledge of the proposed assassination, but maintained that he had been told of it only a few hours before the perpetration of the deed, and had then positively refused to take part in it. Whatever fate the judges meted out to him, Atzerodt could hope for no sympathy.

Lewis Paine, who had attempted the life of Secretary Seward and who had almost massacred his household, cheerfully admitted his complicity. This young giant with the defiant eyes offered no defence and expected to walk to the gallows with his head erect and a joke on his lips. He was a Confederate soldier who had done his duty as he had seen it. A plea in his favour was a mere formality and a waste of time. But to the prison guards he was a hero, and they showed him what little

[1] War Department Archives, statement by his brother, John C. Atzerodt, and consular correspondence; see also supplementary note to chapter xxi, 'A Confession by Atzerodt'.

favours they could under the circumstances. Even on the scaffold the executioner assured him that he would make death as easy as possible for him; but in his anxiety to do so he bungled his job, and Paine died in the horrible agony of slow strangulation.[1]

Edward Spangler, the happy-go-lucky scene-shifter at Ford's Theatre, could not be connected with the crime by any evidence the prosecution could gather against him, and so escaped with a six-year prison sentence.

Michael O'Laughlin and Sam Arnold had been anxious to help Booth in the abduction of the President, but had drawn the line at assassination. They had retired from the adventure after the failure of 20 March.

The conspiracy trial has been described by able writers, and an account of it here is therefore unnecessary. There are some features of it, however, that have never been fully brought out, because all the material was not at the disposal of the recording historians. They pertain particularly to Herold, Dr. Mudd, and Mrs. Surratt.

David E. Herold, a young man of twenty-two years at the time of the assassination, is usually dismissed from serious consideration because of the general reputation he bore. Friendly witnesses described him as something of an imbecile; pleasant, trifling, but irresponsible. A physician who had known him for six years considered him a very light, trivial, unreliable boy with a leaning toward practical jokes, and with the mind of an eleven-year-old child.[2] His counsel doubtless thought this the best line of defence. Nevertheless, it does not appear that all evidence which might have mitigated Herold's offence was put to proper use.

After his return to Washington on 27 April Herold was subjected to a thorough examination by Assistant Judge-Advocate John Bingham. His statements have never reached the printing-press, although they are of considerable interest. According to his own story Herold was not in Washington after eight o'clock on the evening of 14 April. He had an opportunity to sell a horse in Maryland, he said, and was on the other side of the Potomac

[1] Townsend, op. cit., p. 75.
[2] Pitman, op. cit., p. 97.

when the tragedy at Ford's Theatre was enacted. Riding back
to town, he met Booth at approximately half-past eleven o'clock,
at the bottom of Soper's Hill, about eight miles out of the capital.
The actor used all his powers of persuasion to induce the boy to
accompany him to Bryantown, where the two were to start out
on a hunting party. But soon Herold became suspicious, because
Booth was heavily armed and because he could not hide the
injury to his leg; in the end, the latter's insistence prevailed and
the pair rode together as far as Bryantown, where they separated.
Next morning they met again, and Herold saw that his friend's
leg had been set. Buying some provisions by the wayside from
a man whose name Herold had forgotten, the travellers continued to the house of a Mr. Thomas. He refused them food;
but a thicket in the neighbourhood of his house provided a good
hiding-place, and there the fugitives lived for a week, buying
and begging food and drink from chance passers-by. All this
time Herold, so he claimed, kept protesting that he wanted to
return to Washington, as by then the murder had become known
to him; but Booth kept him in line by promises of big rewards
and by threats of death. A few days later Herold accidentally
found an old boat on the Potomac, in which he and Booth finally
crossed.

From this point on, Herold's story became more compatible
with provable facts and dates. He began to introduce names and
places, and his memory suddenly improved remarkably; for he
could well imagine that the authorities, independent of his own
testimony, were in a position to check up on his trip through
Virginia.[1]

Herold's statements are significant, for they mirror the character of their author more accurately than anything that has been
told about him. His story hangs together tolerably well; the
most remarkable thing about it, though, is the care with which
he tried to protect all those who befriended him and Booth
during their flight. He avoided mentioning Dr. Mudd's name
in fairly good fashion; he disguised Cox's name; he accounted
for the provisions furnished to him and to Booth while they
were hiding without dragging Jones into the picture. Where
he wished to remember things he did so; where his disclosures
might injure a friend he became vague and indefinite. It is doubt-

[1] War Department Archives.

ful if Bingham received a great deal of satisfaction from his interview with the reputedly childish prisoner.

Herold's attorneys could have partly corroborated his statements had they taken the trouble to do so. He had said, for instance, that he was on the Maryland side of the Potomac when the assassination took place. This may have been the case, though it is not probable. On the occasion of the attempted abduction of Lincoln on 20 March his part had been to hang around Lloyd's tavern at Surrattsville and to provide the kidnappers with additional implements upon their arrival. Now, there were only two people who claimed to have seen Herold in Washington on the evening of 14 April: John Fletcher, the stable-man, who met him on Pennsylvania Avenue about ten o'clock; and Sergeant Cobb, who permitted him to pass across the bridge. Fletcher was not very close to him at the time and might have mistaken him in the uncertain light of the gas lamps; he probably was more certain of the horse than of the rider. Sergeant Cobb did not really identify Herold at all.

'I brought him up before the guard-house door', he testified, 'so that the light shone full in his face and on his horse.' At this point in Cobb's examination Herold was directed to stand up for identification. 'He is very near the size of the second horseman,' declared Cobb, 'but, I should think, taller, although I can not be sure. . . . He had a lighter complexion than this man.'[1]

One would think that a clever lawyer might have made something out of this testimony; and it is barely possible that, with good legal protection, Herold would have been considered by the court merely an accessory after the crime. But Frederick Stone, who conducted the defence for the unfortunate youth, did little more than apologize for pleading his client's case. The very introduction to his closing argument was not happily chosen.

'*May it please the Court*,' he commenced. 'At the earnest request of the widowed mother and estimable sisters of the accused, I have consented to act as his counsel in the case now before the Court.' Such an inept beginning was clearly prejudicial to Herold's interests. 'Of the fact that this boy, Herold,' he said later in his speech, "was an aider and abettor in the *escape* of

[1] Pitman, op. cit., p. 85.

254

Booth, there is no rational or reasonable doubt. He was clearly guilty of that crime, and must abide by its consequences.'[1]

There is a possibility that with a well-conducted fight in his behalf David Herold might have been sent to the Dry Tortugas rather than to the gallows, and if he had lived through the epidemic of yellow fever there he might have attained as ripe an old age as Arnold.

Of more interest than the fate of Herold is that of Dr. Samuel A. Mudd, the country physician of Bryantown, whose chief crime was the setting of a broken bone for a stranger who came to him for medical aid in the middle of the night. The events that connected him with the assassination of Lincoln and finally brought him as a manacled prisoner face to face with the military commission are, perhaps, in fairness to Dr. Mudd's memory, best set forth in his own sworn statement before Colonel Wells on 22 April, the day after his arrest. This statement was never given to the public and is of singular interest:

'Last Saturday morning April 15, about four o'clock, two men called at my house and knocked very loudly. I was aroused by the noise, and as it was such an unusual thing for persons to knock loudly, I took the precaution of asking who were there before opening the door. After they had knocked twice more I opened the door, but before doing so they told me they were two strangers on their way to Washington; that one of their horses had fallen by which one of the men had broken his leg.[2] On opening the door I found two men. One on a horse led by the other man who had tied his horse to a tree nearby. I aided the man in getting off his horse and into the house, and laid him on the sofa in my parlor. After getting a light I assisted him in getting up stairs where there were two beds, one of which he took. He seemed to be very much injured in the back, and complained very much of it. I did not see his face at all. He seemed to be tremulous and not inclined to talk, and had his cloak thrown around his head, and seemed inclined to sleep, as

[1] Pitman, op. cit., pp. 268, 272.
[2] The original statement says 'sprained or fractured', which is crossed out and replaced by 'broken'.

I thought, in order to ease himself; and every now and then he would groan pretty heavily. I had no proper pasteboard for making splints, and went and got an old bandbox and made one of it, and as he wanted it done hastily I hurried more than I otherwise would. He wanted me to fix it up anyway, as he said he wanted to get back, or get home and have it done by a regular Physician. I then took a piece of the bandbox and split it in half, doubled it at right angles and took some paste and pasted it into a splint. On examination I found there was a straight fracture of the tibia about two inches above the ankle. My examination was quite short and I did not find the adjoining bone fractured in any way. I do not regard it a peculiarly painful or dangerous wound. There was nothing resembling a compound fracture. I do not suppose I was more than three quarters of an hour in making the examination of the wound and applying the splint.

'He continued still to suffer and complained of severe pain in the back especially when being moved. In my opinion pain in the back may originate from riding. I judge that in this case it originated from his fall and also from riding, as he seemed to be prostrated. He sometimes breathed very shortly and as if exhausted. He was a man I should suppose about five feet ten inches high and appeared to be pretty well made; but he had a heavy shawl on all the time. I suppose he would weigh 150 or 160 pounds. His hair was black and seemed to be somewhat inclined to curl. It was worn long. He had a pretty full forehead and his skin was fair. He was very pale when I saw him and appeared as if accustomed to in-door rather than out-door life. I do not know how to describe his skin exactly, but I should think he might be classed as dark, and his paleness might be attributed to receiving this injury. I did not observe his hand, to see whether it was small or large. I have been shown the photograph of *J. Wilkes Booth* and I should not think that this was the man from any resemblance to the photograph; but from other causes I have every reason to believe he is the man whose leg I dressed as above stated.

In order to examine and operate upon his leg, I had occasion to cut his boot longitudinally, in front of the instep. It seems that when he left my house this boot was left behind. Yesterday morning my attention was called to this boot which is a long top-boot.

On making an examination of it I find written on the inside in apparently a German hand, what I take to be "*Henry Luz*, maker, 445 Broadway, *J. Wilkes*". I did not notice the writing in this boot until my attention was called to it by Lieut. Lovett, (Boot produced and identified by deponent as the one taken from the leg of the wounded man.) I have seen J. Wilkes Booth. I was introduced to him by Mr. J. C. Thompson, a son-in-law of Dr. William Queen, in November or December last. Mr. Thompson resides with his father-in-law, and his place is about five miles Southwesterly from Bryantown, near the lower edge of what is known as Zechiah Swamp. Mr. Thompson told me at the time that Booth was looking out for lands in the neighborhood or in this county; he said he was not very particular where, if he could get such a lot as he wanted, whether it was in Charles, Prince George, or St. Mary's Co.; and Booth inquired if I knew any parties in this neighborhood who had any fine horses for sale. I told him there was a neighbor of mine who had some very fine traveling horses, and he said he thought if he could purchase one reasonable, he would do so and would ride up to Washington on him instead of riding in the stage. The next evening he rode to my house and staid with me that night, and the next morning he purchased a rather old horse, but a very fine mover, of Mr. George Gardner Sr., who resides but a short distance from my house. I would know the horse if I should see him again. He is a darkish bay horse, not bright bay, with tolerably large head and had a defect in one eye. Booth gave eighty dollars for the horse.

'I have never seen Booth since that time to my knowledge until last Saturday morning. When I assisted the wounded man into my house on Saturday morning last, the other party with him, who appeared to be very youthful, took charge of the horse, and said he would keep it and the other one until they could be put in the stable; as soon as I could I woke my colored man Frank Washington and sent him out to put the horses in the stable; and the young man came into the house. After setting the wounded man's leg the best I could for the time, I think I walked around to my farm-yard and gave some directions, and when I returned breakfast was ready, and as this young man was up and knocking about, I asked him to come to breakfast. He did so, but the other man remained up stairs in bed. I did not know who this young man was, but he remarked that he had seen me. He appeared to be a very fast young man and was very talkative. He was about five feet, two or three inches high, I would not be positive as to his height. He had a smooth face and appeared as if he had never shaved; his hair was black, and I should consider his complexion dark. I did not notice his eyes very particularly. He wore a dark-colored business coat. I have seen the photograph of Herold but I do not recognize it as that of this young man. He seemed to be well acquainted throughout the whole country and I asked his name. He gave it as Henston, and that of the wounded man as Tyser or Tyson. I did not hear either of them address the other by the first name. The only thing that excited my suspicion, upon reflecting upon these circumstances was that after breakfast, when I was about to leave for my farm-work, this young man asked me if I had a razor about the house, that his friend desired to take a shave, as perhaps he would feel better. I had noticed that the wounded man had whiskers and a moustache when he came into the house. After dinner I went to see the patient and although he kept his face partly turned away from me, I noticed that he had lost his moustaches but still retained his whiskers. I did not pay sufficient attention to his beard to determine whether it was false or natural. This young man asked me if I could fix up, clumsily, some crutches for his friend to hobble along with, and I went down to the old Englishman I had there, who had a saw and augur, and he and I made a rude pair of crutches out of a piece of plank and sent them to him.

'This young man mentioned the names of several parties in this neighborhood whom he knew; among others several here in Bryantown. . . . After dinner between twelve and one o'clock . . . this young man and I rode over to my father's place in order to see if we could get a carriage for the wounded man; but I found that the carriages were all out of repair except one, and we could not get that one. He then concluded to go to Bryantown for a conveyance to get his friend over as far as his friend Mr. Wilmer. I then went down to Mr. Hardy's and was in conversation with him fully an hour, when I returned home leisurely and found the two men were just in the act of leaving. The young man inquired of me the nearest way to Mr. Wilmer's. I told him there were two ways; one was by the public road leading by Bryantown; the other led across the Swamp directly across from me, by which they could save a mile; both are easterly. This road from my house is directly across in a strait line. It is not a public way, but by taking down a fence you can get through. They concluded to take this latter route, and I gave them the necessary directions. I did not see them leave my house. The man on crutches had left the house when I got back, and he was some fifty to seventy yards from me when this young man came to me and began to inquire of me the direction. I do not know how or where Booth got a conveyance away from my house. He did not go in a carriage but he undoubtedly went on horseback. When they came there in the morning this young man said that one of the horses would not stand without tying and asked that both of them should be put in the stable. He held one of the horses until I returned into the house with the wounded man, when I called a colored boy named Frank Washington, and sent him round to take the horses to the stable. I have also a white man named Thomas Davis who has charge of my horses, and I judge that he saw the horses which were in the stable during Saturday.

'I judge that between four and five o'clock on Saturday afternoon they left my house. I do not know where they went. I have not been spoken to by any one for professional advice in their behalf since that time, and have not seen either of them since. It is about four miles across from my house to Parson Wilmer's; and by the public road it is about five miles. I suppose they could go in about an hour or an hour and a half by walking their horses. I suppose in a day or two swelling would take place in the wounded man's leg; there was very little tumefaction in the wound, and I could discover crepitation very distinctly. It would be necessary to dress it again in two or three days if it were left in a recumbent posture, but if moved at a moderate rate, I do not know as it would aggravate it very much unless it was struck by something. I do not know much about wounds of that sort; a military surgeon would know more about those things.

(Signed) SAMUEL A. MUDD.[1]

There is on file in the War Department another statement by

[1] War Dept Archives.

Dr. Mudd which contains some details worth adding. He relates there that he graduated in Baltimore in 1856 and practised in the neighbourhood of Bryantown for nine years. Although the village itself was small, comprising only eight or ten houses, there were two or three other physicians there to share his work. Most of Dr. Mudd's time, therefore, was devoted to farming and not to his medical profession.

The second of Dr. Mudd's statements also stresses that, contrary to general belief and tradition, the bandaging of Booth's leg did not take place on the sofa in the parlour, but was performed on a bed upstairs, as soon as candles could be procured. He further tells of a rather clever story by means of which Herold tried to reconcile two apparently contradictory statements—one, that they were on the way to Washington, and the other, that they were headed south. The fugitives were in a hurry to reach the Potomac, going south, Herold claimed, that they might find a boat to take them back north to the capital.

Dr. Mudd was at home almost the entire day, he said, and saw his guests at short intervals; nevertheless, he had little conversation with them. The fee of twenty-five dollars for his services was pressed on the doctor, although he had told his patient that a smaller one would suffice.

'I had always called myself a Union man,' maintained Dr. Mudd, 'though I have never voted with the administration party.' Nothing was said by the two strangers to lead Dr. Mudd to infer that they had been engaged in any such deed as the assassination of the President.

From this small nucleus a powerful case was built up against Dr. Mudd by the judge-advocate-general. The gentle, kindly country practitioner, who enjoyed nothing more than a peaceful hour in the circle of his own family, was accused of having known of the crime beforehand and of having opened his house to the assassins as a haven of security; he was held guilty of having tried to secure his father's carriage to help Booth continue his flight. It was further asserted that he had recognized Booth at once and had withheld his knowledge from the authorities. Some of the detectives who had examined him even averred that he had denied to them the presence of any strangers at his residence. The star witness for the prosecution, Louis Wiechmann, duly came forth to swear that Dr. Mudd had met Booth, Herold, and Surratt at a hotel in Washington during January 1865, and that the doctor had drawn some queer lines on the back of an envelope, talking to Booth meanwhile in a low voice. Finally, to cap the climax, the accused had denied recognizing his patient as Booth from the photograph shown him by the detectives.

John Bingham brought to bear on Dr. Mudd every weapon in his imposing arsenal. How unfair some of his thrusts were is exemplified by the following. After the physician had gone to Bryantown in the afternoon of Saturday, 15 April, he stopped by the wayside to talk over with some of his neighbours the news that Booth was the murderer of the President, and Boyle the assailant of Mr. Seward. This was natural, as Lieutenant Dana had spread this information around his headquarters. But Dr. Mudd, so Bingham exclaimed, 'took care to make the further remark that Booth had brothers, and he did not know which of them had done the act. When did Dr. Mudd learn that Booth had brothers?'[1]

If Bingham had not had the closing argument, would he have dared to pretend indignation at the awful secret possessed by Dr. Mudd—and shared by millions of other theatre-goers and newspaper readers—that Booth had brothers? Two of them, Edwin and Junius Brutus, were then well on their way to fame; but, secure in his unassailable position, the assistant judge-advocate went still further in his attack. He even accused Dr. Mudd of having taken away the horses of the fugitives.

'. . . what became of the horses which Booth and Herold rode to his house, and which were put into his stable, are facts nowhere disclosed by the evidence. The owners testify that they have never seen the horses since. The accused give no explanation of the matter. . . .'[2] The last sentence amounts to nothing more than an ill-timed joke, considering that the question had not been asked during the trial and that the prisoners never were given a chance to speak for themselves. If Dr. Mudd had let the fugitives proceed on foot he would have sealed their doom and should have been entitled to part of the reward; to hold the

[1] Pitman, op. cit., p. 398.
[2] Ibid.

prisoners responsible for giving no explanation of this matter, gagged as they were in their cells and condemned to silence in the court, is something so biased and unethical that it would have aroused bitter resentment in the hearts of any unprejudiced jury. But even if Dr. Mudd had been a horse-thief, would it not have been the height of folly to steal the well-advertised animals of pursued murderers?

When Dr. Mudd returned home on 15 April, after the strangers had left, his wife informed him that one of them had worn false whiskers. These had become partly detached as he went downstairs, and he had hastily tried to readjust them. This observation, in connection with the fact that Booth had also borrowed a razor to shave off his moustache, aroused the suspicions of the household, and at church the next morning Dr. Mudd described the incidents to his cousin and teacher, Dr. George Mudd of Bryantown, with the specific request to relay the information to the authorities. While not anxious to have his own name known, because of fear of retaliation from Boyle's guerrillas, the accused had expressed perfect willingness to give additional information directly, if it should be necessary.[1] This action on the part of the doctor so clearly indicated his innocence that the prosecutors made desperate attempts to prevent its inclusion in the court records of the trial.

When, therefore, Dr. George Mudd was asked by General Ewing to 'state whether he [Samuel Mudd] said any thing to you about any persons having been at his house', the judge-advocate objected violently.[2] The whole case depended on the answer to this question. Of course, in a military trial, the judge-advocate is expected to remain unbiased, and it is his duty to ascertain the facts, not to prosecute the accused.

General Butler, attacking Bingham from the floor of the House two years later, brought this point into strong relief.

'The gentleman [he remarked] says he was "the advocate of the United States only". Sir, he makes a wide mistake as to his official position. He was the special judge-advocate whose duty it was to protect the rights of the prisoner as well as the rights

[1] Mudd, op. cit., pp. 96, 100.
[2] Pitman, op. cit., p. 206.

of the United States, and to sum up the evidence and state the law as would a judge on the bench.'[1]

Neither Holt nor Bingham nor Colonel Burnett, however, made the slightest pretence, then or at any other time during the proceedings, to work in the interest of truth. Holt opposed Ewing's efforts with every ounce of his fiery energy; but the counsel for Dr. Mudd was equally determined to have his client's statement go on record. Defeated by the first decision of the court, he crossed swords with Bingham again, and once more the decision of the nine officers went against him. Then something unusual must have happened behind the scenes. Some of the judges evidently insisted on hearing Dr. Mudd's whole story, perhaps out of curiosity, perhaps out of a sense of justice. Ewing's clear and unimpassioned reasoning may also have had its effect; at any rate, a few days later the witness was recalled and allowed to tell what he had been forbidden to tell before—that at half-past eleven o'clock on Sunday, 16 April, Dr. Samuel Mudd had requested his cousin to inform the authorities of his suspicions regarding the two strangers.

The judge-advocate took his defeat in bad enough grace. He could not help proclaiming that he thought the admission of such a statement to be irregular; he wished the court to have the benefit of everything that could possibly aid it in arriving at a correct conclusion. He was 'willing that the statements of the prisoner . . . shall be heard,' he declared; but there his assumed fairness left him, for he added maliciously, 'and taken for what they are worth'.[2]

It was through this information supplied by the accused that on Monday, 17 April, Lieutenant Dana at Bryantown finally heard of the two fugitives; he, in turn, did nothing at all about it, but on the following afternoon Dr. George Mudd took four detectives from Major O'Beirne's staff to his cousin's house.[3]

When in his final plea the assistant judge-advocate discussed the delayed visit of the officers to the doctor's home he tried to prove that the prisoner had denied ever having sheltered the two strangers. Two of the detectives had stated this on the witness

[1] DeWitt, *Assassination*, p. 178.
[2] Pitman, op. cit., p. 210.
[3] Ibid., p. 208.

stand; according to another, Dr. Mudd had hesitated to answer the questions put to him. Only Lieutenant Lovett, the leader of the party, testified truthfully: 'We first asked whether there had been any strangers at his house, and he said there were.'[1]

The statements of these detectives were given due consideration by Ewing in his argument for the defence; with the logic of events on his side, he had only to emphasize that it was 'in consequence of this [Dr. Mudd's communication] and *of this alone*, [that] Lieut. Levett and the detectives did, on *Tuesday*, go to the house of the accused. . . .' Dr. George Mudd informed his cousin that he had brought the detectives in accordance with the latter's own request and that the officers wished to confer with him in reference to the two strangers. It would have been absurd on his part to deny Booth's visit in the presence of Dr. George Mudd, who was his cousin's special messenger in this affair. 'The three detectives', said General Ewing, 'are manifestly mistaken; either from infirmity of memory, or from some less pardonable cause. . . .'[2]

General Ewing never knew what the 'less pardonable cause' was, although his lawyer's instinct may have flashed him a warning; but Holt knew and so did Bingham. In their files was Lieutenant Lovett's statement showing that he and his aides had listened to Dr. Mudd's description of his visitors, and had concluded that they were Booth and Herold. Lieutenant Lovett was the only one who testified in accordance with the facts. The rest had good reason to do otherwise; for the report they had submitted upon their return to Washington showed that they had failed to acquaint their superiors with what they had found out, and that they had kept to themselves the knowledge imparted to them by Dr. Mudd. This they had done in order to entrap Booth in the surrounding swamps, where they thought he was hidden, and so pocket all of the reward money.[3]

One must admire Lovett's courage under these conditions; and one wonders what General Ewing would have done if the report of the detectives had been at his disposal.

[1] Poore, op. cit., I, p. 258; see also supplementary note to chapter xxi, 'Lieutenant Lovett's Report'.

[2] Pitman, op. cit., p. 329.

[3] See supplementary note to chapter xxi, 'More About Dr. Mudd'.

Bingham's final *coup* came with a recital of Colonel Wells's testimony. Wells had examined Dr. Mudd several times; finally he showed him Booth's photograph, but Dr. Mudd did not recognize it as a picture of the man he had treated, although he had met Booth before and admittedly knew him slightly. This damaging testimony appears in Pitman's account as follows:

Col. H. H. Wells. I exhibited to him a photograph of Booth, but he said he could not recognize him from that photograph.[1]

In Poore's stenographic version, Wells's testimony shows a curious difference:

'I then exhibited what was said to be a photograph of Booth; and he said, that, from the photograph, he could not recognize him.[2]

Bingham, in his argument, also was careful in his statements about the photograph; he said that Dr. Mudd 'could not recognize him [Booth] from the photograph which is of record here'.[3]

Why all this gentle side-stepping around a picture that had been introduced into the evidence as 'Exhibit 1—Photograph of John Wilkes Booth'?

The answer to this query is amazing: *the photograph of Booth used throughout the whole trial was not a picture of John Wilkes Booth at all, but one of his brother Edwin.*

How such an error—if it was not wilful fraud—could be perpetrated and maintained, is a riddle which staggers one's imagination. Over twenty people identified the photograph during the proceedings, and on only two occasions did the witnesses display any doubt. One Mrs. Van Tine, a boarding-house keeper in Washington, whose business probably required a sharp eye for faces, said she recognized the picture as a likeness of Booth, but 'should not call it a good one'. She thought the assassin was 'a better looking man'.[4]

Mrs. Van Tine's testimony was given in the early stages of the trial, on 15 May. But even on the very first day Henry Von

[1] Pitman, op. cit. p. 169.
[2] Poore, op. cit., I, p. 284.
[3] Pitman, op. cit, p. 400.
[4] Ibid., p. 222.

Steinacker had shown some hesitancy in identifying the photograph.

Q. Look at that photograph.
A. There is a resemblance; but the face was fuller.
Q. You think it is the same person, but he had a fuller face than this?
A. I believe it is.[1]

Counsel for the defence, it would be thought, should have had their curiosity, if not their suspicion aroused, when Von Steinacker wavered in his recognition of Booth's likeness. One look at the picture would have established the fact that the judge-advocate was not acting in good faith. Did the Government officials substitute Edwin's picture for that of John Wilkes deliberately, and if so, for what purpose? And if the substitution was unintended, how could such unbelievable negligence be accounted for? Where were the lawyers for the defence all that time? Did no one know the faces of these two famous brothers well enough to tell them apart? Their photographs were on sale in public stores, and the merest routine check-up would have thrown out of court the testimony of a score of witnesses for the prosecution and wrought lasting damage to its whole cause. Yet, the photograph went unnoticed into the files of the trial, and history has failed to record this slip—one of the most tragic mistakes in American jurisprudence.

This incredible error at Washington headquarters—if error it can be called—must have brought about other serious consequences. The detectives who showed Dr. Mudd the wrong photograph hardly took it along to ensnare their victim; more likely they were convinced that they were carrying a genuine photograph of John Wilkes Booth. The other detectives on the hunt were probably supplied with copies of the same likeness. If this supposition be correct, it follows that *all the pursuers of Booth were equipped with the wrong pictures*. Then how could they have been expected to be successful in their mission? When Dr. Mudd told Colonel Wells that the picture shown to him was not that of the man he had harboured he spoke the absolute truth; when he admitted that Booth had been his patient he did

[1] Poore, op. cit., I, p. 21.

Booth's Photograph
8 No 1.

Payne

On the left, a photograph of Edwin Booth used throughout the conspiracy trial as that
of John Wilkes Booth. On the right, a photograph of John Wilkes Booth

Original in War Department Archives

so not from the likeness shown him, but in spite of it. How many other people who had seen John Wilkes Booth may have been misled when Edwin Booth's picture was held before their eyes? And how many detectives might have met J. Wilkes Booth in person and let him pass as not being the man they were after?

Of all the mysteries and problems arising out of Lincoln's assassination, the enigma of how Edwin's picture came to be substituted for that of his brother is one of the most intriguing. The careful language of Wells and Bingham in alluding to the photograph—not to mention Pitman's changed wording—makes it appear highly probable that they were aware of the substitution. The fact is, then, that Dr. Mudd never denied having housed Booth; he did deny, quite rightly, that he had harboured the man whose picture was shown to him.

Perhaps the best defence for Dr. Mudd was offered, many years later, by one of the very men who had prosecuted him, Assistant Judge-Advocate Colonel Burnett. In a paper read in 1892, he said:

'When I entered upon the duty of assisting in the investigation of the murder of the president, on the 19th of April . . . it was not positively known who had assassinated the president. . . .

'. . . while it was rumored and generally believed that J. Wilkes Booth was the assassin, for some days this rested only upon the statements of some of the persons at the theatre that they believed it was Booth; they thought they recognized him as he ran across the stage, but could not be certain about it.[1]

If the Government did not know on the nineteenth who had shot Lincoln, how was Dr. Mudd to know it on the fifteenth? His knowledge could have come to him only from the murderer himself; but there was not one shred of evidence that Booth had confided in his host, nor was there any allegation made to that effect.

Colonel Burnett then informed his audience how the legal luminaries of the Government were finally convinced that Booth really had committed the murder:

'It was known that the assassin had injured himself when he

[1] Burnett, op. cit., pp. 592, 596.

jumped from the president's box, that he limped as he ran across the stage, and it was subsequently ascertained that he had broken one bone of his left leg. He was traced to Dr. Mudd's house, near Bryantown, Maryland, and there, on the 21st, was secured the boot which Dr. Mudd had cut from his leg. . . . On the inside of the boot was the number of the boot and the name of the maker, and the words "J. Wilkes". As soon as the boot was received at the War Department, I had ex-Marshal Murray put aboard a special engine and sent to New York to look up the maker and ascertain for whom the boot was made. That night a telegram was received from him saying the boot was made for J. Wilkes Booth. This settled the identity of the assassin in our minds beyond all doubt. . . .'[1]

This is Burnett's long-winded explanation of how a fact, well established in the minds of all others, was finally brought home to the representatives of the Government. The explanation is a trifle muddle-headed, for it puts several carts before their respective horses. It was *not* known that Booth had injured his leg and that he had limped across the stage until the officers who were watching Dr. Mudd saw fit to reveal their discoveries. The boot was *not* found, even by them, until the twenty-first, when Dr. Mudd voluntarily produced it. Booth was *not* traced to Dr. Mudd's house because it was known that he would require the services of a physician, but things happened the other way around: the finding of the physician led to the disclosure of Booth's injury. Nevertheless, it stands to reason that if the judge-advocate's office was not convinced that it was dealing with Booth until a shoemaker in New York informed them of that fact, Dr. Mudd could have pleaded ignorance on the same grounds, especially since no testimony was ever introduced to show that he had even looked at the label inside the boot.

If Colonel Burnett had stated on the witness stand in 1865 what he stated from the speaker's platform in 1892, he would have destroyed his own case against the physician.

Dr. Mudd's lot was an unhappy one, and the false position into which he was forced through Booth's unwelcome visit made him behave in a hesitating manner that impressed even his

[1] Burnett, op. cit., p. 596.

counsellors unfavourably. The fact was that the young physician apparently could not reconcile the evidence of his own eyes with the stories that were told him and which he believed to be true. He had probably recognized Booth, but at that time had not known of the assassination. When he heard of the crime he was assured by Lieutenant Dana that Booth was still in Washington during the night of 14 April, and that the assassin's companion was the bandit Boyle; he was certain that Herold bore no resemblance to that dreaded marauder. He must have wondered why his advice to the authorities at Bryantown brought no more than a delayed and half-hearted response; and when he was shown the wrong photograph, his bewilderment must have been complete.

One of the strongest arguments advanced against Dr. Mudd was that he did not advise the authorities more promptly. But Mrs. Mudd averred that her husband had been anxious to go to Bryantown at once after his suspicions had been aroused. It was only when she pleaded with him not to leave her alone in the house that he postponed notifying the soldiers. As the next day would be Sunday, he decided to wait and send word from church to the officer in charge; this he did.[1] Lieutenant Dana's loose statement that the assassin was accompanied by a bandit was the cause of Mrs. Mudd's fear and indirectly of the delay in reporting Booth's whereabouts to the authorities.

The prosecution in the conspiracy trial was careful not to touch upon this matter; and it was not brought out by the defence.

The remaining accusations against Dr. Mudd were shattered by General Ewing, even before Bingham made his final attack on the prisoner.

The physician had attempted to secure his father's carriage for Booth. Would a man jeopardize the safety of his father by such an unwise move, asked General Ewing, if he harboured the slightest suspicion against the two strangers? Did not his very readiness to procure the vehicle show that he considered their request entirely legitimate?

Then, alluding to the mysterious drawings on the envelope which had so disturbed Mr. Wiechmann, the counsel asked pertinently whether it was reasonable to assume that any one but an

[1] Mudd, op. cit., p. 33.

idiot would discuss a murder plot with a man he had met only a few minutes before. Is it likely that he would have discussed it in the presence of a witness who was not believed to have been concerned in the conspiracy and who was known by all others present to be in the employ of the Government?

Dr. Mudd's residence was not on the direct route from Washington to Port Tobacco; would Booth have chosen such a circuitous route at a time when every minute counted?

If the assassin had not injured his leg, would Dr. Mudd ever have been involved in this tragedy?

Booth and the accused physician had not met between 23 December 1864 and the night of the crime. The former meeting was admittedly accidental. If they had been in conspiracy would it not have been necessary for them to communicate more frequently?

One by one the arguments and suspicions against Dr. Mudd were thus invalidated.[1]

Had Ewing known of the fraudulent photograph he would have exposed it and thereby removed the last bad impression left with the judges. The case against the accused doctor would probably have collapsed and he would have been acquitted, perhaps even by the court-martial, certainly in the judgement of posterity.

But did anything really matter with the nine judges? 'The military commission', wrote Townsend in the *New York World*, before the sentence was announced, 'works as if it were delegated not to try, but to convict, and Dr. Mudd, if he be innocent, is in only less danger than if he were guilty.'[2]

One statement, made in behalf of Mudd, is perhaps more convincing than all the others combined. In the intimacy of their companionship on the Dry Tortugas, the doctor told his fellow prisoner Arnold that there never had been any connection between himself and Booth. When Arnold recorded this conversation Mudd had been dead over twenty years and most other participants in the great drama had likewise died.[3] Arnold's statement may therefore be implicitly believed, and so for ever clears Dr. Mudd's name of any complicity in the death of Abraham Lincoln.

[1] Pitman, op. cit., pp. 321–32. [2] Townsend, op. cit., p. 68.
[3] DeWitt, op. cit., p. 263.

CHAPTER XXII

The Woman in the Case

The centre of interest in the trial was, of course, the woman in the case—Mrs. Mary E. Surratt. At that time this lady was about forty-five years of age. Newspaper reporters of the day described her according to their moods and affiliations, either as a handsome brunette, verging on obesity, or as a rather stupid looking female with feline eyes that darted furtively from point to point.[1] Her husband, John Harrison Surratt, at one time had made some money as a contractor and had bought a little farm ten miles south of Washington, where he had built a tavern. The tiny settlement of which Mr. Surratt became postmaster was named for him. Long before the war broke out family troubles had arisen, and Mrs. Surratt became much concerned about the fate of her three children, Isaac, John, and Anna. In a letter to her parish priest, written from Surrattsville, 17 January 1858, she said:

"As Mr. Surratt will not send Isaac to [s]chool and I have sent him as long as I have any means I must now put him to doing of something to get his liveing and it seams imposible to get him a place in Washington. . . . O I hope Dear Father you will try and get him something to do as it will be so much better for him. . . . O, I could not tell you what a time I see on this earth. I try to keep it all from the world on account of my poor Children. I have not had the pleasure of going to Church on Sunday for more than a year. I hope I shall be able to send John to [s]chool next year. . . . .'[2]

In 1862 John Harrison Surratt died. The slaves began to

---

[1] Townsend, op. cit., p. 64.
[2] Original letter in possession of Mrs. Thomas F. Madigan, by whose courtesy it is quoted.

scatter after Lincoln's Emancipation Proclamation. Soldiers tore down fences and stole the livestock, and the widow decided to move to Washington and open a boarding-house. She rented her farm and tavern to a man by the name of John M. Lloyd, who, several years before, had been a constable in Washington, but who by this time had degenerated into an inveterate drunkard.

After strenuous efforts through personal solicitation and newspaper advertisements, Mrs. Surratt succeeded in filling her boarding-house fairly well. One of her earliest and steadiest boarders was a former theological student named Louis J. Wiechmann. He was a college mate of John Harrison Surratt, Jr., and a favourite with all the family, except possibly with Anna, who on one occasion had seen fit to slap his face. According to Wiechmann's own admission, Mrs. Surratt had treated him like her own son, and the two young men shared both room and bed. The Surratts were devout Catholics, and Wiechmann often accompanied Mrs. Surratt to church services. The uncontradicted testimony of all witnesses showed that Mrs. Surratt was a pious, industrious housewife, a devoted mother, and a capable business woman.

John Surratt, Jr., was an avowed secessionist and a dispatch-bearer for the Confederate Government. So far as is known, his mother never expressed any political opinions, but it may safely be assumed that her sympathies were with the South. She may have suspected her son's routine activities, but it is not likely that she was acquainted with his complicity in the kidnapping plot. It was a difficult task for the Government to connect her with the conspiracy to murder the President of the United States. At first Mrs. Surratt was not even suspected, and it was a queer error that put the detectives on her trail. Susan M. Jackson, a coloured servant and a most unreliable witness, let it be known that on the night of the assassination, while she was sleeping in the basement, Mrs. Surratt and her niece Olivia Jenkins, in company of three men, entered her quarters. Miss Jenkins, so Susan claimed, stooped over to make sure that the coloured girl was fast asleep. The three men then asked for permission to change their clothes, and mentioned in the course of the conversation that John Surratt had been in the theatre during the assassination. After they had changed their clothes, the strangers left.[1]

[1] War Department Archives.

This information, which did not reach the War Department until Monday, 17 April, was probably pure fiction. If it had not been the Government certainly would have availed itself of the story during the Surratt trial, when it was of such importance to establish John Surratt's presence in Washington on the night of the assassination.

In the days following the tragedy, however, this information was considered correct, and Mrs. Surratt was hammered mercilessly by interrogators regarding the incident, of which she naturally professed complete ignorance. It was this clue that led the officers to Mrs. Surratt's house on the evening of the seventeenth with an order to arrest all inmates, and, by a strange coincidence, brought about the capture of Lewis Paine, who happened to walk into the house just as the detectives with their prisoners were about to depart. Susan Jackson was paid $250 of the reward money that had been promised for Paine's capture.[1] It was gratitude for this, or else the hope of getting more, which made the girl perjure herself two years later by claiming that John Surratt had eaten at his home on the night of the assassination.

The detectives who broke into Mrs. Surratt's house as early as two or three o'clock on Saturday morning, 15 April, were not Government agents, but members of the Metropolitan Police Force acting under the orders of Major Richards. These two groups of officers worked independently of each other, and usually at cross-purposes.[2]

The question of how the city detectives came to descend upon Mrs. Surratt's residence before dawn on the night of the assassination is not easy to answer.

One possibility is that Fletcher's disclosures led the officers in that direction. His account is contained in that part of the testimony which Pitman suppressed and may therefore have escaped general notice. It will be recalled that the livery foreman identified Atzerodt's saddle and bridle in General Augur's office about two o'clock in the morning. Atzerodt may have been known as an occasional guest at Mrs. Surratt's boarding-house, or perhaps the police were aware of his acquaintanceship with John Surratt.

[1] Laughlin, op. cit., p. 314.
[2] DeWitt, *Assassination*, p. 274.

Fletcher was in the company of a city detective named Stone while at Augur's headquarters; therefore the police were as well acquainted with these developments as was the War Department, and a search of Mrs. Surratt's house seemed in order.

It is by no means certain, however, that the police followed the clue given them in this fashion. For when Wiechmann revealed the story of the kidnapping plot to the authorities he chose an officer named McDavitt as his confidant. Whether this man was identical with the detective McDevitt, who was among those intent on searching Mrs. Surratt's house, has not been established; but even if he was not it is quite conceivable that the police knew the members of Booth's crew and were keeping them under surveillance. Had not John Surratt refused to sleep under his mother's roof on 3 April, and stayed instead at the National Hotel that night for fear that detectives were looking for him?

The district attorney at the Surratt trial, in 1867, was satisfied that 'the officers of justice, by a sort of intuition, found their way to 541 H Street'. But Mr. Bradley, counsel for the defence, strove to gain some real information on the point; evidently he had less faith than his opponent in the intuitive powers of the local detective force. Having elicited the fact of the officer Clarvoe's visit to the Surratt boarding-house, he asked: 'Was that in response to information you had received, and for what purpose did you go?'[1]

It is extremely unfortunate that at this point Mr. Bradley chose to embody two entirely separate subjects in one query. Clarvoe disregarded the first and answered only the second question, as was quite natural. But Bradley did not return to the unanswered portion of his inquiry, and history thereby lost what might have proved important information. Clarvoe's answer was: 'I went for the purpose of capturing Booth, and also to arrest John H. Surratt.'

With such an object in view, it is noteworthy that it was the city police and not the War Department which followed whatever clues were leading to Mrs. Surratt's boarding-house.

A great point against Mrs. Surratt, made in an affidavit by Wiechmann after the trial, was that she had exclaimed when the

[1] *Surratt Trial*, I, p. 688
[2] Ibid.

police came to her house: 'For God's sake, let them come in! I expected the house to be searched. . . .'[1] If Wiechmann's story is true, this ejaculation was probably a result of fear that her son would sooner or later be arrested as a dispatch-bearer.

General Harris stressed Paine's return to the boarding-house on H Street as a particularly damaging piece of evidence against Mrs. Surratt. In a letter to the *New York Sun* in 1901 he explained:

'But there was other evidence. It will be remembered that on the night of April 17 Payne returned to her house, with pick-axe on his shoulder and cap made from his shirt sleeve on his head. . . .

'The very act of this red-handed murderer fleeing to her home at such a time, was in itself, the strongest and most damning evidence against her.

'Take away these two items of evidence—the terrible story of the shooting irons and Payne's return, wipe them out, remove them from the record, and Mr. Weichmann's evidence as to what he saw and heard in Mrs. Surratt's house . . . falls harmlessly to the ground.'[2]

Fair enough. Putting aside for the moment the 'terrible story of the shooting irons', there remained General Harris's conclusion that the arrival of Paine at her home was the most damning evidence against Mrs. Surratt.

But is it really any evidence at all—damning or otherwise— to receive a call from a visitor, who may have been unexpected and unwelcome? Paine might as well have stepped into General Harris's residence, if a whim to do so had seized him. Would that have made the general an accomplice? Paine knew only the two places in Washington where he had stayed before—the Herndon Hotel and Mrs. Surratt's boarding-house. He was tired, desperate, starved.

When Captain Wermerskirch, Captain Smith, and Captain Morgan, belonging to two different branches of the Government service, met at Mrs. Surratt's in the late evening of 17 April, due to the erroneous information given them by Susan Jackson, they did not expect to make the catch they did. Their stories of the events that followed differ in some essentials. Smith asserted

[1] Pitman, op. cit., p. 421.
[2] *New York Sun*, 4 Aug. 1901.

positively that Mrs. Surratt, on being confronted by Paine, lifted her hand and swore by God that she had never seen the man before. Captain Morgan, who was present all the time, did not hear the exclamation. Another point at issue was whether or not the lights were turned low enough at that time to make recognition difficult. Her failure to identify Paine told heavily against Mrs. Surratt, although it was shown that her eyesight was extremely defective, especially under artificial light. Another important point in her favour was that Paine, whom she had last known as an immaculately clad Baptist preacher, was disguised as a labourer. There was a self-made turban on his head, his hands were dirty, and he carried a pick-axe over his shoulder; at least one of the boarders, Honora Fitzpatrick, did not recognize him either.

'I did not recognize him [Paine] at the house,' she swore on the witness stand, 'but I did at General Augur's office, when the skull-cap was taken off his head.'[1]

Miss Fitzpatrick, by the way, also testified that it was she who had bought a picture of John Wilkes Booth and had taken it to Mrs. Surratt's boarding-house; and, in conformity with many other witnesses, she described her landlady's eyesight as very poor.

'Mrs. Surratt has complained that she could not read or sew at night on account of her sight. I have known of her passing her friend, Mrs. Kirby, on the same side of the street, and not see her at all.'[2]

There were other circumstances that bore strongly against Mrs. Surratt. On Tuesday, the eleventh, she had sent Louis Wiechmann to Booth to borrow his carriage for a trip to Surrattsville. Booth had sold his carriage but gave Wiechmann ten dollars to hire one. For a man of Booth's generosity and easy ways this was a natural impulse. To the jury of scantily paid military officers this liberality was incriminating. To the tight-lipped judge-advocate it was the acknowledgement of a conspiracy.

'She sends to Booth for a carriage . . . [and] Booth . . . gives to the agent she employed ten dollars, with which to hire

[1] Pitman, op. cit., p. 132.
[2] Ibid.

a conveyance. . . . And yet the pretence is made that Mrs. Surratt went on the 11th to Surrattsville exclusively upon her own private and lawful business. Can any one tell, if that be so . . . how it comes that he, of his own accord . . . should send her ten dollars with which to procure it? There is not the slightest indication that Booth was under any obligation to her, or that she had any claim upon him. . . .'[1] All of which must have sounded strange to the multitude of Booth's friends who had accepted the boundless hospitality of the young actor whose money came so easily and was spent so freely.

This whole episode appeared in an entirely different light when, two years later, a witness came forth to whom Wiechmann had confided in the meantime. This man, whose name was Lewis Carland, made some startling revelations while under oath:

'Did Mr. Weichmann', he was asked, 'state to you . . . that he was very much troubled in his conscience about the testimony he had given at that trial?'

'He did . . .', Carland answered.

'Did he tell you', the questioner continued, 'that when Mrs. Surratt learned that afternoon he [Wiechmann] had a half holiday, that she said she would like to go to Surratsville, but did not know where to get a buggy, and that he then told her to send for Booth, and that she replied she did not know Booth was in town?'

'Yes, sir,' was the reply.[2]

How many distorted inferences could have been avoided if the truth about the hiring of this conveyance had been known sooner.

But now to 'the terrible story of the shooting-irons'.

When the carriage in which Mrs. Surratt and Wiechmann were driving passed Uniontown at the south end of the Anacostia Bridge they met a buggy containing her tenant, Lloyd, and his sister-in-law, Mrs. Offut. Both teams were halted and Mr. Lloyd stepped over to speak to his landlady. According to Lloyd Mrs. Surratt told him, after a few introductory remarks which he could not interpret, 'to get them [the shooting-irons] out ready; that they would be wanted soon'.[3] Wiechmann, who was

[1] Pitman, op. cit., p. 392.
[2] *Surratt Trial*, II, pp. 814, 815.
[3] Pitman, op. cit., p. 85.

sitting within a few feet of Lloyd and next to Mrs. Surratt, stubbornly maintained that he had not heard the conversation.

When asked on the witness stand in what tone of voice this conversation between Mrs. Surratt and Mr. Lloyd was carried on, he answered: 'It was in that kind of a tone that I did not hear.' But Lloyd did not bear him out in this statement. In fact, in an unguarded moment he related that Mrs. Surratt had 'laughed very heartily' at some time during this short passage of words.[1] True, this admission did not come out until two years later; had it been known in 1865 it might have thrown serious doubt on the whole testimony of the besotted tavern-keeper. A conspirator in alluding to a coming assassination is not likely to break out into hearty laughter.

Lloyd denied at all times that there had been any secrecy about the whole conversation. Even Wiechmann had to admit this, when cross-examined in the Surratt trial:

Q. On the way to the prison . . . when Lloyd was with you [in the carriage] . . . Did you not tell him that you had testified that she [Mrs. Surratt] had spoken in a whisper?
A. Yes, sir.
Q. What did he say?
A. He expressed astonishment.[2]

On the day of the assassination Mrs. Surratt again asked Mr. Wiechmann to drive her to Surrattsville on some business transaction. This time she gave Wiechmann money of her own to hire the conveyance. When Wiechmann returned from the livery stable preparatory to the trip to Surrattsville he noticed that Booth and Mrs. Surratt were talking to each other in the parlour. The conversation lasted only a few minutes; it was then about half-past two in the afternoon. Just as Mrs. Surratt was stepping into the buggy she remembered that Booth had asked her to take a package, later shown to have contained a field-glass.

Mrs. Surratt and Wiechmann did not stay in Surrattsville very long and were on the point of returning home when Lloyd arrived in a state of heavy intoxication. He had been to Upper Marlboro for a court proceeding and had imbibed freely on the

---

[1] *Surratt Trial*, I, pp. 280, 389.
[2] Ibid., p. 416.

way back. As he carried some fish and oysters into the house, he met Mrs. Surratt, who had been detained by a defect in the carriage. According to Lloyd, she again reminded him of the shooting-irons and informed him that they would be wanted that night.

We have it from General Harris's letter in the *New York Sun* that it was Lloyd's testimony which condemned the unfortunate woman. Without Lloyd's confirmation he asserted that Wiechmann's testimony would not have been sufficiently incriminating to bring about her death sentence.

'Now let me say in all candour, and I speak by the record as a member of the commission,' wrote General Harris, 'that it was not Weichmann's evidence at all that condemned Mrs. Surratt. . . . Had it depended on what he said not a hair of her head would have been harmed. The man who did the mischief was John M. Lloyd. . . .'[1]

It is strange that the statements of a self-confessed drunkard should have carried such weight with the officers of the commission. It becomes still stranger when it is considered that Lloyd was deeply involved in the plot, had been intimate with most of the conspirators and had furnished them the hiding-place for their weapons. Moreover, when some officers of the police department stopped at his bar early on Saturday morning he stoutly denied that any one had passed his house during the night, and when he was asked by one of his former mates on the police force for a tip on the probable route of the assassins he sent the inquirers off to Piscataway on a roundabout road that led back to Washington.

But even Lloyd was not sure that Mrs. Surratt had talked about the firearms when he had met her at Uniontown.

'It was a very quick and hasty conversation,' he admitted. 'I am confident that she named the shooting-irons on both occasions; not so positive about the first as I am about the last; I know she did on the last occasion.'[2]

Three times he was led to repeat this statement; each time he varied his phraseology, but not his meaning. 'I am quite positive about that, but not altogether positive,' he declared once; and on cross-examination he said, 'I am quite positive, but

---

[1] *New York Sun*, 4 Aug. 1901.
[2] Pitman, op. cit., p. 86; Poore, op. cit., I, pp. 121, 122.

cannot be determined . . . that she said "shooting-irons". . . .'[1]

This was the sort of evidence produced to convince judges of General Harris's calibre that Mrs. Surratt was guilty. If it had not been for this testimony, he said, 'not a hair of her head would have been harmed'.

Whether Wiechmann spoke the truth during the trial is a question that has been argued pro and con for many years. Wiechmann was not a bad man, but his life was at stake and he was acting under terrific pressure. By his own confession on the witness stand he was a coward, while he admitted at another time that egoism was a predominant feature in his make-up. 'I always look out for self-interest,' he stated glibly.[2]

'Physically and intellectually he was a giant,' said D. H. L. Gleason, his colleague in the War Department, 'but in bravery I should call him a dwarf.'[3] Nevertheless, Wiechmann did his best to praise Mrs. Surratt when he could do so without endangering his own position. With the exception of his statement that he did not hear the conversation between Lloyd and Mrs. Surratt it is doubtful if he ever spoke a deliberate lie on the witness stand. It was more what he insinuated than what he said that fastened the noose tighter and tighter around the neck of the woman who had treated him like a member of her own family.

To the end of his life Wiechmann carried with him the knowledge of the part he had played in convicting Mrs. Surratt; and this knowledge must have weighed heavily upon him, for his last action, so dramatically described by Lloyd Lewis in *Myths After Lincoln*, speaks for itself:

'When he was dying he asked us [his two sisters] to get a pen and paper and told us to write: "June 2, 1902; THIS IS TO CERTIFY THAT EVERY WORD I GAVE IN EVIDENCE AT THE ASSASSINATION TRIAL WAS ABSOLUTELY TRUE; AND NOW I AM ABOUT TO DIE AND WITH LOVE I RECOMMEND MYSELF TO ALL TRUTH-LOVING PEOPLE."

'Then he signed it "Louis J. Weichmann" and died.'

[1] Poore, op. cit., I, pp. 117, 121.   [2] *Surratt Trial*, I, p. 408.
[3] Gleason, op. cit., p. 59.

The Woman in the Case

Wiechmann's last statement rings like the agonized plea of a man with a guilty conscience, begging for clemency and absolution. Though he died naturally, he was, according to Lewis, old and broken far beyond his sixty years, and when the doctor filled out the death certificate, in the space after the word 'cause', he put down 'extreme nervousness'—that was all.[1]

Through recent researches it can now be positively demonstrated that Wiechmann did not, as he claimed, speak without fear of consequences to himself. A letter written to the assistant judge-advocate, Colonel Burnett, from Carroll Prison and dated 5 May 1865, began with these words: 'I have the honor to call your attention to the following additional facts in my recollection. *You confused and terrified me so much yesterday that I was almost unable to say anything.*'[2] Needless to say, this letter was never offered in evidence by the prosecution.

When Wiechmann confided in Mr. Carland after the execution of Mrs. Surratt he said, 'it would have been very different with Mrs. Surratt if he had been let alone'. He said further that a statement had been prepared for him, that it was written out for him, and that he was threatened with prosecution as one of the conspirators if he did not swear to it.[3]

James J. Gifford, who was in prison with Wiechmann, corroborated Carland's testimony.

Q. Did he [Wiechmann] say in your presence that an officer of the Government had told him that unless he testified to more than he had already stated they would hang him too?
A. I heard the officer tell him so.[4]

It can also now be positively stated that Wiechmann did hear the conversation between Lloyd and Mrs. Surratt when the two parties met at Uniontown. Captain William P. Wood, in charge of the Old Capitol Prison, took a statement from Wiechmann as he was delivered into his care on 30 April, just after his return

[1] Lewis, op. cit., p. 267.
[2] War Department Archives. Author's italics; see also supplementary note to chapter xxii, 'The Value of Wiechmann's Testimony'.
[3] *Surratt Trial*, II, p. 815.
[4] Ibid., p. 820.

from Canada, and before he had a chance to confer at length with any one else. In his report Captain Wood stated that 'on or about Tuesday 11th of April Wiechmann and Mrs. Surratt drove in a buggy to Surrattsville also to Capt. Givins [Gwinn's] residence. On the road to Surrattsville she met her tenant Lloyd *with whom she had some conversation in relation to the man Howell, stating that she would like to have him released on taking the oath of allegiance and would see Judge Turner about it'*.[1] This seemingly irrelevant sentence, if it had been known to the defence, probably would have saved Mrs. Surratt's life; but it was not a matter that could be brought out in cross-examination without previous knowledge of the facts, and in the face of the ignorance on the part of his interrogators it was easy for Wiechmann to maintain his stolid attitude.

A trace of this conversation did filter into the record, however, and it was only by a close margin that Mrs. Surratt's attorneys failed to get at the truth. Pitman's report has Wiechmann say:

'I did not hear the conversation that took place between Mrs. Surratt and Mr. Lloyd at Uniontown. Mrs. Surratt leaned sideways in the buggy, and whispered, as it were, in Mr. Lloyd's ear.[2]

On this point the testimony as reported by Poore differs characteristically:

Q. Did she [Mrs. Surratt] state any thing to you afterwards of what the conversation was about?
A. No, sir. The only conversation that I heard at that particular time was between her and Mrs. Offutt. She was talking about the man Howell.
ASSISTANT JUDGE-ADVOCATE BINGHAM. I object. There is nothing of that in the case.[3]

One can almost sense the relief of Holt and Bingham when this line of questioning was not pursued farther. What turn would the trial have taken here if Reverdy Johnson had not abandoned his client, or if her defence had been in equally capable hands?

[1] War Department Archives. Author's italics.
[2] Pitman, op. cit., p. 118.   [3] Poore, op. cit., I, p. 372.

Quite naturally, counsel for Mrs. Surratt tried to shake Wiechmann's testimony, but in only one instance could they positively prove that his statements were inaccurate. Wiechmann testified that on 2 April he had visited Booth in his room at the National Hotel and had found there Mr. McCullough, a well-known actor. It was shown by incontrovertible evidence that McCullough had not been anywhere near Washington within three weeks of the time specified.[1] It was a small matter, but important. *At least, it was important enough for the official recorder to leave this part of the testimony out of his report.*

'On the 2d of April', read Wiechmann's testimony in Pitman, 'Mrs. Surratt asked me to see J. Wilkes Booth, and say that she wished to see him on "private business". I conveyed the message, and Booth said he would come to the house in the evening, as soon as he could; and he came.'[2]

Mark how different this testimony is in Poore:

'It was on the 2d of April when Mrs. Surratt sent me to the hotel; and I at that time found in Booth's room Mr. John McCullough, the actor; and I communicated my message to Booth. I told him that Mrs. Surratt would like to see him. . . .'[3]

Is it possible to avoid the thought that the bias of the War Department against the defenders survived the trial and left its traces in what purports to be a strictly accurate official record?

It is interesting to speculate on what the outcome of the trial would have been if Louis Wiechmann and John M. Lloyd had been made defendants instead of state witnesses. A survey of all the points that could have been charged against any of the three, Wiechmann, Lloyd, and Mrs. Surratt, offers a striking comparison. In the argument to the court the prosecution cited the following against Mrs. Surratt:

Her house was the headquarters of the conspirators. Admittedly so. But Wiechmann lived there, too, and although the latter's own evidence shows that he had reason to suspect the existence of a plot, nothing in his testimony proved that Mrs. Surratt knew of the things that were going on under her roof.

[1] Pitman, op. cit., p. 243. [2] Ibid., p. 113.
[3] Poore, op. cit., I, p. 82.

She is inquired for by Atzerodt, she is inquired for by Paine and she is visited by Booth. Mrs. Surratt was running a boarding-house; is it strange that people looking for rooms should inquire for her? And Booth did not visit her alone; he visited the whole family. A letter from John Surratt, addressed to a cousin of his, and dated 6 February 1865, gives an intimate picture of Mrs. Surratt's household on the occasion of a call from the handsome young actor.

'I have just taken a peep in the parlour. Would you like to know what I saw there? Well, Ma was sitting on the sofa, nodding first to one chair, then to another, next the piano. Anna sitting in a corner, dreaming, I expect of J. W. Booth. . . .

'But hark! the door-bell rings, and Mr. J. W. Booth is announced. And listen to the scamperings of the ——. Such brushing and fixing.'[1]

This letter was in Colonel Baker's possession and naturally known to Judge-Advocate Bingham when he made his denunciation. Mrs. Surratt taking a nap on her chair previous to Booth's arrival—was this the picture in his mind as he described the meeting of the two alleged conspirators?

Booth's photograph, together with that of the chief conspirator, Jefferson Davis, is found in her house. Booth's photograph, as has been stated before, was bought by Miss Fitzpatrick, not by Mrs. Surratt. The picture of the President of the Confederacy may have been obtained while he was still a senator in Washington. There was no evidence offered that Mrs. Surratt acquired the photograph or even owned it. In any case, the possession of the picture in no way connected its owner with Lincoln's assassination.

On 11 April she sends to Booth for a carriage to take her on to Surrattsville. This argument has been dealt with before, as has been the story of the meeting between the accused and Mr. Lloyd.

On the day of the assassination she again sends for Booth, has an interview with him in her own house, immediately goes again to Surrattsville, and then, about six o'clock in the afternoon, she delivers to Lloyd a field-glass and tells him to have two bottles of

[1] War Department Archives; also L. C. Baker, op. cit., p. 562.

*whiskey and the carbines ready, as they would be called for that
night.* This really was the crux of the indictment against the
widow; for how could she anticipate at six o'clock, as the prosecution was careful to point out, that these arms would be called
for and would be needed that night, unless she were in the
conspiracy?

Everything depended, in the final analysis, on the truth of
Lloyd's statement that Mrs. Surratt uttered 'the terrible story
about the shooting-irons' as she conversed with him alone in the
backyard of his tavern, just as he had returned from Upper
Marlboro, where he had attended court and from where he had
brought some oysters and fresh fish.

According to Mrs. Offut, Lloyd's sister-in-law, the tavern
keeper 'was very much in liquor' at that time, so much so that
she had to help him take off his coat. She then insisted on his
lying down. In a few minutes he got up, however, saying that he
was too sick, and would go into the dining-room; but he went
into the bar room instead. In fact, Lloyd himself did not deny
his condition on that fateful evening.

'I was right smart in liquor that afternoon,' he admitted on
cross-examination; 'and after night I got more so.'[1]

Two years later Lloyd had to mount the witness stand again,
much to his chagrin. 'I do not wish to go into the examination
of Mrs. Surratt,' he protested, '. . . I do not wish to state one
solitary word more than I am compelled to.' His reluctance to
testify again was of no avail, however. He had to tell about
things as they appeared to him in his 'confused memory', and
finally revealed that he had been hopelessly drunk when he had
met Mrs. Surratt, toward sundown.[2]

'I knew what effect liquor had on me . . .', he confessed. 'It
makes me forget a great many things.'

'How much did you drink . . . ?' he was then asked.

'I drank enough to make me drunk . . .' he replied pointedly.
'I was so drunk that when I lay down I felt sick. I could not
lie down.'[3]

There were some other questions and answers in this interrogation that are significant:

[1] Pitman, op. cit., p. 87.
[2] *Surratt Trial*, I, pp. 279, 280, 281.
[3] Ibid., p. 293.

Q. When you went to speak to Mrs. Surratt, did you stagger?
A. That I do not recollect.
Q. Did you fall down?
A. Really, I cannot remember such a thing.[1]

Such admissions should have invalidated this drunkard's evidence. What little reliability it had was jeopardized by Lloyd's statement that his testimony was forced out of him by threats of no uncertain character. In the Surratt trial the following colloquy took place while the tavern keeper was on the witness stand:

'While I was there in Carroll Prison, this military officer came there and told me he wanted me to make a statement, as near as I remember. I told him I had made a fuller statement to Colonel Wells than I could possibly do to him under the circumstances, while things were fresh in my memory. His reply was that it was not full enough.

Q. What else did he say?
A. He said that it was not full enough. . . .
Q. Did he say anything to you in the way of offering a reward, or use any threat towards you, for the purpose of getting you to make it fuller?
A. When I told him what I had repeated before . . . he jumps up very quick off his seat, as if very mad, and asked me if I knew what I was guilty of. I told him, under the circumstances I did not. He said you are guilty as an accessory to a crime the punishment of which is death.[2]

Colonel Baker, on taking charge of the pursuit of Lincoln's assassins, had admonished his minions in an official order 'to extort confessions and procure testimony to establish the conspiracy . . . by promises, rewards, threats, deceit, force, or any other effectual means.'[3]

It is not known what means the agents of the Washington authorities used with Wiechmann and Lloyd. That they were adequate is obvious.

[1] *Surratt Trial*, I, p. 298.
[2] Ibid., p. 290.
[3] DeWitt, *Judicial Murder of Mary E. Surratt*, p. 7.

An indication of what military pressure was used on Lloyd—if pressure was needed—may be gleaned from the following. Lieutenant D. D. Dana, in his story in the *Boston Globe* of 12 December 1897 tells of hanging an old man to a tree in Surrattsville and thereby wringing from him the confession that Booth and Herold had stopped at the Surratt inn on the night of the assassination.[1] Whether Dana's story, which comes to us in a somewhat confused way through the pen of a reporter, relates to Lloyd is an open question. It probably does not. But it clearly demonstrates the method used to make recalcitrant witnesses more pliable. Lloyd, with his body and mind weakened through the excessive use of alcohol, would have been in a poor condition to withstand either torture or threats. Be it said in honour of the man, however, that he maintained for ever afterward that he considered Mrs. Surratt innocent of the crime for which she died. At Lloyd's death, on 21 December 1892, the Washington correspondent of the *New York World* wrote:

'Although Lloyd's testimony was most damaging against Mrs. Surratt, and probably condemned her, he himself never believed in Mrs. Surratt's guilt, and said she was a victim of circumstances. Her association with the real conspirators, he always held, was the cause of her conviction.'

Bingham must have realized the bad impression the tavern-keeper had left behind, for in his closing argument he made an attempt to defend him: 'An endeavour is made', he declared, 'to impeach Lloyd. But the Court will observe that no witness has been called who contradicts Lloyd's statement in any material matter. . . .'[2]

Was the judge-advocate in earnest when he spoke these words? Lloyd had chosen to relate only two conversations with the accused woman, one of which had been held in the absence of other witnesses. How, then, could the defence have brought forth evidence to disprove his words, when Mrs. Surratt's own lips were sealed? No one could have refuted Lloyd's testimony but the judge-advocate himself. He could have done it from the records of his own preliminary investigations during which

[1] *Boston Globe*, 12 Dec. 1897; also quoted in Finis L. Bates, *Escape and Suicide of John Wilkes Booth*, pp. 99, 100.

[2] Pitman, op. cit., p. 393.

Mrs. Surratt had given her account of the talks with her tenant. This, of course, he did not do, and therefore it behoves the historian to quote from these sheets, now yellowing in the Washington archives, the exact words of the condemned woman prisoner.

The verbatim record of a hearing given Mrs. Surratt by Colonel Olcott of the Bureau of Military Justice on 28 April 1865 is still accessible:

Q. How long a conversation did you have with Mr. Lloyd?
A. Only a few minutes conversation. I did not sit down. I only met him as I was going home.
Q. Where was Mr. Wiechman?
A. He was there.
Q. He heard the conversation?
A. I presume he did. I don't remember.
Q. What did the conversation relate to?
A. He spoke of having fish and oysters. He asked me whether I had been to dinner, and said that he could give me fish and oysters. Mr. Wiechman said that he would return home as he was in need of his bread and butter.
Q. What did you say about any shooting irons or carbines?
A. I said nothing about them.
Q. Any conversation of that kind? Did you not tell him to have the shooting irons ready, that there would be some people there that night?
A. To my knowledge no conversation of that kind passed.
Q. Did you know any shooting irons were there?
A. No, sir, I did not.[1]

According to both the prosecution and the court, as represented by General Harris, the life of Mrs. Surratt depended on the truth of Lloyd's uncontradicted statement that she had asked him on the afternoon of 14 April to have the shooting-irons ready. Mrs. Surratt reported that the conversation with her tenant had been about nothing more offensive than fish and oysters. The justice of the verdict against this woman, therefore, hangs on the balance of veracity between Lloyd, a drunkard in fear of his life, and Mrs. Surratt, a woman of probity with an unsullied reputation. Lloyd claimed that she had told him to

[1] War Department Archives.

have the carbines ready, a message entirely superfluous, as the guns were hidden where they could be reached in a moment's notice; more than that, it would have been extremely hazardous, when so much depended on absolute secrecy, to give instructions of this kind to a man in liquor. Mrs. Surratt's statement that the innkeeper, who had just come in with a load of fish and oysters, offered her some of them to take home for supper, is in line with what one might expect under the circumstances. Certainly no civil court jury would have hanged the poor woman on Lloyd's unsupported assertion, which she had declared to be false.

As Mrs. Surratt was at no time allowed to speak in her own defence, it is only fair to add one more of the statements she made to Colonel Olcott:

Q. Did your son or Mr. Booth or Herold, or Port Tobacco [Atzerodt] ever tell you that they had engaged in a plot to kill the President?
A. Never in the world if it was the last word I have ever to utter.[1]

Captain Wood, the keeper of the Old Capitol Prison and one of Stanton's intimates, in later years published in the *Washington Gazette* a strange story about Mrs. Surratt's death. Unfortunately, the date of the publication is not known. Wood was aware that Wiechmann had overheard the first conversation between Mrs. Surratt and Lloyd and could, perhaps, have saved the life of the accused woman if he had come forward in time.

'Some time after the execution of Mrs. Surratt, President Johnson sent for me and requested me to give my version of Mrs. Surratt's connection with the assassination of President Lincoln. I did so, and I believe he was thoroughly convinced of the innocence of Mrs. Surratt. He assured me he sincerely regretted that he had not given Mrs. Surratt the benefit of Executive clemency, and strongly expressed his detestation of what he termed the "infamous conduct of Stanton" in keeping these facts from him. I asserted my unchangeable friendship for Mr. Stanton under all circumstances, and while I regretted the course adopted by the Secretary of War towards Mrs. Surratt,

[1] War Department Archives.

I would never hesitate to perform any act of kindness for him. President Johnson commended me for my devotion to friends, and the subject of the assassination was never afterwards discussed between him and myself. The great War Secretary of the Union was no longer in power. He was a plain citizen of our Republic, broken in health and tottering between life and death.

'The Republican leaders had, after much pleading, induced President Grant to name Mr. Stanton for a judge of the Supreme Court. The Senate promptly confirmed the nomination, but Grant, for some reason best known to himself, did not put his signature to the commission, or if he did sign the commission he did not forward it to Mr. Stanton. It was at this time the latter sent for me, and I called at his residence on K Street. When ushered into his presence I was startled at his woe-begone and wretched appearance. He inquired if I knew the reason why that man (meaning President Grant) withheld his commission. I told him. Then we drifted in our talk to the executions herein referred to, and he rebuked me for not making greater effort to save the woman that was hanged. He said he would have trusted his life in my keeping; that I would have saved him the torments of hell had I been more persistent in my efforts. I reminded him of my call on President Johnson to plead for mercy for Mrs. Surratt, and that I was met by L. C. Baker at the entrance of the President's house, and Baker produced an order over his (Stanton's) signature which set forth that I should not be permitted to enter the building or communicate with the President.

' "Too true," he responded, "and the Surratt woman haunts me so that my nights are sleepless and my days miserable, and Grant aids my enemies by refusing to sign my commission, which would afford me temporary relief and perhaps prolong my life. He will not do it, and, Wood, this is at last the end." Placing his hands to his head he continued: "I cannot endure the pressure; I am dying, dying surely, dying now!"

'A few parting words were exchanged between us, and the following day the death of Edwin M. Stanton was publicly announced. . . .'[1]

The points which could have been brought out against Louis

[1] Clipping from the *Washington Gazette*—no date.

Wiechmann and John M. Lloyd as defendants, rather than as state witnesses, would certainly have presented a formidable array.

Against Wiechmann the prosecution at one time must have weighed these factors, none of which was in dispute and most of which appeared as evidence in the trial.

Wiechmann lived in the midst of the conspirators, was intimate with most of them, and particularly so with John H. Surratt.

Wiechmann introduced Atzerodt and Paine to the remainder of the household. He permitted Atzerodt to wear part of his uniform which Wiechmann, as a member of the Washington defence corps, was allowed to possess. This matter was very forcefully brought out at the Surratt trial in the testimony of John T. Holahan, one of Wiechmann's fellow boarders.

Q. After you went there to board, state whether there was any intimacy between Atzerodt and Louis Wiechmann or not?

A. They appeared to be very intimate.

Q. State whether you ever saw them come there [to Mrs. Surratt's house] together or not?

A. Frequently.

Q. Do you know of any other evidence of their intimacy in regard to clothing, or anything of that kind?

A. One day I met them on the street, between Sixth and Seventh streets. Atzerodt had on Wiechmann's military coat and cape.

Q. While they were in the house together, will you state whether there was any intimacy between them or not?

A. They were as intimate as friends could be.[1]

The boots that Paine wore when captured had been borrowed by Wiechmann from a co-worker. This is a fact which was known to the Government but was never permitted to leak out.

Wiechmann knew that both Spencer Howell and a Mrs. Slater were blockade-runners and therefore traitors to the country. At no time did he make any attempt to reveal this to the authorities.

Wiechmann was found in possession of a secret code, which Howell had taught him.

A false moustache was found in the room of the star boarder.

[1] *Surratt Trial*, I, pp. 669, 670.

According to his story, which is unsupported by any other testimony, this moustache was Paine's property and had been hidden by Wiechmann as a joke.

Wiechmann had made incriminating remarks to some of his fellow clerks indicating that he could easily have made a large sum of money, about $30,000, if he had been willing to participate in an enterprise in which several of his friends were engaged.

In Wiechmann's room were found a number of franked envelopes belonging to the office of the commissioner of prisons.

Facsimile of telegram sent by Booth to Louis J. Wiechmann. The meaning of this message has never been fully cleared up, but it shows the intimacy existing between the assassin and the star witness for the Government.

Original in the Archives of the War Department

At various times Wiechmann had made attempts to go to Richmond for the avowed purpose of finishing his studies there.

Wiechmann had divulged office secrets, pertaining to the number of Confederate prisoners, to Howell and others.

It was to Louis Wiechmann that Booth had telegraphed on 23 March 1865: 'TELL JOHN TO TELEGRAPH NUMBER AND STREET AT ONCE.'

Finally, it was Wiechmann who had taken Mrs. Surratt to Surrattsville on 11 and 14 April.[1]

No wonder Major O'Beirne, in his report to the War Department, in December 1865, stated that 'Wiechman was an accomplice of the conspirators but whose status was subsequently changed'.[2]

'It seems extremely improbable that Wiechman was ignorant of the entire plot, if he was not an accomplice,' wrote Colonel John A. Foster in a report on Wiechmann to the judge-advocate-general.[3]

What a strong net the skilful hands of Holt and Bingham could have constructed from these threads. There is no doubt but that this circumstantial evidence was used to influence his testimony, and, regardless of guilt, stouter hearts than Wiechmann's might have faltered under the implied threats.

Against John M. Lloyd the evidence was overwhelming and self-admitted.

He had hidden the carbines, the monkey-wrench, and the rope, together with the ammunition, at the request of the would-be kidnappers. He had sent his wife to Allen's Fresh a few days before the assassination and was bringing her back on 17 April when he was arrested. She did not know why she had been sent away.[4]

He had misled the police officers and soldiers by his failure to report the midnight visit of Booth and Herold after the murder. By doing so he had greatly delayed the pursuit. He then had impeded it still further by sending the officers of the Metropolitan Police Force to Piscataway instead of to Bryantown.

He was a drunken sot who was held in general contempt, and his hanging probably would have been approved by every one.

Some writers have concluded that Stanton and Holt were looking for victims to appease the public's lust for revenge, and that this was why Mrs. Surratt was sacrificed with the others to expiate Lincoln's death, regardless of her guilt or innocence.

[1] Pitman, op. cit., p. 118.
[2] O'Beirne papers.
[3] War Department Archives.
[4] Townsend, op. cit., p. 45.

This explanation—assuming, of course, that the Government officials knew of her innocence—does not appear to cover the case. Atzerodt, Paine, and Herold had no friends and no one of importance particularly cared about them. Their participation in the murder plot was well enough established. Then, there were Spangler, a rough-looking carpenter and scene-shifter, and O'Laughlin and Arnold, ex-Confederates. Public prejudice could have been much more easily aroused against these men than against Dr. Mudd and Mrs. Surratt. Yet it was to convict these last two prisoners that the prosecution exerted itself to the utmost; it was Mrs. Surratt especially who was singled out to bear the brunt of the prosecution. Throughout the trial she was put foremost among the defendants; Bingham's plea to the military court was entitled *A reply to the several arguments in defense of Mary E. Surratt and others*; it was Mrs. Surratt who was robbed of her attorney in chief by means of insults that made him more of a liability than an asset to his client. In the end, when even the military commission shuddered at pronouncing the death sentence over all the defendants, and when Dr. Mudd, O'Laughlin, Arnold, and Spangler escaped the extreme penalty, it was Mrs. Surratt against whom Holt and his aides directed a final *coup* that made her hanging a certainty. The judge-advocate, unable to muster the necessary number of votes to hand her over to the hangman, induced the commission to sign her death-sentence, with the understanding that a petition for mercy, addressed to the President, would be attached to it. This left the final decision of Mrs. Surratt's fate in the hands of the Chief Magistrate. The guileless officers followed Holt's pleadings, as they had done throughout the trial. But Johnson stated that he had never seen the petition for mercy. When he signed the death-warrant on 5 July he did not know that a majority of the court wanted the woman prisoner to live. No one was permitted to see the President until after the execution, and a frantic appeal by one Mr. Brophy, to whom Wiechmann had confessed that he had lied to save his own life, went unheeded. A letter from the special provost-marshal, General Hartranft, with a statement from Lewis Paine asserting Mrs. Surratt's innocence, was likewise disregarded, although it bore the general's endorsement that he believed Paine was telling the truth.[1]

[1] War Department Archives.

Two days later, shortly after noon on 7 July, the four prisoners were hanged.

The reason for the special vindictiveness of the Bureau of Military Justice toward Mrs. Surratt remains shrouded in mystery. Even David DeWitt, who wrote such a complete defence of this hapless woman that no one else has since found much to add to his arguments, is at fault at the end of the trial. He ventured the half-hearted opinion that, in holding the mother, the baffled authorities were really hoping to get the fugitive son into their power. It is difficult to concur with this opinion. If John Surratt had been watching for the outcome of the trial—which he was not allowed to do—he would have hoped for the acquittal of his mother and would not have returned until her fate had been definitely determined. But if her death sentence, as may have been argued by Holt and Bingham to the officers of the military commission, was simply a bait to bring back her son, the execution of the sentence should have been delayed until news of it could reach the fugitive. Instead, the hanging was ordered with indecent haste. It is now known that the Government officials did not want to prosecute John Surratt even after they learned his whereabouts. This makes the reason for Mrs. Surratt's brutal treatment more obscure than ever. The contention that Southern women had been the worst transgressors during the recent conflict and that hence it was decided to make an example of the Washington boarding-house keeper hardly seems valid, since the war was over. The determination of the authorities to see Mrs. Surratt die and their efforts to bring this about by fair means or foul, must have been due to other reasons.

Perhaps Mr. Merrick, counsel for Mrs. Surratt's son in 1867, perceived some of the hidden springs of this attempt to hound a woman to the gallows when he said this to the jury:

'I regret that it will become my painful duty to speak some truths that I would leave unspoken. I regret that it will become my painful duty to inquire into the motives that are influencing the conduct of men; and I am inclined to believe . . . that the inquiry which I will make may lead you to the conviction, that . . . there have been other conspiracies in higher places to commit a murder through the forms of law, and in utter disregard of every high principle that should govern the man of honor. . . . Why is it that all these appliances, this vast machinery, are in this case? . . . What do they represent? . . . there are two sets, one that represents the government in its assumed offended majesty, and the other that represents some officers of the United States seeking for their own purposes the shedding of innocent blood.[1]

What were the 'conspiracies in higher places' that Mr. Merrick suspected?

[1] *Surratt Trial*, II, pp. 1155-6.

CHAPTER XXIII

The Conspirators who went Free

Besides Louis Wiechmann and John M. Lloyd, the Government had a wide choice of victims who could have been held guilty of harbouring, aiding, and abetting the conspirators. On his trip south, from Dr. Mudd's house to his final refuge at Garrett's Farm, Booth was helped on his way by many people, some friendly and some neutral.

On 27 April General Hancock, who had gone to Bryantown to get in touch with Colonel Wells, then engaged in the hunt for Booth, received news that the actor had been killed and that Herold had been captured. Thereupon he wired to Washington as follows:[1]

> BRYANTOWN, APRIL 27, 1865.
>
> HON. E. M. STANTON,
>
> I SHALL RETURN TO WASHINGTON TO-NIGHT. I HAVE CHARGED COLONEL WELLS WITH THE DUTY OF FOLLOWING THE TRACK OF BOOTH AND HEROLD, TO FIND ALL PERSONS WHO GAVE THEM ASSISTANCE IN ANY WAY.
>
> WINF[IEL]D S. HANCOCK,
>
> MAJOR-GENERAL.

There is no doubt that Colonel Wells obeyed these instructions. The Official Records fail to disclose what he found; but this can scarcely evoke surprise. In any event, the persons who gave assistance to the conspirators were never mentioned in those reports that were allowed to reach the public.

[1] *Official Records*, I, vol. 46, part 3, p. 987.

Why the files of the War Department do not always yield information on delicate matters is intimated by Donn Piatt, one of Stanton's friends. This jurist, on one occasion, had served as judge-advocate in a court-martial and after its conclusion reported to the War Minister.

'Mr. Stanton', Judge Piatt wrote when describing this interview, 'examined me at length as to what had been proven, and I saw an expression very like heat-lightning flash over his face when I told him that a certain pet of his had suffered severely. After the death of the Secretary it was discovered that the entire record had disappeared.

'I have my own opinion as to the cause of that disappearance, but it is only an opinion, and I do not care to state it.'[1]

The first home that Booth and Herold reached on the night of 15 April was that of Captain Samuel Cox, about seven miles from Bryantown. Near his house, in a hidden tobacco patch surrounded by a thicket, the fugitives fretted the time away until Friday evening, 21 April. Both Cox and his step-brother, Thomas A. Jones, who supplied their guests with food and newspapers, were fully aware of their identity. Whether the assassins were royally entertained in Cox's dining-room upon their arrival after midnight has not been definitely ascertained. According to local tradition, after Booth had proved to Cox by tattooed initials on his hand that he really was the murderer of the President, the Maryland planter invited his nocturnal visitors to partake of his hospitality. The only witness to this repast, a young negro girl named Mary Swann, later denied under oath that Booth had ever entered her master's house.[2] Cox is said to have rewarded her loyalty by providing her with a life pension. The Washington archives bear out Mary Swann's denials, but they leave the matter of entertainment in doubt. In 1933, when interviewed by the author, this coloured woman, now Mrs. Kelly, stated frankly that she no longer remembered what had happened on that night.

Be these things as they may, it cannot be doubted that Cox

[1] Donn Piatt, *Memories of the Men Who Saved the Union* (Belford, Clarke & Co., Chicago, 1887), p. 67.
[2] Thomas A. Jones, *John Wilkes Booth* (Laird & Lee, Chicago, 1897), p. 121.

and Jones either knew at once that they were harbouring the assassins of Lincoln, or else found it out within a short time. Jones provided the pair with a boat so that they could cross the Potomac and actually guided them through the darkness to the spot from which they embarked. On the day preceding Booth's departure from Cox's farm, Secretary Stanton had issued his proclamation stating that

'All persons . . . secreting said persons [the fugitives] . . . or aiding or assisting in their concealment . . . will be treated as accomplices in the murder of the President . . . and shall be subject to trial before a military commission and the punishment of death. . . .'[1]

It therefore remained only to establish the fact that Cox and Jones had assisted their two visitors, and the case against these staunch Southern sympathizers would be strong enough to have them marked for death.

The files of the War Department reveal that the Government possessed positive evidence that Cox's farm had been Booth's first stop after leaving Dr. Mudd's residence; for the negro who had conducted the assassins on their night ride told the story. According to the account of this coloured man—his name was Oscar Swann—he met them near his home, about two miles from Bryantown, on Saturday night, 15 April, at nine o'clock. He was asked the way to the house of a Mr. Burtle, and started to take them there, but, changing their minds *en route*, the strangers, whose features he could not discern in the darkness, requested to be conducted to Cox's plantation. The party reached this place about midnight. Booth and Herold went inside and stayed three or four hours, while their guide waited in front of the house. Booth then came out, paid Swann twelve dollars, made some uncomplimentary remarks about Cox, and departed.

As a result of Swann's statement, Colonel Wells had Captain Cox arrested and brought to Bryantown, where an examination took place on 8 May, the results of which are found in a report of businesslike brutality.

'Col. H. H. Wells says that in the examination he gave to Samuel Cox at Bryantown the evening he was brought there

[1] DeWitt, *Assassination*, p. 67.

about 11 o'clock p.m., Cox denied all knowledge of either of the two persons named being or having been at his house; and on being told by Col. Wells that he could make a statement if he pleased, but if he did make one, it must be true, and that if he made a false one the Colonel would tie him up by his thumbs, he asked for time for reflection. The Colonel told him he could have until 4 o'clock the next morning to reflect. At 4 o'clock in the morning he was brought in by the guard and said he desired to talk with the Colonel, and the first expression he made use of was that it was no use concealing the fact that the two men were at his house, but he did not know who they were.'[1]

The evidence of Oscar Swann together with the admission of Captain Cox, exacted from him under the persuasion of threatened torture, should have placed Booth's host among the hooded and manacled band in the bilge of some monitor. However, it was really Thomas Jones who carried the major responsibility of caring for the assassins and bringing about their escape. Jones was taken into custody, but it is doubtful if he could have been made to tell what he knew. For one thing, he was a man of taciturn habits, inured to dangers of all kinds and not easily frightened; besides, he had everything to lose and nothing to gain by giving away his secrets. Nevertheless, the authorities could have made out a strong case against him; for while Jones was confident that his negro servant, an ex-slave named Henry Woodland (Woodlawn), would be as close-mouthed as himself, the detectives had no trouble in making him talk. The story he told furnished his interrogators with an excellent lead to the manner in which Booth and Herold had made their way across the Potomac, and Jones certainly appeared to have been involved. When Oldroyd met Woodland in 1901 the negro spun for his visitor a beautiful yarn of how he had misled the Government agents by showing them an imaginary spot where he claimed to have sunk the only boat Jones had in his possession.[2] The files of the Bureau of Military Justice show Jones's trusted servant in a much less heroic light. In fact, he told the detectives enough to let them guess the truth, or come very close to it, and he did not spare his master at all.

[1] War Department Archives.
[2] Oldroyd, op. cit., p. 272.

'"There have been a great many suspicious men knocking about our place," he stated to the government agents on April 30, "and the only man I know of who talked with them was Mr. Jones."'

A rather inauspicious beginning from Jones's point of view; but apparently the supposedly loyal ex-slave needed little coaxing to go further in his insinuations, for he continued:

'A week ago last Thursday [20 April] Mr. Jones had a boat brought up from Allen's Fresh, and . . . he told me to take it up . . . about half a mile . . . I did as he commanded me and supposed the boat was still there until this morning when I went with a detective to show him where it was when I found the boat was gone. Mr. Jones must have hid the boat some where for I could not find it. He told me I must not say anything about the boat unless I was questioned, and that if I were questioned I could answer whatever I chose. On this week about 12 o'clock or after in the day Mr. Jones went away from his house and I did not see anything more of him until the next morning about sunrise; where he went I don't know.'[1]

This story is a remarkably accurate record of Jones's activities. For as Booth and Herold crossed the Potomac on Friday, the twenty-first, Woodland's statement that the boat was provided on the twentieth is in full accord with the facts. But this coloured witness went still further to increase the suspicion of the detectives. He told his inquisitors that within the past year he had often seen signal lights flashed across the Potomac and that they were answered by Mr. Jones; he told of boats crossing under cover of darkness, and of mail being taken from one shore to the other. At such times, he would miss his master who, to his evident disappointment, never told him where he was going.

All in all, Woodland came very near putting a rope around Mr. Jones's neck.

The officers probably could have dispensed with Woodland's testimony altogether and still have learned all the details of Booth's sojourn in the pines and his subsequent flight southward; for they had Herold in their clutches and, although this young man had shown plenty of pluck and loyalty, there is no

[1] War Department Archives.

301

question but that the truth could have been tortured out of him sooner or later. The military pressure that made the ex-policeman Lloyd talk, the threats that opened the mouth of Captain Cox, the measures that were used to cow Wiechmann—is it conceivable that Herold could have indefinitely resisted such influences?

To complete their case, it was essential for the Government detectives to piece together the full story of Booth's adventures. They knew of his arrival at Cox's farm; they had picked up the trail again on the south shore of the Potomac on 23 April. Would they rest content without making strenuous efforts to bridge the intervening gap?

One may assume that Stanton's men knew the itinerary of the fugitives, hour by hour, before the investigation was dropped. If by that time the guilt of Cox and of Jones was not fully demonstarted, a very damaging case, at any rate, could have been worked up against them, certainly a much stronger one than that against Dr. Mudd. The latter had aided a stranger before the news of the tragedy at Washington was generally known and had sent him on his way as soon as he was sufficiently rested. He could be blamed only for keeping secret the visit of the assassins whose disguise he was supposed to have somehow penetrated. In Cox's house the fugitives used no disguise; on the contrary, it was necessary for them to establish their identity in order to gain admission. The news of Lincoln's assassination had, by that time, reached even this lonely spot in southern Maryland, and a few days later the harbouring of suspects was declared a capital offence by proclamation. If Mudd failed in his duty to the Government, he at least did not defy Stanton's decree; but Cox and Jones did, and were, therefore 'subject to trial before a military commission and the punishment of death'.

Yet, in the face of all this evidence, no indictment was brought against either Cox or Jones, and both were released after a few weeks of incarceration.[1]

The punishment meted out to these two well-known Southern sympathizers, one of whom, Jones, had had charge of the Confederate mail for years, was no worse than that experienced by Dr. Richard H. Stewart, whose sole guilt consisted in furnishing a meal to the two culprits after denying them the hospitality of

[1] Jones, op. cit., pp. 125–6.

his home and even refusing to inspect Booth's leg. A Mr. Bryant who had conducted them to the country home of the physician went scot-free. The negro Lucas, on whose wagon the next lap of the journey was covered, was not molested; neither were the boatmen who ferried the assassins across the Rappahannock.

When Booth and his companion reached this ferry at Port Conway they fell in with three Confederate soldiers—Captain Jett, Lieutenant Ruggles, and Lieutenant Bainbridge.[1] Telling them who he was, Booth threw himself on their mercy. These Southern officers were only boys in their teens, but they were gentlemen at heart. Probably unaware of Stanton's proclamation, but fully apprised of the enormous reward awaiting a betrayal of their charges, they followed the generous impulse of their natures and hid the assassin on Garrett's Farm. On them the full wrath of the military prosecutors could well have descended. Here was an acknowledged attempt to balk justice and, from Stanton's point of view, there could be no mitigation of the offence. Not only did these officers hide the fugitives but they even watched over them; for when Lieutenant Doherty's party crossed the river and started on its ride toward Bowling Green, the Federal soldiers saw themselves observed by these Southern sentinels; they gave chase, but were unsuccessful. Bainbridge and Ruggles then rode up to Garrett's Farm and warned Booth that soldiers were on his track and that he had best leave at once.[2]

What more treasonable crime could any one have committed in the eyes of Stanton and of the judge-advocate? If Booth had followed the advice of these newly found friends he would have avoided his pursuers altogether—and there are some who claim that he did, and that it was some one else who was shot in the barn. He would then have had a start of twelve hours before they could have followed the new trail. The assassin might have made good his escape; if he failed to do so, it was not the fault of the Confederate officers.

Jett, Bainbridge, and Ruggles were made prisoners and taken to Washington; they never denied their respective parts, but

[1] See supplementary note to chapter xxiii, 'The Ranks of Jett, Bainbridge, and Ruggles'.
[2] L. C. Baker, op. cit., p. 535.

none of them was prosecuted, and Jett even appeared as a witness for the Government.

After this it was only logical that the Garrett family should not have been molested. Booth had been introduced to them as a soldier named Boyd, and the story he told was credible. They were technically guilty of housing Lincoln's assassin, but not of wilfully defying the Washington Government.

The Bureau of Military Justice divided its prisoners into two groups. The first was treated with extreme severity and the conviction of its members was sought by all possible means. The second received unexpected leniency.

Between these groups there was a line of demarcation, determined by unknown factors, separating those who were to be condemned at any cost from those about whose fate the War Department was indifferent.

Those whom Stanton had put on his death list were:

MRS. MARY E. SURRATT. Her hanging would not be popular and would antagonize a large section of the population, particularly the Catholics. Her conviction would not be easy to bring about.

DAVID E. HEROLD. Guilty as an accessory before or after the crime, his death would be considered just punishment.

DR. SAMUEL A. MUDD. Absent from Washington at the time of the assassination, his guilt as an accessory after the crime could be established only by circumstantial evidence.

LEWIS PAINE. Self-confessed conspirator. His conviction was inevitable, and the public demanded it.

GEORGE A. ATZERODT. His death was a foregone conclusion and undoubtedly would be considered deserved.

MICHAEL O'LAUGHLIN and SAMUEL B. ARNOLD. There was no evidence of their complicity in the assassination plot, but they had conspired to kidnap Lincoln.

ED. SPANGLER. A lonely, unimportant figure, whose connection with any plot was problematical.

The roster of those whose names could have been added to the list of defendants, but who were not prosecuted, comprises:

LOUIS J. WIECHMANN. There was as much evidence against

him as against Atzerodt, and more than existed against any of the others except Herold and Paine. His conviction could have been brought about with ease.

JOHN M. LLOYD. His part in the abduction plot was plainly demonstrated. He certainly aided and comforted the fleeing assassins and misled the pursuers. There was no sympathy with him as a witness, and he would have had none had he been one of the prisoners.

SAMUEL COX and THOMAS A. JONES. Guilty of hiding and feeding the fugitives and of defying Stanton's proclamation. Confederate sympathizers, they made no pretence of loyalty to the Washington Government. Conviction would have been certain and popular.

JETT, RUGGLES, and BAINBRIDGE. They actively abetted the escape of Booth and Herold. They were Confederate soldiers. Their death would have satisfied both those who were clamouring for a moral lesson to the South and those who wished to vindicate the War Department's proclamation of 20 April.

DR. STEWART, BRYANT, GARRETT, and LUCAS. These were but minor figures, and their fate was of no particular interest, one way or the other.

At first glance, there seems to be no reasonable system in the grouping of these suspects. Sympathizers for the Southern cause are about evenly divided between the two lists; in each there are people of refinement and people of little culture; one finds in both groups persons whose conviction, in the excitement of the times, would have found an echo of public approbation. Yet, somewhere there must be a key that solves the puzzle. Why did the Bureau of Military Justice, guided by Stanton and Holt, bear with such uncommon severity on one group, while they exercised a leniency toward the other that was noticed and even mildly censured by a friendly congressional committee?[1] Why was Jett snatched from the jaws of death to give irrelevant testimony that did no more than add continuity to the history of Booth's flight? And why were Lloyd and Wiechmann transferred from the row of prisoners to the line of state witnesses in order to secure the conviction of the one woman in the case?

[1] House of Representatives, 39th Congress, First Session, Exec. Doc. No. 90, p. 7.

The Conspirators who went Free

There is, apparently, only one theory that offers a plausible explanation for these vagaries. This theory takes into account the strange hooding and gagging of the prisoners whom the War Department had chosen as its victims and Booth's escape from Washington under circumstances which justify the suspicion that some powerful influence was exerted to safeguard his flight. The assassin, of course, was fully aware of whatever secret arrangements may have been made in his behalf. His silence, after he had fled from Washington, could be depended on; for, once out of reach of pursuit, the actor wanted to be the hero of his beloved Confederacy. He would never have confessed that he owed his miraculous escape to the intervention of a hated Yankee. Had there been a bargain Booth could have been counted on to carry out his end of it—to keep his lips sealed and to make good his escape; if by any chance he should fail, the penalty would be death.

But how about his associates in the capital? Would he tell them of his powerful connections in order to swing them into line for final action? He could assure his followers that the risk which they were taking had been minimized through his skilful preparations. Of course, none but the cultured few among them would be trusted with this information. Booth was not in the habit of talking confidentially with people like Lloyd; he mistrusted and disliked Wiechmann; but he would confide—if he confided at all—in Mrs. Surratt and her son John, whom he considered his social equals; and he naturally might whisper a word of encouragement to his helpmates, Herold, Paine, Atzerodt, Arnold, and O'Laughlin. Of the remainder, only Spangler, whom he had asked to hold his horse, and who was his ever-willing slave, might have shared his secret over a glass of the actor's favourite brandy.

It was Mrs. Surratt's misfortune that Wiechmann had seen her conferring with Booth in the parlour of her house on the day of the assassination, just as she and her favourite boarder were about to leave for Surratsville.

'Just before leaving the city,' so Wiechmann's testimony reads, 'as I was going to the door, I saw Mr. Booth in the parlour and Mrs. Surratt was speaking with him. They were alone.'[1]

When this information reached the Bureau of Military Justice,

[1] Pitman, op. cit., p. 113.

it probably spelled the death of Mrs. Surratt. If anything else was needed to increase Stanton's alarm, it was Wiechmann's further statement that about nine o'clock on the evening of 14 April the door bell of the boarding-house was rung and that Mrs. Surratt had answered it.

'I heard footsteps go into the parlour, immediately go out again, and down the steps,' Wiechmann had reported.[1] These footsteps, at that time, were supposed to have been those of Booth.

So the murderer had spoken privately to Mrs. Surratt twice on the day of the tragedy. This probably was the poor woman's real guilt in the eyes of the War Department. To remove her for ever was doubtless considered a matter of self-preservation for the high Unknown—if there was any such person—who had used the assassin as his pawn.

But what was an open sesame for Booth in Washington would work for his undoing as soon as he arrived at the fringe of the Confederacy. Captain Cox would have quickly shown him the door had he suspected that Booth was a member of a conspiracy engineered by Northerners. Thomas A. Jones would never have risked his liberty for him; and the Confederate officers at the Rappahannock ferry hardly would have helped him escape if they had guessed that the assassination had been planned by the bitterest foes of the South.

Thus the dividing line between the group that had to be silenced and the one which was of no interest to Booth's hypothetical allies in Washington was drawn automatically. Those whom the assassin had known intimately before his deed and whom he might have taken into his confidence were silenced first by hoods and later by death or by virtual burial in an isolated fortress. Those who had not been closely allied with Booth, but had only helped him during his flight, were permitted to go free. Neither their lives nor their freedom was a matter of concern to the powers in Washington.

The position of Dr. Mudd was uncertain. If the fugitive had merely accepted his medical aid and his hospitality the unfortunate physician probably would not have been molested. But investigation showed that the two had known each other for several months past and, since Mudd was a Southern gentleman

[1] Pitman, op. cit., p. 116.

of position and refinement, an intimacy between him and Booth could reasonably be suspected. It became known that Booth had once slept at the Mudd residence; and Wiechmann's testimony showed that the country doctor had not only walked in Booth's company through the streets of Washington but had also drawn mysterious lines for him on the back of an envelope. It was not his behaviour at Bryantown, but the possibility that Booth had confided in him that decided Dr. Mudd's fate. If he and Booth had been strangers to each other perhaps the harmless physician would have suffered nothing worse than temporary confinement.

The assumption that intimacy with Booth, or else lack of such relationship with him, is the common denominator that separates the two groups of suspects appears to cover the case. It explains all the known facts and is not inconsistent with any of them. Such an assumption therefore can be adopted as a working hypothesis. It cannot be more than that; for there is no proof of it, nor is there evidence of any contact between Stanton's clique, who wished to punish the South, and the hot-headed actor who believed that he was freeing the South from a tyrant.

Perhaps future research will bring to light new data which will either convert this hypothesis into an historical fact, or else demolish it for ever. In the meantime, judgement should be withheld.

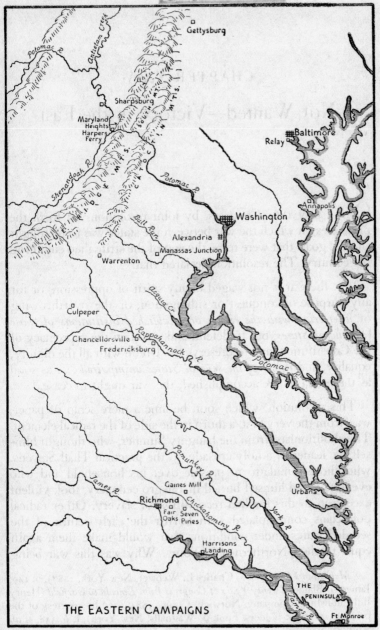

CHAPTER XXIV

Not Wanted—Victory in the East

On 26 July 1861 Congress, by joint resolution, set forth the principles on which the war between the states was to be fought and the goals that were to be the end of the strife then engulfing the country. The resolution declared that:

'... the war is not waged in any spirit of oppression, or for any purpose of conquest or subjugation, or the overthrowing or *interfering with the rights or established institutions of those [Southern] States*, but to defend and maintain the supremacy of the Constitution, and to preserve the Union with all the dignity, equality, and *rights of the several States unimpaired* ... as soon as these objects are accomplished, the war ought to cease.'[1]

This resolution, which soon became a mere scrap of paper, was, from the very first, a thorn in the side of the radical element. The abolitionists, from the haughty Sumner, who thought himself the leader of a holy crusade, to the practical Thad Stevens, who chose a mulatto to preside over his household and who eventually had himself buried in a negro cemetery, took violent exception to this implied recognition of slavery. Other radical politicians contemplated with horror the early return of the seceded states under conditions that would make them again equal to their Northern neighbours. Why was this war being

[1] *McClellan's Own Story* (Charles L. Webster, New York, 1887), p. 149; James G. Blaine, *Twenty Years of Congress from Lincoln to Garfield* (Henry Bill Publishing Company, Norwich, Conn., 1884; used by courtesy of the present copyright-holders, Funk & Wagnalls, New York), I, p. 338, *et al.* Author's italics.

carried on, anyway? If slavery were to be restored, the start of
another armed conflict was only a matter of time. The preservation of the Constitution? They cared nothing for the Constitution. What they did care about, and what was really a question
of political life or death to them, was the preservation of their
party. The Republicans were a new faction, far from homo-
geneous, and a minority group at best. In 1860 Lincoln had not
received the majority of all the ballots, even disregarding the
votes from the Secession states, and could not have been elected
against a solid Democratic opposition. If the Southern states
returned to Congress with their voting strength unimpaired, the
end of Republican domination was in sight. This is what had
to be prevented, regardless of negro rights and the provisions
of the Constitution.

As early as December 1861 Mr. Chase, Lincoln's Secretary
of the Treasury, Senator Wade of Ohio, and Congressman
Ashley of the same state, tried to formulate a policy to accomplish the desired end.

If a state attempted to secede, declared Chase, the state
organization was forfeited, and it lapsed into the condition of a
territory. Such territories were to be governed by Washington,
and the erstwhile states would from time to time be taken back
into the Union as Congress should provide.[1] That such statements were not mere oratory is attested by the fact that this very
doctrine, absurd as it was, was approved after Lincoln's death.
But so long as Lincoln was alive he kept it from gaining the
ascendancy.

At the outbreak of the war the Radical Party represented only
a negligible percentage of the nation. Abolitionists were still
regarded with abhorrence by the great majority. If the contest
had come to a close within a year or two the Southern states
would have been welcomed back into the fold as repentant
'erring sisters'. Therefore, the war had to last long enough to
embitter the Northern sections to a point where the populace,
saturated with propaganda and embittered by the loss of relations
and friends, would become as vindictive as the Radical leaders.
Secretary of War Stanton was quite outspoken about this. When
a commission from New York called on the President early in

[1] Robert B. Warden, *Private Life and Public Services of Salmon P. Chase*
(Wilstach, Baldwin & Company, Cincinnati, 1874), p. 390.

1862 to urge upon him a more vigorous support of General McClellan, it found Stanton with the Executive. Stanton then stated:

'. . . the great . . . aim of the war was to abolish slavery. To end the war before the nation was ready for that would be a failure. *The war must be prolonged, and conducted so as to achieve that.*[1]

The Northern people were not yet prepared to agree with Stanton, hence it was necessary to keep General McClellan from succeeding until the public had been worked up to such a pitch that Stanton's policy would be endorsed. It is said that Lincoln was present as his Secretary of War delivered this strange declaration. There is no record of his having protested.

General McClellan, who knew the value of secrecy and who was fully aware that Washington was filled with Southern sympathizers, had kept his plans to himself; but when Stanton became War Minister he was forced to divulge them. They proved to be simple and sound. An army of 300,000 men was to be raised to make possible a decisive victory. A garrison was to protect the capital; the remainder, with the exception of a strong guard in the Shenandoah valley, was to be thrown to Urbana on the lower Rappahannock; from there Richmond could be reached by a short overland march.[2] The navy could protect the army almost to the gates of the Southern stronghold, and the line of communication with headquarters in the north was safe from interruption, since the Confederacy was without a fleet worthy of the name.

McClellan's plan at once aroused a storm of opposition on the part of Stanton, who constantly instilled into Lincoln the fear of laying the capital open to a surprise attack. In vain McClellan assumed all responsibility for the safety of Washington; Lincoln even went so far as to accuse his general of an attempt at treason for leaving the capital defenceless.[3] Two years later Lincoln allowed General Grant to strip the Washington fortifications of defenders to such a degree that Jubal Early could have

[1] *McClellan's Own Story*, pp. 150-1. Author's italics.
[2] Ibid., p. 227.   [3] Ibid., 196.

marched into it had he arrived a day earlier. Grant was then merely engaged in siege operations and his negligence was inexcusable; but if he was reprimanded, no proof of it has ever been found.

Against McClellan alone, of all his generals, Lincoln, under the influence of Stanton's intrigues, showed a strange and only thinly veiled animosity. Perhaps he sensed a future rival in this idol of the army and was not particularly anxious to help him gather laurels; but Stanton and his Radical friends carried their hatred to the point of conspiring to sacrifice him and the whole army for the purpose of prolonging the war.

The events that followed showed whether or not the war was conducted so as to achieve the postponement of the end.

Stanton had assumed the post of Secretary of War on 20 January 1862. When his confirmation by the Senate was under debate Senator Sumner had come out bluntly with the declaration that '. . . he [Stanton] is one of us'.[1] Stanton was confirmed.

Only a week later Lincoln, evidently at Stanton's urging, issued his famous War Order No. 1, directing a simultaneous advance of all Union armies:

Executive Mansion
Washington, January 27, 1862.

Ordered, That the 22d day of February, 1862, be the day for a general movement of the land and naval forces of the United States against the insurgent forces. That, especially, the army at and about Fortress Monroe; the Army of the Potomac; the Army of Western Virginia; the army near Mumfordville, Ky.; the army and flotilla at Cairo, and a naval force in the Gulf of Mexico, be ready to move on that day.

That all other forces, both land and naval, with their respective commanders, obey existing orders for the time, and be ready to obey additional orders when duly given.

That the heads of Departments, and especially the Secretaries of War and of the Navy, with all their subordinates, and the General-in-chief, with all other commanders and subordinates of land and naval forces, will severally be held to their strict

---

[1] Jeremiah S. Black, 'Mr. Black to Mr. Wilson' in *Galaxy Magazine* (Feb. 1871), pp. 257 ff.

and full responsibilities for the prompt execution of this order.[1]

ABRAHAM LINCOLN.

In a Special Order, dated 31 January 1862, the President gave particular instructions to the Army of the Potomac, directing it to advance on Manassas Junction, near the site of the first battle of Bull Run.

These war orders, the first ever given out by a President of the United States, were monstrous from every point of view— a 'curious specimen of puerile impatience', Ropes called them in his *Story of the Civil War*.[2] To begin with, it was poor discretion to announce publicly the programme of a campaign, thereby advising friend and foe alike. Far more serious, however, was Lincoln's decision to force an army of raw recruits out into the Virginia mud at a time when the roads there were all but impassable. As a result of General McClellan's energetic protests, the order for his instant departure was not pressed, even though it was never officially withdrawn. In 1863 the spring campaign did not begin until May; the following year Grant started his troops the same month, and, even in 1865, when Southern resistance was nearly broken, the attack on Petersburg was not initiated until the end of March.[3] If McClellan had obeyed Lincoln's orders the Northern contingents would have been hopelessly mired, just as General Burnside's troops were a year later at that season.

'The forcing of the army out in March, 1862', says Campbell, 'was idiotically premature. General Grant was made supreme commander on the 9th of March, 1864. He did not stir until two months later, and even then only on his own volition. For what was he waiting? For the rains to stop. McClellan was pushed out seven weeks earlier, in a "phenomenal and unprecedented season", . . . In 1862 General Grant would not have moved until the middle of June. . . .'[4]

Admittedly, Campbell was a champion of McClellan, but his logic appears unimpeachable, none the less.

[1] John C. Ropes, *The Story of the Civil War* (G. P. Putnam's Sons, New York, 1894), pp. 226–7.

[2] Ibid.

[3] Ibid., p. 261.

[4] James H. Campbell, *McClellan* (Neale Publishing Co., New York, 1916), p. 125.

To Grant President Lincoln wrote in 1864: 'The particulars of your plans I neither know nor seek to know,'[1] but to McClellan he had dictated a plan that was suicidal and had given it damaging publicity. He admitted to Grant that, although he did not know how campaigns should be conducted, he had been forced by political pressure to issue his series of early military orders. 'He did not know but they were all wrong,' Grant wrote in his *Memoirs*, 'and did know that some of them were.'[2] But Lincoln never sought to square himself with the man to whom he had given them.

When Grant lay idle until the beginning of the real spring without communicating his ideas to the President or to Stanton or to Halleck, he remained unmolested; but when McClellan, in midwinter (on 12 January), refused to move his troops to certain disaster Lincoln sneeringly remarked at a Cabinet meeting that if General McClellan did not want to use his army, he himself would like to borrow it.[3]

In the end, neither McClellan's plan of campaign, nor Lincoln's pet project of the straight overland march to Richmond was adopted. A compromise was reached, according to which the army was to issue forth from Fort Monroe as a base and work up the Virginia peninsula. The army was to be supported by the navy on the James and the York rivers surrounding this narrow tongue of land, which was almost entirely within range of the naval guns. Any Confederate army on the peninsula was in immediate danger of being shelled out or captured, and no serious opposition need therefore be expected until the invading army was a few miles east of Richmond. But the ships were never sent. McClellan constantly pleaded the importance of this matter to the Secretary of War, and he sent officers directly to Assistant Secretary Fox of the navy. Yet the fleet at no time received orders to assist the army, and this vital part of the plan fell through.[4]

'It was the President, counseled and advised by . . . Mr.

---

[1] *Abraham Lincoln: Letters*, II, pp. 22–4, quoted in Campbell, op. cit., p. 102.

[2] Grant, *Memoirs*, II, p. 122.

[3] Campbell, op. cit., p. 84, *et al.*

[4] John Formby, *American Civil War* (Charles Scribner's Sons, New York, 1910), p. 108, as quoted in Campbell, op. cit., p. 127

Stanton, who was reponsible for the inaction of the navy,' says Campbell. 'Stanton's . . . acts about this time indicate that this was but one of many methods used to make failure certain. . . .'[1]

McClellan had originally estimated that he would need 150,000 men for offensive operations, with 35,000 men to garrison Washington and another 20,000 to 25,000 to guard Harper's Ferry, Baltimore, and Annapolis. On 15 March he had a total of 203,000 men, which should have given him 146,000 for active duty, to which a force of 10,000 was to be added from Fort Monroe. This seemed sufficient at the time, but the President's accusation of treasonable intent still rankled in McClellan's breast, and he insisted that the whole plan of his campaign be submitted for approval to twelve generals. The general-in-chief was not present at the conference; nevertheless, his plan was endorsed by eight and opposed by only four. Thereupon Stanton urged that the result should be viewed as a vote of four to one against McClellan, for the eight were 'McClellan men' and their votes should be counted as one. Lincoln would not follow this sophistry, but he offered no objection when Stanton immediately created four army corps, which McClellan did not want, and appointed as corps commanders three of the four generals who had opposed their chief.[2]

In the latter part of March, a few days before McClellan was to leave for the front, he met Lincoln by appointment at Alexandria. There the President stated that he was being strongly pressed to remove Blenker's German division of 10,000 men from the Army of the Potomac and assign it to Fremont's mountain department.

'He suggested several reasons against the proposed removal of the division,' reported McClellan, 'to all of which I assented. He then said . . . that he would not deprive me of the division.'[3]

But on 31 March, a few hours before he sailed, McClellan received the following letter:[4]

---

[1] Campbell, loc. cit.

[2] Ibid., p. 89; *McClellan's Own Story*, pp. 196, 222; Flower, op. cit., p. 139.

[3] *McClellan's Own Story*, p. 164.

[4] Ibid., pp. 164–5.

Executive Mansion,
Washington, March 31, 1862.

Maj.-Gen. McCLELLAN:

My dear Sir: This morning I feel constrained to order Blenker's division to Fremont; and I write to assure you that I did so with great pain, understanding that you would wish it otherwise. If you could know the full pressure of the case I am confident that you would justify it, even beyond a mere acknowledgment that the commander-in-chief may order what he pleases.

Yours very truly,

A. LINCOLN.

The last sentence may have emanated from Lincoln's pen, but it surely did not emanate from his mind. It is too unlike Lincoln in its diction and in its brutality. McClellan was moved to comment tartly that even the Commander-in-Chief had no power to do with the army 'what he pleases', but could only order what he considered to be right. That the removal of Blenker's division was not right Lincoln himself had implied in his letter.

'. . . the President had already assured me', said McClellan, 'that he knew this thing to be wrong, and had informed me that the pressure was only a political one. . . .'[1] But Stanton and the Radicals had greater influence over Lincoln than military necessity.

'The President', commented Ropes, '. . . did another thing very difficult to understand, and so difficult to justify that we will not attempt the task. He took a whole division—that commanded by General Blenker—from the Army of the Potomac. . . .'[2]

Still, there were another 10,000 men to be picked up at Fort Monroe, so the loss of Blenker's division, while serious, would not be fatal. But when McClellan arrived at Fort Monroe, on 2 April, he received a telegraphic order withdrawing this base from his command and forbidding him to remove any troops from the fortress without sanction of the general commanding there.[3] *No reasons were ever given for this order.*

[1] *McClellan's Own Story*, p. 165.
[2] Ropes, op. cit., i, p. 255.
[3] *McClellan's Own Story*, p. 257.

A day later the following telegram was dispatched to McClellan:[1]

Adjutant-General's Office
April 4, 1862.

Gen. McCLELLAN:

By directions of the President, Gen. McDowell's army corps has been detached from the force under your immediate command, and the general is ordered to report to the Secretary of War; letter by mail.

L. THOMAS,
Adj.-Gen.

In addition, nine regiments of cavalry that had been promised to McClellan were withheld from him. Thus of the 150,000 men needed, only 85,000 remained.

But General McClellan was still to receive his worst blow. Two days after he left Washington recruiting was stopped all over the country. It was stopped so thoroughly that an immediate strengthening of the army became impossible. This was done on the very eve of an advance into enemy territory, with the certainty of losses, and in full knowledge of the fact that the invading force was already undermanned, having been deprived of about one-third of its troops.

General Order No. 33

Adjutant-General's Office, U.S.A.
Washington, April 3, 1862.

III. The recruiting service for volunteers will be discontinued in every State from this date. The officers detached on the Volunteer Recruiting Service will join their regiments without delay, taking with them the parties and recruits at their respective stations.

The superintendents of the Volunteer Recruiting Service will disband their parties and close their offices, after having taken the necessary steps to carry out these orders. The public property belonging to the Volunteer Recruiting Service will be sold to

---

[1] *McClellan's Own Story*, p. 261.

the best advantage possible, and the proceeds credited to the
fund for collecting, drilling, and organizing volunteers.

By order of the Secretary of War.

L. THOMAS
Adj.-Gen., U.S.A.[1]

'Common sense and the experience of all wars', declared
General McClellan, 'prove that when an army takes the field
every possible effort should be made at home to collect recruits
and establish depots, whence the inevitable daily losses may be
made good with instructed men as fast as they occur, so that the
fighting force may be kept up to their normal strength. Failure
to do this proves either a desire for the failure of the campaign
or entire incompetence. Between the horns of this dilemma the
friends of Mr. Stanton must take their choice.'[2]

What McClellan could not know was the nature of the campaign from the rear which was conducted against him by the
War Department. A characteristic picture of one scene has been
preserved by Orville Browning, then senator from Illinois.
While Browning was in conversation with Lincoln, on 2 April,
just after McClellan had left for the front, Stanton entered the
room.

'Supposing he had private business I proposed to leave [reads
the entry in Browning's diary], but both he and the President
insisted that I should remain. . . . He [Stanton] then took from
his pocket a letter, which he said he had just received from one
of the first men of the Nation . . . but whose name he would
not mention, and read from it a passage stating that McClellan
some time in 1860 had been initiated as a Knight of the Golden
Circle by Jeff Davis—that Davis still had great power and
influence over him, and that he would do nothing against the
rebels which would be inconsistent with his obligations as a
Knight of the Golden Circle. . . . Stanton added that he did
not believe these imputations of disloyalty. . . .'[3]

This is what Stanton said to Lincoln behind McClellan's back.
To the general himself he expressed himself a little differently.

[1] *McClellan's Own Story*, p. 258.
[2] Ibid.
[3] Browning, *Diary*, i, p. 538.

Washington, July 5, 1862.

'. . . there is no cause in my heart or conduct for the cloud that wicked men have raised between us for their own base and selfish purposes. No man had ever a truer friend than I have been to you and shall continue to be. You are seldom absent from my thoughts, and I am ready to make any sacrifice to aid you.'[1]

Only six days later Halleck was appointed general-in-chief. The preparations for his promotion had been in full swing for several days when Stanton wrote this loving epistle.

Against such insidious and underhand intrigues, together with the manifest withdrawal of support from the War Office, McClellan was powerless to defend or sustain himself.

Under Stanton's influence, Lincoln wrote singular letters to McClellan. 'I always insisted', he maintained at one time, 'that going down the bay in search of a field, instead of fighting at or near Manassas, was only shifting and not surmounting a difficulty; that we should find the same enemy, and the same or equal entrenchments at either place.'[2]

When Lincoln expressed this opinion he was not only flying in the face of all military axioms, but also in the face of all good judgement. In plain English, he wanted McClellan to fight the enemy on the latter's chosen ground, instead of on one of his own selection. The President apparently cared nothing about topographical obstacles, preferred frontal attacks where flank movements would answer the purpose and, in general, displayed a painful ignorance of all strategical principles. He never was guilty of impressing his views on his generals in later years.

It was becoming evident that Stanton was conducting the war according to his promise, so as to achieve a postponement of the end.

On 12 May the *Merrimac*, the Confederate terror of the seas, was blown up by its own officers. After that there was no reason why the land forces should not have had the full support of the

[1] *McClellan's Own Story*, p. 476.
[2] Colin R. Ballard, *Military Genius of Abraham Lincoln* (Clarendon Press, Oxford, 1926), p. 112.

navy. McClellan begged that McDowell's corps, which had been removed from his command, be sent to him by water. Instead he received, after much procrastination, a promise from headquarters that McDowell would be sent to the peninsula by land in order to keep the troops between the enemy and the Northern capital.

'. . . *you will give no order*', McClellan was told by Stanton, 'either before or after your junction, *which can put him out of position to cover this city. . . . The President desires that Gen. McDowell retain the command of the Department* of the Rappahannock and *of the forces with which he moves forward.*'[1]

This order, dated 18 May, settled the fate of McClellan and of his campaign. For in order to comply with it McClellan had to split his army; the left wing remained on the south bank of the Chickahominy, while the right wing had to be moved to the north bank in order to connect with McDowell's corps. His position would have been faulty even with the expected reinforcements; without them it was desperate. And though promised repeatedly, McDowell never arrived.

In the meantime McClellan fretted over the obstacles that were continually thrown in his way.

'I regret the state of things as to Gen. McDowell's command,' he wrote on 21 May. '. . . One division added to this army . . . would do more to protect Washington than his whole force can possibly do anywhere else. . . . The rebels are concentrating from all points. . . . I would still, most respectfully, suggest the policy of our concentrating here by movements on water. I have heard nothing as to the probabilities of the contemplated junction of McDowell's force with mine. I have no idea when he can start . . . or when he may be expected to reach this vicinity.'[2]

Unexpectedly, Lincoln replied in person, restoring McClellan's command over McDowell's forces and announcing that the latter would move shortly.

'McDowell and Shields both say they can and positively will move Monday morning (May 26th),' he wrote his general-in-chief.[3]

[1] *Official Records*, I, vol. 11, part 1, p. 27; *McClellan's Own Story*, pp. 345–6. Author's italics.
[2] Ibid., p. 349.
[3] Ibid., p. 351.

At this moment the Confederate leaders, well aware of Lincoln's and Stanton's exaggerated fear of endangering their capital, sent Stonewall Jackson on a quick raid into the Shenandoah valley. Thereupon McDowell's order for co-operation was immediately suspended. If it had been revoked in its entirety it would have been better; its mere suspension made it more hazardous than ever for McClellan to continue his straddling position across the Chickahominy, the more so as this river was rising steadily because of persistent rains. Eighteen of the twenty bridges that had been built were inundated, thus practically separating from each other the two wings of the Northern army.[1]

'McDowell saw the blunder,' wrote Blaine, 'but his directions were peremptory and nothing was left but to obey. He telegraphed to the Secretary of War, "The President's order is a crushing blow to us".'[2] He then pleaded for permission to proceed on his course to aid McClellan: 'I obeyed your order immediately,' he wired to Lincoln, 'for it was positive and urgent, and, perhaps, as a subordinate, there I ought to stop. But . . . I shall gain nothing for you there [in the Shenandoah valley], and lose much for you here. . . . I have a heavy heart in the matter. . . .'[3]

Blaine thought that when McDowell turned back he was doing precisely what the President of the Confederate states would have ordered, could he have done so. 'The president [Lincoln]', observed Blaine, 'was led into this course by the urgent advice of the Secretary of War.'[4]

The Confederates were not slow to take advantage of this situation. On 30 May they fell with great violence on McClellan's exposed left wing; there ensued the battles of Fair Oaks and Seven Pines. It was only great skill and pluck that saved the Union forces south of the Chickahominy from destruction.

Almost a month passed. McClellan was held in his vulnerable position by orders from Stanton and was waiting for McDowell,

[1] *McClellan's Own Story*, pp. 364, 365.
[2] Blaine, op. cit., I, p. 367.
[3] Wm. R. Plum, *Military Telegraphy in the Civil War* (Jansen, McClurg & Co., Chicago, 1882), I, p. 157.
[4] Blaine, op. cit., pp. 367–8.

who was still expected. Then General Lee, who had taken charge of the Southern army, suddenly pounced on the right wing of the Northern troops and, in the battle of Gaines's Mill, brought it into gravest danger. On that evening, 28 June, McClellan sent this telegram to Stanton:

I NOW KNOW THE FULL HISTORY OF THE DAY. . . . ON THE LEFT BANK [OF THE CHICKAHOMINY] OUR MEN DID ALL THAT MEN COULD DO, ALL THAT SOLDIERS COULD ACCOMPLISH, BUT THEY WERE OVERWHELMED BY VASTLY SUPERIOR NUMBERS. . . .

I AGAIN REPEAT THAT I AM NOT RESPONSIBLE FOR THIS, AND I SAY IT WITH THE EARNESTNESS OF A GENERAL WHO FEELS IN HIS HEART THE LOSS OF EVERY BRAVE MAN WHO HAS BEEN NEEDLESSLY SACRIFICED TODAY. . . .

I KNOW THAT A FEW THOUSAND MORE MEN WOULD HAVE CHANGED THIS BATTLE FROM A DEFEAT TO A VICTORY. . . .

I FEEL TOO EARNESTLY TO-NIGHT. I HAVE SEEN TOO MANY DEAD AND WOUNDED COMRADES TO FEEL OTHERWISE THAN THAT THE GOVERNMENT HAS NOT SUSTAINED THIS ARMY. IF YOU DO NOT DO SO NOW THE GAME IS LOST.

IF I SAVE THIS ARMY NOW, I TELL YOU PLAINLY THAT I OWE NO THANKS TO YOU OR TO ANY OTHER PERSONS IN WASHINGTON.

YOU HAVE DONE YOUR BEST TO SACRIFICE THIS ARMY.[1]

It is doubtful if in the history of any war such an indictment was ever hurled by a commanding general at his own Government.

In spite of everything, McClellan did save his army and with it his supplies and his wagons. A week of fierce and clever fighting brought him safely to the banks of the James River, where he had desired to be for some time past, and to which place he had ordered material to be shipped many days before Lee's attack. The army was now where it should have been in the first place. Secure in its front and in its rear, and within a few miles of the Southern capital, it needed only time for recupera-

[1] *Official Records*, I, vol. 11, p. 61; *McClellan's Own Story*, pp. 424-5.

tion before resuming the offensive. Two years later it took Grant several weeks to discover this vantage point, and a whole army was lost before he realized that it was useless to 'fight it out along these lines, if it takes all summer'—*these lines* being the overland route to Richmond. Lincoln also perceived this now. With Stanton temporarily absent from Washington, due to sickness in his family, the President's spirits rebounded. On 4 July he wired McClellan in his own inimitable style, evidently free for the moment from sinister influence: 'IF YOU CAN HOLD YOUR PRESENT POSITION WE SHALL HAVE THE ENEMY YET.'[1]

Nevertheless, rumours continued to be heard that a recall of the army was being contemplated. On 28 July McClellan wired to Washington:

MY OPINION IS MORE AND MORE FIRM THAT HERE IS THE DEFENCE OF WASHINGTON, AND THAT I SHOULD BE AT ONCE REINFORCED BY ALL AVAILABLE TROOPS TO ENABLE ME TO ADVANCE. RETREAT WOULD BE DISASTROUS TO THE ARMY AND THE CAUSE.[2]

Commodore Wilkes of the navy implored Secretary Gideon Welles to prevent the removal of the army, and wrote on 5 August:

'The withdrawal of the Army of the Potomac would be the most suicidal act that any administration could commit, and be attended with every disaster that could befall our army—causing its utter demoralization and total destruction . . . and I must say, if anything can, would entirely ruin the Union cause. . . .

'The naval force has now under its control the supply of the army . . . the moment I receive the additional vessels the Department is to supply me I am ready for active offensive operations, and with the aid of the army on the north bank of the James River I have no doubt that Richmond can be taken.'[3]

Welles, watching things critically, gave a vivid description of how the fatal withdrawal of the Union army from the environs of Richmond was brought about. Carrying with him the letter

[1] *McClellan's Own Story*, p. 486.
[2] Ibid., p. 490.
[3] *Official Records*, I, vol. XI, p. 356.

from Commodore Wilkes, Secretary Welles called on Halleck, by now general-in-chief of all Federal armies.

'. . . he seemed stupid, said there was no further use for the Navy. . . . When I suggested that it appeared to me important that the naval force should remain, with perhaps a small number of troops to menace Richmond, he rubbed his elbow first, as if that was the seat of thought, and then his eyes. . . . I questioned then, and do now, the wisdom of recalling McClellan and the army; have doubted if H., unprompted, would himself have done it. It was a specimen of Chase's and Stanton's tactics.'[1]

Welles was wrong on this occasion in coupling Chase's name with that of Stanton. The Secretary of the Treasury had written on 26 June, 'that a small force . . . might contribute largely to the taking of Richmond, if sent immediately up James River'. Although Chase had no confidence in McClellan's ability to handle a great army, and did not regard him as loyal to the administration, he thought it of importance to send reinforcements from Fortress Monroe and Norfolk, and kept insisting that McDowell be sent forward, instead of being recalled while pursuing Jackson. 'Our troops were called off when they were just upon him,' he declared on 2 August. 'The course of the whole movement was changed, for no reason that I could see.'

Chase was no friend of McClellan and had many chestnuts of his own in the fire; but even he conceded that 'a wide door for Jackson to Richmond was opened . . . he . . . fell . . . on McClellan's right, left unsupported as if to invite disaster. . . . Sad! sad! yet nobody seems to heed.' A strange fatality, he thought, seemed to preside over the whole campaign.[2]

On 4 August McClellan sent General Hooker out to clear away the first obstacles to a march on the Confederate capital, only fourteen and three-quarter miles distant. It was too late; for in the meantime the Government had decided on a different course. On the day before, the following dispatch had left Washington for McClellan's headquarters:

IT IS DETERMINED TO WITHDRAW YOUR ARMY FROM THE PENINSULA TO ACQUIA CREEK. YOU WILL TAKE IMMEDIATE

[1] Welles, *Diary*, I, p. 121.
[2] Warden, op. cit., pp. 435, 436, 440, 445.

MEASURES TO EFFECT THIS, COVERING THE MOVEMENT THE
BEST YOU CAN.[1]

The final blow had fallen. McClellan protested desperately, but in vain: 'Here is the true defence of Washington; it is here, on the banks of the James, that the fate of the Union should be decided.

'Clear in my convictions of right . . . knowing that no ambitious or selfish motives have influenced me from the commencement of this war, I do now what I never did in my life before—I entreat that this order may be rescinded. . . .

'Whatever the result may be . . . I . . . have sought to do the best in my power to avert disaster from my country.'[2]

No direct reply to this appeal was vouchsafed the despairing commander. Secretary Welles wrote in his diary that he did not understand 'the object of bringing the army back to Washington, in order to start a new march overland and regain the abandoned position . . . unless it was to get rid of McClellan'.[3]

General Dix had written to General Halleck on 2 August:

'If we can ever reach Richmond, it seems to me the object can be best effected from the position we now occupy. At all events I feel a painful conviction that we cannot bear a retrograde movement at this moment. I have conversed freely with General Burnside on this subject . . . and he concurs with me entirely.'[4]

It was, as McClellan had contended, on the banks of the James, or at least in their immediate vicinity, that the fate of the Union was finally decided. But it was not decided until the powers in Washington considered the time ripe for the termination of the war. In 1862 this time was a long way off; meanwhile suspicion and hatred were being dinned into Lincoln's ears by the Radicals and their outpost in the Cabinet, the Secretary of War.

If Lincoln's mind could be sufficiently poisoned against McClellan, the President and his commanding general would continue to work at cross purposes, and victory could be postponed indefinitely.

[1] *McClellan's Own Story*, p. 495.   [2] Ibid., pp. 497–8.
[3] Campbell, op. cit., p. 300, as quoted from *Lincoln and Seward*, p. 193.
[4] *Official Records*, I, vol. 11, pp. 347–8.

The Radical Congressman Julian once described how Senator Chandler, and others of his kind, had succeeded in working the President into a passion. 'I well remember', he wrote, 'the delight and exultation of the Michigan Senator [Chandler] as he related the circumstances to me. . . . "Old Abe", said he, "is mad, and the war will now go on".'[1]

The war will go on. This was the goal—no truce, no peace, until the South was obliterated as a political entity. And so the war did go on.

In the meantime Halleck had been appointed general-in-chief and Pope had assumed command of the Army of the Potomac, leaving McClellan 'gnawing a file', as Lincoln contemptuously expressed it.[2] But in the midst of this 'gnawing' news of the second battle of Bull Run reached Washington, and panic seized Halleck as well as Stanton, whose intrigues had produced such dire consequences. In this emergency Lincoln took it upon himself to reinstate McClellan. Possibly Pope's telegram of 2 September had something to do with the President's decision. It read:

UNLESS SOMETHING CAN BE DONE . . . TO RESTORE TONE TO THIS ARMY, IT WILL MELT AWAY BEFORE YOU KNOW IT.[3]

The bitterness of Stanton over McClellan's reinstatement knew no bounds. Montgomery Blair, Lincoln's postmaster-general, is authority for the statement that Stanton would have preferred to see the capital fall. To the end he refused to sign the order for the general's reappointment.[4]

If Lee had fondled any hope of entering Washington in the wake of Pope's demoralized army, he quickly abandoned it when he heard that his old opponent was again at the head of the Federal forces. Instead, the Southern leader threw his troops across the Potomac into Maryland. His men needed rest as badly as did their enemies, and he deemed it wise to replenish their supplies from the rich granaries of the Catoctin valley; perhaps

[1] Rice, *Reminiscences of Abraham Lincoln*, p. 53.
[2] Campbell, op. cit., p. 340.
[3] Rhodes, op. cit., IV, p. 135.
[4] *McClellan's Own Story*, p. 545.

he also hoped to gain a large number of recruits. At any rate, Lee occupied a position of some advantage, threatening Washington and Pennsylvania at the same time, without endangering his own line of communications.

McClellan at once set out to give him battle. Reorganizing with astounding speed the shattered divisions of Pope's army, he marched them in three columns up the north shore of the Potomac. Before leaving Washington, however, he suggested to his superiors a move that might have changed the history of the war. He recommended that the garrison at Harper's Ferry, numbering about 12,000 men, be withdrawn and either sent to join him, or at least ordered to occupy Maryland Heights, thus forming a left wing for his advancing forces. If McClellan's advice had been followed, Lee could hardly have withstood the onslaught. But no attention was paid to this admonition. On 10 September McClelland again wired Halleck:

COL. MILES IS AT OR NEAR HARPER'S FERRY, AS I UNDERSTAND, WITH NINE THOUSAND TROOPS. HE CAN DO NOTHING WHERE HE IS, BUT COULD BE OF GREAT SERVICE IF ORDERED TO JOIN ME. I SUGGEST THAT HE BE ORDERED TO JOIN ME BY THE MOST PRACTICABLE ROUTE.[1]

To this Halleck sent the following reply:

THERE IS NO WAY FOR COL. MILES TO JOIN YOU AT PRESENT; HIS ONLY CHANCE IS TO DEFEND HIS WORKS TILL YOU CAN OPEN COMMUNICATION WITH HIM.[2]

'Great Heavens! what a General-in-Chief!' wrote Welles in his diary a few days later.[3] Colonel Davis marched Miles's cavalry out of Harper's Ferry on the fourteenth; there is no question but that Miles could have done the same with his entire force four days sooner. But Stanton and Halleck decided otherwise, and when Lee saw the prize within his easy grasp he took it. On 15 September Colonel Miles surrendered Harper's Ferry with 12,520 men, seventy-three pieces of ordnance, 13,000 muskets, hundreds of wagons, and a tremendous amount of clothing, so badly needed by the Southern army.

[1] *McClellan's Own Story* p. 558.
[2] Ibid, p. 559.
[3] Welles, *Diary*, I, p. 153.

'Why Halleck . . . did not issue such a command [to evacuate Harper's Ferry] is not entirely clear,' wrote Rhodes. 'McClellan advised it . . . and had it been done it is difficult to imagine how Lee with all his fertility of resource could have saved himself. . . .'[1]

Wooden-head is what Gay of the *New York Tribune* called General Halleck even at this early season.[2]

With the fall of Harper's Ferry, one of the greatest opportunities to deliver a decisive stroke for the cause of the Union was irretrievably lost. The prolonging of the conflict was still being accomplished.

While Stonewall Jackson was besieging Harper's Ferry McClellan drove the advance-guard of Lee's army from South Mountain and, on 17 September, fought the battle of Sharpsburg. To General Burnside had been assigned the task of storming one of the stone bridges across Antietam creek; but, although urged to attack time and again, his attempts were so feeble that Lee withdrew the bulk of his forces from that section in order to support his staggering left wing.

If Burnside had made a determined thrust the resistance of his opponents would have crumbled; but it was not until one o'clock in the afternoon that the bridge was finally carried. Two more hours passed before the crest of the hill behind it was taken. Just when Burnside's troops entered Sharpsburg and Lee seemed hopelessly beaten A. P. Hill's division from Harper's Ferry came marching in and threw the victorious Federals back to the banks of the Antietam. Burnside did not cross the bridge in person at any time during the battle.[3]

Lee never again had such a narrow escape during the entire war. If Hill had been a few minutes later—or Burnside a few minutes earlier—the whole Southern army must have been destroyed or thrown into the Potomac. Years later, when Lee lay in a delirium on his death-bed, he kept murmuring, 'Tell Hill he must come up!'[4] If Burnside had done what was expected

[1] Rhodes, op. cit., IV, p. 147.
[2] Ibid., p. 185.
[3] *McClellan's Own Story*, pp. 604–11.
[4] R. E. Lee, *Recollections and Letters of General Robert E. Lee* (copyright 1904, 1924, by Doubleday, Doran & Company, Inc., Garden City, N.Y.), p. 439.

of him on that fateful 17 September Lee's star would have set that night, and the cause for which he fought so valiantly would have received its *coup de grâce*.

With Lee's withdrawal into Virginia the immediate danger to Washington was removed. When McClellan proudly wired to Halleck on 19 September:

I HAVE THE HONOR TO REPORT THAT MARYLAND IS ENTIRELY FREED FROM THE PRESENCE OF THE ENEMY . . . NO FEARS NEED NOW BE ENTERTAINED FOR THE SAFETY OF PENNSYLVANIA. . . .[1]

he probably did not expect a reply devoid of congratulations or even of ordinary courtesy:

WE ARE STILL LEFT ENTIRELY IN THE DARK IN REGARD TO YOUR OWN MOVEMENTS AND THOSE OF THE ENEMY. THIS SHOULD NOT BE SO. YOU SHOULD KEEP ME ADVISED OF BOTH, SO FAR AS YOU KNOW THEM.[2]

To this McClellan replied:

YOUR TELEGRAM . . . RECEIVED. I TELEGRAPHED YOU YESTERDAY ALL I KNEW. . . . I REGRET THAT YOU FIND IT NECESSARY TO COUCH EVERY DESPATCH . . . IN A SPIRIT OF FAULT-FINDING, AND THAT YOU HAVE NOT YET FOUND LEISURE TO SAY ONE WORD IN COMMENDATION OF THE RECENT ACHIEVEMENTS OF THIS ARMY. . . .[3]

Even Lincoln started again to send nagging messages to McClellan. On 14 October the general had made urgent requests for augmentation of his cavalry. The President responded by sending the following wire:

I HAVE JUST RECEIVED YOUR DESPATCH ABOUT SORE-TONGUED AND FATIGUED HORSES. WILL YOU PARDON ME FOR ASKING WHAT THE HORSES OF YOUR ARMY HAVE DONE SINCE THE BATTLE OF ANTIETAM THAT FATIGUES ANYTHING?[4]

[1] *McClellan's Own Story*, p. 621.
[2] Ibid., p. 622.
[3] Ibid.
[4] Ibid., p. 634.

This communication, so entirely unworthy of Lincoln, failed to arouse McClellan to a display of temper. Instead, he set about to demonstrate to the Chief Magistrate that the dispatch had not only been conceived in bad taste but also in utter ignorance of the most elementary military ideas. Like a teacher talking to a child the General painstakingly explained to the President that, even while there are no battles being fought, the cavalry is kept busy scouting, foraging, and protecting the flanks of the army.[1] While there was no visible response to this lecture, it may be taken for granted that its sarcasm was understood. The serious aspect of the matter was the urging of another premature advance that could have ended only in disaster.

On 26 October McClellan had finished his preparations for the campaign and started to cross the Potomac into Virginia. His plan was to move south along the eastern side of the Blue Ridge Mountains and to seal up each pass as he went, thus making it possible to throw his own forces into Lee's rear at any time, while holding the enemies at bay, should they attempt similar tactics.[2] McClellan's advance was so rapid that when he reached Warrenton, on 9 November, Lee's army was still split, one half opposing the Union troops near Culpeper, while the other was scattered west of the Blue Ridge Mountains, unable to join its comrades without forcing the passes. 'The march from the Potomac . . . to Warrenton . . . was a magnificent spectacle of celerity and skill,' stated Rufus Ingalls, chief quarter-master of the Army of the Potomac, in an official report on 17 February 1863.[3]

Lee himself, in a letter to Jefferson Davis, remarked that his adversary was 'moving more rapidly than usual, and it looks like a real advance'.[4] It is said that for the first time in the war Lee was bewildered. As it turned out, however, he had no cause for alarm. On 5 November McClellan was suddenly removed from his position as general-in-chief. 'The announcement came with a shock,' wrote Welles, who was no friend of the deposed commander.[5]

[1] *McClellan's Own Story*, p. 324.
[2] Campbell, op. cit., p. 400; Rhodes, op. cit., IV, p. 189; Ropes, op.cit., II, p. 440.
[3] *Official Records*, I, vol. 19, part 1, p. 96.
[4] Ibid., part 2, p. 698; Rhodes, op. cit., IV, p. 189 (footnote).
[5] Welles, *Diary*, I, p. 183.

A still more extraordinary development was that, of all officers, General Burnside was appointed as his successor— General Burnside, to whose blundering McClellan ascribed the indecisive victory of the Union troops at Sharpsburg. Unless it was considered meritorious to win no battles, there was nothing in his past achievements to commend him to his superiors, and his subsequent career did not belie his past.

'It is not surprising', one reads in Rhodes's *History of the United States*, 'that McClellan was relieved, but it is no less true that his removal was a mistake. . . . Burnside and Hooker were tried, and the army met with two crushing defeats such as it would never have suffered under its loved commander. It is worthy of note that Grant was not suggested.'

The last sentence is worth pondering.

Rhodes continues:

'We have no right to judge the President by our knowledge of the event, but even on turning back to the time itself, we may easily see that the substitution of Burnside for McClellan can in no wise be defended. Burnside had given no proof of his fitness, had refused the place twice, and had told the President and Secretary of War over and over again that he was not competent . . . and that McClellan was the best general for the position.'[1]

If Stanton wished to postpone the end of the war he was certainly using effective methods.

In March 1863 Lincoln discussed with some journalist friends the reasons why he had dismissed General McClellan, and was quoted as having said:

'I do not, as some do, regard McClellan either as a traitor or an officer without capacity. He sometimes has bad counselors, but he is loyal, and he has some fine military qualities. I adhered to him after nearly all my Constitutional advisers lost faith in him. But do you want to know when I gave him up? It was after the battle of Antietam. The Blue Ridge was then between our army and Lee's. We enjoyed the great advantage over them

[1] Rhodes, op. cit., IV, pp. 188–9.

which they usually had over us: we had the short line, and they the long one, to the Rebel Capital. I directed McClellan peremptorily to move on Richmond. It was eleven days before he crossed his first man over the Potomac; it was eleven days after that before he crossed the last man. Thus he was twenty-two days in passing the river at a much easier and more practicable ford than that where Lee crossed his entire army between dark one night and daylight the next morning. That was the last grain of sand which broke the camel's back. I relieved McClellan at once.'[1]

Lincoln's explanation could not have stood up under any sort of examination. On 3 September the Army of the Potomac had been a disorganized mob; by the fourteenth McClellan had galvanized it into victorious action after a fifty-mile march. But this feverish state could not be kept up indefinitely. Most of the horses had broken down and become diseased, which put nearly 4,000 of them out of service. Shoes, clothing, and other materials were wanting; most of the camp equipment had been lost or left behind during the campaign of the last weeks. When Lee crossed the Potomac after the battle of Antietam the means of transportation at McClellan's disposal 'were inadequate to furnish a single day's supply of subsistence in advance'.

Spurred by his own desire as well as by Lincoln's peremptory orders to take up the pursuit, McClellan made strenuous efforts to refit his troops. He at once consulted with Colonel Ingalls, his chief quartermaster, who believed that the necessary articles could be supplied in about three days. But now there occurred one of those inexplicable delays which characterized the War Department at that time, the same sort of delay that ruined Burnside's chances at Fredericksburg a few weeks later. The promised supplies failed to come. Corps commanders were officially advised from Washington that they were to receive their requisitions at certain dates and by certain routes, but when they sent for them the wagon trains were forced to return empty. In some instances they travelled back four or five times before obtaining their supplies, and one corps commander even re-

[1] Albert D. Richardson, *The Secret Service, the Field, the Dungeon and the Escape* (American Publishing Company, Hartford, Conn., 1865), pp. 323–4.

ported that his wagons had travelled more than 150 miles before there were any loads to bring back.

'I made every exertion in my power . . .', wrote McClellan, 'to have these supplies hurried forward rapidly; and I was repeatedly told that they had filled the requisitions at Washington, and that the supplies had been forwarded. But they did not come to us. . . .'

Of all this Lincoln said nothing, probably knew nothing. But he must have remembered what had occurred when he visited McClellan during the first days of October.

'He told me', reported McClellan, 'that he was entirely satisfied with me and . . . that he would stand by me against "all comers"; that he wished me to continue my preparations for a new campaign, *not to stir an inch until fully ready*. . . .'[1]

McClellan's dismissal was the signal for libellous attacks upon him such as have had few parallels in American history. Stanton was in possession of the telegraph office and could give to the Press such news items as he wished, together with his own interpretations. If he had been content up to then to envenom only official Washington against his ablest general, he now used every measure within his vast power to blast McClellan's reputation. That the deposed leader was a great organizer could not well be denied; but he was pictured to the public as hopelessly slow, forever harrassing the administration with demands for additional troops, magnifying the strength of the opposing forces, and hesitating to strike a decisive blow. The fact was suppressed that McClellan had asked for only those troops which had been promised him. Lincoln once had expressed the opinion that his general had the 'slows', but he forgot to mention that he himself had wired him on 24 May 'to move cautiously and safely'. During the march of the Union troops to Sharpsburg Halleck had complained incessantly to McClellan that he thought the movement was too precipitate.[2] As to the size of the Confederate armies, McClellan could rely only on the advice of his superiors and of the secret service, over whom he had no control at all. As late as 1883 Allan Pinkerton still maintained steadfastly

---

[1] *McClellan's Own Story*, pp. 623, 627–8, 629, 636. Author's italics.
[2] Welles, op. cit., I, p. 105; *McClellan's Own Story*, pp. 351, 554, ff.

that he had been correct twenty-one years earlier when he had estimated Lee's army during the peninsular campaign at 200,000 men.[1]

'The rooted belief in Lee's preponderance of numbers had been chronic in the army during the whole year,' said General Jacob C. Cox. 'That belief was based upon the inconceivably mistaken reports of the secret service organization . . . permeating downward . . . till the error was accepted as truth by officers and men, and became a factor in their morale which can hardly be over-estimated.'[2]

On 15 August Secretary Chase asked General Halleck what the hostile forces totalled at Richmond. The general-in-chief thought that they numbered 75,000 to 80,000 men. Besides, he calculated that the Confederates had another 60,000 men confronting Pope.

On 11 September a similar conversation revealed Halleck's belief that Lee had 150,000 men in Maryland and in the vicinity of Washington, of which he estimated 100,000 to be in Maryland.

It is now known that the Confederate troops in Maryland amounted to no more than 35,000 men, and that the Confederate army in Virginia had been similarly overrated by Halleck. Yet it was on the basis of these estimates made by his superiors, that McClellan had to plan his campaign. In view of their calculations can any one blame him for his caution and for his continuous demands for reinforcements? Either Stanton and Halleck were grossly misinformed themselves, in which case McClellan was the victim of circumstances over which he had no control, or else the War Minister and his general-in-chief knew the true size of the enemy forces and purposely misled the commander in the field. There seems to be no third alternative.

Stanton's propaganda, which McClellan was too proud to combat, bore its expected fruit. Even to-day most historians consider McClellan a failure as an aggressive general and declare that his dismissal was justified. The lie, a thousand times repeated, has become history.

[1] Pinkerton, *Spy of the Rebellion*, p. xxx.
[2] *Battles and Leaders of the Civil War*, II, p. 658.

On the other hand, a relative of General Lee once asked him: 'Who, in your opinion, was the ablest Northern general of the war?'

'McClellan, by all odds,' replied Lee.[1]

An interesting sidelight on the McClellan controversy is furnished by Hugh McCulloch, Secretary of the Treasury under Lincoln. McCulloch's opinions are particularly noteworthy because he was one of the few men filling a high position in the Federal Government who viewed the Southern side of the contest with judicial impartiality.

'In the slave-holding States [he declared] the prevailing opinion was, that the Government was a league between sovereign States, which had united for certain governmental purposes, and that their sovereignty, which had been conditionally relinquished, might be resumed by them, or by any of them, whenever, in their judgment, their interests required it. I have not, therefore, spoken of the civil war on the part of the Southern States as treasonable, nor of those who were on that side engaged in it, as having been traitors. Open rebellion is attempted revolution—not treason. Successful rebellion against real, or even supposed, oppression is always and everywhere honored; it does not become treason by unsuccess.'[2]

The ideas of such a clear and fair mind are worthy of consideration. Reviewing McClellan's career with a balanced judgement far removed from the frenzy of war times, he wrote a quarter of a century later:

'The plan of the [Peninsular] campaign, although consented to, was not heartily approved by the President. The general who was to conduct it . . . had incurred the ill will of Mr. Stanton. . . . How powerful this ill will was, was exhibited during the war in numerous instances besides that of McClellan. That a campaign commenced under such circumstances would be a failure, ought to have been expected. Was its failure chargeable to McClellan? I thought it was when the campaign ended . . . but

---

[1] Campbell, op. cit., title-page.
[2] Hugh McCulloch, *Men and Measures of a Half a Century* (Charles Scribner's Sons, New York, 1888), p. viii.

. . . I thought differently when I became acquainted with its history.'[1]

McCulloch then cited the prevalent opinion that McClellan was overcautious, lacking in self-confidence, slow. '. . . I have looked in vain in his military history for the evidence of such defects as have been attributed to him,' he said, and then added significantly: 'The evidence of General McClellan's deficiencies are found, not in a correct history of his military career, but *in the press and in the dispatches of the War Department.*'[2]

A Confederate general who served with distinction in the army of Virginia under Johnson and Lee told McCulloch, in 1874 that there was no Union general the Southerners dreaded as much as they did McClellan. They could always tell when he was in command by the way in which the Union troops were handled and by the number of their own dead and wounded. 'We received the blows, and we knew who dealt the heaviest ones,' he remarked dolefully.

'Did you consider him the ablest of the generals of the Army of the Potomac?' McCulloch inquired.

'Certainly we did,' was the answer; 'he had, as we thought, no equal.'[3]

Burnside immediately discarded McClellan's plan of campaign and substituted one of his own; he would turn the proposed manœuvres into feints, but in reality throw his main force across the Rappahannock into Fredericksburg, fortifying the heights beyond, threatening Richmond, and forcing Lee into a hasty retreat to protect his capital. It was not a bad plan, but its success depended on speed. Lincoln endorsed it, and Halleck promised to look after docks, railways, and pontoon bridges. Evil influences soon made themselves felt again, however. Of them General Oliver O. Howar wrote pointedly in his autobiography:

'The story of the moving of the bridge train from Harper's

[1] Hugh McCulloch, op. cit., p. 305.
[2] Ibid., p. 316. Author's italics.
[3] Ibid., p. 317; see also supplementary note to chapter xxiv, 'Stanton and McClellan'.

Ferry and Berlin to our front at Falmouth is a strange one. It seems to indicate, judging by the uncalled-for delays, the misunderstandings, changes of orders . . . and final inadequacy of the transportation provided, that Halleck himself was playing a part, and possibly hoping to get Burnside well into winter quarters without anybody being particularly to blame. . . .

'As it required thirteen days to do a piece of work which could easily have been done in three days, it would be a marvelous stretch of charity to impute it to mere bungling.'[1]

By the time the Union army was ready to cross into Fredericksburg Lee had fortified the heights beyond. Burnside, goaded by the Washington authorities whom he had consulted, tried to storm Lee's position by a frontal attack. The result was the slaughter known to history as the battle of Fredericksburg.

The historian of *Appleton's Cyclopædia* gives a condensed view of the situation which confronted the Union general, leaving his opinion half hidden between the lines of his carefully worded statement: '. . . on 10 Nov. [1862] Burnside reluctantly assumed command. At this time the Confederate army was divided, Longstreet and Jackson commanding, respectively, its right and left wings, being separated by at least two days' march. McClellan and Burnside were always warm personal friends, and the former gave his successor in command the benefit of his projected plans.

'. . . The movement began 15 Nov., and four days later the army occupied the heights opposite Fredericksburg, but with the river intervening and no pontoon-train ready. The responsibility for this failure has never been charged to Gen. Burnside, nor has it ever been definitely fixed upon any one save a vague and impersonal "department"; but it necessitated a fatal delay, for Lee had moved nearly as rapidly as Burnside, and promptly occupied and fortified the heights south of the river. During the period of enforced inaction that followed Gen. Burnside went to Washington and expressed his doubts as to the policy of crossing the river, in view of the failure of the attempt to divide Lee's forces. But he was urged to push a winter campaign against

---

[1] Oliver Otis Howard, *Autobiography* (The Baker & Taylor Co., New York, 1907), i, pp. 315, 318-19.

Richmond, and, returning to the front, gave orders to place the bridges.'[1]

A few weeks later Burnside planned to retrieve his fortune by endeavouring to cross the Rappahannock some miles farther upstream. In this venture, famous as the 'Mud March', the whole army became hopelessly mired, and the campaign had to be abandoned. Lincoln's wish to have the army undertake a campaign in midwinter on Virginia soil was thus gratified. What McClellan had refused to do, Burnside tried. Five days after he was forced to give up the attempt the President dismissed him from command and appointed General Hooker in his place.[2]

Burnside had told the President and the Secretary of War that he was not competent to command so large an army. He had twice refused the post of general-in-chief.[3] It took thousands of lives, a severe defeat, and a complete demoralization of the army to convince Lincoln that this leader knew his own limitations.

The one man in the North who emerged victorious from all these developments was Stanton. Lincoln's Proclamation of Emancipation had been issued on 22 September 1862 and had gone into effect on New Year's Day, 1863. Stanton's hope that the war would be prolonged until slavery had been abolished and until the North and the South were bitterly estranged was on the way to fulfilment.

Lee defeated Hooker at Chancellorsville and, about 3 June, moved forward to invade Pennsylvania. Hooker, covering Washington and the whole eastern seaboard, followed the Confederate army northward, paralleling its march. Perceiving that the columns of his adversary were stretched out on a long and vulnerable line, Hooker decided to strike it somewhere near the Potomac. For this purpose he wanted the garrison of Harper's Ferry, totalling about 10,000 men, to reinforce the corps he had selected for the attack. But, although the troops at Harper's Ferry

[1] *Appletons' Cyclopædia of American Biography* (see under 'Burnside'), I, p. 464.
[2] *Battles and Leaders*, iii, p. 118; see also supplementary note to chapter xxiv, 'General Burnside at Antietam'.
[3] Welles, *Diary*, I, p. 124.

had this time been withdrawn to Maryland Heights—the step that in the previous year McClellan had urged in vain—Halleck already seemed to have forgotten the previous disaster. Hooker remonstrated that the troops were of no earthly use at Harper's Ferry and pleaded that they be ordered to join his forces. He even begged that his dispatch be shown to the President and to the Secretary of War. Curiously enough, he wired in his resignation at the same time. Halleck did submit the telegram to Lincoln, whereupon Lincoln made a quick and strange decision. Disregarding his own principle of not swapping horses in midstream, he relieved Hooker of the command without ceremony. Meade was appointed in his place and was told to do as he pleased with the garrison on Maryland Heights; he withdrew it immediately.[1]

On the same day Welles wrote in his diary:

'Whether the refusal to give him [Hooker] the troops at Harper's Ferry was intended to drive him to abandon the command of the army, or is in pursuance of any intention on the part of Halleck . . . to overrule the general in the field, is not apparent. The President has been drawn into the measure, as he was into withholding McDowell from McClellan, by being made to believe it was necessary for the security of Washington. In that instance, Stanton was the moving spirit. . . . It is much the same now, only Halleck is the forward spirit, prompted perhaps by Stanton.[2]

It is interesting, almost amusing, to read Stanton's own narrative of Hooker's removal, brought about by Halleck and the master mind behind him. The report comes to us through Congressman George Boutwell, one of the War Minister's most faithful and unquestioning partisans.

'On the eve of the battle of Gettysburg, General Hooker resigned the command of the army. This act was a painful, a terrible surprise to Mr. Stanton and the President. Mr. Stanton's account to me was this: "When I received the dispatch my heart sank within me, and I was more depressed than at any other moment of the war. I could not say that any other officer knew

[1] Rhodes, op. cit., IV, pp. 280, 281.
[2] Welles, *Diary*, I, p. 349.

General Hooker's plans, or the position even of the various divisions of the army. I sent for the President to come to the War Office at once. It was in the evening, but the President soon appeared. I handed him the dispatch. As he read it his face became like lead. I said, 'What shall be done?' He replied instantly, 'Accept his resignation.'" [1]

Nine years after giving to the world Stanton's own account of Hooker's resignation, Boutwell offered a new explanation for this change in commanders.

'Hooker was in Washington Thursday of the week before the battle [of Gettysburg], and at a conference with the President and the Secretary of War, it was agreed to hold Harper's Ferry, which, the year before, had been surrendered with great loss of men and materials of war. Upon his return to headquarters General Hooker changed his opinion, and, without reporting to the Secretary of War, he ordered General Wilson to evacuate the post and join the main army. This order Wilson transmitted to the Secretary of War. Mr. Stanton, assuming that there had been an error in the dispatches, or a misunderstanding, countermanded Hooker's order. Thereupon Hooker, without seeking for an explanation, resigned his command.' [2]

This leaves several questions unanswered. Why, for example, did General Wilson submit the order of his superior officer to the Secretary of War? His business was to obey it and to obey it without delay. And why did Stanton, instead of wiring for an explanation, countermand the order—an open insult to Hooker? By going over the head of the commanding general he practically forced him to offer his resignation. But even then, if Stanton was as perturbed as he claimed, he still could have refused to allow Hooker's retirement at so critical a moment. A simple appeal to his patriotism would probably have sufficed.

Is the answer to this riddle that Stanton was anxious to bring about a change in the high command when it would cause a temporary setback to the Northern cause?

Why Boutwell amplified his first story is not clear, unless it had satisfied no one, not even himself.

[1] Rice, op. cit., p. 128.
[2] *Abraham Lincoln: Tributes from His Associates*, pp. 72–3.

The real story of Hooker's resignation probably has never been told. Stanton was one of the few men who knew it, and he would, of course, have been the last man to divulge it. Some facts regarding the matter, however, have been revealed by one of his clerks, Charles F. Benjamin, who occupied responsible and confidential positions at the headquarters of the Army of the Potomac and in the War Department.

According to Benjamin it appears that as soon as Hooker had recrossed the Rappahannock after the battle of Chancellorsville, Lincoln 'grasped General Halleck and started for the front post-haste'. Following their return to Washington they called a conference with Stanton, and it was decided that Hooker must not be entrusted with the conduct of another battle. The victim of Lee's ingenious strategy at Chancellorsville had offered Halleck his resignation; it was then and there, of course, that it should have been accepted; but it was not. Benjamin continues:

'. . . Hooker's diligent and skillful management of his army rapidly brought matters back to the hopeful state they were in before the late battle. But Mr. Stanton was determined that the deliberate decision of the council of war, held after Halleck's return from the front, should not be set aside, and he was now the master of the situation. Hooker was so full of hope and energy that *severe measures had to be resorted to in order to wring from him that tender of resignation.* . . .'[1]

This, then, is part of the inside story. Hooker's resignation was not voluntary, but was wrung from him by 'severe measures'. He was not only provoked to the point of exasperation, but in the end compelled to quit when he did not want to. How the provoking was done is shown by an exchange of telegrams between Halleck and himself.

On 25 June Hooker had wired:

IS THERE ANY REASON WHY MARYLAND HEIGHTS SHOULD NOT BE ABANDONED. . . .

and was answered the following day:

MARYLAND HEIGHTS HAVE ALWAYS BEEN REGARDED AS AN IMPORTANT POINT TO BE HELD BY US, AND MUCH EXPENSE

[1] *Battles and Leaders*, iii, pp. 240–1. Author's italics.

AND LABOR INCURRED IN FORTIFYING THEM. I CAN NOT APPROVE OF THEIR ABANDONMENT, EXCEPT IN CASE OF ABSOLUTE NECESSITY.

This dispatch caused Horace Greeley to exclaim, that 'Surely, the translator of Jomini can find no parallel for such strategy. . . .'[1]

Hooker replied with sarcasm and ill-concealed scorn.

I HAVE RECEIVED YOUR TELEGRAM . . . I FIND TEN THOUSAND MEN . . . HERE, THEY ARE OF NO EARTHLY ACCOUNT. . . . SO FAR AS HARPER'S FERRY IS CONCERNED, THERE IS NOTHING OF IT. AS FOR THE FORTIFICATIONS . . . THEY REMAIN . . . NO ENEMY WILL EVER TAKE POSSESSION OF THEM. . . .

A few minutes later Hooker sent in his resignation. It is at least possible to surmise that, having been forced to abdicate, the hapless general availed himself of this last opportunity to tell Halleck what he thought of him and then quit before he was removed for speaking his mind.

'Such a change of commanders [comments Horace Greeley], for no more urgent reasons, on the very brink of a great battle, has few parallels in history. . . . Hooker was loved and trusted by his soldiers. . . . Had that army been polled, it would have voted to fight the impending battle under Hooker *without* the aid of . . . 11,000 men, rather than under Meade *with* that reënforcement.'[2]

Which, more likely than not, was the very reason why the change was made.

Even the Radical committee on the conduct of the war, which usually did Stanton's bidding, reached the conclusion 'that Hooker had not been fairly dealt with', and condemned his removal.[3]

Meade was appointed commanding general on 27 June and on 1 July the battle of Gettysburg began. How dangerous it was

[1] *American Conflict*, ii, p. 374.
[2] Ibid., pp. 374-5.
[3] *Life of Zachariah Chandler* (*Detroit Post and Tribune*, Detroit, 1880), p. 244.

343

to change military leaders under these circumstances can readily be seen. Flower, Stanton's biographer, said that the secretary's reasons for this sudden shift 'are not recorded'.[1] Meade himself protested against the promotion, which entailed a '. . . responsibility so suddenly placed upon him in presence of the enemy and when he was totally ignorant of the positions and dispositions of the army he was to take in charge. . . .'[2] But it was all of no avail. The change had been decided on, and Meade had barely a day in which to prepare to fight Lee.

'It is unfortunate', was Welles's crisp comment, 'that a change could not have been made earlier.'[3]

Gettysburg was a tactical victory for Meade, but unless Lee could be destroyed before he recrossed the Potomac the victory was wasted. Lincoln perceived this clearly, and a conference was held at the White House between Lincoln, Halleck, and Stanton. Lincoln inquired of Stanton:

'What shall we do with your man Meade, Mr. Secretary?'

'Tell him', said Stanton to Captain Haupt, who had come up from Meade's headquarters, 'that Lee is trapped and must be taken. . . .'

Then turning to Lincoln, he added: 'He can be removed as easily as he was appointed. . . .'[4]

To Halleck Lincoln expressed the fear that Lee would retreat unharmed after all. He sent this dispatch to his general-in-chief:

I LEFT THE TELEGRAPH OFFICE A GOOD DEAL DISSATISFIED. . . . THESE THINGS ALL APPEAR TO ME TO BE CONNECTED WITH A PURPOSE TO . . . GET THE ENEMY ACROSS THE RIVER AGAIN WITHOUT A FURTHER COLLISION. . . .'[5]

In response to the President's promptings, Halleck wired to Meade on 7 July:

PUSH FORWARD AND FIGHT LEE BEFORE HE CAN CROSS THE POTOMAC.[6]

[1] Flower, op. cit., p. 199.
[2] *Battles and Leaders*, iii, p. 243.
[3] Welles, *Diary*, I, p. 349.
[4] Flower, op. cit., p. 201.
[5] Bates, *Lincoln in the Telegraph Office*, p. 156.
[6] Rhodes, op. cit., IV, p. 294.

Lincoln was then at his country residence, the Soldier's Home. Perhaps the fact of his absence from Washington accounts for two other dispatches sent by Halleck which were in inexplicable contradiction to the President's orders. One of them reads:

DO NOT BE INFLUENCED BY ANY DESPATCH FROM HERE AGAINST YOUR OWN JUDGMENT. . . . REGARD THEM AS SUGGESTIONS ONLY[1]

and the other:

I THINK IT WILL BE BEST FOR YOU TO POSTPONE A GENERAL BATTLE UNTIL EVERYTHING IS READY.[2]

Again the ever-watchful Secretary of the Navy made a significant entry in his diary. 'I fear the Rebel army will escape, and am compelled to believe that some of our generals are willing it should. They are contented to have the War continue. Never before have they been so served nor their importance so felt and magnified, and when the War is over but few of them will retain their present importance.'[3]

Stanton knew whom he was selecting when he had 'smuggled' Halleck in as general-in-chief, which is the way his colleague in the Navy Department callously styled it.[4]

Even Chase, who had helped bring the General from the west, later began to consider him '. . . perfectly useless, a heavy incumbrance, with no heart in the cause, no sympathy for those who have'.[5]

'Lee retreats toward the Potomac,' wrote Gurowski in his diary. 'If they let him recross there, our shame is nameless.' On the sixteenth the crossing had been accomplished, and Gurowski was in despair. 'Lee recrossed the Potomac! Thundering storms, rising waters, and about 150,000 men at his heels! Our brave soldiers again baffled, almost dishonored by know-nothing generalship. We have lost the occasion to crush three-fourths of the rebellion!'[6]

---

[1] Rhodes, op. cit., p. IV, p. 234.
[2] Ibid.
[3] Welles, *Diary*, I, p. 368.
[4] Ibid, p. 392.
[5] Ibid., p. 402.
[6] Chittenden, *Personal Reminiscences*, p. 322. Gurowski was a Radical of Polish birth; for a time he acted as translator in the State Department.

Commenting on this outburst Chittenden, Registrar of the United States Treasury and Stanton's partisan, wrote: 'Does any critic ask why I have quoted these notes of Gurowski? It is because he did not hesitate to say what the masses of the American people thought, what their leaders knew but had not the courage to declare.'[1]

Nevertheless, Stanton kept Halleck in his position. The hour to bring the war to its culmination had not yet come.

Thus Lincoln's change of commanders on the eve of a great battle and the intrigues of the War Department combined to permit Lee's escape. It was a triumph for the war coterie. The emancipation of the slaves had been proclaimed without causing an upheaval. The mood of the Northern population was gradually undergoing a change as the war went on without an end in sight. Lee had decamped and the Confederacy was far from beaten. Stanton and his Radical friends had every reason to congratulate themselves.

For once a shadow of suspicion crossed even the mind of Lincoln. Overtaking his Secretary of the Navy on the lawn in front of the White House, he said with a voice and a countenance that Welles could never forget that there had seemed to him for a full week a determination that Lee should be allowed to slip away.

'There is bad faith somewhere,' the President exclaimed. 'What does it mean, Mr. Welles? Great God! what does it mean?'[2]

For one short moment Lincoln must have suspected that he had been betrayed by those who wished to continue the bloodshed until it suited their purpose to stop it. But the moment passed and the President's confidence in his military advisers returned.

Thereupon the work of the war clique was resumed with impunity.

[1] Chittenden, *Personal Reminiscences*, p. 323.
[2] Welles, *Diary*, I, p. 370.

CHAPTER XXV

Not Wanted—Victory in the West

In the meantime, equally strange events had taken place on the battlefields of the west. General Grant, subordinated to General Halleck at St. Louis, conceived the idea of moving against Fort Henry on the Tennessee River and, after strong urgings, ob-

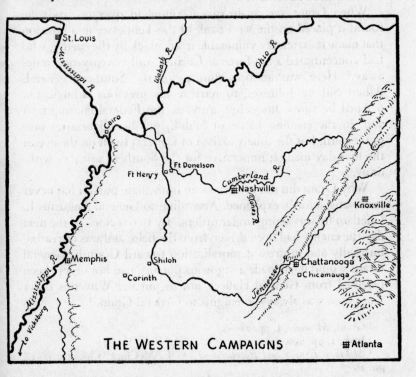

THE WESTERN CAMPAIGNS

tained the reluctant consent of his superior officer. Fort Henry fell, and a few days later, on 17 February 1862 Fort Donelson surrendered. It was the first great victory of the Northern armies.[1]

Halleck, who did not even know that an attack on Fort Donelson had been contemplated, and who had foolishly ordered Grant to entrench at Fort Henry, immediately took all the credit for the success and threw such aspersions on Grant that McClellan advised placing the victor of Fort Donelson under arrest. Halleck had no proof and hesitated. Interrupted telegraph lines, it appeared, had been responsible for the misunderstanding, and the rumours that the new idol of the North had taken to drink were baseless gossip. Halleck then assured his subordinate that he had reinstated him in the good graces of the War Department; but Grant did not know until many years afterwards that it had been Halleck's own jealous insinuations which had made such reinstatement necessary.[2]

When Grant was again given command over his army he found it placed on the west bank of the Tennessee in a position that made it extremely vulnerable to an attack by the enemy, who had concentrated a big force at Corinth, only twenty-odd miles away.[3] Here was an opportunity for the Southern general, Albert Sidney Johnson, to retrieve his previous failures. On 6 April he threw his entire army on the Federal encampment and, in the ensuing battle of Shiloh, put his adversaries into grave peril; but the timely arrival of General Buell on the eve of the first day made it imperative for the Southern army to withdraw.

Why Grant did not undertake an immediate pursuit has never been satisfactorily explained. According to General Augustus L. Chetlain he was acting under orders. 'By two o'clock of the next day the enemy had been driven from the field, and was retreating hurriedly and in great demoralization toward Corinth. General Grant would have made a vigorous pursuit, had not orders been received from General Halleck not to pursue. Why this order was given was always an enigma to General Grant.'[4]

[1] Grant, *Memoirs*, I, pp. 286–8.
[2] Ibid., I, pp. 296, 326–7.   [3] Ibid., I, p. 330.
[4] *Military Essays and Recollections* (A. C. McClurg, Chicago, 1891), pp. 26–7.

General Wallace made similar comments on Grant's failure to follow up the advantage of the battle of Shiloh.

'The pursuit anticipated was not undertaken; exactly why I did not know. Since coming to a better understanding of the situation, however, it has been my surmise that after the battle General Grant was as much under General Halleck's order not to do anything as before it.'[1]

Soon Grant was relieved of further responsibility. Two days after the battle Halleck wired that he was going to take personal charge of the combined armies of the Ohio and the Tennessee, and, on 11 April he appeared on the scene. With reinforcements, his troops soon numbered about 120,000 men, while Beauregard, who had taken command of the Confederates, counted only about 50,000 under him. And now something incredible happened. It took Halleck with his army six weeks to crawl a distance of fifteen or twenty miles, and this in spite of the fact that the advancing troops encountered practically no resistance. During these six weeks no word was received from Washington demanding explanations or urging greater speed. When the huge army finally arrived at Corinth it found the town evacuated.

'With one hundred and twenty thousand men', General Lew Wallace wrote, 'he was moving against fifty thousand, whose recent defeats more than neutralized their advantage of fortifications.

'He was moving at the rate of a mile a day, throwing up works at every halt. That is, he gained a mile every day to go into besiegement every night. At the end he would have spent a month doing what General Johnston [Johnson] had done in three days.

'Beginning his approaches twenty miles from the town, and confining them entirely to one side, he left the enemy free to choose which of the other three sides it would be best to retire by when the time came, and what all to take away with him.

'Finally he placed his armies, all three, under a peremptory order not to bring on an engagement. 'It is better', he instructed them, "to retreat than to fight".'[2]

Grant said in his *Memoirs* that the officers of his army be-

[1] Lew Wallace, *Autobiography* (Harper & Bros., New York, 1906), II, p. 570.
[2] Ibid., II, p. 577; Grant, *Memoirs*, I, p. 377.

lieved a well-directed attack would have at least partially
destroyed the army defending Corinth.

'For myself', he concluded, 'I am satisfied that Corinth could
have been captured in a two days' campaign commenced
promptly on the arrival of reinforcements after the battle of
Shiloh.'[1]

A war correspondent of the *New York Tribune* apparently
agreed heartily with Grant's views.

'The grand army was like a huge serpent . . . large enough to
eat up Beauregard at one mouthful; but Halleck crept forward
at the rate of about three-quarters of a mile per day. Thousands
and thousands of his men died from fevers and diarrhœa.

'There was great dissatisfaction. . . . Pope was particularly
impatient. . . . General Palmer, who commanded on the front,
reported that he could hold it against the world, the flesh, and
the devil; but Halleck telegraphed to Pope three times within
an hour not to be drawn into a general engagement.'[2]

Halleck himself blamed the slow advance of his troops on
weather conditions. 'The whole country here is one mass of
mud,' he wrote to Senator Latham, on 20 April. 'We are obliged
to construct roads before we can move.' It did not seem to occur
to the general that his enemies had traversed the same roads,
equally muddy, in three days or less. 'But no mud can stop for
a long time the advance of this western army,' he continued
boastfully. 'What we cannot bridge over, we will canal through,
and, if necessary, turn the Mississippi.'[3]

When Corinth finally was occupied by Halleck, he proudly
wired to Stanton, under date of 4 June:

GENERAL POPE, WITH FORTY THOUSAND [MEN], IS
THIRTY MILES SOUTH OF CORINTH, PUSHING THE ENEMY
HARD. HE ALREADY REPORTS TEN THOUSAND PRISONERS
AND DESERTERS FROM THE ENEMY, AND FIFTEEN THOUSAND
STANDS OF ARMS CAPTURED. THOUSANDS OF THE ENEMY
ARE THROWING AWAY THEIR ARMS.[4]

[1] Grant, *Memoirs*, I, p. 381.
[2] Richardson, op. cit., p. 250.
[3] Letter in author's possession.
[4] Wallace, op. cit., II, p. 582.

There was not one word of truth in this message. General Beauregard remarked caustically that the statement 'contained as many lies as lines'; and General Pope, the alleged hero of the pursuit, later flatly denied ever having sent in any such report and even demanded its exhibition from the files. This request was evaded, and the dispatch was never produced.[1]

General Halleck, having triumphantly entered Corinth, and 'not knowing what better to do, busied himself in hastily dissipating his magnificent army, sending detachments of it here and there, apparently without object'. This at least was the opinion of General Wallace.[2]

Grant evidently entertained similar ideas, for he wrote in his *Memoirs*:

'After the capture of Corinth a movable force of eighty thousand men, besides enough to hold all the territory acquired, could have been set in motion for the accomplishment of any great campaign for the suppression of the rebellion. . . . But the work of depletion commenced. . . . If he [Buell] had been sent directly to Chattanooga as rapidly as he could march, leaving two or three divisions along the line of the railroad from Nashville forward, he could have arrived with but little fighting, and would have saved much of the loss of life which was afterwards incurred in gaining Chattanooga. Bragg would then not have had time to raise an army to contest the possession of . . . Tennessee and Kentucky; the battles of Stone River and Chickamauga would not necessarily have been fought; Burnside would not have been besieged in Knoxville without the power of helping himself or escaping; the battle of Chattanooga would not have been fought. These are the negative advantages, if the term negative is applicable, which would probably have resulted from prompt movements after Corinth fell into the possession of the National forces. The positive results might have been: a bloodless advance to Atlanta, to Vicksburg, or to any other desired point south of Corinth in the interior of Mississippi.'[3]

The opportunity of marching practically unhindered through Southern territory, which had presented itself after the fall of Fort Donelson, and which had not been improved then, now

[1] Wallace, op. cit., II.
[2] Ibid.
[3] Grant, *Memoirs*, I, pp. 383, 384.

appeared for a second time; again no advantage was taken of it by Halleck. When Grant, second-in-command after Shiloh, suggested to his chief, 'Why not press on to Vicksburg before it can be strengthened?' he received the curt reply: 'When your advice is needed, it will be asked.'[1]

'If he [Halleck] desired to serve the country,' wrote the redoubtable Butler . . . 'he was utterly careless of his duty, for . . . there was nothing so important to be done . . . as to capture Vicksburg and open the river . . . there were not four thousand available armed men between Vicksburg and Halleck. . . .

'The truth is not to be disguised that Halleck did not want to capture Vicksburg. . . .'[2]

Even Stanton's biographer, Gorham, wondered at Halleck's inexplicable failure to free the Mississippi from Confederate control.

'When we consider the vast expenditure of lives, time, and money made during the ensuing year to secure the capture of Vicksburg . . . that the whole year could probably have been saved, and the position taken in July, 1862, instead of July, 1863, if Halleck would but have extended his hand . . . his failure to do so seems unaccountable and unpardonable.'[3]

Strange how often critics of that era are moved to say that the events they review are past understanding.

During this period Halleck skilfully undermined Grant's standing at Washington. Reports were afloat in the country that Grant had been drunk at the battle of Shiloh, and the manner in which he was being ignored by Halleck must have lent credibility to these libellous tales.

'The President desires to know', wired Stanton to Halleck, 'whether any neglect or misconduct of General Grant or any other officer contributed to the sad casualties that befell our forces on Sunday [at Shiloh]. . . .'

[1] Coolidge, op. cit., p. 95.
[2] Benjamin F. Butler, *Butler's Book* (A. M. Thayer & Co., Boston, 1892), p. 458.
[3] George C. Gorham, *Life and Public Services of Edwin M. Stanton* (Houghton Mifflin Co. Boston, 1899), I., p. 325.

To this Halleck replied evasively: 'The casualties were due in part to the bad conduct of officers utterly unfit for their places. . . . I prefer to express no opinion in regard to the conduct of individuals till I receive reports of commanders of divisions. . . .'

While thus insinuating things he dared not put down as facts, he kept Grant deceived by saying that 'For the last three months I have done everything in my power to ward off the attacks which were made upon you.'[1]

At this juncture Halleck was called to Washington as general-in-chief of all Union armies, a position he held to the end of the war. The reasons for his promotion are hard to fathom. Up to this time he had, to all appearances, demonstrated only that he was good at intriguing and bad at campaigning.

Edward Bates, who at first had found Halleck 'a frank, straightforward man . . . imputed to have high military ability', later was forced to change his opinion. 'It does *appear* that Halleck is determined that we shall not take Vicksburg—if he can prevent it,' he admitted in his diary on 28 February 1863. 'He *refused* to take it when Beauregard evacuated Corinth[.] Then, only 8 or 10,000 men were needed to ensure the capture. . . . . When sharply question[ed] in C.[abinet] C.[ouncil] he pretended that he had not troops to spare! Yet at that very time, Curtis, with his 20,000, lay demoralizing and rotting at Helena!'[2]

Halleck's personality made a strange impression on people who dealt with him. He had a peculiar way of carrying his head sideways 'and a habit of looking at people with eyes wide open, staring, dull, fishy even, more than owlish', as if he were talking to some one over his listener's shoulder.[3]

Donn Piatt left a word picture of the general-in-chief that even outdoes this contemptuous description by General Wallace. He said that Halleck reminded him of two lines in an old ballad:

> *His head being larger than common*
> *O'erbalanced the rest of his fat.*[4]

[1] Coolidge, op. cit., pp. 96, 97.
[2] Edward Bates, *Diary*, pp. 201, 283.
[3] Wallace, op. cit., pp. 570-1.
[4] Piatt, op. cit., p. 66.

The attorney-general recorded in his diary, under date of 23 May 1863, that Isaac Newton, commissioner of agriculture, had told him that Halleck was a confirmed opium-eater. 'That he is something bloated, and with watery eyes, is apparent,' was Bates's comment. 'But whether from brandy or opium I cannot tell.' After that he usually referred to the general-in-chief as 'that poor thing—Halleck'.[1]

Secretary Welles looked upon Halleck with undisguised contempt and repulsion. He thought the general 'heavy-headed' and 'in all military matters . . . destitute of resources, skill, or capacity', possessing no originality and 'little real military talent'. What irritated Welles immeasurably was Halleck's habit of rubbing his elbows whenever he was asked a question; in the end he seldom gave an intelligent reply. 'He seemed stupid,' Welles wrote in his diary, soon after he had made Halleck's acquaintance.[2] The President himself, when free from Stanton's influence, indicated that he was fully aware of Halleck's incompetence; for when McClellan's forthcoming removal was discussed in a Cabinet meeting Secretary Bates quietly suggested that the general-in-chief should take command of the army in person. But the President remarked, and all the Cabinet concurred in the opinion 'that [Halleck] would be an indifferent general in the field, that he shirked responsibility in his present position, that he, in short, is a moral coward. . . .'

Admiral Foote was more outspoken in his opinion. He thought Halleck 'a military imbecile'.[3] And McClellan stated:

'Of all men whom I have encountered in high position Halleck was the most hopelessly stupid. It was more difficult to get an idea through his head than can be conceived by any one who never made the attempt. I do not think he ever had a correct military idea from beginning to end.'[4]

In justice to General Halleck it should be noted that he did not replace General McClellan through his own intrigues. 'I must say', he stated in a letter on 20 April, '. . . that the clamor against McClellan is not well founded. He is a very able military

[1] Edward Bates, *Diary*, pp. 293, 479.
[2] Welles, *Diary*, I, pp. xxix, xxx, 119, 121.
[3] Ibid., I, pp. 120, 180.
[4] *McClellan's Own Story*, p. 137.

General Henry W. Halleck

From a photograph in possession of author

man and no better head of the army can be found. . . . Unless I am greatly deceived in the character and capacity of the man, I could not consent to become his rival.'[1]

McClellan may have sensed the ties which bound Stanton and Halleck so closely together when he wrote:

'. . . a day or two before he [Halleck] arrived in Washington Stanton came to caution me against trusting Halleck, who was, he said, probably the greatest scoundrel and most barefaced villain in America; he said that he was totally destitute of principle, and that in the Almaden Quicksilver case he had convicted Halleck of perjury in open court. When Halleck arrived he came to caution me against Stanton, repeating almost precisely the same words that Stanton had employed.'[2]

Compare this with a paragraph in a letter from Senator Latham to Halleck on 6 April: 'Stanton is your friend—get Judge Blair and you have the living active element of the cabinet on your side.'[3]

Secretary Chase, who had also been instrumental in bringing Halleck to the capital, held the private opinion that Halleck was good for nothing, and that everybody knew it but the President.[4] He was almost as blunt in this regard as Welles, who thought that Halleck's presence at headquarters was a national misfortune. 'He has suggested nothing [in this summer's campaign],' he wrote, 'decided nothing, done nothing but scold and smoke and scratch his elbows. Is it possible the energies of the nation should be wasted by the incapacity of such a man?'[5]

'After Burnside had made his ghastly failure before Fredericksburg he advised Lincoln to remove both Stanton and Halleck,' wrote Macartney. When Burnside contemplated another campaign Lincoln sought Halleck's advice but learned nothing. He finally lost patience with his chief military counsellor and wrote him to confer with the general in the field. '. . . gather all the

[1] Letter in author's possession.
[2] *McClellan's Own Story*, p. 137.
[3] Letter in author's possession.
[4] Clarence E. Macartney, *Lincoln and His Generals* (Dorrance & Co., Inc., Philadelphia, 1925; used by courtesy of the author), p. 186.
[5] Welles, *Diary*, I, p. 373.

elements for forming a judgment of your own,' he wrote to Halleck, 'and then tell General Burnside that you do or that you do not approve his plan. Your military skill is useless to me if you will not do this.'[1]

Halleck responded to this letter by offering to resign his position. Whereupon Lincoln, instead of accepting the offer, rescinded his own criticism. The copy of the letter to Halleck bears the following meek endorsement in Lincoln's hand: 'Withdrawn because considered harsh by General Halleck.'[2]

Hooker, upon succeeding Burnside, first of all asked Lincoln's permission to act without consulting Halleck. When the President agreed, Hooker, ignoring the general-in-chief, communicated directly with Lincoln. Possibly this was the reason for Halleck's narrow-minded determination not to let Hooker withdraw the garrison from Harper's Ferry. That this refusal might have endangered the fate of the Union was a contingency which did not seem to enter into Halleck's calculations.

General Butler expressed his opinion of Halleck in his usual frank manner:

'Now there is General Halleck, what has *he* to do? At a moment when every true man is laboring to his utmost, when the days ought to be forty hours long, General Halleck is translating French books at nine cents a page; and, sir, if you should put those nine cents in a box and shake them up, you would form a clear idea of General Halleck's soul!'[3]

Many people have wondered why Lincoln kept such a man in high office. 'The strange thing', said Macartney, 'is not that Lincoln should have chosen Halleck for commander-in-chief in the summer of 1862. . . . The strange thing is that after his incapacity had been so strikingly demonstrated Lincoln should have kept him in command. . . . Halleck is a contemptible, almost ridiculous figure. One would laugh at him, were it not for the fact that his incompetence was one of the chief factors in the repeated and tragic reverses which befell the Union armies.'[4]

[1] Macartney, op. cit., p. 195; Rhodes, op. cit., IV, p. 201.
[2] Macartney, op. cit., p. 196.
[3] Ibid., p. 199.
[4] Ibid., p. 202.

On 15 July 1864 Bates spoke his mind 'very plainly, to the Prest. (in presence of Seward, Welles and Usher) . . . '. He expressed his opinion about 'the late military operations', and his contempt for General Halleck.[1]

Perhaps the retention of Halleck will be understood when it is recalled that he willingly took orders from Stanton and that the secretary had vowed that the war should not be finished until the Northern people had been worked up to the proper pitch—proper, that is, for the purpose of the Radicals whom he represented in the Cabinet, unbeknown to his chief. To end the war before this goal was reached, Stanton had said in 1862, would be equivalent to failure.

The selection of Halleck as head of the Federal armies made it all but certain that the war would be just one military fiasco after another.

'Had I been successful in my first campaign', wrote McClellan, 'the rebellion would perhaps have been terminated without the immediate abolition of slavery. . . . I believe that the leaders of the radical branch of the Republican party preferred political control in one section of a divided country to being in the minority in a restored Union. Not only did these people desire the abolition of slavery, but its abolition in such a manner and under such circumstances that the slaves would at once be endowed with the electoral franchise . . . and permanent control thus be secured through the votes of the ignorant slaves. . . .'[2]

Even Halleck could see this point clearly; at least he had seen it before he became general-in-chief. 'I am satisfied', he had written in a confidential letter, 'that if the ultra-abolition sentiment of the north should get the ascendency in the administration of the Govt., there can be no peace, but the war will be interminable. . . . Our only hope is that the President will stand firm in his conservative policy.'[3]

·

On 4 July 1863 General Grant took Vicksburg and with it 31,600 prisoners, 172 cannon, and a large amount of ammunition. Meade had failed to annihilate Lee, but Grant had crushed all

[1] Edward Bates, *Diary*, p. 385.
[2] *McClellan's Own Story*, p. 154.
[3] Letter in author's possession.

opposition on his immediate front, and was now able to reap the fruits of his victory. He proposed to march forthwith against Mobile.[1] In his *Memoirs* he wrote:

'Having cleaned up about Vicksburg. . . . I suggested to the General-in-chief the idea of a campaign against Mobile. . . . Halleck disapproved of my proposition . . . so that I was obliged to settle down and see myself put again on the defensive. . . . It would have been an easy thing to capture Mobile at the time I proposed to go there . . . the troops from Mobile could have inflicted inestimable damage upon much of the country from which his [Bragg's] army and Lee's were yet receiving their supplies. I was so much impressed with this idea that I renewed my request later in July and again about the 1st of August. . . . Both requests were refused.'[2]

The proposed move would have cut the Confederacy in two and probably would have ended the war. It did not seem to occur to Grant that this might have been the reason it was refused. Instead this army of 75,000 men, flushed with victory, was broken up into small detachments and employed in unimportant expeditions. The result was the *débâcle* of the Northern armies at Chickamauga. Halleck, not even suspecting that the enemy was concentrating its forces, had made no preparations to meet an attack.

'I expressed surprise to the President', wrote Welles, 'at the management and his forbearance, and it touched him. I asked what Meade was doing with his immense army and Lee's skeleton and depleted show in front. He said he could not learn that Meade was doing anything, or wanted to do anything.'

Yet Lincoln now made no remark about desiring to borrow the army as he had done in McClellan's day. All the President complained about was that ' "It is . . . the same old story . . . Imbecility, inefficiency . . . Oh," ' he groaned, ' "it is terrible, terrible, this weakness, this indifference of our Potomac generals. . . ." '

But Stanton and Halleck held fast to their position, and Lincoln did not censure them. 'Better, perhaps, if he did,' thought Welles.[3]

[1] Grant, *Memoirs*, I, p. 572.   [2] Ibid., I, pp. 578–9.
[3] Welles, *Diary*, I, p. 439.

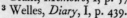

CHAPTER XXVI

The Case against the Radicals

The year 1864 arrived and with it a great change came over the administration. The time for dawdling was over; elections were approaching. Now was the moment to begin the war in earnest. First of all Halleck had to be side-tracked. This was accomplished by appointing Grant lieutenant-general, while the former chief of the armies was reduced to a mere figurehead and left to his own devices. By this time Lincoln himself admitted that ever since Pope's defeat two years before Halleck had been little more than a first-rate clerk.[1] There was no stinting of men now. Stanton's biographers point with pride to Grant's testimony before the committee on the conduct of the war, given in May 1865, in which he gave credit to the Secretary of War for hearty co-operation.[2] But this was only natural. The war had to come to an end some time.

Matters in the rear were not going quite so well as the Radicals had hoped. While the prolonged conflict and the hysterical out-bursts of the administration press had produced a feeling of bitter hatred against the South, they had also swelled the ranks of those who wanted peace at any price. Unless a decided victory could be won in 1864 the Democrats might win the election, and all the bloodshed would go for nothing. Lincoln saw his pet plan of an overland attack on Richmond put into operation. He saw Grant lose in six weeks more men than Lee had in his entire army. After that the lieutenant-general found himself almost

[1] Horace White, *Life of Lyman Trumbull* (Houghton Mifflin Co., Boston, 1913), p. 227.
[2] Flower, op. cit., p. 387.

exactly at the same spot on the James from which McClellan had been recalled. But this time there was no recall; no Pope was entrusted with an army in front of Washington. There were no reproaches; only the lines in Lincoln's face deepened and his eyes assumed a sadder expression.

By July Grant had depleted all of the Union reserves. The fortifications of Washington, which then required 37,000 men to defend, were manned by only 9,000 convalescent soldiers and green recruits.[1] In 1862 McClellan had left the capital protected by 19,000 men, with many times that number near enough so that they could be summoned at need. Grant left Washington so bare that Jubal Early could have walked into it if he had stayed on the south shore of the Potomac, or if General Wallace had not thrown the garrison of Baltimore into his way to delay him;[2] but Lincoln did not say a word. If he thought of McClellan at all, he was not magnanimous enough to offer his former general-in-chief an apology.

Then came new hope. General Johnston, perhaps the cleverest of all the generals then in the field, who had opposed Sherman in the west, was suddenly relieved of his command. It was the worst blunder of which Jefferson Davis was guilty—a godsend Sherman called it—and ushered in the dusk of the Confederacy. Atlanta fell on 2 September; a few weeks later Sheridan was victorious over Early and drove him from the Shenandoah valley. The danger was over. Lincoln was re-elected.

Now that Lincoln's incumbency seemed assured for another four years grave misgivings must have arisen in the minds of the Radicals as to whether he was really the man they wanted in the White House. It would have been much safer for them to have had Chase or Chandler or Wade there; but all political manœuvring to replace Lincoln on the Republican ticket had come to naught, because it was recognized that without Lincoln at the head of it the party would fail at the polls. While the President had, somewhat doubtfully, signed the Proclamation of Emancipation, he still did not seem over-enthusiastic in back-

[1] Welles, *Diary*, ii, p. 72.
[2] Campbell, op. cit., p. 131.

ing the abolition of slavery.[1] In 1862 he had written to Horace
Greeley of the *New York Tribune*.

'If I could save the Union without freeing any slave, I would
do it; and if I could save it by freeing all the slaves, I would do
it; and if I could save it by freeing some and leaving others alone,
I would also do that.'[2]

To the Radicals, these sentiments were far from satisfactory,
contrary though they were to the Chicago platform and the congressional resolutions of 1861, according to which slavery was
not a war issue but was to be left for state regulation. In the
summer of 1864, when Greeley had proposed peace negotiations,
Lincoln had insisted that the abandonment of slavery was a
sine qua non for a termination of hostilities. Later, at the time
of the Hampton Roads conference in January 1865, Lincoln was
to submit again a memorandum of instructions in which he would
insist that there be no receding on the slavery question.[3] But
now rumours were rife that the President was weakening, and
was so desirous of peace that he was willing to make the re-
establishment of the Union the only real condition of a settlement.

'I said [to General Singleton]', wrote Orville Browning in
his diary on 24 November 1864, 'I thought the President would
make the abolition of slavery a condition precedent to any settlement. He replied that he knew he would not—that he had a
long interview with him before the election—that the President
showed him all the correspondence between himself and Greeley
. . . and said . . . [it] put him in a false position—that he did
not mean to make the abolition of slavery a condition, and that
after the election he would be willing to grant peace with an
amnesty, and restoration of the union, leaving slavery to abide
the decisions of judicial tribunals. . . .'[4]

On 26 November Browning recorded that Singleton had
again received word from the President that the slavery issue
should not stand in the way of adjustment and that he intended
to say so in his message. Singleton, by the way, was to be one

[1] Rhodes, op. cit., IV, p. 159, *et al.*
[2] Ibid., IV, pp. 74, *et al.*
[3] Ibid., IV, pp. 513, 514.
[4] Browning, *Diary*, I, p. 694.

of the peace commissioners if negotiations with the South were decided upon.[1]

Browning naturally was incredulous of Lincoln's reported attitude, and on 24 December went to the White House himself to get authoritative and first-hand information on this point. The entry in his diary for that day leaves no doubt of what was in Lincoln's mind:

'In the evening went to the President's and had an interview. . . . During the evening the President showed me all the correspondence between him & Greely in regard to the negotiations at Niagara in July last with Clay and Tucker, and assured me that he had been misrepresented, and misunderstood and that he had never entertained the purpose of making the abolition of slavery a condition precedent to the termination of the war. . . .'[2]

Radicals could not regard these sentiments of the Chief Executive as anything but treason to his party. They believed that Lincoln was transcending his delegated powers. In July 1864 he had killed, through a pocket veto, the congressional plans for the restoration of the Union, and his opponents had attacked him fiercely in the Wade-Davis manifesto for trying to usurp the rights of the legislative arm of the Government. Now that Lincoln had been re-elected with the understanding that slavery would be destroyed they could not concede to him the right to change the policies of his party. But Lincoln soon put a new fear into the hearts of the Radicals, and one that made them almost forget the problem of slavery.

The Wade-Davis manifesto had made it clear that Congress meant to deal with the problem of Reconstruction without interference from the White House. The President, on the other hand, still anxious to abide by the half-forgotten resolution of 1861, was determined to restore all civil and political rights to the Confederate States immediately upon their return into the Union. He therefore decided on a shrewd move. He arranged matters so that the generals in the field should conclude an armistice

[1] Browning, *Diary*, I, p. 695.
[2] Ibid., I, p. 699.

that practically amounted to a peace without penalties; the nation would then be confronted with a *fait accompli* against which the rage of the politicians would beat in vain. The people were with Lincoln—the elections of 1864 had demonstrated that—and in the general ecstasy of joy accompanying the end of hostilities, all opposition would be drowned out. Congress was not to meet until December, and by then it would be too late to undo what had been accomplished.

And so, on 27 March 1865, Lincoln went to meet Grant, Sherman, and Admiral Porter in the cabin of the *River Queen*. There he gave secret orders to his military leaders for what Lloyd Lewis called 'one of the most cunning examples of the "double-cross" that the whole range of American politics, before or after him, could show.'[1] These orders were, in short, to grant to the opponents at the proper time a truce that embraced a formula for peace on the basis of the situation as it had existed before the outbreak of the war.

'It was not to help Grant that Lincoln went down to the battle-front,' said Lewis in his *Myths After Lincoln*. 'It was to help Lee. The question in his mind was not who would win, but what the winner would do with the vanquished.'[2]

When Sherman signed the truce with Johnston, on 17 April, he only followed the rules laid down by Lincoln. The agreement entered into stated that the President of the United States was to recognize the state governments on the condition that the officers and legislators would take the oath prescribed by the Constitution. The Federal courts were to be re-established, and the people of the late Confederacy guaranteed their political rights, as well as their rights of person and of property. A general amnesty was to be announced and the war declared over.[3]

When this tentative agreement reached Washington, on 21 April, Stanton prevailed upon President Johnson to call a Cabinet meeting without delay. At first Stanton raved alone in his denunciation of Sherman, but he finally carried the Cabinet with him to the extent of having the armistice disapproved. The secretary went even beyond this. Without the knowledge of the President he released to the Associated Press a diatribe that

[1] Lewis, op. cit., p. 30.
[2] Ibid., p. 20.
[3] Milton, op. cit., p. 173.

practically stamped Sherman as a traitor. The armistice, Stanton stormed, '. . . gave terms that had been deliberately, repeatedly, and solemnly rejected by President Lincoln, and better terms than the rebels had ever asked in their most prosperous condition.'[1]

But Admiral Porter, who had taken notes during that historic conference on the James River, felt that the terms of the truce

'. . . were exactly in accordance with Mr. Lincoln's wishes. He [Sherman] could not have done anything which would have pleased the President better. Mr. Lincoln did in fact arrange the (so considered) liberal terms offered General Joseph Johnston, and whatever may have been General Sherman's private views, I feel sure that he yielded to the wishes of the President in every respect. It was Mr. Lincoln's policy that was carried out. . . . I was with Mr. Lincoln all the time he was at City Point, and until he left for Washington. He was more than delighted with the surrender of Lee, and with the terms Grant gave the Rebel general, and would have given Joseph Johnston twice as much had the latter asked for it. . . .'[2]

Sherman's peace negotiations took place, of course, after Lincoln's death. But the late President had given enough evidence in the weeks just before his assassination to allow his Radical opponents—and advisers—a clear insight into the workings of his mind. 'Give Lee anything he wants if he will only stop fighting,' he had told Grant.[3]

On the day before Richmond fell Lincoln had a conference with Judge Campbell of Virginia, during which it was arranged

---

[1] Flower, op. cit., p. 265; Gorham, op. cit., II, p. 188.

[2] Milton, op. cit., pp. 703-4. Although Sherman could never be induced to speak of the conference on the *River Queen*, he made some significant remarks in a letter written on 19 Oct. 1868, addressed to Admiral Porter:

'You will remember that last spring when I wrote you about . . . the interview of Mr. Lincoln, yourself Grant and me, at City Point, you wrote me a letter very full and descriptive . . . [and] gave me at length the subjects therein discussed, principally that *Mr. Lincoln plainly foreshadowed the course to be pursued when the Rebel Armies were defeated* . . . tell me the substance of your memory of *what Mr. Lincoln did say, likely to influence me in offering to Jos Johnston the favorable terms I did*. . . . Being an interested party, I would prefer the testimony to come from you. . . .'

(Original letter in possession of author. Author's italics.)

[3] Flower, op. cit., p. 260.

that 'the gentlemen who had acted as the legislature in support of the Rebellion' should be permitted to meet in the Confederate capital for the purpose of withdrawing the Virginia troops. General Wietzel was instructed to give the legislators the necessary protection.[1]

When Stanton learned of this decision of the President he became panicky. On his own responsibility and plainly insubordinate to his chief, he gave orders to disobey Lincoln's instructions and, when Lincoln returned to Washington, managed to obtain his consent to withdraw the permit. Lincoln had made his arrangements in private and had hoped to have the legislature in session before the Radicals could be advised of the event; but treachery on the part of a subaltern officer gave the scheme away and thereby prevented its execution.[2]

By this time the Radicals must have been fully aware that Lincoln was determined to thwart their desires and to restore to the South its former rights, even if it meant the eclipse of his own party.

Senator Yates of Illinois, in a debate during the spring of 1867, delivered a speech on the floor of the Senate, in which he remarked that:

'Whoever that man may be, whether President of the United States or any other person, who stands in the path of this country for union, to honor and to glory, should be taken out of the way. I am not saying how.'[3]

Had Lincoln stood, according to Radical principles, 'in the path . . . to honor and to glory', whatever that may mean? And had he to 'be taken out of the way'?

How many desperate meetings took place to devise means of overcoming what, to the Radicals, was outright treachery? There was no use arguing with Lincoln, who could be as stubborn as a mule. There was no beating him in the game of politics or at the polls. Many a Radical may have hoped that Lincoln might die so that his own political and financial existence could endure; for short of killing the President there did not seem to be any chance of stopping him. As Stanton's biographer put it:

[1] Flower, op. cit., 269.   [2] Ibid.
[3] DeWitt, *Impeachment of Andrew Johnson* (Macmillan & Co., New York, 1903), p. 218.

'Lincoln and Sherman labored under the same disability. . . . The latter has suffered severely in history on account of his attempt to fix the political status of the rebellious sections . . . yet Sherman was only a soldier, whose terms could be . . . reversed and annulled, while Lincoln was president of the United States . . . with supreme discretion in military affairs. Therefore, when, by the secret letter to General Weitzel, he undertook to hand over to the Virginia legislature that which the Confederate armies had been unable to secure . . . he entered the vortex leading to destruction. . . .'[1]

Lincoln did indeed enter the vortex leading to destruction by making his gesture of peace; for the day after he had done so, death eliminated him for ever from the political arena.

There is not a shred of evidence in existence to connect the Radicals with Lincoln's death. Neither is there any proof that Stanton and the Radicals had any secret meetings previous to this tragedy. What we do know is this. On Sunday evening, 16 April, before two full days had elapsed since Lincoln's assassination, a meeting of Radical leaders took place in Stanton's office, at which time the Secretary of War read a programme he had developed for the 'reconstruction' of Virginia and North Carolina. This programme Stanton had submitted to the last Cabinet meeting at which Lincoln had presided; there it had met with opposition, as it contemplated the elimination of existing state lines.[2]

Although the matter was still pending in the Cabinet, the Secretary of War did not hesitate to submit it for general discussion to his Radical friends.[3] This shows that he considered himself a sentinel for the Left wing of the Republican Party and ready to do its bidding. That he undertook to oppose the President without the promptings of the Leftists is quite unthinkable. During Johnson's administration the Secretary made little effort to disguise his position as a Cabinet spy for the Radical leaders.

Stanton's proposal would have placed Virginia and North

[1] Flower, op. cit., p. 270.
[2] Milton, op. cit., p. 167; Welles, *Diary*, II, pp. 281, 282.
[3] Welles, *Diary*, II, p. 291.

Carolina in a single military department under supervision of
the War Department, and it seemed to Welles 'a plan of subjugation, tending and I think designed to increase alienation and
hatred between the different sections of the Union'.[1] Lincoln
had asked Stanton to change his plan so as to preserve State
individuality. It was further proof, if such proof was needed,
that the President was incorrigible. Living, he would for ever
present an almost insurmountable obstacle to Radical plans.

But Fortune smiled on the Radical Party. Lincoln was murdered.

'It is usual today [says George Fort Milton in his *Age of
Hate*], to depict the death of Lincoln as having occasioned an
universal outburst of grief throughout the North and particularly among the leaders of the Republican party, by whom "the
Great Emancipator" has since been made a party god. When a
searcher for the truth examines the private records of the time,
he can scarce repress a feeling of surprise, for the fact is that the
Radical leadership of the Republican party, while not pleased
with the sacrifice of Lincoln, the individual, almost rejoiced that
Lincoln, the merciful executive, had been removed from the
helm of state.'[2]

Julian, one of these Radical leaders, boldly stated that the
accession of Andrew Johnson to the presidency would prove a
blessing to the country. In this sentiment he was not alone. On
15 April, only a few hours after Lincoln's death, a caucus of
Republican leaders was held, at which the tragedy was described
as a gift from Heaven, and it was decided to get rid of Lincoln-
ism. Ben Butler was chosen to be Secretary of State. Unfortunately for that plan, Seward's injuries were not fatal, and his
position did not become vacant.[3] Blunt Senator Wade told the
new President: 'Johnson, we have faith in *you*. By the gods, there
will be no trouble now in running the government!'[4] Johnson
had been ranting for weeks past that secession was treason, that
treason must be made odious, and that all Confederates should
be hanged.

[1] Milton, op. cit., p. 158.
[2] Ibid., p. 168.
[3] Ibid., op. cit., pp.168–9.
[4] Ibid., p. 169.

From the pulpit the Radical sentiments poured forth with astounding frankness. 'I accept God's action as an indication that Lincoln's work as an instrument of Providence ended here,' said the Reverend Martin R. Vincent, in the First Presbyterian Church of Troy, New York, 'and that the work of retribution belonged to other and doubtless fitter instruments. I will not positively assert that his policy toward traitors was so much too lenient that God replaced him by a man who, we have good reasons to think, will not err in this direction. Yet I say this may be and it looks like it.'[1]

The Reverend Warren E. Cubworth, in Boston, also expressed his satisfaction: 'His [Lincoln's] death under God will do as much for the cause he had at heart as did his life. We know that already several of the leading supporters of his administration had taken issue with him on Reconstruction in the rebel states.'[2]

The Reverend Mr. Crane was convinced that the assassination was the work of Providence. 'Abraham Lincoln's work is done,' he stated solemnly. 'From the fourteenth of this April his work was done. From that time God had no further use for him. . . .'[3]

In the West, too, there arose strange ministerial sentiments. 'Most of the prayers, and speeches were impressive and in good taste,' wrote Bates; 'but I could not help feeling [regretful] at the tone and manner of Dr. Post—Harsh, vindictive and out of keeping with his usually bland and amiable character. . . . I cannot help fearing that his ardent temperament has been worked upon by crafty partizans. . . . For I know that it is the present scheme of the extreme radicals (who never were Lincoln's friends) to make party capital out of his flagitious murder.'[4]

It is remarkable how closely the wishes of the Radicals and the ways of Providence chanced to meet on 'the fourteenth of this April'. If the Radical preachers had wished to stress the point they could have easily shown that the mysterious workings of Providence had accomplished more than the removal of the President. An attempt had also been made on the life of Seward, the only other prominent Republican who was lenient and con-

---

[1] Lewis, op. cit., pp. 93, 94.
[2] Ibid., p. 97.
[3] Ibid., p. 99.
[4] Edward Bates, *Diary*, p. 474.

ciliatory. While some steel bandages made Providence fail in this instance, it worked perfectly again in the case of Andrew Johnson, in so miraculously sparing him from the knife of an assassin, just as Grant and Stanton had been preserved for the Cause. It is true that such puzzles as the stage-setting in Atzerodt's room, the unrepaired door-bell in Stanton's house, and the successful flight of the assassin across the Anacostia Bridge still remained unsolved. But the ways of Providence are proverbially hard to fathom, and the ministers of the Gospel probably felt they had gone as far as they could to explain them.

The Reverend S. D. Brown of Troy, without intending to do so, came perhaps closer than any one to summing up the case against the Radicals. 'God has a purpose in permitting this great evil . . .', he declared. 'It is a singular fact that the two most favorable to leniency to the rebels, Lincoln and Seward, have been stricken. Other members of the Cabinet were embraced in the fiendish plan, but as to them, it failed.'[1] Singular indeed.

Only one man ventured to utter publicly the suspicion that the Radicals had been instrumental in causing Lincoln's death. That man was Andrew Johnson. In a speech from the steps of the White House, on 22 February 1866, he announced that there had been

'innuendos in high places . . . that the "presidential obstacle" must be got out of the way, when possibly the intention was to institute assassination. Are those who want to destroy our institutions and change the character of the Government not satisfied with the blood that has been shed? Are they not satisfied with one martyr? Does not the blood of Lincoln appease the vengeance and wrath of the opponents of this Government? . . . Have they not honor and courage enough to effect the removal of the presidential obstacle otherwise than through the hands of the assassin?'[2]

So far as motives go, the Radicals had a greater stake in Lincoln's death, and expected more benefit from it, than all the Southern leaders could have hoped for by any stretch of the imagination; but as to tangible evidence of their complicity in the assassination, there simply is none.

[1] Lewis, op. cit., p. 82.   [2] Rhodes, op. cit., V, p. 577.

CHAPTER XXVII

The Case against John Wilkes Booth

The motives that prompted John Wilkes Booth to kill Lincoln have been the subject of many conjectures. During the days and months following the tragedy, when the public mind was still inflamed by the passions of war, suspicion naturally was directed, not to say diverted, toward the Southern leaders as the real instigators of the crime. Nevertheless, a most thorough, almost desperate, search for proof of the charge against them cleared them of all guilt. No connection between Booth and the Confederate leaders was ever established. In a letter the assassin left behind, and which was turned over to the authorities by his brother-in-law, John S. Clarke, the actor plainly absolved all others of complicity, by signing it:

A Confederate Doing Duty upon His Own Responsibility
J. WILKES BOOTH.[1]

This closing phrase was supposedly written in January 1865. The letter had been deposited with Clarke in the previous November. Booth asked for the paper in January and added this postscript, which is in a different ink from the rest. He then returned the letter to his brother-in-law.[2]

That Booth's services had been hired and paid for by some mysterious power was too obvious an idea to escape notice; but such a supposition disregarded the fact that money meant very little to a man of his type. Besides, his own earning power was quite above the average. '. . . my profession alone has gained

[1] Laughlin, op. cit., p. 24; also contemporary newspapers.
[2] *Richmond Whig*, 24 Apr., 1865, *et al.*

me an income of more than twenty thousand dollars a year,' he wrote in the Clarke letter.[1] John T. Ford stated to Colonel Olcott on 28 April 1865 that the season before he had paid Booth $500 for six nights' engagement. In 1863 Booth had evidently been making even more than that. To Ben DeBar, a St. Louis theatre manager who was related to him through the marriage of his brother Junius Brutus, he had written on 22 September:

DEAR BEN—

Yours of the 20th rec'd. All right. Book me for the two weeks to begin Jan. 4th/64. Share after $140 per night, and benefit each week.[2]

Money could hardly have been an inducement to Booth, who, if he had acted more and idled less, would soon have been able to accumulate a small fortune.

In casting around for other possible motives it has been asserted that Booth killed Lincoln to avenge the execution of a friend and former classmate named John Yates Beall.

Captain Beall was a young Virginian who had been given a commission as acting master in the Confederate navy. He soon distinguished himself by capturing some enemy vessels in Chesapeake Bay and by similar exploits, such as the partial destruction of the Cape Charles lighthouse. Eventually he joined an expedition that captured two steamers on Lake Erie for the purpose of releasing the Southern prisoners on Johnson's Island. This venture failed. Later he was arrested by Government agents at Suspension Bridge and lodged in Fort Lafayette, in the bay below New York City. He was accused of having attempted to derail some passenger-cars near Buffalo, with the intention of liberating a number of Confederate prisoners of war who were *en route* from Johnson's Island to Fort Warren in Boston Harbour. Tried by a court-martial under the direction of General Dix, he was sentenced to be hanged on 24 February 1865.[3]

---

[1] Laughlin, op. cit., p. 23 ; War Department Archives.
[2] Ibid.
[3] Isaac Markens, *President Lincoln and the Case of John Yates Beall*, p. 2, ff.; Virginia Lucas, 'John Yates Beall: An Appreciation" in *Confederate Veteran Magazine*, Aug., Sept. 1927.

Extraordinary efforts were made to obtain a commutation of his sentence. Orville H. Browning of Illinois, a personal friend of Lincoln, and the man who had served as United States senator after the death of Stephen Douglas, was retained by Beall's friends. Browning secured for his client a petition bearing the signatures of six senators and eighty-five members of the House. Among these were such prominent names as those of Speaker Colfax and James A. Garfield, the latter preceding his signature with the words: 'I recommend a temporary reprieve at least.'

The petition, dated 17 February 1865, set forth:

'Your petitioners respectfully represent that John Yates Beall . . . was arrested on the 16th day of December last and . . . tried by a military commission . . . upon charges . . . of . . . "Acting as a spy", and after a hasty trial was found guilty. . . . As it is admitted that the said Beall is a Captain regularly commissioned in the rebel service and that Jefferson Davis by a manifesto . . . assumed all responsibility for the acts . . . and thus publicly asserted that the several acts . . . were done under his authority and direction, we therefore respectfully recommend your Excellency a commutation of the sentence of death pronounced against him.'[1]

The petition went unheeded, as did visits to Lincoln by John W. Garrett, president of the Baltimore and Ohio Railroad, Richard S. Spofford, librarian of Congress, Governor John Andrew of Massachusetts and, strange to relate, Thaddeus Stevens of Pennsylvania.

To some of his callers Lincoln showed a telegram from Dix stating that Beall's execution was necessary for the security of the community. The stern commander at New York undoubtedly had in mind the recent attempt to burn that city. At any rate, in spite of all the influence brought to bear on him, Lincoln remained obdurate, and the prisoner was hanged on 24 February 1865.[2]

Soon after the assassination of the President a story sprang up connecting his death with that of Captain Beall. It was asserted that Beall and Booth had been friends, had attended the

[1] Markens, op. cit., p. 7.
[2] Ibid., p. 8; *Memoir of John Yates Beall* (John Lovell, Montreal, 1865).

same school, and had been inseparable before the war. When Beall was captured, it was whispered that Booth went to Washington and induced Senator Hale, whose daughter he was expected to marry, to call with him and McLean of Ohio on the President. At midnight the three men were driven to the White House. Lincoln was aroused, and Booth implored him to exercise clemency. It was reported that Booth knelt at Lincoln's feet, clasped his knees, and begged him to spare his friend's life. At last the President, with tears streaming down his face, took Booth by the hands and promised a pardon; but next morning Seward interfered and forced Lincoln to break his promise. Beall was executed, and Booth swore to avenge his friend at the first opportunity by killing both Lincoln and Seward.

This is the substance of the story that has been told often and in many variations. So far as can be ascertained, it has no foundation. While its genesis is doubtful, there is reason to believe that it originated in the brain of Mark M. Pomeroy, editor of a sensational weekly published shortly after the war.[1]

Neither in Beall's correspondence nor in his diary does the name of Booth appear. Albert Ritchie, who was with Beall at Fort Lafayette to the end, receiving his last statement and will, never heard of Booth's intimacy with Beall, nor did he remember the latter even mentioning the actor's name. Browning, in his diary, does not say that Booth was present at his interview with the President, but after the assassination he recorded the following observation:

'I am at a loss as to the class of persons who instigated the crime—whether it was the rebel leaders—the copperheads among ourselves in conjunction with foreign emissaries, gold speculators, or the friends and accomplices of Bealle who was recently hung at New York. I am inclined to the latter opinion.'[2]

Contrary to Mr. Browning's thoughts on the subject, there is no apparent correlation between Beall's hanging and Booth's plans. Aside from lack of positive evidence that the two men even knew each other, the probabilities are that Booth, an impulsive man of deep passions, would not have nursed his revenge for two months before striking. He had had an opportunity to kill Lincoln on 4 March, as he confided to the actor Chester, but

---

[1] Markens, op. cit., p. 11.
[2] Browning, *Diary*, II, p. 19.

he had not availed himself of it.[1] Beall had been hanged only about a week before. Is it reasonable to assume that the assassin would have waited another six weeks to cool his wrath when the intended victim was in his power only a few days after Beall's execution?

The possibility of any connection between these two tragic events becomes still more remote when it is considered that Booth's scheme for abduction dated back to the fall of 1864, long before Beall had run afoul of the Washington authorities.

In his diary Booth wrote that he knew no private wrong, and that he struck for his country alone. Even the hard-headed Butler was willing to concede that the diary was 'the dying declaration of a man, assassin though he be, who was speaking the truth, probably to himself, as between himself and his God'.[2] And so, seeing that Booth expressly disavowed any private motives the conclusion is justified that he was not avenging Beall when he shot Lincoln, and that the fate of the young Virginian who died a martyr's death in New York Harbour, had no bearing on the designs of the assassin.

At the conspiracy trial the prosecution endeavoured to prove that the plan to kill Lincoln had been in Booth's mind for many months past. This was not the case. The intent to kill did not enter into his calculations until a day or two before the deed was done.[3] Under date of 13 April Booth declared that 'Until today, nothing was ever thought of sacrificing to our country's wrongs. For six months we had worked to capture, but our cause being almost lost, something decisive and great must be done.'[4]

That the diary was a truthful account of Booth's adventures and sentiments is generally admitted. At least it is in entire accord with all the known facts. But when Booth wrote that 'Until today nothing was ever thought of sacrificing to our country's wrongs', he probably did not mean to have the word *today* interpreted literally. He had been brooding, ever since Lee's surrender, over the realization that all he had hoped to gain for the South by abducting the President was now un-

[1] Pitman, op. cit., p. 45.
[2] Booth, *Diary*; also DeWitt, *Assassination*, p. 179.
[3] *Impeachment Investigation*, p. 286; Booth, *Diary*.
[4] Ibid.

attainable. In a letter written to a girl in New York on 12 April he must have given vent to his feelings, to judge by her reply, which is still in the archives of the judge-advocate-general's office in Washington. To this young lady Booth could unburden himself freely, and her response, in spite of its *demimonde* flavour, mirrors the depressed sentiments of the actor:

New York, April 13th.

DEAR WILKES

I received your letter of the 12th (stating you would be in this City on the 16 inst.) this morning, and hasten to answer it. On account of a misunderstanding between my Landlady and your humble servant, I have been obliged to leave her hospitable mansion, and am now for the time being, stopping at the New York Hotel, after your arrival, should you not approve of my present location, it can easily be changed to suit your convenience.

Yes, Dear, I can heartily sympathize with you, for I too, have had the blues ever since the fall of Richmond, and like you, feel like doing something desperate. I have not yet had a favorable opportunity to do what *you* wished, and *I* so solemnly promised, and what, in my own heart, I feel ought to be done, I *remember* what happiness is in store for us if we succeed in our present undertakings, therefor, do not doubt *my* courage, have faith, 'for even as you put your faith in me, so will I in you' and Wilkes hath said *vengeance* is mine.

My removal has consumed the means you gave me when we parted, take this as a gentle hint to bring a good supply, 'for money makes the mare go' now a'days. I do as you desired and keep as secluded as a nun, which is not agreeable to me as you have found, but ere this, but any thing to oblige you, darling. If anything *should* happen (as I trust there will not) to prevent your coming to the City, please let me know, and I will join you (as agreed upon) at the house of *our* mutual friend A——s. 'Don't let anything discourage *you*.'

believe me *yours* and *yours* only

ETTA

P.S. Annie who is acting the maid to perfection, wishes to be remembered to her dear ahem!!! Sam.

Au revoir

ETTA[1]

---

[1] War Department Archives.

No one ever has found out who 'Etta' was. For Stanton's detective force it should have been an easy task; but it was never undertaken.

After the armistice Booth reluctantly gave up his plan for kidnapping Lincoln. He still felt that something heroic had to be done; but it was no longer a matter of aiding the South—it had become a matter of revenge. There is no reason to doubt that he acted, to use his own expression in the letter left with his brother-in-law Clarke, as 'A Confederate Doing Duty upon His Own Responsibility'.[1] His duty, as he saw it, was to kill Lincoln.

It was probably between the day of Lee's capitulation and 14 April that the idea of assassination gradually developed in Booth's mind. But he had not yet decided how it should be executed, except that the killing must be done spectacularly, in a theatre and while a performance was going on, just as the abduction was to have been effected. He had set his heart on this particular background for the deed which he imagined would make him the idol of the Southern people.

Booth told the Confederate officers who secured for him temporary shelter at Garrett's Farm that he had no idea the war was really over with Lee's surrender; for he would not have struck had he believed that the struggle was ended when the flags were lowered at Appomattox Court House.[2]

Grant arrived in Washington on 13 April. Booth felt sure that a theatre party would be arranged in honour of the general. In fact, he felt so sure of it that for the fatal evening he engaged a box at Grover's Theatre, the other leading playhouse in the city. To accomplish this he moved stealthily. One John Deery, then billiards champion of America, kept a large saloon directly over the front entrance to Grover's Theatre. On Friday, 14 April Booth entered Deery's office and asked the proprietor to procure a box for that night's performance. The actor's explanation was that he did not wish to ask for the box himself, as this would put him under obligation to the manager of the theatre, who probably would insist on Booth's accepting complimentary tickets. Deery took the money the conspirator handed him and did as requested.

[1] Laughlin, op. cit., p. 23.
[2] Ruggles's 'Narrative' in *Century Magazine* (Jan. 1890), p. 445.

'. . . if Mr. Lincoln had visited my theatre that night,' asserted Mr. Grover, 'Wilkes Booth would have had the adjoining box.'[1]

No such preparations were necessary at Ford's Theatre, where Booth was much more at home, and where he spent a great deal of his time.

On the day of Grant's arrival Booth wrote in his diary that until *to-day* no thought of murder had crossed his mind. The party in honour of Grant would provide the opportunity, and with the opportunity there came the final resolve.

The plans of the conspirators now matured rapidly. Booth's little band had dwindled by this time, until only Paine, Herold, and Atzerodt remained. Paine was dispatched to spy out Seward's whereabouts in order to insure a successful attack on the morrow. Atzerodt registered at the Kirkwood House, and was sent out pleasure-riding, while Booth and Herold entered his room and planted the clues they wished the authorities to find there. A last meeting of the four plotters was held at the Herndon House at eight o'clock in the evening. Thus the dress-rehearsal for a great drama took place while, only a few doors away, the curtain was rising on the last play Lincoln was destined to see.[2]

The case against John Wilkes Booth is complete. From the very first there never was any doubt of his guilt. Yet, with one of the world's most momentous crimes proven against him, students have disagreed about his motives, and legends had to be invented to satisfy the popular demand for more convincing ones. Some historians have attributed his act to the influence of strong drink, some to insanity. But through each report on the great tragedy one can trace the lingering perplexities of the writer. No one seems sure of his own conclusion. The student is as puzzled as the man in the street. A great political crime was committed without an adequate motive, unless a desire to avenge the sufferings of the South and to be applauded as the last champion of a lost cause may be so considered.[3] But if Booth really acted under the misapprehension that Lee's surrender had not ended the war Lincoln's assassination stands out as the most useless murder in all American history.

[1] Leonard Grover, 'Lincoln's Interest in the Theatre' in *Century Magazine* (Apr. 1909, D. Appleton-Century Co., New York), p. 949.

[2] Pitman, op. cit., p. 307.

[3] See supplementary note to chapter xxvii, 'The Spurious Confession'.

CHAPTER XXVIII

The Case against Andrew Johnson

When William G. Shepherd, in 1924, investigated for *Harper's Magazine* the story of John Wilkes Booth's alleged escape, he stated that he was not going to name a very high official who, it was whispered to him, appeared implicated in this mystery. 'It is part of the ... legend', he protested, 'that a certain government official of great power and position planned the killing of Lincoln and helped Booth to escape. Let his name be Blank.'[1]

There was really no necessity for Shepherd to be so secretive. Had he read nothing more sensational than the *Congressional Globe* for the year 1867 he would have known that Mr. Blank's name was then on many lips and that he was being publicly denounced as Lincoln's murderer. Mr. Blank was none other than Andrew Johnson, seventeenth President of the United States.

When Johnson became the Chief Executive of the nation the Radicals began to have pleasurable visions of wholesale massacres and executions that would depopulate the South; for the new President had expressed his hatred of traitors in terms that were immoderate and unmistakable. Yet week after week passed and, except for the hanging of the so-called conspirators and of Captain Wirz, the former commandant at Andersonville, no deed of violence took place. On the contrary, pardon followed pardon; and worse than that, the President undertook to re-establish state governments along the lines Lincoln had advocated. At first the Radicals were bewildered; then astonishment gave way

[1] William G. Shepherd, 'Shattering the Myth of John Wilkes Booth's Escape' in *Harper's Magazine* (Nov. 1924), p. 708.

to unbridled fury.[1] When it was discovered that John Surratt had been found in Europe, and that the Government had made only languid efforts to have him returned for trial, Johnson's enemies seized the opportunity to vent their wrath against him. They insinuated that the President did not dare have the fugitive returned to justice because he dreaded a confession.

On 24 January 1867 Benjamin Loan, a representative from Missouri, declared in the House:

'In the beginning . . . the assassination [of Lincoln] had been thought the deed "of a reckless young man. . . . But subsequent developments have shown it to have been the result of deliberate plans adopted in the interest of the Rebellion. . . ." An assassin's bullet wielded and directed by Rebel hands and paid for by Rebel gold made Andrew Johnson President. . . . *The price that he was to pay for his promotion was treachery. . . .*'[2]

Congressman Ashley of Ohio—who, it will be noted without surprise, was one of Stanton's intimates—spoke of 'the man who came into the Presidency through the door of assassination', and of 'the dark suspicion that crept over the minds of men as to his complicity in the assassination plot'. But, as usual, it was General Butler who came out most brazenly in his accusation. He was interested in discovering, he said, 'who it was that could profit by assassination who could not profit by capture and abduction [of the President]; who it was expected [by the conspirators] would suceed to Lincoln, if the knife made a vacancy.'[3]

An unheard-of thing had come to pass; a president of the United States had been accused on the floor of Congress of having instigated the assassination of his predecessor.

It now rested with the accusers to prove their case. On Butler's motion the House authorized a special committee to investigate 'all the facts and circumstances connected with the assassination tending to show who were the persons engaged in the conspiracy . . .'. That there should be no doubt against whom this was aimed the resolution stated gratuitously that many of those suspected were holding high positions of power and authority,

[1] Milton, op. cit., pp. 236 ff.
[2] Ibid., p. 404; DeWitt, *Assassination*, p. 174.
[3] DeWitt, *Assassination*, pp. 174, 180.

but had probably acted through inferiors who were their tools.[1]
This seemed like prejudging the case, but the committee was not
in a mood to shy at trifles. Offers of amnesty were made to every
one contributing evidence which would bring the true facts to
light; but the only visible result was the reappearance of the
convicted perjurer Conover. He could prove, he stated, that
Booth and Johnson had corresponded with each other, that
originally the assassination of Lincoln had been planned for the
day of the second inauguration, and that Johnson had become
intoxicated on that occasion in an endeavour to steel himself
against the announcement of the murder which he momentarily
expected.

But all this backstairs tittle-tattle did not get the committee
anywhere. It therefore decided to send an agent to Fort Jefferson
to obtain statements from the three surviving prisoners, Dr.
Mudd, Arnold, and Spangler. To each of them it was intimated
that a successful implication of the proper persons would be
rewarded by immediate release. The result of these interviews
was disappointing. The condemned men did not wish to say
anything at all and even appealed to the governor of the island
for protection.[2] In desperation the committee finally summoned
Congressman Ashley to force from him a complete disclosure
of all he knew. His testimony, however, was vague, even though
his belief appeared unshaken.

Q. You are the member of Congress who preferred the charges
   in the House of Representatives against the President for
   impeachment?
A. I am.
Q. Have you produced to this committee all the testimony of
   which you have any knowledge to sustain these charges?
A. All that I can present to the committee at this time.[3]

After references to Conover and some irrelevant matters, the
questioning continued:

Q. Have you not stated to members of the House of Representatives that you had evidence in your possession which would
   implicate Mr. Johnson in the assassination of Mr. Lincoln?

[1] DeWitt, *Assassination*, p. 180.
[2] Arnold, *The Lincoln Plot*; DeWitt, *Assassination*, p. 181.
[3] *Impeachment Investigation*, p. 1194.

A. No; not evidence in my possession. I may have said that I had statements made, in writing and otherwise, by this man and that, which induced me to believe it. I may have said that.

Q. Have you ever brought that evidence on which you believe it before this committee?

A. No, sir.

Q. Why did you not?

A. I have spoken to members of this committee about it. I have had no evidence which I regarded as valid; it was only an isolated statement of parties here and there, and not sufficiently strong to warrant me in presenting it.

Q. Then do you say before this committee that you had no evidence against Mr. Johnson which you considered as valid?

A. Yes. I had no evidence which I regarded as sufficient for the conviction of a criminal before a jury. . . .

Q. Then you state now, as you did before, that you know of no other evidence. . . .

A. I know of none at present . . . or I should bring it. I have given General Butler all the matters that I regarded as of sufficient importance. . . .[1]

Ashley's testimony was the last the committee took. As soon as he had left the stand it adjourned, never to meet again.

Butler evidently made herculean efforts to unearth damaging material against the President, but finally had to confess failure. 'Johnson had been suspected by many people of being concerned in the plans of Booth against the life of Lincoln or at least cognizant of them,' he wrote many years later. 'A committee . . . of which I was the head, felt it their duty to make a secret investigation of that matter, and we did our duty in that regard most thoroughly. Speaking for myself I think I ought to say that there was no reliable evidence at all to convince a prudent and responsible man that there was any ground for the suspicions entertained against Johnson.'[2]

Failing in their endeavours to bring forth tangible evidence of Johnson's complicity in Lincoln's death, the foes of the President

[1] *Impeachment Investigation*, pp. 1198, 1201.
[2] *Butler's Book*, p. 930.

concentrated their efforts on pointing to some peculiar circumstances that seemed to throw his behaviour into an unfavourable light. For one thing, Johnson had not stayed long at Lincoln's bedside; in fact, it was questioned whether he had been there at all at any time during the night. This controversy has long continued among writers, but it appears from papers found recently that Johnson did go to the Petersen house when he heard of the tragedy, even if he did not go there of his own accord.[1]

The Vice-President contrary to his usual custom, apparently went to bed very early that night. Former Governor Farwell of Wisconsin, who witnessed the assassination at Ford's Theatre, bethought himself of the danger Lincoln's successor might be in and rushed to the Kirkwood House to advise Johnson of what had happened. It was not easy to arouse the sleeping man. According to Farwell's statement Johnson was deeply shocked at the news and wept on his visitor's shoulder. Still, his sympathy with the dying President did not prove strong enough to make him take the obvious course of going to the Petersen house, where all the Cabinet members, and many other men of lesser station, were assembled. It was only when Stanton sent Major O'Beirne for Johnson that the latter accepted the summons; even so, he stayed only a short time, and was then escorted back to his hotel.[2]

Half an hour later, about two o'clock, Johnson had a long and serious talk with his private secretary, Mussey, on the duties devolving upon the new Chief Executive.[3] According to some reports the Vice-President spent the next few hours indulging in heavy drinking; he kept walking up and down in his room, roaring blasphemous threats at the assassins and at Southerners in general.[4] Just what happened after that no one seems to know with certainty.

Senator Stewart of Nevada claimed to have found Lincoln's successor in a drunken stupor at eight o'clock in the morning. According to this informant Johnson's hair was matted with mud, and he was in such a disgraceful condition that a doctor

---

[1] O'Beirne papers; see also supplementary note to chapter xxviii, 'The Visitors at Lincoln's Bedside'.

[2] Pitman, op. cit., p. 152; O'Beirne papers.

[3] *Washington Daily Morning Chronicle*, 29 Aug. 1873.

[4] Howard, *Civil War Echoes*, p. 82.

and a barber were rushed to the Kirkwood House to make him presentable for the ceremony that was to install him as President a few hours later. Stanton was the only other person alleged to have known of this disgraceful episode.[1] But when Salmon P. Chase, then Chief Justice of the Supreme Court, swore Johnson in as the new incumbent at the White House, not one of those present discerned anything unusual in his appearance, and all praised his solemn and dignified manner.

Out of this welter of conflicting testimony only two facts emerge that are uncontradicted; one, that Johnson did not go to Lincoln's bedside without solicitation, and the second, that he did not linger there for more than a few minutes, or at the most half an hour. Neither one of these actions is creditable. The first shows a lamentable lack of good breeding; the second is more serious. Lincoln could have recovered consciousness at any time before he expired; some physicians were of the opinion that the dying President was partially aware of what was going on around him and they half expected that a flickering of the flame, before it went out, would enable Lincoln to confer with his entourage for a few moments.[2] Johnson must have known that he, especially, should have remained with his chief until the end. He saw that no one else was leaving and, Stanton's orders to the contrary notwithstanding, he should have stayed on, if for no other reason than to avoid giving cause for the undesirable comments that were certain to follow.

Johnson's supporters must have appreciated the importance of this matter, for one of them tried afterwards to correct the bad impression that had been created. Farwell, who had spent some time with Johnson that night, presented him with an engrossed account of the events as he recalled them. Unfortunately, Farwell's memory was faulty. According to his story, it was Johnson who had ordered Major O'Beirne to take him to the Petersen house; this statement is erroneous. It was Stanton who had sent O'Beirne on his mission to act as escort for the Vice-President. Another assertion made by Farwell, that Johnson stayed at Lincoln's bedside until the end, is equally at variance with the facts as otherwise reported.

There is some question why the former governor of Wisconsin

[1] William M. Stewart, *Reminiscences*, pp. 194, 195.
[2] Lewis, op. cit., p. 61.

383

should have found it necessary to write any account at all in defence of the new President's action. That it was within Johnson's power to remove him from the Federal pay-roll clouds the issue still more. No other writer on this subject, except DeWitt, has accepted Farwell's statements as credible.[1]

Senator Foote, in some *Reminiscences* published in 1873, wrote, 'that late on the morning after the act of killing, when almost all Washington was astir, Mr. Johnson was keeping himself closely immured, as if fearing injury from some sudden ebullition of popular rage against those suspected to be concerned in the deed of blood . . . '. As an astute politician Johnson should have known that such criticism was to be expected.

Foote, in building up a case against Johnson, cited the following points:

'First, Mr. Johnson's well-known and anxious desire for the highest official honors which the country could bestow upon him, for the space of at least twenty years before the "deep damnation" of Mr. Lincoln's "taking off" had blurred so unfortunately the historic record of our country.

'Second, The utter extinction of his hopes of Presidential advancement along *the accustomed pathway* to promotion, by his shameless drunkenness on the day of his being sworn into office as Vice President.

'Third, His falling out with Mr. Lincoln soon after, and delivering a speech on Pennsylvania avenue . . . in bitter denunciation of . . . humanity and moderation. . . .

'Fourth, That Booth . . . called at Mr. Johnson's private room, only a few hours before the murder occurred, and on finding him absent wrote upon a card the deep disappointment which he felt at not having met with the only human being on earth who could possibly profit by Mr. Lincoln's death, and who was at the same time the only individual in the world who could give assurance to his murderer of his own pardon. . . .'

Foote also took this occasion to refer to Johnson's behaviour after the adjournment of the military commission which condemned the conspirators; his suspected suppression of the

[1] DeWitt, *Assassination*, p. 54.

petition for mercy relating to Mrs. Surratt: his refusal to admit to the White House all who wished to intercede in her behalf; and his suspension of the *habeas corpus* in regard to this unfortunate woman.[1]

Shortly after the execution of the four conspirators, a curious incident took place. Had Johnson's enemies been aware of it they would have taken advantage of it with relish.

The President had been reported ill ever since the end of June and, on 9 July, two days after the hanging of Mrs. Surratt, Welles recorded in his diary that Johnson still looked pale and listless. The faithful secretary urged an excursion down the Potomac. During the conversation Attorney-General Speed came in and not only joined Welles most earnestly in his suggestion, but begged that Stanton be taken along. The War Minister was not at all well either; it was thought that he was overworked. Speed expressed the wish that the trip be made on the President's yacht, the *River Queen*, on which Lincoln had been in the habit of travelling. Plans were made accordingly, and General Mussey, the President's secretary, ordered that the craft be prepared to sail the next day.

Welles was slightly disturbed, as the *River Queen* was not under his jurisdiction, and therefore went to the White House to change the arrangements. But this proved unnecessary; for Mussey brought him the startling information that Johnson would not set foot on the yacht. The President came in shortly afterward and confirmed the message of his aide; he demanded a naval vessel for the excursion.[2]

No one seems ever to have made further reference to this strange affair, which is made more significant by Johnson's almost superstitious avoidance of Lincoln's name in his speech of acceptance when he was made President in a Kirkwood House parlour.

'... an unpleasant impression was created', wrote Blaine, 'by its evasive character respecting Mr. Lincoln. The entire absence of eulogy of the slain President was remarked. There was no mention of his name or of his character or of his office.'[1]

---

[1] *Washington Chronicle*, 29 Aug. 1873.
[2] Welles, *Diary*, II, p. 329.
[3] Blaine, op. cit., II, p. 9.

Later, when Robert Lincoln sought to sell the various Lincoln carriages to the new President, the latter declined to buy them. The Johnson files fail to show any reason for this refusal on his part.[1]

The attacks on Johnson, intended to arouse suspicion against him, date back to the days following his proclamation of 2 May 1865, in which Jacob Thompson, Beverly Tucker, and other Confederate leaders in Canada were being openly accused by the President of having been a party to the conspiracy. These Southern gentlemen were not slow in responding and were savage in their own defence.

'I know', said Jacob Thompson in a public letter, 'there is not half the ground to suspect me as there is to suspect President Johnson himself.

'First. There was an absence of all motive on my part. . . .

'*Second. A paper is found in President Johnson's room . . . signed by the assassin himself* . . . this note is from a private citizen to a high official, and it is certain that if it had been sent by any other man at any other time . . . it would have implied previous intimacy . . . and a wish to have an interview without witnesses. . . .

'Third. President Johnson goes to bed on the night of the assassination at the unusual hour, for Washington, of 9 o'clock, and is asleep . . . when an anxious gentleman leaves . . . to inform the new incumbent of his great good fortune, which filled him with unutterable distress.'

Mr. Thompson made it clear that he did not really suspect Johnson, but suggested that if such circumstantial evidence could have been secured against a citizen of the South the Bureau of Military Justice would have considered it 'testimony as strong as proofs from Holy Writ'.[2]

Beverly Tucker struck at Johnson in the same vein, but with still more vigour: 'He . . . must expect to be dealt with as a man, not as a potentate,' he exclaimed. 'He shall not escape me by a dastardly attempt to throw the responsibility on the . . . tools . . . in his employ. I intended to strike at the head, not at

[1] Milton, op. cit., p. 229.
[2] Howard, *Civil War Echoes*, pp. 101, 102.

the tail, and if God spares my life, Andrew Johnson, and not I, shall go down to a dishonored grave.'

Tucker also pointed to the established law of evidence that no man shall be adjudged guilty who cannot be shown to have benefited by the crime. *Cui bono?* None but Johnson. Whence did the intimacy between Booth and the Vice-President arise? '*Is it impossible*', he asks, '*that Booth may have met Mr. Johnson in that lower circle they were both known to frequent.* . . .'

For twenty years 'all the arts and appliances which the fruitful brain of the unscrupulous demagogue could invent and employ have been exhausted to . . . reach the position of second civil officer of the Government. Then the prize, so long dazzling his vision, seemed within his grasp. . . . But the illusion was shortlived. . . .'

The disgraceful scene of Johnson's drunkenness on his inauguration day destroyed his hopes and made him desperate, Tucker believed. 'The crimsoned blush of indignation and shame mantled the cheeks of ambassadors, senators, justices . . . while . . . Abraham Lincoln . . . on the evening of the same day, at the inauguration ball, declined to recognize him.' Thus Johnson's future political hopes seemed blasted for ever. He might become President by succession, but never by election.

'. . . this, it is true [Tucker concluded], is but hypothesis, and yet, when you support it by the fact that . . . Booth was not captured alive, as he unquestionably could have been, we must induce some one more plausible ere we wholly reject this. Dead men tell no tales, and the wantonly hushed voice of this unhappy man leaves behind his bloody tragedy a fearful mystery.'[1]

At the time these events occurred there lived in Washington the son of Senator Howard of Michigan. This young man, whose given name was Hamilton, acted as secretary to his father and in this capacity acquired knowledge of some facts which were not given to the public until he printed them in 1907 as *Civil War Echoes—Character Sketches and State Secrets*. One of the chief items related by Howard is Governor Salomon's account of his experiences. It appears that Johnson and Salomon, ex-governor

[1] Howard, *Civil War Echoes*, pp. 102, 106, 107.

of Wisconsin, were well acquainted and occupied adjoining rooms at the Kirkwood House. Salomon had witnessed the assassination at Ford's Theatre and hastened to Johnson's room to apprise him of the murder. When he reached the door he tried to open it without ceremony, as was his wont, but to his surprise he found it fastened. Knocking loudly he was at last answered by Johnson, who appeared in his nightshirt, as if he had just arisen from his bed. Salomon was surprised because he knew Johnson's fixed habit of sitting up late. The Vice-President gave his visitor no reasons for having gone to bed so early.

Salomon then described Johnson's blasphemous threats against all traitors, his weeping fit, and his indulgence in whiskey.

Early the following morning Governor Salomon discovered in his mail the famous card—'Dont wish to disturb you Are you at home?'—and found that this message had been left for Vice-President Johnson by a fine-looking gentleman. Salomon now felt that he held in his possession a highly important State secret. After worrying for some time about the best course to pursue, he finally decided to hand Johnson his tell-tale card while the new President was in the midst of a meeting with the members of his Cabinet. But the expected sensation did not materialize. Johnson took the card and, after examining it with placid and unruffled countenance, remarked that he did not know Wilkes Booth, had never seen him, and that it was nothing but sheer presumption on the part of the actor to leave such a message.

'He spoke deliberately,' said Salomon, 'and with much dignity and unction.'

Salomon finished his recital to Senator Howard with the remark that he had private suspicions which he did not wish to reveal. This left Howard far from satisfied, and, calling upon Secretary Stanton shortly afterward, the senator volunteered his personal opinion and belief that Johnson was an accessory before the crime. The only reply he received from his listener was a shrug of the shoulders, which Howard interpreted as 'I could disclose a great deal of very interesting information on that particular subject, but it will not do to tell even you. . . .'

What struck Howard as particularly damnable was the fact, established by a senator who was anxious to impeach the President, that Johnson did know Booth and that his dignified denial at the Cabinet meeting apparently did not conform to the truth. While Johnson was military governor of Tennessee he and John Wilkes Booth had kept two sisters as their mistresses in Nashville and had been frequently in each other's company. This information came to young Howard from his father, who subsequently became chairman of the Senate committee on President Johnson's impeachment. The story had been uncovered through the efforts of private detectives.[1]

The value of Hamilton Howard's story is greatly impaired by his obvious prejudice against Johnson. Having associated largely with the most radical element in Congress, he naturally was hostile toward the Vice-President. His bias makes him even relate as evidence the opinion of a doorkeeper's wife, who exclaimed, when she heard of the assassination, '*Yes, and Andy Johnson has had a hand in it.*' When asked on what she based her opinion she replied that it was founded on her intimate knowledge of Johnson's character; that while a senator and boarding with her he had always sat up drinking strong liquor until early in the morning and that his associates had been hard and tough-looking customers; that he had been generally very drunk by midnight, had been disloyal to the Union, and had consorted with rebels. The doorkeeper assured Howard that his wife was a 'right smart woman', and believed she was 'almost generally right'.[2]

This is a type of evidence that even the managers of a military commission might have hesitated to parade in open court.

What is perhaps more to the point is that Hamilton Howard is inaccurate in some of his statements which are subject to verification. He confuses General David Hunter with General Winfield Scott Hancock, and cites the latter as the president of the conspiracy trial commission. The story attributed to Governor Salomon more probably concerned former Governor Farwell of Wisconsin, who swore on the witness stand that:

'On the evening of the 14th of April last, on leaving Ford's Theater, I went immediately to the Kirkwood House, to the room of Vice-President Johnson. I should think it was between

[1] Howard, op. cit., pp. 83, 84.
[2] Ibid., p. 79.

10 and half-past 10 o'clock. I found the room door locked. I rapped, but receiving no answer, I rapped again, and said, in a loud voice, 'Governor Johnson, if you are in the room, I must see you.'' I believe the door was locked, but am not certain. . . .

'I remained in Mr. Johnson's room about half an hour. I took charge of the door, and locked and bolted it. . . .'[1]

Can it be possible that two former governors of Wisconsin should have had identical experiences on the same night? No; the chances are that the statement attributed by Howard to Salomon really emanated from Farwell.

Moreover, Salomon's elaborate account of Booth's visiting card is flatly contradicted by the sworn statement of William A. Browning, private secretary to Johnson, who claimed that this singular piece of pasteboard was handed to him by the clerk of the Kirkwood House in the late afternoon of 14 April. Robert Jones, the clerk mentioned by Browning, corroborated this testimony while on the witness stand.[2]

It may also be worthy of note that Gideon Welles, who attended Johnson's first Cabinet meeting and accorded it a full description in his diary, made no mention of the dramatic incident which Governor Salomon described with such minute care.

In their attempt to connect Johnson with the untimely death of his predecessor the Radicals tried to secure the aid of John Surratt, who had been brought back from Egypt and was about to be put on trial for his life. What Ashley, Stanton's close friend, promised him in return can only be imagined. But the prisoner knew nothing against the President and could not be induced to give the desired testimony. News of this reached Johnson through a physician whom Anna Surratt, John's sister, had summoned as a messenger. She also had been tempted by Butler and Ashley, but when she sent word that she would be interviewed only in the presence of her lawyer their interest seemed to wane, and they declined to see her at all.[3]

The last warrior to enter the lists against Johnson was none other than Judge Holt, the judge-advocate-general who had

[1] Pitman, op. cit., pp. 151, 152.
[2] Ibid., p. 70.
[3] Milton, op. cit., p. 413.

fought so fiercely to place the guilt on the shoulders of Jefferson Davis and other Southern leaders and to incriminate the eight shackled prisoners who, thanks to his efforts, had been duly sentenced.

Holt's accusation came in 1873 and was the outcome of a controversy with the former President regarding the petition of mercy for Mrs. Surratt. Holt insinuated that, in 1865, there might have been reasons that 'would in all probability have operated against any development of the facts of this case'. But he goes even farther than that. 'There must have been', he sneered, 'something very fearful in his [Johnson's] contemplation to lead him to disregard an imperative public duty . . . rather than suffer the field of inquiry in relation to the conspiracy and assassination to be again opened. Was it apprehended that in the shadows of the field an accomplice or accomplices might be lurking who could not be safely dragged to light?'

Holt's attack took place in 1873, four years after Stanton's death. Johnson did not deign to reply to it.[1]

This is the evidence in the case against Andrew Johnson.

To it there may be added the docility with which he obeyed Stanton's orders to come to Lincoln's bedside and leave it again, and his continued unwillingness to rid himself of his Secretary of War long after the latter's treachery had become evident.

'The failure of the President', wrote Secretary McCulloch, 'to exercise his undoubted right to rid himself of a minister who differed with him upon very important questions, who had become personally obnoxious to him, and whom he regarded as an enemy and a spy, was a blunder for which there was no excuse.'[2]

No excuse—and no explanation. None of Johnson's contemporary friends could account for his strange patience with Stanton, and none of his biographers and apologists has put forth any plausible justification for it. It has remained to this day an unsolved mystery.

---

[1] DeWitt, *Assassination*, p. 246; H. L. Burnett, 'Controversy Between President Johnson and Judge Holt' in *Washington Chronicle*, 25 Aug. 1873, p. 32.

[2] McCulloch, *Men and Measures*, p. 391.

CHAPTER XXIX

The Case against Stanton

There was one man who profited greatly by Lincoln's death; this man was his Secretary of War, Edwin M. Stanton.

Brusque, insolent, cruel, Stanton was without doubt the most unpopular member of Lincoln's administration; but the President in spite of strong pressure, had been loath to let him go while the conflict was raging; he seemed to think that no one else could do the work as well.

'Find the man,' he had said. 'Show me that he can do it. He shall.'[1]

After the war was over, however, it seemed only a question of time when Lincoln would divest himself of a secretary who was fast becoming both a personal and a political liability to him.

No author has ever painted a picture of Stanton that was acceptable to all. 'The character and career of Edwin M. Stanton', wrote DeWitt, 'are so enveloped in enigma that we are compelled to pause . . . to gain, if possible, some adequate conception of the man.' But difficulties presented themselves even to this careful investigator.

'. . . alternately appearing and disappearing before the eye of the inquirer . . . there are two Stantons—one the direct contradictory of the other. Listening to the chorus of panegyrists, we see a war-minister greater than the elder Pitt; an organizer of victory more skilful than Carnot. . . . Listening to the voice of his detractors, we see . . . a life-long dissembler . . . a Cabinet

---

[1] Gamaliel Bradford, *Union Portraits* (Houghton Mifflin Co., Boston, 1916), p. 180.

officer obsequious to his superiors or his equals . . . to the point
of servility, and insolent . . . to his inferiors to the point of
outrage; governed by no loftier motive than the lust for office
and the power that office gives; an official parasite battening upon
the life-blood of his chief. . . .'[1]

One of his colleagues, Attorney-General Bates, expressed this
opinion after the Secretary of the Treasury had resigned in 1864:
'I should not be a bit surprised', his diary recorded, 'if Stanton
soon followed Chase. In that I see no public misfortune, for I
think it is hardly possible that the War Office could be worse
administered.'[2]

Stanton first became a figure in national life when, on 20
December 1860 Buchanan appointed him attorney-general,
apparently not without misgivings. In doing so he respected the
wishes of Jeremiah S. Black, his new Secretary of State, a former
law partner of Stanton.

'He was always on my side,' Buchanan wrote his niece in
1862, 'and flattered me *ad nauseam*.' Black also was sometimes
overwhelmed with excessive demonstrations of thankfulness and
friendship. All of which did not hinder Stanton, immediately
after joining the President's inner council, from starting an
intrigue with Buchanan's political enemies in Congress; for,
knowing that a Republican administration was to come into
power within a few weeks, he deemed it wise to secure a foothold
among its friends, while at the same time pretending limitless
fidelity to his Democratic chief and colleagues. Verification of
Stanton's duplicity comes to us from first-hand sources.

Senator Sumner, representing the Radical abolitionists whom
Stanton professed to abhor, wrote that in January 1861 he called
on the new secretary at the latter's office. '. . . he [Stanton]
received me kindly, seeming glad to see me . . . he whispered
that we must be alone. . . .' Passing from room to room without
finding the desired privacy, they finally reached the corridor,
and there Stanton proposed to call on Sumner at his residence at
one o'clock that night to tell him of the 'fearful condition of
affairs'.[3] The clandestine meeting took place, and soon Stanton

[1] DeWitt, *Impeachment*, pp. 241–2.
[2] Edward Bates, *Diary*, p. 381.
[3] DeWitt, *Impeachment*, pp. 251, 254.

was in daily communication with the Republicans in Congress and, according to one of them, Henry Wilson, he kept them well informed of what was going on in the Cabinet.[1]

While Stanton was flattering Buchanan to his face he did something behind his back that one reads about with bated breath. He outlined for the Republicans in Congress 'a basis for articles of impeachment of President Buchanan if such a course should become necessary'. With his associate Watson he spent hours in consultation about laws covering such a procedure. Flower cited some of Stanton's friends as witnesses for this and related the story with apparent pride.[2]

This peculiar sort of apparent double-dealing has never been denied. Stanton's apologists have pronounced it a deed of super-patriotism. In fact, it was nothing but a bold attempt to curry favour with both of the contending factions.

In his avidity for immediate recognition by the incoming party Stanton was doomed to disappointment. His name was not included among the War Democrats Lincoln selected for his Cabinet. Stanton's feeling of wrath was intense; the man who could flatter *ad nauseam* showed that he could be venomous as well. He designated the party that had snubbed him as *Black* Republicans; he blamed the 'imbecility of this Administration' for the disaster at Bull Run. He referred to Lincoln as 'the original gorilla', and he told McClellan that, with Lincoln in the White House, Paul du Chaillu had made a mistake in going all the way to Africa to look for an ape. Stanton's ire appeared to have overcome even his renowned patriotism, for he expressed the ill-concealed hope that Jeff Davis might 'turn out the whole concern'.[3]

It was well for Stanton that his contempt and hatred did not become known until many years later; for gratitude on the part of the *Black* Republicans was not altogether wanting. Seward, Sumner, and Chase had not forgotten the helpful espionage of President Buchanan's attorney-general, and when Cameron's management of the War Department began to arouse antagonism Stanton was remembered. It first was necesssary to be rid of

[1] H. Wilson, 'E. M. Stanton' in *Atlantic Monthly* (Feb. 1870), p. 237.
[2] Flower, op. cit., pp. 89, 90.
[3] DeWitt, *Impeachment*, p. 263; *McClellan's Own Story*, p. 152.

Edwin M Stanton

From an original painting by Nast   *Print in possession of author*

Cameron, however, and it was well known how reluctant Lincoln was to change his Cabinet officers. Finally, the appointment of Stanton came about through one of the neatest moves in the annals of Washington politics.

Secretary Cameron, in his annual report, had chosen to insert an explicit recommendation in favour of arming negroes, although this sentiment was then distasteful to Lincoln. Before transmitting the document to the President Cameron asked the advice of Stanton, who was acting as his attorney. The latter wrote an additional paragraph which was adopted and printed in the final report. It read in part as follows:

'Those who make war against the Government justly forfeit all rights of property . . . and, as the labor and service of their slaves constitute the chief property of the rebels, such property should share the common fate of war. . . . It is as clearly the right of this Government to arm slaves when it may become necessary as it is to use gunpowder or guns taken from the enemy.'[1]

By writing this paragraph Stanton succeeded in killing two birds with one stone. He widened the breach between Lincoln and his Secretary of War, and he showed to the Radical Republicans of Sumner's type that he was willing to be their representative in the Cabinet. To increase Lincoln's embarrassment, Cameron—possibly on Stanton's advice—sent advance copies of this report to the leading newspapers. When Lincoln discovered the paragraph about the freeing and arming of slaves, he objected and demanded its excision; but Cameron did not yield, and although Lincoln himself eliminated this part of the report before sending it to Congress, the papers published the unexpurgated document, thereby humiliating the President and making a reconciliation with Cameron impossible.

'There was reluctance on the part of the President to remove Mr. Cameron,' wrote Welles, 'and only a conviction of its absolute necessity and the unauthorized assumption of executive power in his Annual Report would have led the President to take the step.'[2]

Stanton had done his work well and soon had his reward. His selection as Cameron's successor was immediately proposed by

[1] Flower, op. cit., p. 116.
[2] Welles, *Diary*, I, p. 58.

Seward, and Lincoln sent his name to the Senate on 13 January 1862. It was then that Sumner moved its acceptance with the memorable words, 'He is one of us'.[1]

'Interesting, indeed [proudly wrote Stanton's biographer, Flower] is the fact that Lincoln was unaware that the iron-willed giant he was putting in was more stubbornly in favor of . . . arming the slaves . . . than the man he was putting out. Lincoln was also unaware that the recommendation which, with his own hand, he had expunged from Cameron's report and which was the means of forcing its supposed author out, was conceived and written by the very man now going in . . . and so it may be said that Stanton wrote his own appointment!'[2]

Yes, Mr. Flower, this *is* interesting.

But should not Stanton, in all fairness to his new chief, have made him acquainted with his views? And what would Lincoln have done had he known them?

With due disapproval of Stanton's tactics, one feels like doffing one's hat before such simple efficiency in the art of deceit.

The only man to object to Stanton's appointment was Postmaster-General Montgomery Blair. Secretary of the Navy Welles merely recorded in his diary that he had reason to know that Stanton was engaged with discontented and mischievous persons in petty intrigues to impair confidence in the administration; but he said nothing. Blair, on the other hand, when Stanton had previously been considered for district-attorney at Washington, had stated reluctantly that he doubted his integrity, relating at the same time 'an instance which had come to his knowledge and where he has proof of a bribe having been received . . . '. There could be no mistake, be averred.[3] The details of this alleged case have never been divulged, but Blair and Welles remained aloof from their colleague in the War Department ever after.

'I am going to be Secretary of War to Old Abe,' confided Stanton to his friend Judge Piatt a few days before he entered upon his new duties.

---

[1] H. Wilson, 'Jeremiah S. Black and Edwin M. Stanton' in *Atlantic Monthly* (Oct. 1870), p. 466.

[2] Flower, op. cit., p. 117.

[3] Welles, *Diary*, I, pp. 57, 127, 128.

'What will you do?' Piatt asked, curious about Stanton's plans to reconcile his own and Lincoln's widely separate points of view.

'Do?' was Stanton's reply; 'I intend to . . . make Abe Lincoln President of the United States.'[1]

Just what Stanton meant by these words is something of a riddle; for he was certainly professing no love for the President at that time.

Piatt was not the only one to doubt the compatability of Lincoln and Stanton, for Chittenden also thought that men of Mr. Stanton's temperament could not be the favourites of President Lincoln. Nor was it merely divergence of temperament which erected a barrier between them, for, to quote Chittenden further:

'There were also reasons of a personal character which would have barred his entrance into the Cabinet, if Mr. Lincoln had been an ordinary man. . . . Both had been counsel for the same party in an action in which . . . Mr. Lincoln was entitled to make the argument. . . . It was an action in which he took a deep interest professionally. . . . But Mr. Stanton . . . in a domineering manner not uncommon with him . . . coolly assumed control and crowded Mr. Lincoln out of his own case.'

Lincoln was deeply hurt in this instance and for the first time seemed 'to have claimed in his own favor any question of precedence'.[2]

Stanton undoubtedly remembered the success of his presumption in the above-mentioned trial. Could it have been the ease with which he had dominated Lincoln in that case which made him assert so confidently to Piatt that he was going to 'make Abe Lincoln President of the United States'?

The new Cabinet officer had hardly started his duties before he manifested his genius for disseminating views that were favourable to himself. On 9 February 1862 Seward's friend, Thurlow Weed, published a story in the London *Observer* which quickly made its rounds through American newspapers. On 27

[1] Donn Piatt, *Memories of the Men Who Saved the Union*, pp. 57–8.
[2] Chittenden, *Recollections*, p. 185; see also Albert J. Beveridge, *Abraham Lincoln, 1809–1858* (Houghton Mifflin Co., Boston, 1928), I, pp. 575–83.

December 1860, according to this account, when President
Buchanan appeared to be yielding to the demand of South
Carolina that Major Anderson and his garrison be removed from
Fort Sumter, Stanton stepped forward in a Cabinet meeting,
denounced two of his colleagues as financially dishonest, and
delivered an ultimatum to the chief of the nation either to stand
firm or to accept Stanton's resignation. When Black, Holt, and
Dix seconded the motion, it 'opened the bleary eyes of the
President' and forced him to decide on the patriotic course so
sternly demanded.[1]

It is characteristic of Stanton's ability as a propagandist that
this tale, although lacking any foundation, has persisted to this
day and is given universal credence.

Morgan Dix, writing the biography of his father, stated that
'this highly colored narrative was not only untrue, but may be
taken as a specimen of the numerous inventions of a time of
excitement'. He had the written testimony of two of the men who
were supposed to have taken part in this discussion that no such
thing had occurred at any time while they were in the Cabinet.
Even the date assigned to it by the inventors of this canard was
wrong, as Dix at that time had not yet been appointed. Judge
Black also denounced the account as false; and Stanton himself,
when appealed to for verification, explained 'how and by whom
it had been fabricated, but said it was not worth a contradiction;
for every man of common intelligence would know it to be a
mere tissue of lies'.[2]

When Henry Wilson repeated the story in eulogies of Stanton
after his death, Judge Black fiercely demanded proof. Wilson
turned to Holt, who was supposed to have been present, but
failed to enlist his support. Finally, the evidence simmered down
to the testimony of the wife of Congressman Dawes, who 'distinctly remembered hearing Stanton tell at her house the story
of that terrible conflict in the Cabinet'.[3]

There can be no doubt, then, as to who invented this tale, or
as to what methods were used to circulate it.

---

[1] William N. Brigance, *Jeremiah Sullivan Black* (University of Pennsylvania Press, Philadelphia, 1934), p. 74.
[2] Morgan Dix, *Memoirs of John A. Dix*, I, p. 379; Jeremiah S. Black,
'Senator Wilson and Edwin M. Stanton' in *Galaxy Magazine*, vol. IX, 1870.
[3] Brigance, op. cit., p. 75.

Jeremiah Sullivan Black, who had warmly recommended Stanton to President Buchanan, said of him at the time: 'His condemnation of the abolitionists was unsparing for their hypocrisy, their corruption, their enmity to the Constitution, and their lawless disregard for the rights of States and individuals. Thus he won the confidence of the Democrats.' But while, as Black guilelessly imagined, Stanton's political principles were thought to be as well known as his name and occupation, the wily attorney-general of Buchanan's official family was holding nocturnal meetings with the most avowed abolitionists in the country; he even advised them to kidnap one of his colleagues as soon as it was deemed expedient to do so.[1]

Welles's diary has an interesting comment in this connection:

'Mr. Black says that Stanton went into Buchanan's Cabinet under his auspices, and no one has ever questioned it. He further asserts that Mr. Stanton "said, many times, that he was there only that I [Black] might have two voices instead of one. . . ." The same professions and the same expressions were made by the same individual to Mr. Seward when he entered the Lincoln Cabinet, and subsequently, as I heard Mr. Seward say; and I doubt not with equal sincerity to each, though Black and Seward were entirely antagonistic in their political views and principles.'[2]

It is also noteworthy that this indomitable foe of all secessionists, who 'never spoke or wrote of those at war against the Government, but as rebels and traitors',[3] was, while a member of Buchanan's Cabinet, distinctly of the opinion that the Government had no right to make war on a state for the purpose of coercing it to remain in the Union. Black stated that Stanton endorsed this point of view 'with extravagant and undeserved laudation . . . and the special message of the eighth of January, 1861, which expressed the same principles with added emphasis, was carefully read over to him before it was sent to Congress, and it received his unqualified assent. . . . The evidence', so Judge Black contended, 'is "direct as well as circumstantial, oral

[1] DeWitt, *Impeachment*, p. 247; Welles, *Diary*, I, p. 355.
[2] Welles, *Diary*, I, p. 60.
[3] A. E. H. Johnson, 'Reminiscences of the Hon. Edwin M. Stanton' in *Columbia Historical Society Proceedings*, vol. 13, 1910, p. 75.

as well as documentary, and some of it is in the handwriting of Mr. Stanton himself".'[1]

F. P. Blair's imputations surpassed even those made by Black; according to Welles Blair professed to have positive and unequivocal testimony that Stanton had acted with the secessionists early in the war and had favoured a division of the Union.[2]

But after Stanton had joined hands with the Radicals and been assigned a seat in Lincoln's Cabinet his memory suffered a strange lapse; for he once told Congressmen Dawes and Washburne that Buchanan, before writing his annual message, had sent for him to answer the question of whether a state could be coerced. For two hours, so Stanton claimed, he had battled against the President, and had finally conquered temporarily the heresies in the head of the 'old-broken-down man'. Yet, it was with this ruin of a man that Stanton kept up a lively correspondence during 1861, praising his administration and jeering at Lincoln because he could do no better than follow the course of his predecessor. 'So far . . . as your administration is concerned', Stanton wrote to Buchanan on 16 July, 'its policy in reference to both Sumter and Pickens is fully vindicated by the course of the present administration.' A policy (so Stanton's greatest apologist, Flower, admits in parenthesis) which was strenuously opposed by Stanton while in Buchanan's Cabinet.[3]

In the same letter Stanton added: 'I think that the public will be disposed to do full justice to your efforts to avert the calamity of civil war. . . .'[4]

No sooner was Stanton firmly established as Secretary of War than his elaborate plans to further his personal ambitions assumed definite shape. The first part of his programme was to prolong the conflict, thereby aiding the abolitionists in their scheme for final disfranchisement of the South and, incidentally, helping to create an army that would be a power for a long time to come and a formidable weapon in the hands of a military idol. That he would be the one to emerge in the end as the popular leader was undoubtedly his cherished dream. He could see no serious competition in the Cabinet. Lincoln he looked upon with more or

[1] DeWitt, *Impeachment*, p. 249.
[2] Welles, *Diary*, I, p. 355.
[3] DeWitt, *Impeachment*, p. 249; Flower, op. cit., p. 1c.
[4] Flower, op. cit., p. 108.

less open contempt. He anticipated no trouble in dominating this uncouth country lawyer, as he had done once before; what he dreaded was the rise of a successful and popular general who might catch the public fancy and capture the prize he coveted for himself. That problem would not have to be dealt with till later, however. Of the ultimate end of the war there could be no doubt. Barring a miracle, the enormous preponderance of the North's numbers, its unlimited resources, and the ever tightening blockade must eventually bring the Confederacy to its knees, no matter how badly the Union generals handled the campaigns.

In the meantime, several manœuvres had to be executed. One of the first was to secure control of all intercourse with the Press.

'From January 1862, when Stanton entered the cabinet, until the war ended', said David Homer Bates, 'the telegraphic reins of the Government were held by a firm and skilful hand. . . . Stanton "centered the telegraph in the War Department, where the publication of military news . . . could be supervised, and, if necessary, delayed. . . ." ' On 25 February 1862 Stanton appointed a military supervisor of telegrams. 'What his blue pencil erased . . .' proclaimed Bates haughtily, 'had to be left out, and reporters frequently spent hours in procuring some choice bit of news which was never transmitted over the wires.'[1]

Before long Stanton swept the management of all the telegraph lines in the United States into the War Department and, on 2 March, he concentrated the telegraph machinery in a room next to his own. Even Lincoln was not allowed a special code and had to send and receive messages through the common channel.[2] This arrangement, together with his censorship over the Press, gave the War Minister a power never before dreamed of, and one which he was not loath to use to his own advantage.

'The telegraph office is in the War Department Building,' recorded Welles, 'which has a censorship over all that passes or is received.'[3]

Stanton could be a man of Machiavellian finesse whenever it suited his purpose. While all his efforts were being directed to destroy McClellan, for example, he informed the Press that the

[1] Bates, *Lincoln in the Telegraph Office*, pp. 39, 108, 109.
[2] Flower, op. cit., p. 217.
[3] Welles, *Diary*, I, p. 365.

fall of Richmond could be expected momentarily. Naturally, these joyous tidings were immediately flashed all over the Northern states. There was nothing in the situation at that time which warranted such optimism, and McClellan certainly had not authorized any such statement. But when Richmond was not taken, and the normal reaction set in, it was not Stanton's reputation which suffered, but McClellan's.[1]

The war went on. McClellan, a most dangerous opponent for future honours, was disposed of; for the moment there was nothing to fear from the other army leaders who followed in rapid succession. But within the Cabinet a new figure arose to challenge Stanton's superiority. This was Salmon P. Chase, the Secretary of the Treasury, who was showing an ambition to run for the presidency in 1864. The relations between Chase and Stanton were neither cordial nor contrariwise; but the Secretary of War had to meet this new situation. He did so in his own inimitable way.

On 11 October 1862 Chase had asked General Hunter, 'What of Stanton?' To which he had received the reply: 'Know little of him. . . . Think, from facts that have come to my knowledge, that he is not sincere. He wears two faces. . . .'[2]

It was not long before Chase had an opportunity to form his own opinion on this subject.

A man named Hurtt had been commissioned on 13 October 1861 as assistant quartermaster of volunteers. He had hardly reached his post in Cincinnati when he began to speculate in forage and supplies. According to revelations which appeared in the *Cincinnati Gazette* after the war (1874), he entered into correspondence with some of Chase's confidential financial agents, and soon the frauds for which he was responsible assumed gigantic proportions. In the midst of these doings General Burnside took command of the Department of the Ohio, and on 28 July 1863 directed one Major N. H. McLean to investigate some of Hurtt's transactions. McLean made his report in September 1863, and on 23 November Hurtt was put on trial before a court-martial. Then something unexpected happened. A tele-

---

[1] Campbell, op. cit., p. 205.
[2] Warden, *Chase*, p. 505.

gram was received from the War Department; the court was declared dissolved, and all papers were ordered to be sealed and sent to Washington. Scarcely enough time had elapsed for an examination of these documents at the War Department when Major McLean was peremptorily removed from his post at Cincinnati and instructed to report for duty at Vancouver, in Washington territory.[1]

A second court was convened in the following year; Hurtt was convicted and dismissed from service. Just before the proceedings of the case were ready for publication the general distribution of court-martial orders was stopped by direction of the War Department.

'Many readers will ask', wrote the *Cincinnati Gazette*, 'why did a man of Mr. Stanton's iron nerve hesitate to put all these offenders, high and low, on trial at once? . . . men so high in the nation's counsels, and in the confidence of the people, were compromised, that to uncover their iniquity . . . would result, as he feared, in destroying the confidence of the people.'

Stanton had reasoned, according to this paper, that it was unwise to let the nation know about a league organized for plunder only, which counted among its members

'. . . the financial agents of the government and some of its most prominent political supporters. . . . And so the court was dissolved, and the officer who knew all the facts, and who had the full confidence of his commanding general, was obliged to leave with his family, in the dead of winter, for the most distant point on American soil, lest the facts in regard to a band of robbers, holding high position, should by any possibility come to light.'[2]

Probably it was only a coincidence that General Burnside himself was sent to Knoxville in August 1863, before Major McLean had made his report on the swindling operations.

It may have been some such incident that Judge Piatt had in mind when, in writing a chapter on Stanton in his *Memories*, he said: 'The true story of the late war has not been told. It probably never will be told. It is not flattering to our people, and . . . unpalatable truths seldom find their way into history.'[3]

[1] Warden, *Chase*, pp. 519 ff.   [2] Warden, *Chase*, p. 518.
[3] Piatt, op. cit., p. 77.

The article in the *Cincinnati Gazette* was written by General Boynton, and he named the Cookes as the financial agents of the Government. To what extent others were involved in this scandal is not relevant. The important thing is that the righteous Stanton had compromised with his conscience, and had done so to save Secretary Chase from serious embarrassment; for Chase's misplaced confidence in these rogues would have given him painful prominence had Stanton chosen not to intervene.

After this Stanton had no reason to fear Chase.

Mere love of subterfuge seems at times to have governed Stanton's actions, even when nothing could be gained by an evasion of the truth. In September 1862 General Butler, desiring reinforcements, addressed a letter to Senator Wilson, asking him to use his influence with the Secretary of War to have them sent to him promptly. Wilson did so and wrote that 'he [Stanton] agreed with me and . . . expressed his confidence in you, and his approval of your vigor and ability'.

But twenty-one days previous to this, by a secret order, Stanton had appointed General Banks to succeed the unsuspecting Butler, and while he was handing those bland assurances to his caller he knew all the time that Butler was no longer the commander. Is it any wonder the latter wrote: 'Can lying, injustice, deceit, and tergiversation farther go?'[1]

During the early months of his incumbency Stanton tried hard to bend the President to his wishes. In the beginning he succeeded with surprising ease. Lincoln issued his rash war orders under Stanton's tutelage and followed the War Minister in his persecution and final dismissal of McClellan. Stanton found, however, that he could not influence his chief beyond a certain point. Lincoln did not mind his secretary's brutal manners, nor his almost open contempt, or if he did, he hid it well behind a mask of tolerant amusement. But behind that mask there lurked resentment.

Encouraged by Lincoln's apparent docility Stanton crept forward craftily. By the summer of 1863 he had succeeded to such an extent that he occasionally ordered Lincoln around like a clerk. When the news of Hooker's resignation reached him

[1] *Butler's Book*, p. 529.

Stanton, according to his own account, 'sent for the President to come to the War Office at once. It was the evening, but the President soon appeared.'[1]

Who else in Washington, not excepting Seward, would have had the audacity to request the Chief Executive to come to his department to read a telegram, rather than take the message to the White House?

In 1864 the inevitable clash came. 'I cannot do it,' exclaimed Stanton on one occasion. '*Mr. Secretary, it will have to be done,*' replied Lincoln.[2] Stanton surrendered. He had challenged the President and had lost. It is possible that from then on Stanton's contempt was blended with hatred.

There were other incidents on record showing how quickly the imperious war lord, when confronted with some one who was not awed by his blustering, could be cowed, in spite of his outward show of combativeness. Once an officer called on him to get a pass for an old man who desired to visit his dying son. Stanton refused the request, whereupon the officer, drawing himself up to his full height, said, 'My name is . . . Walton Dwight, lieutenant-colonel of the One Hundred and Forty-ninth Regiment of Pennsylvania volunteers. You can dismiss me from the service as soon as you like, but I am going to tell you what I think of you.' He did—and got his pass.[3]

A similar case is reported by Maunsell B. Field, Assistant Secretary of the Treasury under Chase. It appears that Secretary Chase had just heard some disagreeable news and was in an ugly mood. 'Mr. Stanton', related the narrator, 'unfortunately for himself, happened to come into the secretary's room shortly after . . . when he received such a verbal castigation at the hands of Mr. Chase as few men would have ventured to inflict upon the great War Secretary. What was more remarkable, however, he bore it with great meekness.'[4]

---

[1] Rice, *Reminiscences of Abraham Lincoln*, p. 128.

[2] Ibid, p. 398; also supplementary note to chapter xxix, 'The Showdown Between Lincoln and Stanton'.

[3] Bradford, op. cit., p. 172.

[4] Maunsell B. Field, *Memories of Many Men* (Sampson Low, Marston, Low & Searle, London, 1874), p. 282.

A third instance is reported by Colonel Burnett, who in the conspiracy trial acted as assistant judge-advocate.

Wiechmann and Holahan were wanted by Stanton; Burnett was instructed by the secretary to take their statements and then let them go. He performed this task, but Stanton in the meantime had discovered his mistake in losing contact with the two men and upbraided Burnett in a most insulting manner. The next day the assistant prosecutor produced his witnesses again, and then said: 'And now, Mr. Stanton, I am through with the service under you. . . . You would have condemned and disgraced me . . . for obeying your own order, and I am damned if I will serve further under any such man. . . . I am through with you. . . .' Thereupon the secretary got up from his desk and humbly begged Colonel Burnett's pardon.[1]

'He [Stanton] believes in mere force, so long as he wields it,' wrote Edward Bates, 'but cowers before it, when wielded by any other hand.' Bates was Stanton's colleague in Lincoln's Cabinet and should have known.[2]

For three years Stanton had held his portfolio and things were working out well for his plan. The war had been prolonged; the slaves had been freed. A new union would have to be built on the ruins of the old, and the party to which he had given his latest allegiance would be firmly in the saddle.

McClellan was out of public favour, and there was no one in the offing to take his place. If no new general who was widely popular arose to mar his designs Stanton was likely to become the hero of the nation; for history showed convincingly that after every great victory the people elevated the man they considered responsible for it to the most exalted position within their power.

Of course, there was Grant. But to most observers in Washington at that time the modest little man appeared dull. Richard Dana of Boston, who happened on the general in the Willard Hotel lobby, wrote of him in this manner: 'A short-round-shouldered man, in a very tarnished . . . uniform. . . . He had no gait, no station, no manner . . . and rather a scrubby look.

[1] Burnett, *Ohio Society of New York*, p. 598.
[2] Edward Bates, *Diary*, p. 483.

. . .'[1] Grant might win battles—no one knew how he did it—but as a politician he would be like clay in the hands of the War Minister.

In 1864 Stanton had insisted on controlling the cipher operator at Grant's headquarters and later on had given instructions to have all of the general's wires copied for inspection. He left Grant's orders unapproved for days until it was 'entirely convenient for him' to sanction them.[2] Stanton probably did this mainly to test the temper of his subordinate; the latter, while slightly irritated, bore no grudge. At any rate, in November Grant told Lincoln that no one was better fitted for the office than Stanton and that he desired no other superior. At that time strong pressure was being exerted on Lincoln to change his Secretary of War. The commendation from the head of the Western armies undoubtedly strengthened Stanton's hold on his position.

Stanton now saw how far he could go without arousing Grant and did everything within his means to belittle the deeds of the victorious commander. In his report on the final operations of the war there is not one word in praise of the general-in-chief. He roughly asserted his superiority over Grant, and sent for him as he would for a lieutenant.[3] Apparently Grant could be bullied; there was nothing to fear from him.

Of the prominent military leaders only Sherman remained. Highly educated, grim-visaged and suspicious of all politicians, the leader of the march to the sea could not be easily pushed aside. But Stanton soon had an opportunity to sink his stiletto into him to the hilt. After this popular officer had proposed Lincoln's own peace terms to Johnston, Stanton, without the President's knowledge or consent, sent to the Press such an account of the general's course of action—including nine reasons why the agreement had been disapproved—that in many an editorial column Sherman was openly accused of treason. By ordering other generals to proceed against the Confederate army at once Stanton practically made sure of such an interpretation.

[1] W. E. Woodward, *Meet General Grant* (Horace Liveright, New York, 1926), p. 309.
[2] Grant, *Memoirs*, II, pp. 104–5; Badeau, op. cit., pp. 79, 80.
[3] Badeau, op. cit., p. 78.

Stanton even dared to suggest to the papers that Sherman had been bribed to make his peace terms and to let Jefferson Davis escape to Mexico or Europe.

'The orders of General Sherman to General Stoneman', his message read, 'to withdraw from Salisbury and join him will probably open the way for Davis to escape to Mexico or Europe with his plunder, which is reported to be very large, including not only the plunder of Richmond banks, but previous accumulations.'[1]

Lest this insinuation should be overlooked the Secretary of War quoted a telegram from Richmond which was still more offensive. Referring to Davis and his partisans, it intimated that 'they hope, it is said, to make terms with General Sherman or some other Southern Union commander, by which they will be permitted with their effects, including this gold plunder, to go to Mexico or Europe.'[2]

Sherman saw through these machinations, but was powerless. He charged Stanton with 'deadly malignity, and expressed the wish to 'see deeper into the diabolical plot . . .'. 'When you advised me of the assassin Clark being on my track,' he wrote, 'I little dreamed he would turn up in the direction and guise he did. . . .'[3] The distinguished general evidently recognized that in a political sense he had been thoroughly assassinated and disposed of.

Thus, with one blow, the idol of the western armies was vanquished by Stanton's artifices and was prevented from becoming a dangerous rival.

Meanwhile, four years of war had not only achieved the result for which Stanton had striven—the preparation of the North for a peace conforming to his own idea—but it had dulled the nation's sense of right and wrong.

'Men who had lived so long under the nervous strain of killing other men while trying to be gentle and chivalrous at the same time finally gave it up as a bad job,' writes Woodward in his book *Meet General Grant*. 'Hard, animal-like streaks are

[1] Gorham, op. cit., II, p. 187.
[2] Ibid.
[3] *Official Records*, I, 47, part 3, p. 454; see also pp. 220, 221.

beginning to appear in his [Grant's] nature,' he continued. 'He has visibly coarsened in fiber.'[1]

So had every one else. Human lives had ceased to mean what they had meant in times of peace. Grant left 30,000 Northern prisoners to die in the camp of Andersonville, although the Confederates were willing to release them unconditionally if steamers would be sent to Southern ports to remove them. Stanton did not disapprove of Grant's pitiless attitude. He and Seward had thrown thousands of prisoners of their own into cells, and it did not seem to hurt their consciences. The principle of *malice toward none, charity for all* afforded small consolation to the unfortunates, estimated at 38,000, who languished in cells for political reasons only, and were kept there without charges and without recourse to court, *habeas corpus* having been suspended by executive proclamation. Stanton's biographer even boasts that 'the number of arrests made under his [Stanton's] so-called "arbitrary" authority during the war, including deserters and bounty-jumpers, reached nearly two hundred and sixty thousand'.[2]

As the war drew to a close Stanton seemed about to reach the zenith of his career; with Chase safely seated on the bench of the Supreme Court and with Grant cowed, the War Minister was second only to Lincoln in public acclaim. Aside from the Chief Executive he recognized no authority higher than his own. According to a lifelong friend, he was 'drunk with the lust of power' and 'fairly rioted in its enjoyment'.[3]

The attorney-general, aroused to impotent indignation by the War Lord's constant encroachments on his own field, expressed the opinion that Lincoln himself was being awed into passive submission. 'I have never interfered', he declared, 'with military seisures for mere military purposes; but I feel it to be my duty to denounce, if I cannot prevent, the frequent instances of needless, groundless and wanton interference of the military, in matters which in no wise concern them, as if the object were to contemn and degrade the civil power. . . . The President's opinions (known and published) are against these arbitrary proceedings, and yet they are boldly practiced. . . . I fear he has to

[1] Woodward, op. cit., p. 342.
[2] Flower, op. cit., p. 133.
[3] Piatt, op. cit., p. 79.

say, in his heart, like King David—"These sons [of] Zeruiah be too hard for me!" '[1]

Was Lincoln afraid of Stanton?

At least one man thought so—John A. Kasson, an Iowa congressman, who later became Minister to Austria. In a chapter contributed to Allen T. Rice's *Reminiscences of Abraham Lincoln*, he used the sub-title, *Lincoln Afraid of Stanton* and justified it by narrating a singular experience.

Kasson had obtained from the President an order for the promotion of an officer; when he took it to Stanton he was brutally insulted, and the execution of the order was refused.

'A few days later . . .' Kasson wrote, 'I reported the affair to the President. A look of vexation came over his face, and he seemed unwilling then to talk of it. . . .'

Shortly after this Lincoln gave Kasson another order and requested him to take it to the War Department. This the Iowan declined to do. ' "Oh," said the President, "Stanton has gone to Fortress Monroe and Dana is acting. . . ." This he said with a manner of relief. . . .'

Kasson soon found an opportunity for revenge. Walking into the House one day he heard Thaddeus Stevens on the floor defending the Secretary of War, who was charged with having confined innocent men in the Old Capitol Prison.

'As soon as Mr. Stevens had finished,' Kasson wrote, '. . . I let loose my denunciations of his [Stanton's] willful and arbitrary action. . . . In three minutes every newspaper and every pen . . . was laid aside. . . . The vote was soon taken, and . . . only six votes were given on the Secretary's side, to one hundred and twenty-five for the resolution. . . .

'The next time I saw Mr. Lincoln, I remember well his change of manner to me. He showed his gratification in his peculiar and familiar manner, by his twinkling eyes, and by his slapping me on the thigh, as I thought quite unnecessarily.'[2]

There was one fly in the ointment, however, from Stanton's

---

[1] Edward Bates, *Diary*, p. 350.
[2] A. T. Rice (Ed.), *Reminiscences of Abraham Lincoln by Distinguished Men of His Time*, pp. 381–4.

point of view. He was not sure that Lincoln would keep him in
the Cabinet when the combat was ended. The War Minister
therefore decided on an adroit move to force the issue. As soon
as the President returned from Richmond Stanton offered his
resignation. There was not the slightest chance that Lincoln
would accept it at this moment of triumph, and Stanton knew
it. But he put the President into a position where, in order to
be consistent, he would have to put up with his Secretary of
War for a while longer, even after sober thoughts had replaced
his first overwhelming joy.

During August of the preceding year it had been rumoured
that Stanton was going to relinquish his position. These reports
were contemptuously dismissed by the Secretary of the Navy.
'If Stanton ever, at any time or under any circumstances, has
spoken in whisper to the President of resigning, he did not mean
it,' he commented, 'for he would be, I think, one of the very
last to quit, and never except on compulsion.'[1] Later events were
to prove how right Welles was and how much compulsion it
took to make the War Minister vacate his place.

Temporarily, Stanton was safe; under his clever management
the future could be trusted to take care of itself. The elections
of 1868 were still far off—but who would then be more available
than the outstanding chieftain of the war?

There is little doubt that Stanton would have brushed Lincoln
aside if he had thought it possible to do so. He once told Welles
that he was under no particular obligation to the President, who
had called him to a difficult position and had imposed labours
and responsibilities on him such as no man could carry. The
obligation, he said, was the other way.[2] It was not gratitude
which kept Stanton the faithful servant of the President, but
prudence. Chase, popular with many politicians, had tried to
replace Lincoln; McClellan had done the same; both had failed.
Lincoln evidently had the voters on his side. It was still safer
to work with him than against him.

When Chase began to aspire to the presidency Attorney-
General Bates thought that Stanton was preparing for the even-

[1] Welles, *Diary*, II, p. 102.
[2] Ibid, I, pp. 98, 149.

tuality of Chase's election; for he saw fit to make a pungent entry in his diary on 9 March, 1864.

'If the President had a little more *vim*, he would either control or discharge Mr. S[tanton]. If I were in his place, I would never submit to have the whole influence of the two most powerful Departments, Treasury and War, brought to bear upon the election—against the Pres. and for the aspiring Secretary.'[1]

Later on in the summer, when the outlook for the Northern cause was more dismal than ever, the opposition Press did not hesitate to put into plain words that it suspected more than mere incompetence in high places. 'The people are demanding of the administration to recall McClellan', wrote the *New York Herald* on 5 August 1864, 'that the country in its trying hour may have the benefit of his superior skill and genius. This demand is so strong that even the radical journals like the *Post* and the *Commercial* join in the cry. Mr. Lincoln must not think from this that the public will be satisfied in placing him in command while he retains Stanton in the War Department to interfere and upset all his plans and defeat his efforts to crush out the rebellion. The only hope for Old Abe is in the immediate removal of all such Marplots as Stanton and Halleck, and in giving McClellan a command commensurate with his ability and skill. Has Mr. Lincoln patriotism enough left to do this?'

It was then that Stanton did something that gave some observers the impression that he was beginning personal negotiations with the Southern leaders, somewhat along the lines he had followed when he had established contact with prominent Republicans while still a member of Buchanan's Cabinet. The *New York Herald* of 19 August 1864 reported sneeringly that Judge Black (Stanton's sponsor and former law partner), Jake Thompson (Jefferson Davis's chief agent in Canada), and General Hooker were all stopping at hotels in Niagara Falls and wondered whether Stanton had upset the peace negotiations of Horace Greeley with the Southern commissioners in order to initiate his own. 'The alarm and fear that have taken possession of Old Abe have given rise to the rumour that Judge Black came with the permission of Secretary Stanton,' wrote a Niagara Falls correspondent.

Stanton, in the opinion of some contemporary critics, would

[1] Bates, *Diary*, p. 343.

not have hesitated to go to considerable lengths in his secret parleys with the enemy. 'The Blairs charge Stanton with infidelity to party and to country,' wrote Welles in July 1863, 'from mere selfish considerations, and with being by nature treacherous. . . . Were any overwhelming adversity to befall the country, they look upon him as ready to betray it.'[1]

Unquestionably Judge Black did make the journey to Canada with Stanton's consent. The former had mentioned accidentally that he was going; whereupon the War Minister 'instantly and very unequivocally' expressed his wish that the visit should be consummated. 'You repeated it not less than three times,' wrote Black.[2]

Black's trip across the Canadian border did not remain unnoticed. It seemed to be the understanding among the exiled Confederates that Stanton was bargaining for his personal safety in case of defeat; the Reverend Robinson wrote as follows:

'Why what will you think . . . when I tell you that I saw, myself, in intimate association, here [in Toronto,] with Messrs. Thompson and Cleary, and elsewhere with Messrs. Clay and others, a distinguished jurist whom I understood to have come directly from Secretary Stanton himself, to consult, during the alarm about the prospective breakdown of the Republican party in August last, and his reported fears of personal violence to the Cabinet from the excited populace of the North?'[3]

There is no definite proof of treachery on Stanton's part in this episode. Black and Thompson were discussing an armistice, but just what the scheming Secretary of War had in mind there is no way of knowing. Lincoln's ticket was not given an even chance of winning at that time, and if the peace party had come into power in the November elections Stanton's downfall was inevitable. The bellicose little War Minister was reputed by Welles, and by others who knew him well, to be a physical coward, and it was rumoured in Washington that he always carried a stiletto in his shirt bosom. The Reverend Robinson's fear of violence on the part of an outraged people was probably shared by Stanton.

[1] Welles, *Diary*, I, p. 356.
[2] Brigance, op. cit., p. 129.
[3] Robinson, *Infamous Perjuries of the Bureau of Military Justice Exposed.*

The battle of Mobile and the fall of Atlanta changed the whole picture abruptly. The peace negotiations came to a sudden end, and Stanton felt insolently serene again.

Unexpectedly the blow fell. Lincoln was deserting his own party by taking steps to restore the Union on its old foundations. The South was to come in again and would vote the Republican party out of office—Lincoln, Stanton, Sumner, and all. If Stanton were to survive politically he would have to turn Democrat once more; but this was probably too big a task even for this skilful dissembler. The future, which had looked so bright, was suddenly shrouded with gloom.

It was then that Lincoln was shot.

Curious thoughts must have coursed through Stanton's mind as he watched the prostrate figure of his dying chief stretched diagonally across a boarding-house bed. This backwoods lawyer with the enormous muscular development that now was plainly visible on the naked body, had not proved so pliable after all. Without a college education, without natural refinement, he had undertaken to establish his authority over every one of his Cabinet members.

Mrs. Lincoln, frightened and distracted, had fallen to the floor in a faint. A sudden rage possessed Stanton. Brutally, he gave orders to take 'that woman' out of the room and not to let her come back.[1] The President was sinking; there was no purpose in still acting like a gentleman to his wife.

But there were other things to be done. Stanton summoned Vice-President Johnson, and sent him home again after a few moments because, as he claimed, his presence annoyed Mrs. Lincoln.[2] If Johnson were imprudent enough to leave, so much the worse for him. How pleasing it must have been to the War Minister to see every one taking orders from him. Even the Vice-President, on the verge of becoming Chief Executive, was acknowledging Stanton's superiority. Of course, Johnson, as war governor of Tennessee, had once been under the authority of the War Department. Perhaps Stanton's autocracy could be

[1] Lewis, op. cit., p. 60.
[2] Storey, 'Dickens, Stanton, etc.', in *Atlantic Monthly* (Apr. 1930), p.465.

made to outlast this night, and, if properly nursed, to perpetuate itself. It was a dream worth dreaming.

'In the back bedroom of Peterson's lodging-house', writes Lloyd Lewis, 'he [Stanton] took charge of the Republic. Through the war this "mad incorruptible" had believed himself to be the real ruler of the nation, guiding with his superior brain the weaker, softer will of Lincoln, and now his hour had come. He was dictator.'[1]

When Lincoln's death was announced Stanton did a queer thing; he slowly, and with apparent deliberation, straightened out his right arm, placed his hat for an instant on his head, and then as deliberately returned it to its original position. To some of those present it must have appeared as if Stanton were crowning himself King of America.[2]

As Stanton surveyed the situation on the morning of Lincoln's death, his triumph seemed complete. The South was conquered and completely at the mercy of the President, as Congress was not in session. Seward was confined to his bed in what was thought to be a critical condition. Grant was under the thumb of the War Department. The President could be depended upon to be stern and uncompromising—and to take orders from his Secretary of War. Besides, as long as Johnson lived, he would walk under the shadow of his great blunder on the day of his inauguration. There was no apparent reason why Stanton could not remain what he had been during the night of 14 April— *de facto* President of the United States.

To demonstrate his affection for the dead President, and incidentally his power, the War Minister ordered the closing of the playhouse in which the assassination had taken place. There was no legal justification whatsoever for this act. 'Nothing could be more despotic,' opined Browning, 'and yet in this *free* Country Mr. Ford is utterly helpless, and without the means of redress.'[3]

'I see by the papers', one reads in the diary of the former attorney-general, 'that the Sec of War has, by his simple fiat, prevented the opening of Fords Theatre. . . . After that, what

[1] Lewis, op. cit., p. 57.
[2] Flower, op. cit., footnote, p. 283; also Lewis, op. cit., p. 60.
[3] Browning, *Diary*, II, p. 38.

may he not do? What is to hinder him from transferring estates from one man to another, annulling land titles and dissolving the tie of marriage?'[1]

There is no denying that Lincoln's death held out a great promise for Stanton.

At the same time it must have occurred to the War Minister that here was an opportunity to link himself dramatically to the unforgettable moment of Lincoln's death. From out of nowhere emerged the pathetic words which the austere secretary was reported to have uttered when it was announced that the end had come:

Now he belongs to the Ages.

A beautiful epilogue. What a pity it probably never was spoken.[2]

As time passed, and the supposedly pliant Johnson followed more and more in Lincoln's footsteps, Stanton's hopes for a continued dictatorship slowly dwindled. Johnson actually grew more self-willed than Lincoln had ever been. He made every effort to restore the South to its place in the Union, and since Congress was adjourned, was making rapid headway toward peace and harmony.

The Radicals were furious, but impotent. Until the legislative bodies of Washington would convene nothing could be done to stop the President. When at last the thirty-ninth session opened in December 1865 Thaddeus Stevens of the House, the bitterest of them all, organized a steering committee of fifteen which was created for only one purpose—to prevent representatives from the South from occupying their seats in the congressional halls. It was a revolutionary measure, desperate, unprecedented, but effective. Against the solid wall of iniquity presented by the Radicals in both Houses, all of Johnson's appeals and arguments were shattered into fragments. To the victors belonged the spoils, and the Radicals would not yield one jot or one tittle, the Constitution of the United States notwithstanding.

All of this Stanton watched with an ever scheming brain. 'The Secretary of War', wrote Milton, 'was reckless in his con-

[1] Bates, *Diary*, p. 491.
[2] See supplementary note to chapter xxix, 'Now He Belongs to the Ages'.

duct toward the President. From the day of Johnson's accession, he kept him surrounded by detectives and spies and made the most of his espionage. Whatever the President said to a White House confidant, would probably be carried straightway to Stanton, who continually betrayed the measures and purposes of the President to the Radicals and concocted schemes against the Administration with them.'[1]

As yet, there was no telling whether the President or Congress would prove more powerful in the end. It was good policy, therefore, to hunt with the hounds and run with the hares, and that is what Stanton set out to do. Again he sat in the inner councils of a President, and again he whispered all he heard and learned to the President's implacable enemies.

'Stanton contrived' [Welles remarked] 'to have the President surrounded most of the time by his detectives, or men connected with the military service who are creatures of the War Department. Of course, much that was said to the President in friendly confidence went directly to Stanton. In this way a constant espionage was maintained on all that transpired at the White House. Stanton, in all this time had his confidants among the Radicals—opponents of the President—in Congress,—a circle to whom he betrayed the measures and purposes of the President and with whom he concocted schemes to defeat the measures and policy of the Administration.'[2]

There is one thing that Stanton probably foresaw before others were cognizant of it. If the President and Congress should remain at loggerheads for any length of time, the country was bound to drift toward anarchy.

During all this confusion, when old standards were crumbling, the army remained the one bulwark of safety. Whoever controlled the army would control the country. Hence, Stanton determined to control the army.

The first move of the Radicals was to pass what was known as the Freedmen's Bureau Bill. Originally the Freedmen's Bureau had been created in March 1865 for the purpose of supervising the hordes of negroes who had been liberated through the advance of the Federal troops. It had been conceived merely as a

[1] Milton, op. cit., p. 276.
[2] Welles, *Diary*, II, pp. 403, 404, footnote.

temporary stopgap until these former slaves could find a place where they would be able to take care of themselves. The new bill, designed to meet political exigencies, contemplated an extension of rights to the negroes. Any offence against its provisions was subject to punishment not by the court but by army officers, for the agents of the Freedmen's Bureau were to work under the regulations of the War Department. Thus what Welles called a 'terrific engine' was to be placed into the hands of Stanton. Johnson vetoed the bill, and the attempt of the Radicals to increase the power of the military arm of the Government was defeated for the moment. In spite of the presidential opposition, a new and still more stringent bill was soon drawn up, however, and became a law over Johnson's veto. The power of the War Minister was beginning to grow.[1]

Soon Stanton's strength was further augmented. How cleverly this was brought about has become known through the autobiography of Congressman Boutwell, who was the secretary's dupe in this cabal. It is a queer story.

'When I arrived in Washington [he wrote] to attend the meeting of Congress at the December session, 1866, I received a note from Mr. Stanton asking me to meet him at the War Office with as little delay as might be practicable. When I called at the War Office, he beckoned me to retire to his private room, where he soon met me. He then said that he had been more disturbed by the condition of affairs in the preceding weeks and months than he had been at any time during the war. He gave me to understand that orders had been issued to the army of which neither he nor General Grant had any knowledge.'[2]

Stanton never told his visitor what these orders were or who had issued them. This is deplorable, for the records fail to confirm the accusation, and Grant registered no such complaint, nor did he ever refer to the matter in any way.

'He [Stanton] then said [so Boutwell continued] that he thought it necessary that some act should be passed by which the power of the President might be limited. Under his dictation, and after such consultation as seemed to be required, I drafted

---

[1] Milton, op. cit., pp. 285–7, 288, 316.
[2] Boutwell, op. cit., II, pp. 107, 108.

amendments to the Appropriation Bill for the Support of the Army, which contained the following provisions: The head-quarters of the General of the Army were fixed at Washington, where he was to remain unless transferred to duty elsewhere by his own consent or by the consent of the Senate. Next, it was made a misdemeanor for the President to transmit orders to any officer of the army except through the General of the Army.'[1]

This outrageous proposal, it should be noted, was attached to the Army Appropriation Bill, making it impossible for Johnson to veto it without arousing violent antagonism on the part of every one connected in any way with the military service.'[2]

One might easily call this manœuvre the 'Perfect Intrigue of the Age'. Unknown to his chief, Stanton summoned an important legislator and, assuming his favourite air of anxiety and dread, literally dictated to him a bill which took from the President an important part of his constitutional power. Johnson was not to be permitted to transfer General Grant, whom Stanton controlled, nor could he evade Grant by giving orders to other generals directly. In plain words, Stanton withdrew the army from the authority of the President, its Commander-in-Chief and, using Grant as a pawn, made himself master of the military branch of the Government.

All this time Johnson's friends kept counselling him against retaining Stanton in his Cabinet. The Philadelphia Convention, meeting in August 1866, was 'strong and emphatic' in its opinion that the Secretary of War should be dismissed. A meeting of ex-service men convened in Cleveland and, a month later, presented to Johnson a round-robin letter, signed by such men as Generals Wool, Granger, Rousseau, Thomas Ewing, and McCook, reciting that 'in discharge of a duty which we owe to you, to the country and to ourselves, we beg leave to say that the Honorable E. M. Stanton, Secretary of War, does not possess the confidence politically or otherwise of any considerable numbe

[1] Boutwell, op. cit., II, p. 108.
[2] Milton, op. cit., pp. 378 ff.; also Lloyd Paul Stryker, *Andrew Johnson, A Study in Courage* (The Macmillan Co., New York, 1930), p. 457 *et al.*

of your friends . . . and that his continuation in that position greatly tends to weaken your administration'.[1]

Gideon Welles had already warned the President in June of Stanton's duplicity, but had accomplished nothing. On the fourteenth of that month the diary of the Secretary of the Navy was enriched by the following entry:

'He [the President] still leans on Seward and seems under his influence, though with doubts and occasional misgivings. Seward himself defers to Stanton,—is becoming afraid of him.' Why was Seward afraid of Stanton? What was it, to use the vernacular, that Stanton 'had' on Seward—if anything? 'That Seward is cheated I cannot believe,' proceeded Welles, 'and if he is not cheated I am constrained to believe the President is. And who is to undeceive him? I have on more than one occasion suggested my doubts, but while he has received my suggestions attentively he has pondered in obvious distress. . . .'[2]

What was it that distressed Johnson? What prevented him from asking for Stanton's resignation?

'The country could not understand why Johnson did not discharge the faithless Secretary [comments Milton in *The Age of Hate*]. Radicals were as amazed as Conservatives . . . Doolittle [senator from Wisconsin] wrote the venerable Francis Preston Blair of a rumor so damnable that Blair sat down immediately to present it to the President, to force the latter to act.

' "For six long months," Doolittle had written, "I have been urging the President to call on Grant temporarily to do the duties [of the] War Department. . . ."

'But Stanton remains, and so the report has spread all over the State, that there is something sinister. It started through the Milwaukee *Sentinel* printing the letter of a correspondent from Washington, which says that Stanton is not removed because it is rumored and believed that Stanton has testimony to show that Mr. Johnson was privy to Lincoln's assassination. . . .'[3]

But in spite of all pleas, Johnson stood pat, and Stanton stayed on. The ugly rumour did not 'force the . . . [President] to act', as his friends had hoped.

---

[1] Milton, op. cit., p. 356.   [2] Welles, *Diary*, II, p. 527.
[3] Milton, op. cit., p. 356.

One of Stanton's prettiest intrigues occurred in the beginning of the year 1867. On 8 January, Congress called on the President for any facts which had come to his knowledge regarding failures to enforce the Civil Rights Bill. This resolution bore all the earmarks of a Radical plot designed to embarrass Johnson; nevertheless, the matter was put before the Cabinet for consideration. Stanton suggested that the head of each department give his statements separately. All the secretaries penned their replies without an hour's delay—all except the War Minister. He did not bring in his answer for a month, and then it was a strange and equivocal document.[1]

Stanton produced a report which he had obtained from General Grant and which included a singular paper from General Howard. The latter cited 440 cases of negro murders and quarrels wholly irrelevant and unreliable. 'McCulloch and Stanberry', wrote Welles, 'each remarked to me before we left that here was design and intrigue in concert with the Radical conspirators at the Capitol. Stanton betrayed his knowledge and participation in it, for ... he could not conceal his part.... He had delayed his answer until Howard ... could hunt up all the rumors of ... malignity, and pass them, through General Grant, on to the President. It would help generate difference between the President and the General, and, if sent out to the country ... would be used ... to injure the President and, perhaps, Grant also.'[2] Again Stanton contemplated harming, with one shrewd move, the only two persons who stood in the path of his own advancement.

On 16 February, Welles had a conversation about this affair with Secretary Browning, who expressed his amazement at Stanton's course, saying that he was forced to believe 'there was design and villainy, if not absolute treachery, at the bottom'.

'It was with reluctance he came to this conclusion,' remarked Welles, 'but it was impossible to do otherwise.'[3]

'It was a mean, malicious thing,' the diary of Browning reads, 'intended to compel the President, for the benefit of radical partizans, to send out to the country ... these prejudiced and in many instances false ... statements, or place himself ... in a

[1] Welles, *Diary*, III, p. 42; Milton, op. cit., pp. 386–7.
[2] Welles, *Diary*, III, p. 44.
[3] Ibid., III, p. 45.

position where they could falsely, but plausibly charge him with the suppression of facts. . . .

'Stanton was very persistent, and manifestly wanted to do the President an injury. . . . He has no sincerity of character, but is hypocritical and malicious.'[1]

Then the Secretary of the Navy decided to call on the President.

'I told him that it was with reluctance I was compelled to express an unfavorable opinion of a colleague. . . . I adverted to the occurrences of yesterday and told him . . . that it was intended the statement of reported murders should go abroad under his name . . . and spread before the country . . . establishing military governments over the Southern States. . . . That report was to be the justification for the act . . . and Radical Congressmen were acting in concert with the Secretary of War. . . . I said . . . *that gradually the Administration was coming under the War Department.*

'The President listened and assented. . . .'[2]

While all this storm was raging around him Stanton calmly continued to build up his war machine. On 13 February 1867 the so-called Reconstruction Bill passed the House. It embodied Stanton's plan to dissolve the Southern states and to divide them into military districts, much along the lines he had advocated, with such indifferent success, at Lincoln's last Cabinet meeting. The former Confederacy, according to the House bill, was to be put under the most arbitrary rule of the soldiery. Military governors with unlimited power were to be appointed, not by the President, but by the general of the army—in other words, by Grant. Behind Grant lurked the figure of the War Minister. The Senate, however, restored to the Chief Executive the right to select the military governors, and it was in this form, probably to Stanton's great disappointment, that the bill finally passed Congress and was laid before the Cabinet on 22 February. Not a single member, with the significant exception of Stanton, advised the President to approve the bill. A few days later Welles called at the White House and Johnson referred to the pitiful exhibition the Secretary of War had made of himself.[3]

[1] Browning, *Diary*, II, p. 130.
[2] Welles, *Diary*, III, pp. 45, 46. Author's italics.
[3] Milton, op. cit., pp. 387–8; Stryker, op. cit., p. 447.

'The President', said Welles in his diary on 25 February, 'wondered if he [Stanton] supposed he was not understood. The sparkle of the President's eyes and his whole manner betokened intense though suppressed feeling.'[1]

But Stanton remained.

Johnson immediately vetoed the Reconstruction measure. He pointed out that it gave the military commanders of the districts as much power as absolute despots, their mere whims being enough to take the place of the law. Of course, this was exactly what the Radicals wanted, and Stanton was more than anxious to be the recipient of this added authority. He now had reached a position where, through the armed forces of the country, he could wield an influence never before vested in any individual.

The only disturbing thought to trouble him must have been the ever-widening breach between the President and himself. If Johnson should finally decide to dismiss him, his political fortune would be greatly endangered. This situation had to be met, and it was met squarely.

At the same time the Reconstruction Bill was under consideration, the Tenure-of-Office Bill was concocted by the Radicals, if not by Stanton himself. For the new measure was admittedly designed to make secure his position as a spy in Johnson's Cabinet. It robbed the President of his constitutional right to remove appointed officials without the express consent of the Senate. The Tenure-of-Office Bill passed Congress simultaneously with the Reconstruction Act, and both were enacted over the President's veto. Again Stanton was apparently backing Johnson and was more emphatic and earnest in the expression of his objections than was any member of the Cabinet. Thereupon Johnson quickly turned on his Secretary of War and asked him to write the veto. But Stanton was not so easily cornered; he declined, claiming that he could not do it because of rheumatism in his arm.[2] Even his enemies must have chuckled at this naïve but efficacious retort.

For reasons difficult to explain Johnson left the appointment of the district commanders in the South to Stanton. A series of

[1] Welles, *Diary*, III, p. 49.
[2] Browning, *Diary*, II, p. 132.

disgraceful episodes followed, in which Stanton's men displayed
an insolence that bordered on insubordination. Finally McCulloch, Secretary of the Treasury, accused Johnson, face to face,
with having 'retained in his Cabinet a man "notoriously opposed
to his Administration . . . who from the beginning had been an
embarrassment . . ." ' yet who had been allowed ' "a controlling
voice and often was the only person consulted" '. The selection
of the military commanders, in particular, on which so much
depended, had been made without advice from any member of
the Cabinet except the 'false and unfaithful one'. Johnson listened
to this reproof and agreed that the Secretary of the Treasury
was right; but, remarked Welles, having 'commenced in error,
he will be likely under the same influence to continue in weakness. . . .' Seward and Randall were weak, Welles thought, but
Stanton was wicked.[1]

'I have no doubt that most of these offensive measures have
emanated from the War Department,' Johnson once said to
Welles.

'Not only that,' replied the secretary, 'but almost all the
officers of the Army have been insidiously alienated. . . .' And
then he ventured to say that all of Lincoln's Cabinet officers
should have been removed—'certainly some who have made it
a business to thwart and defeat your measures. . . .'

'He assented', Welles chronicled in his diary, 'with some
emotion, to the last remark, but expressed a doubt whether he
could have got rid of Stanton.'

Is it surprising that the country wondered then, as the historian wonders to-day, what the bonds were that tied Johnson's
hands and bound him to Stanton, whom he hated and despised
and who had the unheard of effrontery to double-cross the
President before his very eyes?

Johnson told Welles that he presumed his Secretary of War
intended to be a candidate for the presidency. The discovery
came too late; Welles was frankly of the opinion that nothing
mattered any more. 'I remarked . . . [that] he [Stanton] had so
managed with the Radicals as to cripple the Administration until
it was powerless. . . . The President assented. . . .'[2]

Johnson by this time was hopelessly shackled. He could not

[1] Milton, op. cit., pp. 439–40; Welles, *Diary*, III, p. 91.
[2] Welles, *Diary*, III, pp. 123, 155.

force Stanton out without incurring the danger of impeachment. But an impeachment was what Stanton hoped for; it would make him practically dictator of the nation. There being no Vice-President in line for succession, the duty of the Executive would devolve upon Ben Wade, president of the Senate, a man who was not made of presidential timbre and who would lean heavily on his Secretary of War. The South was already in Stanton's grasp; domination over the North was at last attainable. The prospects of the War Minister had never been so bright.

There was no reason now why Stanton should any longer pose as a friend of the President. On 21 June the Cabinet met to endorse certain interpretations of the Reconstruction Act, drawn up by the attorney-general for the purpose of mitigating its severity. Johnson asked each member in turn whether he was agreeable to the proposed orders, and all were in harmony with their chief and endorsed his lenient views—but not Stanton; he answered in the negative every time.[1] The mask had at last been discarded. Stanton stood in open opposition to the President; yet he would not resign. At this open insult, Johnson finally rebelled; if Grant would accept the position of Secretary of War, Stanton must go.

But it soon became clear to Johnson how helpless he was. Stanton's removal could not have been effected against his own will without the consent of the Senate. Grant expressed his views on the matter with great frankness. ' "It certainly was the intention of the legislative branch of the Government to place Cabinet Members beyond the power of executive removal. . . ." And, being at this time still untutored in the ways of politicians, he added brusquely that, ' "it is pretty well understood . . . it was intended specially to protect the Secretary of War" '.[2]

Then a spectre from the past arose to bring an intolerable situation to its long-delayed climax.

On the day that Grant wrote his candid letter to the Commander-in-Chief the junior counsel for the defence was addressing the jury at the trial of Mrs. Surratt's son in Washington. In the course of his speech he made a contemptuous reference

[1] Milton, op. cit., p. 443.
[2] Ibid., p. 450.

425

to the petition for mercy which had been attached to the sentence of that unfortunate woman, now dead more than two years. The President, learning apparently from the papers that such a document existed, sent to the War Office for the findings of the court-martial. This was on 5 August 1867. Before nightfall he discharged Stanton by sending him a curt note:

Sir: Public considerations of a high character constrain me to say that your resignation as Secretary of War will be accepted.

ANDREW JOHNSON
President of the United States.[1]

No one knows whether it was the discovery of the deceit he thought had been practised against him two years before that finally made Johnson take this decisive step. Of course, it was decisive only in forcing the existing breach into the open. For Stanton insolently replied that he would not resign, thus publicly defying the authority of the President.

The immediate consequence of Johnson's action was his impeachment by Congress. This was what Stanton had been playing for. It was a game for big stakes. If Johnson should be found guilty, the War Minister would be the strongest man in the country; and the elections of 1868 were only a little over a year away.

Destiny, however, willed it otherwise. One single senator stood between Stanton and the fulfilment of his dreams. By a vote of thirty-five to eighteen Johnson escaped impeachment. With the announcement of the result, Stanton collapsed. He relinquished his hold on the War Department where he had held forth for months behind barricades and an army of sentinels. His health began to fail. Out of the confusion and strife, it was Grant and not he who had emerged as the man to head the Republican ticket at the next election.

Nothing illustrates Stanton's character better than two episodes in his relationship with General Grant.

On 14 January 1868 Grant relinquished the office of Secretary of War, which he had held temporarily, and Stanton immedi-

[1] DeWitt, *Impeachment*, p. 276.

ately resumed his former position. 'With customary incivility', wrote Coolidge, 'almost his first act was to send a messenger to Grant's office with word that he "wanted to see him". Had it not been before the days of electricity, he would no doubt have pressed a buzzer. . . .'[1]

But four months later Grant was nominated for President. 'Stanton carried him the news,' we are informed by Badeau. 'I was with Grant . . . when the Secretary of War entered the room. . . . this time he did not send for Grant. He came hurriedly up the stairs panting for breath lest some one should precede him . . . and as he rushed in he exclaimed: "General! I have come to tell you that you have been nominated . . . for President of the United States".'[2]

During the campaign of 1868 Stanton once more fought for a position near the top. Speaking in his own city, Steubenville, in favour of Grant as a presidential candidate, he maintained that the general's 'capacity and integrity for civil administration were equally manifest in the vast territory in which he operated.' In Cleveland, Philadelphia, and other places he lauded the Republican candidate in a similar strain.[3]

Grant was elected, but Stanton again was thwarted in his expectations; there was no seat provided for him in the Cabinet. Thereupon he turned against his former general-in-chief with the same venom that he had shown toward Lincoln when the latter had been tardy in recognizing him. Stanton's state of health would not have permitted him to assume the strenuous duties of a secretary, but he did entertain strong hopes of being appointed Judge of the Supreme Court. Day followed day, however, and the sick man heard nothing encouraging. It is then that he struck at the new President. When Senator Sumner called on him in the fall of 1869 Stanton announced to him in a solemn voice that he had something important to say to his visitor. 'I know General Grant better than any other person in the country can know him,' he stated. 'It was my duty to study him, and I did so day and night, when I saw him and when I did not see

---

[1] Coolidge, op. cit., pp. 259, 260.
[2] Badeau, op. cit., p. 144.
[3] DeWitt, *Impeachment*, p. 592.

him, and now I tell you what I know, *he cannot govern this country*.'[1]

It is illuminating to hear from Stanton's own lips that he had given such keen attention to the character of his erstwhile general and that the opinion he had formed was most unfavourable. Sumner, in the speech on the floor of the Senate, in 1872, when he made these revelations, stated that he had always known of Stanton's low estimate of the general's capacity, but that he was astounded at the intensity of the ex-secretary's manner. Finally Sumner had said to his sick host, 'But you took part in the Presidential election, and made a succession of speeches for him in Ohio and Pennsylvania.' 'I spoke,' had been the reply, 'but I never introduced the name of General Grant. I spoke for the Republican Party and the Republican cause.'[2]

The political world, with Stanton's eulogies of Grant fresh in its memory, listened to this report with bated breath and incredulous ears. At last, Senator Carpenter, one of Stanton's staunchest friends—the man who had finally secured his appointment to the Supreme Court bench—broke the silence. 'If Mr. Stanton made that declaration to the Senator from Massachusetts', he asserted, 'under the circumstances detailed by him, if there is a word of substantial truth in that whole paragraph ... then Mr. Stanton was the most double-faced and dishonest man that ever lived.'[3]

A few months before, Stanton's former law partner and protector, Judge Black, after reading Wilson's disclosures of how Stanton had betrayed Buchanan in 1861, had uttered practically the same opinion: 'Surely if these things are true, he was the most marvellous impostor that ever lived or died.'[4]

The story of Stanton, as presented in the foregoing paragraphs, is not based entirely on tangible evidence, but is of necessity strongly interwoven with presumed motives that cannot be known with certainty. Historians must perhaps be

---

[1] De Witt, *Impeachment*, p. 594.

[2] Ibid., p. 595.

[3] Ibid.

[4] Ibid. (quoted from *Galaxy Magazine*, vol. IX, 1870—'Senator Wilson and Edwin M. Stanton').

allowed leeway in interpreting the characters of the men they portray; in most cases they go too far. No lover of truth will contend that he knows positively what he himself may do under given circumstances, and it is preposterous to assume such definiteness in regard to others. If students would indulge more in fact-finding and less in speculation, history would be greatly benefited. Research should be undertaken with a microscope, not with a brief case. If, nevertheless, an attempt has been made here, to sketch Stanton in the light in which an intimate study of the man's activities seem to reveal him, such a picture must be viewed with caution and should be subjected to the closest analysis before it is accepted.

Tracing farther the thread of duplicity that winds itself through Stanton's life, the possibility that he may have been involved in the plot to assassinate Lincoln is at least worthy of discussion. A hypothetical indictment against him could be built up on the following points:

It was to his advantage to have the President out of the way; it would mean a continuance in office, increased power over a new and supposedly weak Chief Executive and a fair prospect of replacing the latter at the next election. Politically speaking, Lincoln's elimination would render harsh treatment of the conquered South certain—at least, Johnson was committed to that course—and insure the dominance of the Republican Party and a more influential role for the friends and sponsors of the War Minister.

As Secretary of War Stanton failed in his duty to protect the President's life after he was convinced that there was danger in the air. He bluntly denied Lincoln's request to be protected by Major Eckert and did not provide a proper substitute.

It was probably due to the efforts of Stanton that all evidence of negligence on the part of John F. Parker was carefully suppressed.

Stanton took especial pains to remove Grant from the scene of the crime.

He directed the pursuit of Booth and allowed it to be conducted in a manner that, but for the assassin's accidental injury, would have allowed his escape.

He kept Booth's name from the public for three critical hours, and hampered the newspapers in divers ways instead of enlisting their aid in the capture of the assassins.

He diverted public suspicion to Southern leaders from the very beginning.

The War Department recalled Major O'Beirne when he reported his proximity to the fugitive murderer.

The actual pursuit and subsequent capture of Booth was reserved for Stanton's own trusted lieutenants; the assassin was not brought back alive.

All suspects known to have been intimate with Booth were silenced by unusual methods and were subsequently removed from contact with the public, either by infliction of the death penalty or by banishment to a desolate fortress. Other prisoners, of at least equal guilt, escaped punishment. The return of John Surratt was delayed; in fact, efforts were apparently made to prevent it altogether.

Actual contact between the War Minister and Booth could have been established through President Johnson who, it was said, knew the actor, and whose private secretary admitted such acquaintance.[1] Stanton had a singular hold over Johnson, who kept him in office for unknown reasons in spite of the War Minister's open treachery.

Plausible as such an indictment may seem, it would stand no chance of surviving a legal attack. There is not one point in this summary that can be proven; it is all hypothesis. Circumstantial evidence, at best, is a dangerous foundation upon which to build. When the accused, as in this case, has no opportunity to defend himself, the historian is forced to proceed with the utmost consideration.

If Stanton had kept a diary or left some notes, it would be possible, perhaps, to form a clearer picture of his devious ways. Without the existence of such documents a search for the truth is baffling. 'It is exceedingly unfortunate', wrote Flower, 'that Mr. Stanton kept no private letter-books and (purposely, as I believe,) left no material for the use of biographers. . . .'[2]

In view of all facts known at this time, an indictment against Stanton cannot be sustained for lack of material evidence.

[1] Pitman, op. cit., p. 70.
[2] Flower, op. cit., preface.

Conclusion

From the record submitted in this volume the story of Lincoln's assassination emerges in a state of confusion. Witnesses who have long since died may have taken with them valuable knowledge which they intentionally or unintentionally withheld during their lifetime. Senator Zachariah Chandler, for example, who, as a member of the committee on the conduct of the war, was deep in the confidence of the Civil War era, knew many things which he thought it unwise to divulge. 'The secret history of these exciting days,' one reads in his biography, 'teeming with incident and concealing many startling revelations, has yet been but sparingly written; it is doubtful if the veil will ever be more than slightly lifted. Mr. Chandler himself guarded scrupulously from public knowledge much that was well known to him and a few associates and would have shed light on the hidden springs of actions of vast moment. This class of information he treated as state secrets, whose perishing with the actors in the great drama was desirable for public reasons.' And Senator Wade, his colleague and friend, once said to a reporter who desired to write some inside history: 'There is no use in telling what we know unless we tell *the whole truth*, and if I tell the whole truth I shall blast too many reputations.'[1]

Was Attorney-General Bates right when he wrote in his diary that 'this assassination is not the act of *one man*; but only one scene of a great drama'?[2]

Historical evidence is largely circumstantial and therefore not wholly reliable; and historical writers themselves are human and cannot always divest themselves of their prejudices. Even

[1] *Life of Zachariah Chandler*, pp. 187, 188, 218.
[2] Bates, *Diary*, p. 473 (15 Apr. 1865).

people who helped shape great events have at times despaired. 'I don't believe the truth ever will be known,' wrote General Meade, 'and I have a great contempt for History.'[1]

A great deal of new evidence must be brought to light before students can write a definite answer to many questions that confront them in their research on Lincoln's death. Facts, facts, and more facts are needed and should be unearthed. In the meantime, hasty inferences are dangerous and may turn out to be unjust. Seemingly perfect nets of circumstantial evidence have at times been torn apart by a single contradictory but incontrovertible fact. Well-established theories have been shattered because they could not be brought into harmony with a single important new revelation, just as the discovery of radium has destroyed the belief of science in the indestructibility of the atom and changed its ideas on the transmutation of elements.

Pending future developments, the story of Lincoln's assassination remains, in many of its phases, an unsolved mystery.

[1] Bradford, *Union Portraits*, quotation page.

Supplementary Notes

Supplementary Notes : Contents

Contents

Supplementary Notes

CHAPTER III

THE ELUSIVENESS OF MR. PARKER

IN the standard books on Lincoln's assassination Parker is referred to as a 'messenger' by Laughlin and DeWitt, as an 'attendant' by Oldroyd, and as a 'servant' by Nicolay and Hay.

That Nicolay and Hay, in their biography of Lincoln, should emulate other historians in the haziness with which they treated the story of his bodyguard is incomprehensible. As members of the presidential household they certainly knew Forbes well and Parker at least slightly; hence it would have been highly desirable if they had referred to the latter by name and not as a 'servant'. There was no other person attending Lincoln who could be so described, as Forbes certainly was not the man whom Booth approached in the audience. Nicolay and Hay had, more than any one else, the opportunity to analyse Parker's behaviour. Why did they fail to do so?

A correspondent of the *Boston Globe* remarks in an article printed 16 April, 1905:

'That there was even an attendant sitting in the dress circle to watch the door that gave access to the box is by no means certain. If there was he must have let Booth in simply because he asked to go in . . . it seems incredible if there had been a better witness [than Captain McGowan] in the shape of the man who actually admitted the assassin to the box that he was not called on to testify.'

437

This question should have occurred to all intelligent newspaper writers of 1865, as well as to the leading detectives of the country. Parker was in Washington until 1868 and therefore easily accessible; it is inexplicable that no one approached him.

Crook, another of Lincoln's bodyguards, states that Parker should have been inside the box; his duty was to stand at the rear, 'fully armed, and to permit no unauthorized person to pass. . . .'

'. . . incredible as it may seem,' adds Crook, 'he [John Parker] quietly deserted his post of duty. . . . It was . . . through this guard's amazing recklessness—to use no stronger words— that Booth . . . accomplished his foul deed.'

He also avers that it was Forbes's duty to close the door of the carriage but fails to say where the footman was, or where he should have been, during the performance.

Why public curiosity was not sufficiently aroused to demand an investigation of Parker's delinquency is easy to understand. Most people were unaware of his existence; they did not know that for some time past their Executive had been protected by a special detail of men. Lincoln was opposed to a guard of any sort and was very sensitive on this subject. When the guards were selected in November 1864 the newspapers did not report it. These members of the police force wore civilian clothes and not uniforms; they walked with the President and not behind him; and their only weapons, Colt revolvers, would not have aroused the attention of a casual observer.

Townsend wrote in the *New York World* that the 'servant' in the President's box, as well as Major Rathbone, challenged the intruding stranger.

David E. Herold, in his statement made on board the monitor *Montauk* before Special Judge-Advocate John A. Bingham, on 27 April, said that Booth told him:

'There was a soldier or officer trying to prevent him from going into the box, and the thought struck him to draw a letter from his pocket and show it to the man, which he did. The man let him pass. He was so agitated at the time, that he fastened the door, he thinks. He advanced toward the President, with the letter in one hand and the pistol in the other.'

Oldroyd stated that, 'It has been said that before Booth went into the President's box he handed his card to an attendant of the President who was on guard, but this assertion is not supported by any testimony that was made public during the trial.' Oldroyd must have completely overlooked Captain McGowan's statement made on the witness stand, on 15 May, and recorded by Pitman on page 78 of his report.

Oldroyd also maintained that the doors to the President's box should have been locked, but that they were not on this occasion, 'and no one connected with the theatre could ever explain why they were left in that condition on that night'.

In this Oldroyd is mistaken. The locks had been out of order for several weeks and the apparent mystery was fully explained at the trial.

At the beginning of March 1865 practically all the members of the presidential guard, as well as other men on the roster of the Metropolitan Police Force, were threatened by the draft. Some of them, like Crook and Smith, had their cases fixed by Lincoln—the word 'fix' being the very expression the Chief Executive himself used on this occasion. Other guards were taken care of through Mrs. Lincoln's influence, although such a task scarcely lay within her province. It is understandable, however, that Mrs. Lincoln might have risen to the defence of her own household, of which these guards formed a part. The motive that prompted her to intervene in the case of two policemen who were outsiders and could hardly have been known to her—and of whose qualifications she knew nothing—is problematical.

Thomas Pendel related that, shortly before peace was proclaimed, he was asked by Alfonso Donn, a White House guard, to see Mrs. Lincoln in behalf of two relatives who wished to be exempted from service. Mrs. Lincoln signed the necessary documents and procured their freedom.

It is odd that Pendel did not disclose the identity of the two relatives, one of whom must have been Parker. He did mention Parker specifically in another part of his book. ' "John, are you prepared?" ' asked Pendel, 'I meant by this to ask if he had his revolver . . . ready to protect the President. . . .'

REFERENCES

John G. Nicolay and John Hay, 'Abraham Lincoln' in *Century Magazine* (January 1890), p. 434.

William H. Crook, *Memories of the White House*, pp. 41, 42; *Through Five Administrations*, pp. 4, 26.

George Alfred Townsend, *The Life, Crime, and Capture of John Wilkes Booth*, p. 7.

War Department Archives, Washington.

O. H. Oldroyd, *Assassination of Abraham Lincoln*, pp. 16, 17.

Benn Pitman, *The Assassination of President Lincoln*, p. 109.

Thomas Pendel, *Thirty-Six Years at the White House*, pp. 30, 40.

THE METROPOLITAN POLICE

The records of the Metropolitan Police Force during the first few years of its existence show a low morale among its officers. The force had been organized in September 1861 and numbered about 155 men at the time of Lincoln's assassination.

During the years 1861 to 1865 a total of 345 policemen were appointed, of whom no less than 140 were later dismissed.

Thirty-six of these were mustered out with two or more charges against them, while 104 were dismissed for the following reasons: twenty-three for violating rules and regulations, fifteen for intoxication, fourteen for neglect of duty, twelve for conduct unbecoming an officer, nine for general inefficiency. The remainder were guilty of disobedience, bribery, or maltreatment of prisoners. Only two of these men were honourably discharged, while four were physically disabled. Among those left nineteen were eventually promoted, 134 resigned, twenty-nine died, seven were pensioned, and the rest were dropped for various other reasons. But even of the nineteen men who were promoted, only five eventually were pensioned. Five others were reduced in rank, four were later dismissed, while the rest followed different lines of occupation. It must be stated, however, that of the 134 men who resigned eighteen did so to accept higher positions.

The percentage of worthy and unworthy men appointed to the police force did not change for the better in the first four years. Of the 173 men appointed in 1861 fifteen were promoted and fifty-two were dismissed. Of the fifty-two men appointed in 1862 one was promoted and seventeen were dismissed. Of the thirty-nine men appointed in 1863 one was promoted and twenty-two were dismissed, and of the fifty-eight men appointed in 1864 two were promoted and thirty-five were dismissed. Of the twenty-five men appointed in 1865, up to the month of April, fourteen were dismissed and none was promoted.

This compilation shows that the Government had more success in selecting the right type of men in 1861 than in later years when the war had thinned out the ranks of available recruits.

REFERENCE

Records of the Metropolitan Police Force, Washington, D.C.

CHAPTER IV

THE FORBES AFFIDAVIT

The following is Charles Forbes's sworn statement regarding his presence in the presidential box at Ford's Theatre on 14 April:

District of Columbia ss:—

On this 17th. day of September A.D. 1892 before me Anson S. Taylor, a Notary Public in and for the District aforesaid, personally appeared Charles Forbes, a resident of the City of Washington, District of Columbia, whose Post Office address is # 1711 "G" st. n.w., Washington, D.C., who being duly sworn declares and says as follows:—

I was the personal attendant of the late President Lincoln from shortly after his first inauguration up to the time when he fell by the assassin's bullet. Shortly after his death, when Mrs. Lincoln was packing her things preparatory to vacating the White House, she gave me the full suit of clothes which the President wore the night of the assassination together with other personal belongings of my friend and benefactor. I asked her, 'What shall I do with them?' she said, 'Do anything you like with them, don't let me see them again.' Mr. F. G. Logan of Chicago, Ill., is now the custodian and possessor of some of these articles, among them being the stock that he wore on the night of the 14th. day of April, 1865, the knife which he ordinarily carried in his pocket, the shawl which was his constant companion, both day and night, winter and summer, and which was the same one brought from Springfield with him, the cane which was made from the old Rebel Merrimac, and which he himself presented to me some time before his death, and the photograph of himself, which contained his last bit of writing in the shape of his autograph: Tad had given me the picture in the afternoon, and I still had it in my pocket when Mrs. Lincoln and her guests were ready to start for the theatre.

The President was engaged, and told them to go ahead and send the carriage back for him. I accompanied them to the theatre and returned in the carriage for the President. When the last visitor had departed and I had helped him on with his great coat, I remembered the picture and said 'Mr. President, Tad gave me a photograph this afternoon, and I wish you would put your name at the bottom of it.' 'Certainly, Charley' replied the President, and picking up a pen he wrote his name on the photograph, and that is the last writing he ever did, for I accompanied him in the carriage, was with him from the carriage to the box in the theatre, and was in the box when the assassin fired his fatal shot.

(Signed) CHARLES FORBES

Sworn to and subscribed before me,

(Signed) A. S. TAYLOR,
Notary Public

(Seal)

Reprinted by courtesy of Mr. Frank G. Logan and the Chicago Historical Society.

THE INACCURACIES OF NICOLAY AND HAY

The exactness of Nicolay and Hay in their account of the assassination is the more remarkable as Hay was at the White House when the news of the tragedy was brought there, and at Lincoln's bedside later on.

The two authors call Rathbone 'Major' on one page, and 'Colonel' on the next; they mention a 'servant' to whom Booth showed his card; they say the bullet lodged behind Lincoln's left eye instead of behind his right one, and their list of persons around the deathbed of the President is carelessly incomplete.

Nicolay and Hay also record that Lincoln went unattended most of the time and that his cavalry guard was installed toward the end of the war, all of which is erroneous.

According to these authors, Grant arrived in Washington on Friday morning, 14 April, instead of on Thursday the thirteenth. This is another glaring misstatement, for Grant spent Thursday evening with Secretary Stanton; his visit there was the subject of much discussion during the conspiracy trial and should not have escaped the attention of any conscientious historian.

REFERENCE

Nicolay and Hay, 'Abraham Lincoln' in *Century Magazine* (January 1890), pp. 428 ff.

CHAPTER V

THE STORY TOLD BY DAVID HOMER BATES

Bates, in his article in the *New York Independent* of 1895 and in his paper of 10 February 1900 made a curious statement which calls for an explanation:

'On the afternoon of Friday, 14 April 1865, the day of his assassination [so the statement reads], Mr. Lincoln made his accustomed call at the War Department telegraph office. He came earlier than usual . . . because, as we afterwards learned, of his expected visit in the evening to Ford's Theatre.

'Although I was on duty at the time I have no distinct remembrance of the occasion, for what occurred a few hours later was so appalling that memory retained nothing clearly, except that which took place after the awful news was received. . . .'

Of course, there may have been many reasons why Bates told his audience that his memory of Lincoln's last visit was hazy; but his neglect to mention the President's request for Eckert's company, on the face of things, seems to vitiate the detailed story related by this witness years afterward.

443

There may have been grounds, however, for his unwillingness to disclose at that time secrets that he was free to divulge later. Together with other cipher operators, he had followed Eckert into the employ of the Western Union Telegraph Company, of which Stanton's former confidant had been made president. Bates's revelations do not show his superior in an enviable light; but by 1907 Eckert had reached the age of eighty-six years; so far as he was concerned, the true story of Lincoln's last visit could then be told.

Bates, who, like Eckert, was a man of high standing and had held positions of trust and responsibility for many years, cannot be suspected of having invented so elaborate a tale. The incident is striking and is told in a straightforward manner. It adds nothing to his fame; moreover, it is anything but favourable to his chief, of whom he constantly speaks in the highest terms of admiration, and of whom he says that 'below the surface there beats a heart full of warm affection for his chosen friends . . .'.

Eckert, in 1907, was still actively and vigorously engaged in various enterprises and was chairman of the board of the business he had served since 1866. If Bates's account had met with Eckert's disapproval, Eckert could and would have strenuously denied it, since it appears highly probable that he was acquainted with a book dealing so largely with his own experiences and written by one of his own associates. Perhaps, as a matter of courtesy, he had even been consulted in its preparation.

Bates, his father, and Stanton were natives of Steubenville. The latter two men had been members of the same Masonic lodge. It is therefore not likely that Bates had anything but friendly feelings toward Lincoln's Secretary of War.

Conceivably Lincoln had asked for Eckert's company during an afternoon visit at the War Department and then called again in the evening. Perhaps Bates had the evening call in mind when he said that he could not remember what happened on that occasion. In the evening, neither Stanton nor Eckert was on duty, and it is quite likely, therefore, that nothing that would impress itself on Bates's mind took place then. This assumption is the more probable as Bates, in his book *Lincoln in the Telegraph Office*, put the time of Stanton's momentous refusal 'on the morning of the 14th'. In this he is obviously mistaken; for at eleven o'clock Ford's Theatre was officially advised of Grant's expected attendance; Lincoln would not have asked for Eckert's company, of course, before Grant had cancelled the engagement.

The former military telegraph operator related the entire incident without a trace of apology; he did not criticize the action of his superior, in whose good faith he must have sincerely believed. 'The stern and cautious Secretary', he wrote, 'again urged the President to give up the theatre-party, and, when he found that he was set on going, told him he ought to have a competent guard.' When Lincoln thereupon broached his request for Eckert's services and was bluntly refused, Bates saw nothing incongruous in it.

In all likelihood the story of Stanton's fateful refusal is true. Whenever history is based on testimony furnished by human minds, it must be judged by the preponderance of evidence, which in this case is plainly on the side of David Homer Bates.

REFERENCES

David Homer Bates, 'Some Recollections of Abraham Lincoln', *History of the Ohio Society of New York*, pp. 635, 636; also letter by William H. Crook in the Hannah Collection, Chicago.

New York Independent, 4 April 1895.

David Homer Bates, *Lincoln in the Telegraph Office*, pp. 366, 367, 408.

CHAPTER VI

THE PLOT TO KIDNAP LINCOLN

Booth's probable intention to abduct the President in January 1865 is also indicated by his efforts to have the actor Samuel Chester on the stage at that time at Ford's Theatre.

When Mathew W. Canning, a theatrical agent in Philadelphia, was arrested on 15 April 1865 he told the authorities that in December 1864 Booth and President and Mrs. Lincoln had attended the same play.

'. . . when the President and lady were passing out [of the theatre]', Canning related, 'he [Booth] moved after them, eyeing them very intently while they waited on the steps some moments for a carriage.'

A few minutes after this incident Canning and Booth were drinking in a saloon. 'I want you to do a great favour for me . . . ', said the actor. 'You know Sam Chester; he is a particular friend of mine; he is dissatisfied in New York and wants to go back to Ford and if I interfere they might get angry with me.'

'But they might get angry with me,' Canning retorted.

'Oh no,' said Booth, 'there's no danger of that; I will give you anything if you will see Ford.'

Canning spoke to Ford, and the latter finally consented to engage Chester. In the meantime Booth had gone to Louisville, and from there wired to Canning: 'Don't fail to hush that matter at once.' This was a perplexing message; but Booth later explained it by blaming the telegraph operator for a typographical error. The dispatch, he claimed, should have read, 'Don't fail to *push* that matter.'

In any event, Booth had made strenuous efforts to bring Chester to Washington. Eventually, Chester stayed at the Winter Garden in New York, and Booth lost further interest in him after his refusal to take part in the kidnapping scheme.

REFERENCE

War Department Archives, Washington.

THE SPELLING OF THE NAMES OF PAINE
AND WIECHMANN

Wiechmann's name has been spelled in almost as many ways as there are writers who have mentioned him. One of the reasons for this divergence is that the young Government clerk was not consistent himself. When called to the witness stand in 1867 he went into the matter in detail.

Q. State your full name.

A. My name is Louis J. Weichman. Before the trial of the assassins I spelled by name Wie. I gave it distinctly to the reporters, as I thought, but they spelled it Wei, and since that I have spelled it that way.

While he was thus gently reproving the reporters, they quickly avenged themselves by failing to remove one of the *n*'s, as Wiechmann had indicated that they should do. They stuck to *Weichmann;* but, as his family spelled the name *Wiechmann,* the latter spelling has been used in this text.

Paine's name is usually spelled *Payne.* There seems to be only one of his signatures available for guidance. This one appeared on his Oath of Allegiance, dated 14 March 1865, as *Paine.*

REFERENCES

Surratt Trial, vol. i, p. 369.
War Department Archives, Washington.

CHAPTER VIII

THE BOGUS PROCLAMATION

On 18 May 1864 during a period of uneasiness and uncertainty following the Battle of the Wilderness, the *Journal of Commerce* and the *New York World* published what purported to be a proclamation by the President, which read in part as follows:

PROCLAMATION BY THE PRESIDENT

A DAY OF FASTING RECOMMENDED.—CALL FOR FOUR
HUNDRED THOUSAND TROOPS

'*Executive Mansion, May* 17, 1864.
'*Fellow-citizens of the United States:*

'In all seasons of exigency it becomes a nation carefully to scrutinize its line of conduct, humbly to approach the Throne of Grace, and meekly to implore forgiveness, wisdom, and guidance.

'For reasons known only to Him it has been decreed that this country should be the scene of unparalleled outrage, and this nation the monumental sufferer of the nineteenth century. With a heavy heart, but an undiminished confidence in our cause, I approach the performance of a duty rendered imperative by my sense of weakness before the Almighty and of justice to the people. It is not necessary that I should tell you that the first Virginia campaign under Lieutenant-general Grant, in whom I have every confidence, and whose courage and fidelity the people do well to honor, is virtually closed. He has conducted his great

enterprise with discreet ability. He has crippled their strength
and defeated their plans. In view, however, of the situation in
Virginia, the disasters at Red River, the delay at Charleston, and
the general state of the country, I, Abraham Lincoln, do hereby
recommend that Thursday, the twenty-sixth day of May, A.D.
1864, be solemnly set apart throughout these United States as
a day of fasting, humiliation, and prayer.

'Deeming furthermore that the present condition of public
affairs presents an extraordinary occasion, and in view of the
pending expiration of the service of (100,000) one hundred
thousand of our troops, I, Abraham Lincoln, President of the
United States, by virtue of the power vested in me by the
Constitution and the laws, have thought fit to call forth, and
hereby do call forth the citizens of the United States between
the ages of (18) eighteen and (45) forty-five years, to the aggre-
gate number of (400,000) four hundred thousand, in order to
suppress the existing rebellious combinations, and to cause the
due execution of the laws. . . .'

This proclamation was a fraud, but it had been perpetrated
very cleverly. It was obviously issued for the sole purpose of
causing fluctuations in the price of gold, stocks, and bonds. The
forgery, written like the Associated Press dispatches on thin
manifold paper of foolscap size, was handed in to the offices of
all city newspapers between three and four o'clock in the morning. 'In handwriting and every other respect it was admirably
calculated to deceive,' stated General Dix, in an official wire to
the War Department. 'None of the responsible editors of either
paper were present. . . . It was printed by the *Herald*, but none
of the copies were issued, the fraud having been discovered
before they left the office.'

It is indeed remarkable that the forgery did not deceive all
the papers and that the deception was recognized as quickly as
it was. The *World* stopped the sale of its issue over the counter
at 8 a.m., announced the imposture on its bulletin boards, and
offered a reward of $500 for the discovery of the man who had
perpetrated it.

The *Tribune* and the *Times* escaped being victimized by only
the narrowest of margins. The boy to whom the proclamation
had been entrusted aroused suspicion by delivering his copy to

the *Tribune* at the wrong door. The editor immediately got in touch with the *Times* to find out the source of the news. The latter paper, which had accepted the message in good faith, was aroused in turn, and when the Associated Press denied its authenticity, both the *Tribune* and the *Times* suppressed it. The *Herald*, finding that the other papers were not printing the document, recalled the 20,000 copies already printed. The *Sun* had gone to press when its copy of the proclamation arrived.

Lincoln at once sent peremptory orders to Dix to arrest and imprison the editors, proprietors, and publishers of the *World* and the *Journal of Commerce*, and, although Dix was convinced early in the day that they were innocent, the Secretary of War forbade their release until the real culprit was found. A strong appeal on the part of the *Herald, Times, Tribune,* and *Sun* was to no avail.

The phraseology of the spurious proclamation was not a bad imitation of Lincoln's style, but the President's much-vaunted sense of humour failed to assert itself on this occasion; and the astounding order to arrest the staff, publishers, and proprietors of the two papers involved was issued over Lincoln's own name.

Stanton immediately went his chief one better. He took possession of the offices of the Independent Telegraph Company in Washington, New York, Baltimore, Philadelphia, and even in far away Harrisburg and Pittsburgh and had the superintendents, managers, and operators thrown into confinement. The charge against them was 'aiding and abetting the circulation . . . of a forged document. . . .'

Two days later the author of the fraud was discovered. He proved to be Joseph Howard, an ex-reporter on the *New York Times*. Howard immediately made a full confession which exonerated all arrested persons from any complicity in the hoax.

Although this brought about the release of the prisoners, Stanton did not restore their offices to the Telegraph Company for forty-eight hours. No apologies were ever made to those who had been illegally held under arrest, among whom there were members of a Washington news syndicate which was in no way connected with the affair.

The perpetrator of what Lincoln had called a 'publication . . . of a treasonable nature, designed to give aid and comfort to the enemies of the United States and to rebels now at war against the Government', went scot-free. He once had been secretary to the Reverend Henry Ward Beecher, and the famous minister made an appeal for the release of his ex-employee. This led to the following characteristic exchange of telegrams between Lincoln and his War Minister:

EXECUTIVE MANSION, WASHINGTON,

22 *August*, 1864.

MY DEAR SIR: I VERY MUCH WISH TO OBLIGE HENRY WARD BEECHER BY RELEASING HOWARD; BUT I WISH YOU TO BE SATISFIED WHEN IT IS DONE. WHAT SAY YOU?

YOURS TRULY,

A. LINCOLN.

I HAVE NO OBJECTION, IF YOU THINK IT RIGHT——AND THIS IS A PROPER TIME.   E.M.S.

LET HOWARD, IMPRISONED IN REGARD TO THE BOGUS PROCLAMATION, BE DISCHARGED.

A. LINCOLN.

REFERENCES

Morgan Dix, *Memoirs of John A. Dix*, vol. II, pp. 97–8, 99, 100.
David Homer Bates, *Lincoln in the Telegraph Office*, pp. 232, 234, 237, 241–2.
James N. Lee, *A History of American Journalism*, p. 298.
'Howard's Bogus Call for Troops' in the *New York Herald* for 11 April 1915.

FLOWER AND PITMAN RE-EDIT HISTORY

Flower wrote that Stanton sent his first telegram to the Press at 11.30 p.m.; he was evidently aware of the inexcusable delinquency of the War Minister and, intentionally or unintentionally, covered it up with an untrue statement. He also appropriated for his idol a message which Stanton never sent and which originated with Gobright, the agent of the Associated Press.

When Wiechmann surrendered to the police, on the morning after the assassination, he stated that he thought the fugitives would take a road through southern Maryland, especially as

450

there was no late train by which they could have left. Was this simple reasoning something to be withheld from the reading public? It would seem so; for when Pitman edited the testimony of the conspiracy trial he omitted all reference to this conversation.

REFERENCES

Frank A. Flower, *Edwin McMasters Stanton*, p. 281.
Benn Pitman, *The Assassination of President Lincoln*, p. 119.
Ben Perley Poore, *Conspiracy Trial*, I, p. 377.

CHAPTER IX

HOW ATZERODT LEFT WASHINGTON

Atzerodt had no particular difficulty in leaving Washington and making his way north to the house of his brother-in-law Richter, in Montgomery County.

According to a report prepared by Colonel John A. Foster, Atzerodt left his hotel in Washington at five o'clock on the morning of Saturday, 15 April, and went to Georgetown, where he took the stage for Rockville.

'On reaching the Forts,' so the report reads, 'in obedience to orders then issued, he and the others were . . . detained there from 9 o'clock to three in the afternoon. During that time he treated the guard to several drinks, and finally induced them to allow him to proceed in a wagon of one John Garther who took him as far as Rockville, when he left him and proceeded to his own house.'

REFERENCE

War Department Archives, Washington.

CHAPTER X

LIEUTENANT DANA SCATTERS THE CHAPEL POINT GARRISON

An indication that Lieutenant Dana's message to Chapel Hill really caused the troops stationed at that point to be sent to the

451

Patuxent River is found in an official telegram which Major John M. Waite dispatched from Leonardtown, Maryland, on 20 April, to Brevet-Colonel J. H. Taylor, chief of staff:

JUST REACHED HERE WITH ONE COMPANY; THE OTHER THREE TOOK DIFFERENT ROADS FROM VICINITY OF PORT TOBACCO. ONE STRUCK THE PATUXENT AT BENEDICT; WILL FOLLOW UP THAT RIVER. ONE WILL SCOUR THE COUNTRY DOWN THE POTOMAC, ALONG THE WICOMICO RIVER AND VICINITY. ALL WILL BE HERE TO-DAY.

Major O'Beirne also partially confirms the story of the disbanding of the troops at Chapel Point; for in his claim for a portion of the rewards, on 27 December 1865, he states that he 'proceeded in person to the lower neck of Maryland running from Kobb Neck and White Point which I reconnotured [*sic*] very carefully with a force of 6 Detectives and 10 enlisted men from the Veteran Reserve Corps from the Command of Lieut Doherty at Chappel Point . . .'.

The name of this last-mentioned officer was Laverty and not Doherty; he is not identical with the young lieutenant in charge of pursuing Booth to Garrett's barn.

REFERENCES

Official Records, series I, vol. 46, part III, p. 870.
O'Beirne Papers, in possession of the author.
L. C. Baker: *History of the United States Secret Service*, p. 489.

CHAPTER XII

BOOTH'S PURSUERS

Townsend's *The Life, Crime, and Capture of John Wilkes Booth* mentions the following names of detectives and military commanders who took part in the pursuit of John Wilkes Booth:
John S. Young, chief of the New York detective force.
Marshal Murray, of New York.
Provost-Marshal Major O'Beirne, Commander of the District of Columbia civil and military police

Officers Radford
    Kelso
    Elder
    Hoey } detective force of Young and Murray
Deputy-Marshal Newcome of New York
Officers Joseph Pierson and
    West of Baltimore

Detectives John Lee
    Lloyd
    Gavigan } immediate aides of Major O'Beirne
    Coddingham
    Williams

Officers Taggert
    George Smith } detachment of Philadelphia detective police force.
    Carlin

Provost-Marshal MacPhail, of Baltimore
Lieut. Commander Cushing
Ex-Marshal Lewis and Angelis, volunteer detectives
Secret police of Richmond
Col. Wells, of the Twenty-sixth Michigan regiment, assisted by
Col. Clendenning, of the Eighth Illinois cavalry
Lieutenant Lovett, of the Veteran Reserves, commanding Maj.
    O'Beirne's First detective party

Detectives D'Angellis
    Callahan
    Bostwick } under Maj. O'Beirne in his second detective party
    Hanover
    Bevins
    McHenry

Capt. Beckwith, General Grant's chief cipher operator
Maj. Waite of the Eighth Illinois cavalry
Total military forces deputed to pursue the fugitives:

    700 men of the Eighth Illinois cavalry
    600 men of the Twenty-second colored troops
    100 men of the Sixteenth New York

CHAPTER XIII

BOOTH'S DIARY

The *New York Times* reported on 27 April 1865 that 'Booth had in his possession a diary, in which he had noted events of each day since the assassination of Mr. LINCOLN. This diary is in possession of the War Department.'

The Booth diary was also mentioned by George Alfred Townsend, of the *New York World*, on 28 April 1865.

REFERENCES

New York Times, 27 April 1865.
George Alfred Townsend, *Life, Crime, and Capture of John Wilkes Booth*, p. 37.

STANTON QUOTES

The story of Stanton's tampering with a copy of the Constitution in a political debate, against none other than John A. Bingham, is told by Walter Gaston Shotwell, who, in his charming book, *Driftwood*, gives Bingham's own account of the incident.

'"And he read his copy, denouncing mine as spurious. But he skipped a line in reading it; and when he closed I had no right to reply. But I was mad and I got on a chair on the platform and charged him with skipping the line and challenged him to another debate. He said that he had to go to Virginia, just across the river, on business the day I named. . . ." '

Later the debate took place, but neither Shotwell nor Bingham reports how Stanton evaded the charge of misquoting the Constitution of the United States for the sake of winning an argument.

Apparently Stanton was an adept in omitting sentences from texts whenever it suited his convenience. Twenty-five years later he took a similar liberty with one of General Grant's dispatches.

It was at the time of the Sherman-Johnston armistice, which the Cabinet rejected. Grant had been sent to see Sherman and reported as follows: 'I reached here this morning and delivered to General Sherman the reply to his negotiations with Johnston. *He was not surprised but rather expected their rejection.*'

When Stanton gave this correspondence to the press, he not only deliberately suppressed the last sentence, but also omitted the remainder of Grant's dispatch in which the general-in-chief palliated what he considered merely a mistake on the part of Sherman.

REFERENCES

Walter Gaston Shotwell, *Driftwood*, pp. 81, 82.
James Ford Rhodes, *History of the United States*, V, p. 175.

CHAPTER XIV

WHO SHOT THE MAN IN GARRETT'S BARN?

Lansing, Michigan
21 September 1936.

DEAR MR. EISENSCHIML,

My father, Lieutenant Luther B. Baker, stated to me repeatedly that it was difficult, if not impossible, to get the men to take up their proper positions around the barn. The candle he held in his hand and later placed on the ground in front of the barn door, made all those who stood in its light easy targets, and this may account for the fact that he alone remained in that exposed position.

The man who had ordered the men into their respective places was not my father, but Conger, an officer who had just been mustered out of service as a Lieutenant Colonel, and to whom my father deferred out of courtesy. Lieutenant Doherty resented Conger's assumption of authority and kept sulking in the background during the besiegement.

Lieutenant Baker was a man of courage and absolute honor. He would have been incapable of firing the shot that killed Booth.

(Signed) LUTHER H. BAKER

CHAPTER XV

THE MYSTERY OF BOOTH'S NOTE TO JOHNSON

The motive behind Booth's note to Johnson, which has puzzled every historian, is explained by Oldroyd as follows:

'The object of this note is not known, but the theories are that Booth wanted to obtain a view of the Vice-President's room, by which he could direct Atzerodt; or expected to receive an invitation from him to call, which would cast suspicion upon Mr. Johnson, and probably implicate him in the assassination of the President.'

The first of these theories is too weak to be defended. There certainly would have been no sense in Booth's merely looking at an ordinary hotel room. The second is tenable only if Johnson's own assassination was not contemplated. If Johnson had been killed, too, no one would have suspected him of complicity. Yet, Oldroyd hesitates to draw the obvious inference that Johnson's life was not in danger.

Clara E. Laughlin writes at some length about Booth's mysterious message to Johnson, but fails to come to a satisfactory conclusion.

'Booth must have known,' she says, 'the Vice-President would hardly be in his room at that time of day, so what he hoped to gain by sending the card is difficult to guess. Perhaps Atzerodt, who took a room at the Kirkwood about one'clock that day, was given the card and told to send it—possibly to implicate Johnson in the crime Booth had just decided to perpetrate that night; possibly to determine for Atzerodt that the Vice-President was out and so make him feel free to explore the neighbourhood of Johnson's room. This latter assumption is ridiculous, however, for Atzerodt was a guest of the hotel and could have prowled about the Vice-President's room all he wished without exciting suspicion, and in the event of his discovering by this elaborate ruse that Johnson was out (which he could easily have done without giving his name or Booth's) he could do no more than that. There is a mystery in that card which has never been cleared, and perhaps never will be.'

George Fort Milton, author of *The Age of Hate*, thought that Booth intended to assign to some one other than Atzerodt the murder of the Vice-President, and was approaching Browning, Johnson's private secretary, to spy out the land. This, to Milton's mind, is the explanation of the card the actor left at the Kirkwood House.

This interpretation is not quite convincing.

The *Albany Argus*, in an edition which appeared a few days after the assassination, was one of the few papers to express a theory on Booth's visit to the Kirkwood House, on 14 April.

'What was the object of Booth in seeking an interview with Vice-President Johnson on Friday morning? Not to kill him; for that would foil the other attempt, and explode the whole conspiracy. Was it not to involve the Vice-President, and cast suspicion on him? To get him to write a note—a simple response to his card would do—"I shall be happy to have an interview with Mr. Booth on ——." This dropped on the scene of the murder would be an evidence of collusion with Mr. Lincoln's destined successor—a shallow device, but one in the fashion of a hundred stage plots. What other theory accounts for the visit to Johnson, the note, the desired interview, and the expected response? If we discard the idea of an intended murder of the Vice-President, this seems the only remaining conjecture.'

Assuming the reasoning of the *Argus* to be sound opens up another query: Who would have benefited from this plan to put Johnson in an awkward position? If the Vice-President had been tricked into writing a polite note to Booth, and if this reply had been discovered among the actor's possessions, its author would have become the immediate object of vitriolic attacks by an outraged public; he might even have been forced to resign the presidency. Or, supposing such a harmless little missive had been found and withheld from publication, it would have become a formidable weapon in the hands of an unscrupulous finder.

REFERENCES

O. H. Oldroyd, *Assassination of Abraham Lincoln*, p. 13.
Clara E. Laughlin, *The Death of Lincoln*, p. 80.
George Fort Milton, *The Age of Hate*, p. 192.
Albany Argus, April 1865.

CHAPTER XIX

A PLOT TO KILL LINCOLN ON 4 MARCH

The only acknowledged plot to kill Lincoln on the day of the inauguration is alluded to in the *Washington Daily Morning Chronicle* (a paper friendly to the Government) in its issue of 6 March 1865. This article is entitled:

ON HIS MUSCLE

'Yesterday afternoon at about two o'clock, a man named Thomas Clemens, who had been imbibing very freely, became very belligerent in his demonstrations in front of Willard's Hotel, wanting to whip everybody. Some large and well-built stranger ventured to take hold of him, but did not get his hands on him before Clemens knocked him down on the pavement. The stranger, fully convinced that he had put himself into bad hands, sought refuge in the hotel, and did not make his appearance again while Clemens was about. Officer Roth, of the Second Ward, then collared him, when Clemens struck him a couple of heavy blows with his fist and kicked him, hurting him considerably.

Mr. Kneass, a Government detective, came to the aid of Officer Roth, and was struck a couple of times by Clemens. They, however, succeeded in getting him to the Second Ward station-house, where he kicked detective Kneass and knocked the stove over.

'Provost Marshal Major O'Beirne called at the station-house, saw Clemens, and said he would send for him. In case the major finds nothing against him he will be remanded to the civil authorities.'

On 7 March 1865 the *Chronicle* reports further on the

THREAT TO ASSASSINATE PRESIDENT LINCOLN

'In yesterday morning's *Chronicle* we gave an account of the arrest of a drunken man, named Thomas Clemens, for disorderly conduct in front of Willard's Hotel, on Sunday afternoon. We also stated that Provost Marshal Major O'Beirne called at the station-house, and asked that Clemens be turned over to him. Clemens was delivered to him as desired. The cause of the Major's request was that two gentlemen had filed with him affidavits, in substance as follows:

'One was that this man Clemens came into the office of the person who made the affidavit, at about 2 o'clock on last Sunday, and there made a declaration that he had come from Alexandria, Va., on the day of the inauguration, for the purpose of killing the President, but that he arrived about a half hour too late, and that was all that saved the President's life, asseverating that he thought he would be doing a national benefit to kill such a tyrant. Witness then went out and reported the charge to Major King, of General Augur's staff.

'The affidavit of the other was substantially as follows:

'On March 8th there came to his house between the hours of twelve and one o'clock a man, in company with one Thomas Clemens, both citizens. They were very disorderly indeed. They seemed to have been drinking very freely. Thomas Clemens, in particular, was very abusive. He said (using gross and profane language) he came here to kill the President, Mr. Lincoln, and that he was late by about one-half hour and that his Saviour would never forgive him for failing to do so. He, Clemens, further said that he would do it that night, namely, the 5th of March, and that he came expressly to do it and he would do it before he left town. He furthermore said that the Government had robbed him of a certain sum of money.

'Clemens was returned to the civil authorities, and Justice Boswell gave him a hearing, and committed him to jail for court.'

JEFFERSON DAVIS'S ATTITUDE TOWARD LINCOLN'S ASSASSINATION

Jefferson Davis's attitude in regard to violent acts against his Northern opponents is not entirely a matter of conjecture. Major Walker Taylor, a nephew of Zachary Taylor and a cousin by marriage to the President of the Confederacy, proposed to the latter the abduction of Lincoln. Davis declined to entertain the suggestion because of the risk of killing the captive in the event of resistance.

In August 1863 a soldier in camp near Fredericksburg wrote to the Confederate Secretary of War offering to assassinate some certain persons filling high places in the North. He received the reply that 'duty requires all such schemes . . . to be discouraged by the Department and to be discarded by you. The laws of war and morality as well as Christian principles . . . forbid the use of such means of punishing even the atrocities of the enemy.'

Lieutenant Ruggles, one of the Confederate officers who helped Booth in his escape, thought that 'though it is contrary to the general belief of the people of the North, I believe that, had the war then been going on, Booth, instead of finding an asylum in the South, would have been taken and surrendered to the United States by the Confederate Government.'

A scheme to kidnap Jefferson Davis was at one time put before the Federal authorities. Stanton was called upon by a group of preachers who intended to abduct the President of the Confederacy. It was a curious thought to have been conceived in the minds of clergymen, but they were so certain that his removal would end the war that they even wished to aid personally in the venture. On advice from Captain William P. Wood, head of the Old Capitol Prison, who was sent to Richmond to investigate the project, the scheme was turned down as impracticable and undignified. The records do not state that Stanton was particularly disturbed about the morality of the plan.

REFERENCES

James Ford Rhodes, *History of the United States 1850–1877*, V, p. 513, 514.

Francis Wilson, *John Wilkes Booth*, pp. 88, 89.

M. B. Ruggles, 'Pursuit and Death of John Wilkes Booth' in *Century Magazine* (January 1890), p. 444.

Frank A. Flower, *Edwin McMasters Stanton*, p. 276 (footnote).

CHAPTER XX

THE LEGALITY OF THE MILITARY
COMMISSION

In connection with the arguments on the legality of the military trial of the so-called conspirators, it is of some interest to note the advice Lincoln himself received on a parallel question.

'Mr. Lincoln was advised [wrote Judge David Davis to Herndon in 1866], and I also so advised him, that the various military trials in the Northern and Border States, where the courts were free and untrammelled, were unconstitutional and wrong; that they would not and ought not to be sustained by the Supreme Court; that such proceedings were dangerous to liberty. He said he was opposed to hanging; that he did not like to kill his fellowman; that if the world had no butchers but himself it would go bloodless. When Joseph E. McDonald went to Lincoln about these military trials and asked him not to execute the men who had been convicted by the military commission in Indiana he answered that he would not hang them, but added, "I'll keep them in prison awhile to keep them from killing the Government." I am fully satisfied therefore that Lincoln was opposed to these military commissions, especially in the Northern States, where everything was open and free.'

The above-named Joseph McDonald told Weik, in 1888, how Lincoln, with kindly shrewdness, expected to let these victims of the Indiana court-martial escape the death penalty.

'I was counsel for Bowles, Miligan, *et al.*, who had been convicted of conspiracy by military tribunal in Indiana. Early in 1865 I went to Washington to confer with the President, whom I had known, and with whom, in earlier days I had practised law on the circuit in Illinois. My clients had been sentenced, and unless the President interfered were to have been executed. Mr. Hendricks, who was then in the Senate, and who seemed to have little faith in the probability of executive clemency, accompanied me to the White House. It was early in the evening, and so many callers and visitors had preceded us we anticipated a very brief interview. Much to our surprise we found Mr. Lincoln in a singularly cheerful and reminiscent mood. He kept us with him till almost eleven o'clock. He went over the history of my clients' crime as shown by the papers in the case, and suggested certain errors and imperfections in the records. The papers, he explained, would have to be returned for correction, and that would consume no little time. "You may go home, Mr. McDonald," he said, with a pleased expression, "and I'll send for you when the papers get back; but I apprehend and hope there will be such a jubilee over yonder," he added, pointing to the hills of Virginia

461

just across the river, "we shall none of us want any more killing done." The papers started on their long and circuitous journey, and sure enough, before they reached Washington again Mr. Lincoln's prediction of the return of peace had proved true.'

REFERENCE

William H. Herndon, *The Life of Lincoln* (Belford, Clarke & Company, Chicago, 1889), vol. III, pp. 556, 557, footnote.

HOLT SHUNS PUBLICITY

Originally Judge-Advocate Holt wished even the charges and specifications against the so-called conspirators to be withheld from the Press. In this respect he went beyond Stanton himself. Eventually, the pressure of public opinion must have prevailed. The letter pertaining to this matter, found in the files of the judge-advocate's office, reads as follows:

War Department
Washington City
Hon. E. M. Stanton   *May 10th,* 1865
    Secy. of War

Sir

This evening you expressed the opinion that the charges and specifications should go to the Associated Press with the synopsis of todays proceedings, but at the same time directed me to consult with Judge Holt in reference to the matter. His opinion is decidedly against any publication of the charges, and in favor only of a very brief synopsis. How shall it be?

I have the honor to be

Very Respy
Your Obt. Svt.
H. L. Burnett
Bvt. Col. & Judge. Adv.

I directed that you should be
governed by the opinion of Judge   [In Stanton's
Holt. You will consider yourself   handwriting.]
under his instructions and to be
governed by his opinion.
    E. M. Stanton

War Department Archives, Washington.

CHAPTER XXI

MORE ABOUT DR. MUDD

Senator Orville Browning of Illinois, Lincoln's friend, who later became Secretary of the Interior under Johnson, helped General Ewing in the defence of Dr. Mudd and Samuel Arnold. He wrote twelve pages of foolscap to be incorporated into the argument in Arnold's behalf.

This fact may throw some light on a disputed remark which General Lew Wallace is said to have made to the senator one morning, at the time of the trial. 'If Booth had not broken his leg, we would never have heard the name of Dr. Mudd.'

Mrs. Browning repeated these words to Mrs. Mudd when she met her several days later in General Ewing's office.

Eldrige Monroe, a son-in-law of Dr. Mudd, thought the transfer of the prisoners to the military prison on the Dry Tortugas was due to a desire on the part of the authorities to place them beyond the reach of the civil courts. After the decision of the Supreme Court in the Milligan case it might have been possible to obtain the release of Dr. Mudd and his companions on legal grounds, if they had been in the hands of civil authorities. This opinion has something in its favour and would be entirely acceptable, were it not for the fact that no decision of this sort could have been anticipated in 1865; nor does Monroe's argument explain the fact that the prisoners were held practically *incomunicado* after their arrival on the island.

REFERENCES
Orville Hickman Browning, *Diary*, II, p. 33.
Nettie Mudd, *The Life of Dr. Samuel A. Mudd*, pp. 37, 38, 14.

A CONFESSION BY ATZERODT

On 25 April Atzerodt made a confession to Colonel Wells, which was published in an amended form in Pitman's report of the conspiracy trial.

Two interesting items in Atzerodt's original statement were significantly omitted from the latter account.

The first pertains to the fact, related by the conspirator, that he was introduced to Booth in the office of the commissioner-general of prisoners. This was Wiechmann's place of employment. It appears therefore that Wiechmann had the effrontery to use the War Department's own premises to foster an acquaintance with an enemy of the Federal Government; for it was Wiechmann's belief, according to his own admission, that a blockade-running scheme was being arranged.

The second item is Atzerodt's account of the road the assassins intended to take after their deed. Atzerodt was to act as their guide, and it was therefore necessary to give him advance notice of the route to be followed.

'They wanted I should show them the road to Indiantown on Maryland Point. they were to go to Surratsville around Piscataway and to strike the Potomac. they were to go through Bumpy Oak. To go to Bumpy Oak you leave the road leading from Washington to Bryantown at Teebee which is about Six miles from Surrattsville you turn off to the right.'

It is manifest, therefore, that the original plan of the conspirators did not include a visit to Dr. Mudd or even to Bryantown. They intended to leave the Bryantown road at Teebee, turning to the right; instead they turned to the left, because of Booth's injury.

That the fugitives were headed for Maryland Point, straight south of Piscataway, is unlikely. Maryland Point is much farther from Washington than Port Tobacco. The chances are that Atzerodt made this misstatement for the purpose of diverting attention from his home town and from the part assigned to him in the escape.

Nevertheless, if the Government had chosen to publish this confession in its entirety Dr. Mudd's name would have been cleared to the extent of proving that a visit to his house had not been contemplated by Booth and Herold.

REFERENCE

War Department Archives, Washington.

LIEUTENANT LOVETT'S REPORT

Lieutenant Lovett's report of the observations which he made at Dr. Mudd's house and withheld from his superiors for several days, were contained in the following report:

We went on to New Port and from there to Bryantown [where we] got information of two strange men being in that vicinity and that one of them had a broken leg and that a man by the name of Dr. Samuel Mudd had set it for him. I then proceeded to Dr. Mudd's farm about four and a half miles from Bryantown. He was not at home, but his wife sent for him and he came in. In about half an hour. But in the meantime I had questioned his wife concerning the two men who had been there, she stated that they were both strangers to her. . . .

When the Doctor came in, I questioned him about the two men that had stopped at his house on Saturday. He seemed to be somewhat excited and said, that they were perfect strangers to him, that he had set one of their legs which had been broken by his horse falling on him, and that was all he knew about them, he was then questioned in regard to the appearance of the men and did not give much satisfaction. . . . Dr. Mudd seemed to be very much reserved and did not care to give much information. I was then satisfied that it was Booth and Herold, and made up my mind to arrest Doctor Mudd when the proper time came. I was under the impression that Booth and Herold were in the neighbourhood and that Dr. Mudd knew where they were and was secretly giving Booth medical attendance. After arranging [*sic*] things so that if Booth and Herold were in the neighborhood and the Doctor go to them we would get the whole of them. . . .

> Very Respectfully
> Your Obet. Servt.
> ALEXANDER LOVETT
> 1st Lt. Comg. 14th Co. 2d Batt. V.R.C.

COL. BURNETT
Judge Advocate of Military Commission

REFERENCE

Statement made by Alexander Lovett, Washington, D.C., May 2, 1865. War Department Archives, Washington.

CHAPTER XXII

THE VALUE OF WIECHMANN'S TESTIMONY

On 7 July 1865, a few hours before the execution of Mrs. Surratt, a man named John S. Brophy urged upon Judge-Advocate Holt a document containing some statements about Wiechmann which threw serious doubt on the value of the latter's testimony.

The document begins by declaring that Wiechmann always was a coward, even according to his own father. It then sets forth that Stanton and Burnett had threatened him with death, and that he had said that he would rather be hooted as a spy than tried as a conspirator.

Wiechmann then made the interesting revelation, so Brophy writes, that 'if Captain Gleason had not informed on him, they (Stanton and Burnett and the rest) "never would have got a word out of him" about any of the parties suspected'; he admitted to Brophy that he was a liar and that he had sworn to a deliberate falsehood on the witness stand.

Mrs. Surratt, the communication states, had wept bitterly and constantly at the thought of her son John going to Richmond; she had begged him to stay at home and not to bring trouble upon himself and his family.

Still more impressive is the following:

'. . . he (Weichmann) told me since the close of the trial, that once while some of these men were in the house with John . . . Mrs. Surratt called . . . (her son) aside and said to him "John! there is something going on I am afraid and I cannot see what it must be. Why do these men come here? Now, John, I cannot allow this, and you must tell me what you are about." Weichman also told me that John did not and would not tell her. . . .'

Finally, Brophy states that Wiechmann was willing to sign a letter to the President asserting Mrs. Surratt's innocence, provided it would be kept a profound secret; the letter was to be handed to Johnson in person.

After stressing that Wiechmann was an avowed secessionist and that he never would have fought for the Northern side,

Brophy reached the climax of his missive. He stated that Wiechmann 'had me summoned to testify to his character, and afterwards, remembering I suppose all that he had said to me, begged me and brought some of the sub-officers of the Court to get me to leave the witness room for fear I would be called upon the stand.'

This important letter actually was presented by Holt to the President at half-past nine in the morning of 7 July, as shown by an endorsement on the envelope. Whether Johnson ever read it is not known.

Previous to writing his final appeal to Johnson, Brophy had unburdened himself to the counsel for Mrs. Surratt.

'We took the proper steps to have him [Brophy] called as a witness,' reported Mr. Clampitt, 'but the Commission, taking advantage of a technical ground, refused to permit him to testify on this *all*-important point.'

If Brophy had been permitted to testify, he might have demolished Holt's entire case against Mrs. Surratt. Why he was not called as a witness in the Surratt Trial of 1867—if he was still alive then—is not clear, unless it was because Lewis J. Carland, another witness, testified to the same effect. Brophy was mentioned in Carland's testimony as having been present during Wiechmann's self-incriminating remarks.

Wiechmann apparently evaded the truth on one occasion when he testified that no officer of the Government had made any threats against him.

Q. Were any threats ever made to you by any officer of the Government in case you did not divulge?
A. No, sir: no threats at all.
Q. Any inducements?
A. No, sir. . . .

Wiechmann told the blockade-runner Howell that his sympathies were with the South and that he wanted to go to the South. He also gave Howell the number of Confederate prisoners in Northern camps.

References

War Department Archives, Washington.
John W. Clampitt, 'The Trial of Mrs. Surratt', in *North American Review* (September 1890), p. 234.

Ben Perley Poore, *The Trial of the Conspirators*, I, p. 377.
Benn Pitman, *Assassination of President Lincoln*, p. 133.

CHAPTER XXIII

THE MILITARY RANKS OF JETT, BAINBRIDGE, AND RUGGLES

The correct military titles of the three young Confederate soldiers, Jett, Bainbridge, and Ruggles, who helped Booth and Herold conceal themselves at the Garrett Farm, are not definitely known; in most instances they are referred to as Captain Jett, Lieutenant Bainbridge, and Lieutenant (sometimes Major) Ruggles.

According to some reports William Jett was a captain in the regular Confederate army. After recovering from a serious wound, he joined Mosby's irregulars, and it is not certain whether or not he gave up his rank in order to serve under this famous raider.

Mortimer B. Ruggles was a mere boy when he joined the army. He, too, earned his officer's stripes but resigned his commission when he became one of Mosby's troopers.

A. R. Bainbridge, it seems, had never risen above the rank of a private.

In a letter written to the author, John T. Goolrick, a cousin of Bainbridge and Ruggles, states that Major Edward Ruggles, with whom the lieutenant is often confused, was an elder brother of Mortimer B. Ruggles.

The records of the United States War Department show that Bainbridge and Ruggles were private soldiers at the time they were imprisoned, following the assassination. This is partially confirmed in a letter written by Nannie Burton Marye to Mrs. Marguerite DuPont Lee in Washington:

'First, I would like to say that neither of the young men you mention, Bainbridge, Ruggles or Jett held any commission in the Confederate army, but were simply enlisted men. My cousin, William S. Jett was only eighteen years old at the time of the surrender, and had been in the army a very short time.'

William Jett, in his statement to the Washington authorities on 6 May 1865, referred to his position at the time by saying, 'I was on my way from Fauquier Co[unty]., where I had been with Mosby's Command. I did not belong to that command, but to the 9th Va. Cavalry, Co[mpany]. C. . . . when Richmond was evacuated I was on duty in Caroline Co[unty]. as Commissary Agent.'

Hence he probably was more than a private soldier.

In his testimony at the conspiracy trial he referred to himself as a commissary agent, to Ruggles as a lieutenant, and to Bainbride as a 'young man'.

REFERENCES

Original letter from Nannie Burton Marye in possession of Mrs. Lee.

War Department Archives, Washington.

Benn Pitman, *Assassination of President Lincoln,* p. 90.

CHAPTER XXIV

STANTON AND McCLELLAN

It is more than probable that Lincoln's rash War Order No. 1 was prompted by Stanton, but that Stanton was in full accord with its headlong strategy is certain. For, on 20 February, the Secretary of War, in a telegram published in the *New York Tribune* over his signature, executed a neat attack on McClellan by deriding the necessity of a well mapped-out campaign. After modestly declining to accept any credit for Grant's recent victories in the west—'no share of it belongs to me'—he penned the following silly effusion:

'Much has recently been said of military combinations and organizing victory. I hear such phrases with apprehension. They commenced in infidel France with the Italian campaign and resulted in Waterloo. Who can organize victory? Who can combine the elements of success on the battlefield? We owe our recent victories to the spirit of the Lord that moved our soldiers to rush into battle and filled the heart of our enemies with dismay.'

Stanton continued his advocacy of frontal attacks, without direct reference to the overland route to Richmond which he wished McClellan to take, and which always led to destruction whenever taken, by saying:

'We may well rejoice at the recent victories, for they teach us that battles are to be won now by us in the same and only manner that they were won by any people, or in any age, since the days of Joshua—by boldly pursuing and striking the foe.'

Evidently it seemed to Stanton that a flank attack on his own general was proper and might be advantageous; but the armed enemy must be attacked in front, and on his own chosen battle-ground. Upon publication of this letter, McClellan was bound to be hurt, whether he did or did not do what the secretary had recommended.

After Stanton had forwarded his dispatch to the *Tribune* he wrote a private letter to Charles A. Dana, then one of its editors, saying that the sole object of the message was to prevent antagonism between the Western troops and himself. He then telegraphed that his revised judgement was against publishing the dispatch, but that he would defer to the editor's judgement. Of course it was published, thus putting the finishing touches on an act that was typically Stantonian from beginning to end.

It is understandable that Flower, in his version of this episode omits Stanton's qualifying clause about deferring to the judgement of the *Tribune*.

In another letter to the *Tribune*, dated 1 February 1862, Stanton furnished a complete defence for McClellan's much criticized delay, although this was probably far from his intention. 'To bring the War Department up to the standard of the times', he wrote, speaking of his own problems, 'and work an army of five hundred thousand . . . is no easy task. . . . All I ask is reasonable time and patience.'

An example of how easily history can be perverted by partisan historians is furnished by Frank A. Flower, Stanton's biographer, who quotes a letter written by General Pleasanton to General Marcy, chief of staff (and McClellan's father-in-law), on 11 August 1862, containing an urgent appeal for permission to attack Richmond at once:

'There are moments when the most decided action is necessary to save us from great disasters. I think such a moment has arrived.

'The enemy before us is weak. A crushing blow by this army at this time would be invaluable. . . . That blow can be made in forty-eight hours. Two corps would do it. . . .

'. . . I think he [McClellan] has an opportunity at this time few men ever attain.'

And this letter, embodying all that McClellan had pleaded and begged for and was not allowed to do, 'clearly establishes McClellan's persistent and disastrous insubordination'. At least, this is Flower's inference.

Stanton executed a clever political move when he appointed Halleck general-in-chief. In a letter addressed to Lincoln McClellan had stated that there should be only one head of all armies. When Stanton announced to the Press the appointment of Halleck he declared that his action was based on McClellan's own advice, as if the latter had been consulted and had suggested the name of another man to supersede himself.

McClellan's telegram to Stanton, accusing him of sacrificing the army, never reached the War Secretary in its entirety. When the message was received at the telegraph office the military supervisor of telegrams read it and declared that it could not go before Stanton as it was. He thereupon directed that it be recopied, omitting the last paragraph.

When Lincoln suddenly changed the tone of his message to McClellan in the early part of July 1862 Stanton was absent because of sickness in his family. It is curious how Lincoln's relief from Stanton's constant pressure expressed itself immediately at that time by a lapse into his former cordiality toward his general.

Welles gives Stanton a clean bill of health so far as Lincoln's first war order is concerned. '. . . we united in requesting Presi-

dent Lincoln to issue his celebrated order of the 27th of January . . .', he writes. 'Such an order had been suggested, before Mr. Stanton's appointment, by the Navy Department. . . .'

But on another occasion he states that 'near the close of January he [Stanton] pressed this subject [McClellan's inactivity] on the President, who issued the order to him and myself for an advance on the 22d of February'.

REFERENCES

Frank A. Flower, *Edwin McMasters Stanton*, pp. 129, 130, 171, 173.
James Havelock Campbell, *McClellan*, p. 291.
David Homer Bates, *Lincoln in the Telegraph Office*, pp. 109, 110.
Gideon Welles, *Diary*, I, pp. 61, 95.

GENERAL BURNSIDE AT ANTIETAM

Burnside's action in the battle of Antietam has been the subject of many controversies. His advocates maintain that he did not receive orders to storm the bridge until nine o'clock and then did all that was humanly possible. On the other hand, McClellan, who was a close friend of the general, speaks of the 'inexcusable delay in attacking', and maintains that if 'Porter or Hancock had been in his place the town of Sharpsburg would have been ours . . .'.

General Cox [Union] thought that the passage of the creek was disputed by four Confederate brigades, while General Longstreet [Confederate] stated that General Toombs alone, with four hundred worn and footsore troops, held back Burnside's entire ninth corps.

Disregarding all this contradictory evidence, it is certain that Burnside did not succeed in turning the battle to the advantage of his cause, regardless of whether the fault was his or not.

REFERENCES

McClellan's Own Story, p. 608.
Battles and Leaders of the Civil War, II, pp. 649, 670.

CHAPTER XXVII

A SPURIOUS CONFESSION

In 1865 there was printed in Paris a book entitled *Confession de John Wilkes Booth*, purporting to be a translation of the actor's own manuscript, written during his stay at Garrett's Farm. Booth, according to this story, handed the confession to a mysterious friend, who later fled to England, where he had it published.

According to this book, which is plainly a crude fabrication, the assassin's hatred of the North was caused by the death of a friend named Maguire, who had been killed by Federal soldiers. This friend's brother and a neighbour named Jarvis are the only other conspirators mentioned.

The most interesting part of the volume deals with Booth's entrance into the box and with the subsequent events at the theatre. In literal translation it reads as follows:

'The President's servant stopped me in the corridor, and I feared that in spite of all my precautions I would see my plans completely upset.

'I told him that I was a senator and that I came by invitation.

'He allowed me to pass.

'I immediately entered the little passage, and as soon as I had closed the door behind me, I adjusted the small bar of wood in order to keep out any newcomer.

'I found myself confronted by Major Rathbone, who asked me if I knew in whose box I was.

'I saluted and drew to one side.

'Then adjusting my pistol with the left hand, I fired.

'Someone threw himself at me, but I struck with my knife and I threw him aside.

'With one leap, I jumped on the railing of the box and from there to the stage floor.

'In my fall, my spur caught in some object, causing my foot to turn, and when I fell to the stage I feared that I had broken my leg.

'I was thrown forward, but by a violent effort I managed to maintain my equilibrium and I faced the audience.

' "Sic Semper Tyrannis", I cried.

'Then I crossed the stage, and almost collided with someone. I do not know with whom.

'Profiting by the surprise and general alarm, I reached the stage door, and mounted my horse and rode away.

'I was supposed to meet some people upon my departure from the theater but for one reason or another, they were not at the appointed rendezvous, and that is how it happened that I had but one companion in my flight.'

The noteworthy part of this account is Booth's alleged statement to the guard that he was a senator and had come to the box by invitation. This explanation of Parker's passive attitude has been repeated many times and may have had its origin in this spurious book.

It is also of some interest that, in this so-called confession, Booth claims to have held the pistol in his left hand.

REFERENCE

Confession de John Wilkes Booth, Assassin du Président Lincoln. publiée d'après le manuscrit original (Poupart-Davyl et Cie, Paris, 1865), pp. 114–16.

CHAPTER XXVIII

THE VISITORS AT LINCOLN'S BEDSIDE

What is claimed to be a complete list of those who visited the Petersen house, during the night of 14 April, is contained in a document signed by all those present on that occasion. It comprises forty-five names, besides those of Lincoln and Mrs. Lincoln. The list given by Nicolay and Hay omits no less than twenty of these, among them such important ones as Robert T. Lincoln and Thomas T. Eckert.

The signed list is supplemented by the printed names of those in attendance, but the names of two men whose signatures do not appear in writing are given in print. They are Lyman B. Todd and General Henry Halleck.

The insertion of Halleck's name is noteworthy. In a Currier and Ives engraving, widely distributed following Lincoln's death, the figure of Andrew Johnson appears prominently at Lincoln's bedside. Two years later, in a re-issue of this print, Halleck was substituted for Johnson.

The original of the declaration, containing the names and signatures of the visitors at Lincoln's bedside, is in the possession of the Chicago Historical Society and reads as follows:

THE LAST HOURS OF LINCOLN

'We the undersigned visited the late President Lincoln at his bed-side during his last hours. We have since sat for a likeness to be used expressly in the composition of the Historical Painting of that event, designed by John B. Bachelder and Painted by Alonzo Chappel.

Andrew Johnson

Hugh McCulloch	G. Marston
Edwin M. Stanton	D. K. Cartter
Gideon Welles	J. C. Hall
J. P. Usher	C. S. Taft
W. Dennison	C. C. Augur
James Speed	Chas. A. Leale
William T. Otto	H. R. Rathbone
Rbt. King Stone	A. F. Rockwell
J. K. Barnes	L. H. Pelouze
Thos. T. Eckert	E. L. Dixon
J. B. S. Todd	Thomas M. Vincent
Schuyler Colfax	Clara H. Harris
Robert T. Lincoln	Constance Kinney
Charles Sumner	R. J. Oglesby
M. B. Field	E. H. Rollins
L. J. Farwell	M. C. Meigs
I. N. Arnold	Mary C. Kinney
C. H. Liebermann	I. N. Haynie
C. H. Crane	B. B. French
J. F. Farnsworth	P. D. Gurley
John Hay	Geo. V. Rutherford

As a matter of fact, many people, possibly not so well known, were also present, although their names were not recorded on this document. Among them were Major O'Beirne, provost-marshal of the District of Columbia, Corporal James Tanner,

who took down the testimony, and Alexander Williamson, tutor
at the White House.

References

John G. Nicolay and John Hay, 'Abraham Lincoln', in *Century
    Magazine* (January 1890), p. 436.
George Fort Milton, *The Age of Hate*, p. 250.
The Chicago Historical Society.

CHAPTER XXIX

'NOW HE BELONGS TO THE AGES'

Nicolay and Hay, whose account of the assassination is so full
of inexplicable errors, related the story of Stanton's famous
utterance in its orthodox form. Major Hay was at the President's
bedside, and it is possible that he may have heard the remark.
At any rate, he reported that it was made immediately after
Lincoln breathed his last.

'At twenty-two minutes after seven he [Lincoln] died. Stanton
broke the silence by saying, "Now he belongs to the ages."'

Stanton's biographer, Flower, pictured the death scene somewhat differently.

'At 7.22 . . . Lincoln . . . gently ceased to breathe. Stanton
touched the Reverend Mr. Gurley on the arm and said: "Doctor,
please lead in prayer".'

After this remark, which showed no great originality, there
followed the prayer.

'Surgeon-General Barnes tenderly drew a sheet over the face
of the martyr and Stanton, as he darkened the windows, said
impressively: "He now belongs to the ages."'

Flower carefully added that by that time most people had
filed out of the room.

Gideon Welles evidently did not hear the classic words, for
his diary makes no reference to them; and Corporal Tanner, in
describing the last minutes of Lincoln's life in his letter of
17 April, said:

'At 6.45 Saturday morning I finished my notes and passed
into the back room . . . I approached quite near the bed . . . I
stood just to the left of General Halleck and between him and
General Meiggs. Secretary Stanton was there trying every way
to be calm and yet he was very much moved. The utmost silence
prevailed. . . .

'As soon as he was dead, Rev. Dr. Gurley . . . offered up a
very impressive prayer. I grasped for my pencil which was in
my pocket, as I wished to secure his words, but . . . my pencil
had been broken in my pocket. . . . The friends dispersed. . . .

'Secretary Stanton told me to take charge of the testimony
I had taken, so I went up to my room, and took a copy of
it. . . .'

Here was one witness who stayed to the last and was eager
to put down in black and white every word that was spoken;
yet, although he stood quite near Stanton, he only heard a few
commonplace words that were not worth recording.

Deviating widely from the generally accepted phrasing,
Chittenden ascribed to Stanton these words:

'There lies the most perfect ruler of men the world has ever
seen!'

But Chittenden was not at Lincoln's bedside, and his source
of information is unknown.

On the other hand, one of Stanton's clerks related that the
War Secretary took the hand of the expired President and said:

'Ah, dear friend! there is none now to do me justice; none to
tell the world of the anxious hours we have spent together!'

This witness was also somewhere else at the critical moment;
then, too, this would not have made a good story.

One report, also difficult to authenticate, was that Stanton
said, 'And now he belongs to the Angels.' A popularization of
this paraphrase would have been nothing short of a calamity.

Maunsell B. Field, who was present at the death of the
President and who stayed on until Stanton locked the door, tells
only of Gurley's prayer. He could hardly have missed any
remarks made in the bedroom; but of Stanton this deponent says
nothing.

On 15 April the *New York Times*, in its evening edition, published a long report, 'The Last Hours of President Lincoln', without any reference to 'The Ages' legend. The *New York Evening Post*, the evening edition of the *Detroit Tribune*, both of 15 April 1865, and the *Philadelphia Inquirer* of 17 April, though they contain special accounts of the scene about Lincoln's deathbed, likewise do not mention it.

But there is one witness to the contrary. Dr. Charles Sabin Taft, who was present all night, wrote on the day following the tragedy: 'When it was announced that the great heart had ceased to beat, Mr. Stanton said in solemn tones, "He now belongs to the Ages."'

It is regrettable that Dr. Taft was an army surgeon when he penned this account, and that he preceded it by saying that the notes 'were made by direction of Secretary Stanton . . .'.

Major O'Beirne, writing fifty years later, said that the War Minister exclaimed, 'Now he belongs to history'; of this the provost-marshal made a memorandum immediately afterwards. 'I was the only one near him', he chronicled, 'when he said it in a sad, heroic, hopeful tone, subdued by his evidently distressed feelings. . . .'

Considering all the evidence available, it appears that Stanton may have spoken the famous words attributed to him in a 'sad, heroic, hopeful tone'; or again, they may have occurred to him after most witnesses had left the room. In any event, he took good care that the beautiful story survived. Perhaps he told it to eager-eared hostesses, as he had done when describing the imaginary battle-scene in Buchanan's Cabinet. Perhaps other subordinates, besides Dr. Taft, made up their accounts under his direction. At any rate, if Stanton had decided to preserve the epigram for posterity, he could be trusted to avail himself of any of the numerous subtle methods so well known to this greatest propagandist of his time.

REFERENCES

John G. Nicolay and John Hay in *Century Magazine*, January 1890, p. 436.
Frank A. Flower, *Edwin McMasters Stanton*, p. 283.

Supplementary Notes

William E. Barton, *The Life of Abraham Lincoln*, II, pp. 472, 473.

L. E. Chittenden, *Recollections of President Lincoln*, p. 186.

Charles F. Benjamin, 'Recollections of Secretary Stanton' in *Century Magazine* (D. Appleton-Century Company, New York), March 1887, p. 760.

Maunsell B. Field, *Memories of Many Men*, p. 326.

Charles Sabin Taft, 'Lincoln's Last Hours' in *Century Magazine* (February 1893), p. 635.

New York Evening World, 21 April 1915.

THE SHOWDOWN BETWEEN LINCOLN AND STANTON

It is only fair to state that on the occasion of the fateful clash between Lincoln and Stanton the latter was clearly within his rights, while the President was exerting his authority in violation of justice, if not of law.

After the draft had been resorted to, county agents were appointed for the purpose of buying men, wherever they could, to save the citizens from fighting in the ranks. One of these agents conceived the idea of buying some Confederate prisoners who were about to be released and had agreed to enlist without bounty in the Union army for service against the Indians.

Being an acquaintance of Lincoln, the agent obtained from him an order to have these men credited to his county. Stanton indignantly refused to allow such a barefaced subterfuge; the men, he argued, already belonged to the United States and had no relation whatever to the county this agent represented.

In defending his point of view, Stanton acted honourably and in the interest of the Government. Lincoln's obdurateness is more difficult to explain. It may have been due to political obligations; it is also conceivable that he was looking for an opportunity to force a showdown with his overbearing Secretary of War.

REFERENCE

Allen T. Rice, *Reminiscences of Abraham Lincoln*, p. 396.

WAS STANTON AN ADDICT?

In his book, *Andrew Johnson*, Winston quotes Dunning (author of *Reconstruction: Political and Economic*) as intimating that 'as time passed Stanton . . . acted with such duplicity as "to strongly suggest the vagaries of an opium-eater"'.

It is extremely improbable that Stanton really was an opium-eater. He was afflicted with what Piatt called a 'determination of blood to the brain', and was subject to gloomy spells; it is known that he also suffered from asthma. To alleviate his pain, he may have taken drugs at times. His untiring energy, however, and the clearness of his brain, which endured to his dying day, preclude the conclusion that he was an addict.

REFERENCES

Robert W. Winston, *Andrew Johnson*, p. 417.
Donn Piatt, *Memories of the Men Who Saved the Union*, p. 62.

Acknowledgements

In the preparation of this book I have received help from many people, to whom I am greatly indebted.

To Paul M. Angle for much competent advice and criticism.

To the Misses Inez Awty, Vivian Bolotin, Sally Holmes, Blanche Novotny, and Sally Owens for their literary judgement, which played an important part in the composition.

To Mr. David Rankin Barbee, who has contributed much to my knowledge and who has given to me some of his treasure of unused data. The chapter on Hanscom is entirely due to his co-operation, and it was he who turned my attention to William P. Wood.

To Mr. Luther H. Baker, son of the late Lieutenant Luther B. Baker, who has imparted to me interesting recollections.

To F. Lauriston Bullard for helpful and valuable criticism.

To Professor John W. Curran, of the DePaul University College of Law in Chicago, who is second to none in his knowledge of the conspiracy trial, and who has assisted me in many ways.

To Mesdames Cathryn Churchill and Meta Caminer for their patience in deciphering and retyping the manuscript.

To Messrs. H. E. Crawford and George E. Mierkle of the Metropolitan Police Department in Washington, who have given me much of their time, and whose records have enabled me to write the chapter on John F. Parker.

To the late John H. Dern, Secretary of War, who permitted the publication of material found in the files of his department.

To Mesdames Gertrude Garrigan, Kathe Thompson, Rea Hyman, Beatrice Jaros, Gertrud Brink, Pearl Hight, Ann Breitowich, Dr. Helen Lemberger, and Mr. Charles Tyng for the time they gave to historical research.

To Mr. Alexander Hannah for his kindness in permitting me to use his collection.

To Miss Clara E. Laughlin for many helpful suggestions on presenting historical evidence.

To Mr. Lloyd Lewis for putting at my disposal some interesting facts from his files, particularly in regard to Dr. Mudd.

To my wife Bertha and to my children, Rosalie, Gerald, and Ralph for help in the reading of proofs and for valuable suggestions.

To the late Mrs. Marguerite DuPont Lee for interesting information.

To Miss Laura Jane Lee for her assistance in gathering facts from newspaper files.

To the Lincoln National Life Foundation of Fort Wayne, Indiana, for valuable support. Its whole library was placed at my service by Dr. Louis A. Warren, and he has repeatedly given me references I could not have obtained elsewhere. His former assistant, Mr. R. Gerald McMurtry, has found for me, among other things, Gleason's important article and a play connected with Junius Brutus Booth in which Lincoln was ridiculed.

To the late Mrs. Ruth M. Mastny for her enthusiasm and encouragement.

To Miss Virginia Maier, who has devoted her entire time for years to historical research, and who has been a vital factor in the completion of the volume.

To Messrs. L. Milton Ronsheim and H. B. McConnell of Cadiz, Ohio, for permission to read and make use of original Wiechmann and Bingham letters in their possession.

To Lieutenant-Colonel Lucius M. Smith, Colonel William A. Graham, Chief Clerk Edwin B. Pitts, and Chief Record Clerk Joseph L. Lyons of the judge-advocate's office, whose unending courtesy has enabled me to go through the archives of the War Department.

To Mr. Forest H. Sweet of Battle Creek, Michigan, who has procured for me many letters, particularly in regard to Stanton and Halleck.

To Mr. James N. Wilkerson of Kansas City, whose criticism has clarified much that was confusing, and who has shared with me many a valuable find.

To the officers and librarians of the Newberry Library in

Acknowledgements

Chicago, the University of Chicago Library, the McCormick Historical Association in Chicago, the Chicago Public Library, the Chicago Historical Society and the New York Public Library, the Union League of Philadelphia, as well as of the Library of Congress and the Smithsonian Institution, who have given me much kindly assistance.

To the Macmillan Company for permission to quote from *Assassination of President Lincoln*, and *Impeachment and Trial of Andrew Johnson*, both by D. M. DeWitt, and also from James F. Rhoades's *History of the United States*.

To many others who have contributed information, original documents, or advice.

Index

Adams, Charles Francis, informed of Lincoln's death, 19–21, 71, 209

Aiken, Mr., defending conspirators, 237, 240–1

Albany Argus, its theory of Booth's visit to Kirkwood House, 457

Anderson, Major, 398

Andrew, Gov. John, his petition for Beall, 372

Antietam, Burnside at, 472

Appletons' Cyclopædia, on battle of Fredericksburg, 338–9

Arnold, Samuel B., his fatal letter to Booth, 52, 56, 57, 210, 213; and kidnap plot, 53, 56–9; and Booth, 59, 306; tortured, 177–82; confined at Dry Tortugas, 182–5; testimony against, 245, 252; vindicates Mudd, 270; his unimportance, 294; on Stanton's death list, 304; refuses to implicate Johnson, 380

Ashley, Congressman, of Ohio, 311; attacks Johnson, 379–81, 390

Associated Press, and news of the assassination, 72–4, 79–82, 83–4; and bogus proclamation, 449

Atlanta Intelligencer, 90

Atzerodt, George A., conspirator, 53, 59, 284; his attempt to kill Johnson, 165, 170–3; tortured, 174–5, 177–82; official description of, 197; at the bar, 251; Fletcher's disclosures concerning, 273; and the Surratt evidence, 291, 294; on Stanton's death list, 304; Booth and, 306; his easy escape, 451; his confession, 463, 464

Augur, Gen. Christopher C., 55, 111, 123, 126; and Richards, 74–5, 116; asks Stanton for instructions, 105, 106; his orders to Slough, 107; his odd conduct, 119, 127, 137; and Fletcher's disclosures, 273, 274

Badeau, Adam, 62, 63, 65; on Stanton, 427

Bainbridge, Lieut. A. R., and Booth, 175, 303–5, 468, 469

Baker, Col. (later Gen.) Lafayette C., 104; and the search for Booth, 120, 123, 125–6, 128–34, 139, 141; his *Secret Service*, 144, 150–6, 186; and Booth's diary, 145–9; Johnson turns against, 149; his death, 156; his orders for conspirators, 183–5; a confidant of Stanton, 191, 192; and Surratt trial, 284, 286, 290

Baker, Lieut. Luther B., and the search for Booth, 129, 130, 132, 137, 140–1, 146, 147–8; and shooting of Booth, 157, 159–64

Banks, Gen., 225, 404

Bates, David H., memoirs of, 41, 42, 47, 48, 60–1, 71, 401; story told by, 443–5

485

Index

Bates, Edward, 431; his opinion of military commission, 231, 244, 245; his opinion of Halleck, 353, 354, 357; on Radical sentiments, 368; on Stanton, 393, 406, 411, 415, 416

Beall, John Yates, his execution as motive for Lincoln murder, 371–4

Beauregard, Gen. Pierre, 349, 353; contradicts Halleck, 351

Beckwith, Capt. S. H., Grant's cipher operator, 52; testimony of, 71; and the search for Booth, 126–8, 130, 133, 136, 139

Beecher, Henry Ward, asks release of Howard, 450

Benjamin, Charles F., and Hooker's resignation, 342

Bingham, Dr. G. W., and the Davis case, 215

Bingham, John A., 182; and O'Laughlin trial, 166–7; and Davis case, 218; assisting Holt with prosecution, 235, 244, 245, 247, 252, 254, 261–3, 265, 267, 282, 284, 287, 293, 295; Herold's statement to, 438; his debate with Stanton, 454

Black, Jeremiah S., and Stanton, 393, 399, 400, 428; and Weed story, 398; his trip to Canada, 413

Blaine, James G., his opinion of McDowell, 322; criticizes Johnson, 385

Blair, Gen. F. P., and Howard's wires, 94, 95; accusation of Stanton, 400

Blair, Montgomery, his estimate of Stanton, 327, 396

Booth, Edwin, 261, 265–7

Booth, John Wilkes, assassinates Lincoln, 15–21, 32; and Parker, 31, mobilizes his band, 53, 54; a monomaniac, 58–9; his kidnap plot, 59; entered box with ease, 70; his name withheld, 72–8,

80–4, 94; likely to be in Richmond territory, 91; the search for, 97–114, 119–39; his actual route, 103–5, 112, 127, 138, 139; his injury, 108–10, 113; his 'perfect crime', 112, 113; his death, 142–3, 157–64; controversy over his diary, 143–9, 151, 152; and plots against the Cabinet, 166, 167, 170–5; his killing deliberate, 187, 188; and Miss Hale, 211, 212; characteristics of, 248; controversy over his photograph, 265–7; Mrs. Surratt and, 276, 277, 282–4; his wire to Wiechmann, 292; helped by many people, 297–308; his motives in killing Lincoln, 370–77; his friendship for Johnson, 388–9; list of his pursuers, 452, 453; his note to Johnson, 456, 457; bogus confession of, 473, 474

Booth, Junius Brutus, 261

Boston Globe, 287; on Parker, 437

Boutwell, Congressman George S., 207; and Davis trial, 226–7; his *Reminiscences*, 229–30; on Hooker's removal, 340, 341; and Stanton, 418, 419

Boynton, Gen., his story in *Cincinnati Gazette*, 404

Bradley, Mr., counsel for Mrs. Surratt, 274

Brophy, John S., his appeal unheeded, 294, 466, 467

Brown, Rev. S. D., sums up case against Radicals, 369

Brown, William, witness of the murder, 75

Browning, Senator Orville H., 51; condemns military commission, 232; describes campaign against McClellan, 319; and Lincoln's attitude toward slavery, 361, 362; defends Beall, 372, 373; on Stanton, 415, 421; and Arnold, 463

Browning, William A., secretary to Johnson, 390

486

tion, 16–22; his failure to punish Parker, 28; ousted from Cabinet, 30; fails to arrest Hanscom, 38; accused by Speed, 40; his failure to protect Lincoln, 41–9, 54, 55, 58, 60, 61; his conflicting testimony, 42, 43; his secret knowledge, 58; warns Sherman, 60, 90; and Grant's refusal to attend theatre, 66, 69–71; his handling of news of the murder, 72–8, 82–4, 86–90; Pinkerton's wire to, 90; and the search for Booth, 100, 101, 102, 104–6, 121, 126, 133, 134; his failure to prosecute, 141; and Booth's diary, 145–9; and Baker's indiscretion, 153–6; entertains Grant, 166; the plot against, 168, 169, 176; his novel torture, 177–87; his loyal assistants, 189–95; and Surratt's flight, 196, 201, 203–7; his desire to make Davis the culprit, 209–13, 216, 227; and Mrs. Surratt's death, 294; and War Department files, 298; his proclamation of capital punishment, 299, 302, 303; his death list, 304, 305; states aim of war, 311, 312; his opposition to McClellan, 312, 313, 316, 319–23, 325, 326, 328, 332, 334–6; emerges victorious, 339; his story of Hooker's removal, 340–4; and Meade, 344; and Halleck, 346, 355, 358; his Radicalism, 346; inquiries into Shiloh failure, 352; co-operates at last, 359; denounces Sherman, 363, 364; becomes panicky, 365; his programme for Virginia and North Carolina, 366, 367; and proposed excursion on *River Queen*, 385; his double-dealing, 392–6; appointed to Cabinet, 395, 396; as a propagandist, 397–402; triumphs over Chase, 402–4; could be cowed, 405, 406; prolongs war, 406–8; his tri-

umph over Lincoln, 411–2; and peace negotiations, 412, 413; his reaction to Lincoln's death, 414–6; his intrigues during Johnson administration, 416–27; relations with Grant, 433, 434; hypothetical indictment against, 429–30; and bogus proclamation, 449, 450; misquotes, 454, 455; and plan to abduct Davis, 460; and McClellan, 469–72; his historic utterance questioned, 476–8; his showdown with Lincoln, 479; question of his addiction to drugs, 480

Stanton, Mrs. Edwin M., declines Lincoln invitation, 69

Stevens, Thaddeus, and the Davis trial, 219; and resolution of Congress, 310; his petition for Beall, 372; defends Stanton, 410; creates steering committee, 416

Stewart, Joseph B., witness of the murder, 75

Stewart, Dr. Richard H., and Booth, 148, 302, 305

Stewart, Senator, accuses Johnson of drunkenness, 382, 383

Stone, Frederick, counsel for Herold, 254, 255

Sumner, Charles, takes exception to resolution of Congress, 310; and Stanton, 313, 393, 394, 396, 428

Surratt, Anna, asked to testify against Johnson, 390

Surratt, John H., conspirator, 53–5, 58; testimony against, 83; his escape to Canada, 196–9; his further wanderings, 201–7; official fear of, 207; charges dropped 208; his death, 271; refuses to testify against Johnson, 390,

Surratt, John H., Jr., his association with Wiechmann, 272–3; letter from, 284; failure to prosecute, 295

Index

Surratt, Mrs. Mary E., conspirator, 177; as a prisoner, 181; hanged, 182, 186; defended by Johnson, 193; counsel for, 237; centre of interest, 271; clue to her arrest, 272–6; evidence against, 276–80; Wiechmann's testimony concerning, 280–4, 306, 307; the prosecution's evidence against, 283–6; Lloyd and, 288–93; Government's vindictiveness toward, 294–6; on Stanton's death list, 304

Taft, Dr. Charles S., and Stanton's historic utterance, 478
Tanner, Corp. James, his testimony against Booth, 77, 78
Taylor, Major Walker, proposes abduction of Lincoln, 459
Thompson, Col., scouts north of Washington, 97, 138
Thompson, Jacob, 214–15; his attack on Johnson, 386
Toronto Globe, and the Davis case, 215
Townsend, George A., 84, 85, 152; describes hunt for Booth, 135; his description of Baker, 150; on death of Booth, 161; on the trial, 270; lists Booth's pursuers, 452, 453
Tucker, Beverly, his opinion of the shooting of Booth, 164; his attack on Johnson, 386, 387

Vicksburg, battle, 352, 353, 357, 358
Vincent, Rev. Martin R., his Radical sentiments, 368
Von Steinacker, Henry, testimony of, 220, 221, 223, 239–42, 266

Wade, Senator, of Ohio, 311; supports Johnson, 367
Wade-Davis Manifesto, 362

Waite, Major John M., and the search for Booth, 99, 126; his wire to Taylor, 452
Wallace, Gen. Lew, 213; member military commission, 232, 233, 240–2; his opinion of Halleck, 349, 353; delays Early, 360
War Department, U.S. See Stanton, Edwin M.
Washington, celebrates Lee's surrender, 13; telegraphically isolated, 84–9; its avenues of escape closed, 97–108; threatened by Lee, 325–30
Washington Chronicle, and news of the assassination, 79, 82, 92, its article on plot against Lincoln, 458, 459
Washington Evening Star, 67, 68
Washington National Intelligencer, and news of the assassination, 78, 79; and conspiracy against Cabinet, 165
Washington National Republican, 33, 36–9
Watson, Peter H., and the McCormick-Manny case, 193, 194
Weed, Thurlow, his story of Stanton, 397
Weitzel, Gen., instructed to protect Confederates, 365
Welles, Gideon, Secretary of the Navy, 182, 236, 328; estimate of, 13; distrusts Stanton, 14; mobilizes navy, 97; in danger, 175–6; comments on Surratt trial, 208; disapproves management of war, 324, 325; and President's suspicions, 346; his opinion of Halleck, 354, 355; criticizes generals, 358, and Stanton's plan for the South, 367; proposes excursion for Johnson, 385; and Cameron's removal, 395; discusses Black, 399, 400; and Stanton, 411, 412, 413, 417, 418, 420–4, 471, 472, 476

497

Index

Wells, Col. H. H., Ferguson's report to, 77; and the search for Booth, 123, 126; testimony of, 266, 267; his instructions from Hancock, 297; arrests Cox, 299, 300

Wiechmann, Louis J., warns of kidnap attempt, 55, 58, 104, 119, 137, 212, 274; and Richards, 123, 124, 199; and the search for Surratt, 199–201; his evidence at the trial, 261, 274–83, 306, 307, 308; his association with the Surratts, 272; his last statement, 280–1; points against, 283, 290–2; Government's treatment of, 286; his confession to Brophy 294; military pressure on, 302; failure to prosecute, 304, 305; value of his testimony, 466, 467

Wilkes, Commodore, his plea to Welles, 325

Wilson, Francis, his *John Wilkes Booth* quoted, 181

Wilson, Gen., 341

Wilson, Senator Henry, and Stanton, 394, 404, 428

Wirz, Capt., 233, 378

Withers, William, Jr., identifies Booth, 77

Wood, Capt. William P., in charge at Mudd's house, 187, 188, 195; a confidant of Stanton, 192; and the McCormick-Manny case, 193, 194; and Wiechmann's statement, 281, 282; his story of Mrs. Surratt's death, 289, 290; advises against abduction of Davis, 460

Woodward, W. E., on Grant, 408, 409

Wray, E. D., witness of the murder, 75

Yates, Senator, of Illinois, 365

1. Envelope found in Lincoln's desk after his death. It contained the Charles Selby letter and was filed by the President with the simple endorsement, 'Assassination'. (*See page* 248)

Original in War Department Archives

2. Envelope in which Secretary of War Stanton kept the 'bullet and bones from the brain and head of Abraham Lincoln'

Original in War Department Archives

Board of Metropolitan Police.

COMPLAINT

AGAINST

*Patrolman John F. Parker
of the 5th* Precinct.

CHARGE.

Conduct unbecoming an officer

Day of Trial *Apr 2, 1865, 10 o'clk P.M.*

RECORD.

"Tried Oct. 14, 1862, for conduct unbecoming an officer, and reprimanded Oct. 16, 1862." "Tried Apr. 1863, for being asleep in his beat, & complaint dismissed Apr 2, 1863." "Tried Mar. 1863, for willful violation of the Rules & Regulations, & reprimanded Apr 2, 1863." "Tried July 1, 1863, for conduct unbecoming and and complaint dismissed July 9, 1863." "Tried May 3, 1865, for neglect of duty, and complaint dismissed June 2, 1865."

Judgment, *Complaint dismissed Apr 30, 1865*

T. A. Lazenby
Secretary

3. Record of John F. Parker, Lincoln's bodyguard
(*See page* 24 *ff.*)

Original in Archives of the Metropolitan Police, Washington

Department of the Metropolitan Police,

483 "TENTH" STREET,

WASHINGTON CITY, *May 1st*, 1865

To *John F. Parker*.

SIR: Take notice that charges have been preferred against you, to the Board of Metropolitan Police, which charges are now on file in the office of the Secretary of the Board, at No. 483 "Tenth" street, and a copy thereof is hereto annexed. You are hereby notified and required to answer the said charges in accordance with, and in the manner required by, the Rules and Regulations for the Government of the Police Force.

You will also take notice that your trial upon said charges will be in order, and will take place, at a meeting of this Board to be held at the office of the said Board, No. 483 "Tenth" street, in said city, on the *third* day of *May*, 1865, at *1* o'clock p. m., and will be continued from day to day until the trial is concluded.

T. A. Lazenby, Secretary.

To the Board of Metropolitan Police:

I hereby CHARGE *Patrolman John F. Parker of the 5th Precinct*

with *Neglect of duty*

SPECIFICATION.

In this, that said Parker was detailed to attend and protect the President Mr Lincoln, that while the President was at Fords Theatre on the night of the 14 of April last, said Parker allowed a man to enter the Presidents private Box and shoot the President

Respectfully,

A. C. Richards
Supt

Witnesses
A. C. Richards
Chs. Forbes at Presidents House

I ADMIT due personal service on me of copies of the within complaint, charges, specifications, and notice of trial, this *1st* day of *May*, 1865.

John F. Parker

4. The charge for Neglect of Duty against Lincoln's bodyguard, John F. Parker
(*See page* 26)

Original in Archives of Metropolitan Police Department, Washington

Head Quarters Middle Department, 8th Army Corps,
OFFICE PROVOST MARSHAL,

Baltimore, *Mar. 14ᵗʰ 1865*

OATH OF ALLEGIANCE.

I, *Lewis Paine Franquir Co 4ᵗʰ Regt* do solemnly swear that I will bear true faith, allegiance and loyalty to the Government of the United States, and support, protect, defend and sustain the Constitution, Government and laws thereof; that I will maintain the National Sovereignty in its integrity, any ordinance, resolution, or law of any State, Convention or Legislature to the contrary notwithstanding. That I will discourage, discountenance and forever oppose secession, rebellion and the disruption or severance of the Union; that I disclaim and abjure all faith, fellowship or sympathy with the so-called Confederate States and Confederate Armies, and pledge my property and my life to the sacred performance of this my solemn Oath of Allegiance to the Government of the United States. And further, I will not attempt to trade or have any correspondence directly or indirectly, or have any business transactions whatever with any person living in the so-called Confederate States, unless under the proper Military supervision and approval. † And that I do this with a full determination, pledge and purpose, without any mental reservation or evasion whatever, and that I will well and faithfully perform all the duties required of me as a true and loyal citizen of these United States. So help me God.

† to go north of Philadelphia & remain during the war

L. Paine

WITNESS:

Edwin Vaughan

Capt. and Asst. Provost Marshal.

---

5. Paine's Oath of Allegiance. This is the only known document bearing his signature
(*See page* 446)

Original in War Department Archives

6. The much discussed card left by Booth for Andrew Johnson. It figured as Exhibit No. 29 in the conspiracy trial. (*See page 15*)

(Copy)

United States Consulate
Toronto C.W. Jany 3 1865

Hon W. H. Serrard
Secretary of State
Washington D.C.
Sir-

The following facts having
been given to me, I hasten to transmit
them directly to you, without losing the
several days time necessary to occupy
by sending through the Consul General.
I shall, however, enclose him a copy
—I am not informed of the names of
parties interested, only their initials,
which I give, as I receive them—

The Rebels in this city have a
quick and successful communication
with Jeff Davis and the authorities
in Richmond in the following
manner — Having plenty of money at
their command, they employ British
Subjects, who are provided with
British passports, and also with
passports from Col—— (probably
Jacob Thompson) which are plainly
(written

7. Letter from the United States Consul at Toronto to the State Department
regarding the so-called underground route to Richmond. (*See page* 105)

Original in War Department Archives

Phonographic Institute
Cincinnati O.

August 14th 1865

Dear Sir

No 4 is wanted to make the book complete. The testimony relates to Booth & Herold at Dr Mudd's on the 15th and at the ferry on the Rappahannock on the 24th and contains no word relating to the flight of the conscience stricken fugitives in the interval. I think the Appendix ought to supply this in the way of a good map, showing the ground over which they travelled. I have all the details ready.

I remember Major Gen. Hancock saying to Judge Holt in my hearing "I have sent those maps showing Booth's route to your office" — the very thing I need.

If you can assist me in making this work complete you will be doing a public good and eternally obliging

Yours very Obdt Benn Pitman

8. Letter written by Benn Pitman, official reporter at the conspiracy trial, pointing out a break in the testimony concerning Booth's flight.
(*See page* 142)

Original in War Department Archives

War Department
Washington City, D.C.
Feb 13 1862

Ordered

That William P Wood be and
he is hereby appointed Superintendant
of the Military Prison called the Old Capital
Prison and that he have possession, Supervision
Control and management thereof, and of the
Prisoners that now are, or hereafter may be
imprisoned therein; under the orders rules and
regulations that shall from time to time be
prescribed by the Provost Marshal with
the authority and Sanction of this Department
or that shall be given by the Secretary of War.

Edwin M Stanton
Secretary of War

Stanton's appointment of William P. Wood as Superintendent of the Old Capitol Prison
(*See page* 192)

Original in possession of author.

"On or about Tuesday 11th of April Wiechmann and Mrs Surratt, drove in a buggy to Surrattsville also to Capt Givins residence. On the road to Surrattsville she met her tenant Lloyd, with whom she had some conversation in relation to the man Howell, Stating that she would like to have him released on taking the Oath of Allegiance and would see Judge Turner about it.

The second buggy ride with Mrs Surratt was on the Friday of the Presidents Assassination, She represented her business to be in relation to some real estate. The buggy was driven to Lloyds place a package of paper was left at Lloyd's house. Wiechmann says he knows of no other business transacted at Lloyds only in relation to real estate, interest and similar matters appertaining to transactions between Mrs Surratt and a man by the name of Nothey. Wiechmann wrote a letter to a party named "Brawner" for Mrs Surratt,

10. Report by Captain William P. Wood embodying a suppressed statement by Wiechmann which might have saved Mrs. Surratt's life. (*See page* 289)

Original in War Department Archives

It is about four miles across from my house to Parson Wilmer's, and by the public road it is about five miles. I suppose they could go in about an hour or an hour and a half, by walking their horses.

I suppose in a day or two swelling would take place in the wounded man's leg; there was very little tumefaction in the wound, and I could discover Erysipelation very distinctly. It would be necessary to dress it again in two or three days if it were left in a recumbent posture, but if moved at a moderate rate, I do not know as it would aggravate it very much, unless it was struck by something. I do not know much about wounds of that sort; a military surgeon would know more about those things.

Saml. A. Mudd

Subscribed & sworn before me this
22d day of April 1865

H. H. Wells
Col. & Pro. Mar. Genl. Dep. So. P.

---

11. Last page of statement made by Dr. Samuel A. Mudd on the day after his arrest
(*See page* 259)

Original in War Department Archives

Executive Mansion,
Washington, D.C. Jany 29, 1869.

General:

The President directs me to request that you will send to him the record of the trial of the assassins of the late President Lincoln, together with the findings and sentences of the Military Commission, the action of the President upon the same, and any recommendation made by members of the Commission with respect to any of the prisoners.

I am General,

Brigadier General   Very respectfully,

Joseph Holt,   Your obedient Servant,

Judge Advocate General,   Wm G. Moore,

U. S. Army.   Secretary.

12. President Johnson's order preparatory to signing a pardon for the surviving prisoners on the Dry Tortugas. (*See page 270*)

Original in War Department Archives

2.

Mrs. Surratt repeats substantially the story that she told on her first examination; but admits that Atzerod boarded in her house a short time; and that, calling himself Wood, a man representing himself to be a baptist Minister and answering in the main to the description of the Seward Assassin occupied rooms there a few days also. She denies in toto having had any conference with Lloyd about firearms, or any conversation with Booth, Herold or others about the projected assassination, or of having known that her Son was implicated in it, or of having done anything prejudicial to the public interest. Her manner throughout was cool and collected.

Samuel ⟨L⟩ Chester an actor from Winter Garden New York, an old and very intimate friend of Booth's is an amiable, rather weak, apparently inoffensive person, with an excellent memory and not lacking in intelligence. He is one of the most important witnesses of the Government that I have examined. He details at great length several conversations with Booth,

13. Report by a Government investigator, containing Mrs. Surratt's own protestations of innocence. (*See page* 288)

Original in War Department Archives

Carroll Prison
Washington D.C
May 5, 1865

Col. Burnett
Judge Advocate
War Department
Washington D.C

Colonel:

I have the honor to call your attention to the following additional facts in my recollection. You confused and terrified me so much yesterday that I was almost unable to say anything.

I was anxious as you and the Government are that all guilty parties should be brought to justice and meet the fate they so well deserve but for God's sake do not confound the innocent with the guilty.

To begin I would state that I have ridden out only twice this year on horseback. Once on the morning of the 2ᵈ of April with Atzerot. Mrs Surratt had sent me out, to tell him that she would like to see him as soon as possible. I found him standing in front of the Pennsylvania house with two horses, I asked him whose horses they were. "One is mine" he said "and the other is Booth's." I then asked him whether he would not let me ride one and he said "yes" We then rode to Mrs. Surratt's where Atzerot saw her, I remained outside waiting for him. On leaving Mrs. Surratt we went to St. Aloysius church and thence to Trinity church in Georgetown. He acted just as a catholic, and on my saying

14. Letter written by Louis Wiechmann from Carroll Prison to the judge-advocate. 'You confused and terrified me so much yesterday that I was almost unable to say anything. . . .'
(*See page* 281)
Original in War Department Archives

U S arsenal
Mil. Prison
Wash. D.C.
July 7, 65

Mr Payne stated to me this morning
that he was convinced Mrs Surratt was
innocent of the Murder of the President
or any Knowledge thereof, — and as to
the abduction of the President, he did not
know that She was Connected with it, although he had frequent conversations with
her, during his stay at her house
I think Payne would state the truth on
this matter,
J. F. Hartranft
Bvt. Maj. Genl.
Comy Prison

15. Letter written by General J. F. Hartranft, special provost-marshal, indicating his belief
in Mrs. Surratt's innocence. (*See page* 294)

Original in War Department Archives

War Department
Washington City
June 28th 1865

Rec'd of Brevet Col. H. L. Burnett,
Judge Advocate, the sum of Two Hundred
and Forty dollars ($240.⁰⁰)
Sanford Conover.

16. Receipt for money paid by the War Department to Sandford Conover, one of the Government witnesses, later convicted for perjury. (*See page* 221)

Original in War Department Archives